DATE DUE

THINGS WHICH
ARE DONE
IN SECRET

THINGS WHICH ARE DONE IN SECRET

by Marlene Dixon

BLACK ROSE BOOKS — Montréal

Black Rose Books No. E 24

First Edition in English 1976

Hardcover — ISBN: 0-919618-68-5
Paperback — ISBN:

Cover Design: Michael Carter

Canadian Cataloguing in Publication Data

Dixon, Marlene, 1945-
Things which are done in secret

ISBN 0-919618-68-5 bd.
ISBN 0-919618-92-8 pa.

1. McGill University. 2. Dixon, Marlene, 1945-
3. Vaillancourt, Pauline. I. Title.

LE3.M22D49   378.714'281   C77-000104-1

LE
3
.M21
D58
1976

BLACK ROSE BOOKS LTD.
3934 rue St. Urbain,
Montréal H2W 1V2,
Québec

Printed and bound in Québec, Canada

CONTENTS

586220

The things which are done in secret are things that people are ashamed even to speak of; but the things exposed to the light will be illuminated and anything exposed by the illumination turns into light

St. Paul

Foreword

This book is dedicated to all those whose thought continues to protest in the name of truth. It is especially dedicated to those militants who were not so fortunate as to fall heir to proofs in documentary form. It is also for those who must support families and who cannot escape and upon whom silence is forced. "Confidentiality" assures that the things which are done in secret, the things people are ashamed even to speak of, *never* become exposed to the light. This book is one long breach of confidentiality in order that the things exposed to the light will be illuminated, which is another way of expressing a protest in the name of truth. The author and the author alone is responsible for the publication of the documents contained in this book.

The reader will note many long quotations. There is a reason for their use. Only very rarely is the voice of the militant heard in the land. It is the author-editor's wish that those who have experienced political repression in the academy speak with their own voices, in their own words, about their common experiences, as much as is possible. The reader is urged to treat the quotations as text, for they *are* texts. This book, in spirit at least, is a collective book (although its faults are those of the author alone).

The reader will note another peculiarity of this book: I have written it in the third person singular. Some people have found this odd. I chose to do so for many reasons. First, because I did not wish to dominate this book — and what is more domineering than the personal pronoun? I have lived a good deal of my life in the public eye, and I find it acutely uncomfortable; there is something painfully public about the first person singular. Every purge and attempted purge (which is to say the history of my academic life) has been largely a public event. I review my own history more to stir the memory than to reveal new details or the anatomy of the purge itself (with the exception of the material in Part VI). Indeed, the basic reason why I appear as one of the actors in this tale is because the story cannot be told without me — the events are all intertwined with my history. I would wish it otherwise.

Perhaps the more important reason for the third person was a desire on my part to be as objective as possible about myself. The personal pronoun is a constant temptation to share one's subjective life and experience with one's reader. This tale is not about my subjective life, but the objective events and mechanisms of academic repression. Yet so strong is the urge to personal comment beyond the limits of the book that I had to censor even in the third person!

9

Finally, I wrote in the third person because I was a different person then (1969-1972) than I am now. All of us who have gone through the experience of McGill have changed in profound ways: I have grown stronger, but there were times when I wondered if I would survive. McGill for me was an assault on my very humanity that led, for a time, to the virtual destruction of my intellectual life. I had become so brutalized by the constant punishment that when I stopped one day to look at myself — I did not recognize *that* person wrapped in an insulation of rage and cynicism, that person I had become. That person, who was a product of the McGill environment, began to pass away only when I decided to leave. It is that person that I am describing in the past tense, from the advantage of hindsight and with the perspective of time and distance.

This book has a final purpose, which is to apply in however insignificant a manner the cardinal principle of a very great teacher:

> *The materialist doctrine concerning the changing of circumstances and education forgets that circumstances are changed by men and that the educator must himself be educated . . . The coincidence of the changing of circumstances and of human activity or self-changing can only be grasped and rationally understood as revolutionary* practice. *(Karl Marx)*

The system runs on the principle of collaboration. We can begin by refusing to collaborate.

Marlene Dixon
South Durham, Quebec
April 1975

Introduction

This book is a documentary history of academic repression as it is practised at one university. Yet the same process and nearly identical documents (one would need only change the signatures) will be found at all universities that have condoned or demanded academic repression. Only a few of the relevant documents have actually fallen into the author's hands. In the offices of the Deans and the Vice-Principal and the Principal and the Board of Governors, in locked filing cabinets, will be found the truly damning documents: letters, memoranda and notes. The true stories never appear as written documents. One would have to "bug" the faculty club, telephones and offices to catch them in frank conversation. For the essence of academic repression is its secrecy.

What is a university? The Liberal ideologues of academia would have us believe that it is a temple of ideas, inhabited by "universal" men generating "universal" ideas, in which "academic freedom" assures that members of the university are "free" to assert what ideas they will. The Liberal ideologues hold above all that the ultimate tool of the university is rational discussion. Indeed, the university is the veritable symbol of the "free world's" freedom. Intellectuals behind the Iron Curtain pine away for the freedom and "liberty" enjoyed by their academic brethren in the liberal democracies of mature capitalism. This liberal mythology of the university is politically necessary to the system of repressive tolerance that disguises the actual conditions of "unfreedom", of repression and persecution which are done in secret.

In reality, the Western university is a necessary and central institution to the social order of mature capitalism. It produces technocrats and technicians. It produces justificatory ideologies for class oppression nationally and internationally. It celebrates the free enterprise system as the apex of human achievement and the Western liberal democracies as the ultimate expression of human social and political freedom. It carries out basic research in the hard sciences and repressive research in the "soft" social sciences: riot control, counter-insurgency, the control and co-optation of mass movements, poverty programs to control the poor, and so on. Within the modern university, whose roots are to be found in the 20th century and whose funds are provided by the State and very big business, academic freedom has never existed and will never exist. The reasons for this and how it is accomplished are presented in Part I. What is important for the public and students and young faculty who have not yet learned the rules is the *necessary* secrecy and hypocrisy; the *necessary* mass of verbiage and endless procedures by which overt repression is disguised, issues confused, and the mythology of "rational discourse" and "freedom of thought" preserved. For it is a mythology, and nothing more.

The true essence of life and thought in our universities is hypocrisy. It permeates every feature of life as a necessary consequence to the maintenance of a Big Lie. Thought which is divorced from action takes on an abstracted character: it becomes possible to justify repression in the name of freedom; war in the name of peace; exploitation in the name of human liberty. Every repressive act, in public presentation, is drowned in a cloying sheath of words, words, words . . . standards, decency, justice, quality, merit, rationality. "In political, ideological and philosophical struggle, words are also either weapons and explosives or tranquilizers and poisons. The whole class struggle can, at times, be encapsulated in the battle for one word against another. Certain words fight like enemies. Others offer the opportunity for vacillation: they are the location of a decisive but as yet undecided battle."*

·   In the universities words have become tranquilizers and poisons as part of the battle against words that are weapons and explosives. So much of the student rebellions of the 1960's expressed consciousness of the corruption of words (the corruption of ideas) to the point where they become meaningless. But, the word-games of repression are only effective so long as the things which are done in secret are kept secret. Outside the wall of confidentiality, a stark reality — repression — becomes a propaganda war: a war of words, of "he said" and "she said" and "they said" and how are people to ever know who said what and its true meaning? The damning documents, even in the rare instances when they actually fall into the hands of dissidents, will usually remain secret. To "violate" the "norms of confidentiality" is the cardinal sin, the unforgivable transgression, for an academic. To tell the truth carries heavy penalties.

Nothing is more dangerous to the mythologies of the liberal university than truth, both simple and complex. The simple truth is that people get fired for being nonconformists, for being too successful, for being independent, for not joining the right faction, for not seeking out the most powerful patron. Yet there is one group that almost always gets fired, no matter what they may do or not do: the Marxists. There are Marxists and Marxists — some are more dangerous than others. The activists who tried to use the mythology of the liberal university — to claim their right to academic freedom and to express what ideas they believe and to *act* upon those ideas — were the first to go. Second were those who *might* become activists, who could not be trusted as conformists. It may even come to be the time for Marxist metaphysicians to go in the near future.

It is also a simple truth that the State and trustees and Boards of Governors exert enormous political pressure to clean out the Marxist infection, the carriers of revolutionary ideas: for who is more fearful of revolution than the exploiter? Yet there are more complex truths as well. Marxists (the dangerous ones) are dialecticians and dialectical analysis is the most dangerous threat to the professoriate, to the veils of ideology by which they disguise their true nature:

> [Dialectical analysis] recovers tabooed meanings and thus appears almost as a return, or rather a conscious liberation, of the repressed! Since the established universe of discourse is that of an unfree world, dialectical thought is necessarily destructive, and whatever liberation it may bring is a liberation in thought, in theory. However, the divorce of thought from action, of theory from practice, is itself part of the unfree world. No thought and no theory can undo it; but theory may help to prepare the ground for their possible reunion . . . .[1]

---

* Louis Althusser, quoted in Maria Antonietta Macciocchi, *Letters from Inside the Italian Communist Party to Louis Althusser*, NLB, 1973, p. 16.

1. Herbert Marcuse, *Reason and Revolution*, Beacon, 1960, p. xii.

Yet nothing is more dangerous than the unity of theory and practice, the linking of thought and action that produces the recovery of tabooed meanings! Such theory and practice exposes the social sciences and scientists to be in fact corporate liberal ideologues and their "science" to be corporate liberal ideology. It exposes the utilization of conflict theory and the study of mass movements in Vietnam and Chile, in Greece and Guatemala, in the Congo and Brazil.

What is dangerous for professors is a thousand times more dangerous for the real employers of professors, for whom the professors manufacture the repressive ideologies and their darker reflection, the facts woven into the repressive fabric of Western imperialism as patterns of containment, counter-insurgency and counter-revolution:

> One did not have to wait for Hiroshima in order to have one's eyes opened . . . Those who enforce and direct this conquest have used it to create a world in which the increasing comforts of life and the ubiquitous power of the productive apparatus keep man enslaved to the prevailing state of affairs. Those social groups which dialectical theory identified as the forces of negation are either defeated or reconciled with the established system. Before the power of the given facts, the power of negative thinking stands condemned.
>
> This power of facts is an oppressive power; it is the power of man over man, appearing as objective and rational condition. Against this appearance, thought continues to protest in the name of truth. And in the name of fact: for it is the supreme and universal fact that the status quo perpetuates itself through the constant threat of atomic destruction, through the unprecedented waste of resources, through mental impoverishment, and — last but not least — through brute force. These are the unresolved contradictions.[2]

Perhaps in the future the power of negative thinking, thought which continues to protest in the name of truth, may flower in our universities, as it did so briefly in the late 1960's before it was almost completely repressed in North America. But if it is to have another chance then its champions must understand its enemies, their machinations, establishments, ploys, and ideologies. It is hoped that this book will contribute to such understanding, and that anything exposed by the illumination turns into light."

---

2. Ibid., p. xiv.

PART I:
Professionalism and Repression

All social life is essentially practical. *All the mysteries which lead theory towards mysticism find their rational solution in human practice and in the comprehension of this practice.*

Karl Marx

The mechanism of ideological control and academic repression is the profession itself. If any single agency can be isolated in the process of repression in the modern university it will be found in professionalism as it is expressed in the interlocking hierarchies of the various professions and university administrations. The fact that the profession is its own policeman is a source of much confusion — for in public, the profession *appears* as the defender of academic rights and the source of the defence of academic freedom.

The mechanisms described in this section were developed in the United States, but they were and are being imported into Canada. Furthermore, the domination of Canadian social studies by American social science assures that professionalism-American-style will be practiced in Canadian universities by reactionary and conservative American professors (particularly of senior rank) and, more importantly, by American-identified Canadian social science professionals. The Simon Fraser purge in 1969 forever shattered any pretensions to greater academic freedom in Canada. In the absence of a determined struggle *not* to follow the model of the U.S.A., it is inevitable that Canadian universities will become carbon copies of Big Brother institutions in the U.S. Repression as a generalized phenomenon may not, as yet, be as prevalent in Canada as it is in the United States — but that can be explained by noting that social turmoil in Canada is not yet at the level that has characterised American society for the last ten years. In Québec, where the independence struggle provoked the federal government to impose a state of seige, Marxist and radical intellectuals have many links with the C.N.T.U., with citizen's groups, with political parties, and many are unionized. The continued existence of radicals and Marxists in French-speaking colleges and universities in Québec is a consequence of the protection provided them by popular mass organizations. An isolated radical intellectual is a sitting duck.

McGill, the main subject of this case study, is to all intents and purposes an American university. It has a large proportion of American professors, principally of right-wing persuasions; it serves American corporate interests; it considers itself part of the U.S. professional community and its professors seek rewards chiefly from the American professional hierarchy. It is no accident that most of the actors in this tale are Americans! McGill represents many things to many people, but surely one of the clearest of its manifestations shows just what an American-style university is like in Canada . . . and what most Canadian universities may come to resemble in the near future. There *is* hope in Canada, given that we never forget that there is no hope without struggle.

The Ideological Hegemony of Corporate Liberalism

A critical analysis of the liberal professions reveals them to be conservative guilds, in which the myth of democratic self-government disguises bureaucratic organization and oligarchic control. The "free market place of ideas" never existed. From the earliest days the ideological hegemony of what the Schwendingers, in the *Sociologist of the Chair,* term "corporate liberalism" has been predominant:

> Our study will show that by the end of the formative years, the leading scholars in American sociology formulated their *own* kingdoms of reason based on principles of equity, tolerance, pluralism, and bourgeois democracy. In charting the nature of these kingdoms, the Americans also employed what they alleged to be "universals" such as synergy and sublimation, conflict and accommodation, social control and cultural lag. Partly because they were markedly ahistorical and extremely general in application, these universal ideas were couched in very formal generalizations. In spite of their formal masks, however, it will be found that they were firmly grounded in liberal doctrines of class harmony and class collaboration. They were also anchored in other tenets of liberalism which justified the corporate-liberal state, social class inequality, the centralization of capital, and modern imperialism. These ahistorical ideas, therefore, were just as much the product of doctrines that justified newly emerging (although much more advanced) capitalist relationships as were the earlier liberal concepts of eternal truth, eternal justice, and natural man.[1]

The ideological hegemony of corporate liberalism was not established in American sociology accidentally. Universities are institutions which require capital to function; the capital to function is derived from State funds or from private endowments. In short, the modern university does not exist as a free institution outside of the State and monopoly capitalism: it is a *product* of the State and monopoly capitalism. The fragility of the university is in fact the fragility of the universities' limited autonomy, an autonomy which at any time may be withdrawn by the funding powers. The autonomy of the university, and the special status, professional, of its teachers (as against being obvious hired heads) depends upon their utility to the ruling bourgeoisie. For the ideological professions, autonomy is the most fragile of all because the deadly microbes of revolutionary ideas are implicit in all of its concerns. Under monopoly capitalism sociology is not a science; it is an ideological and technical *weapon* against insurgency.

The intellectual history of American academic social sciences overwhelmingly reveals that academic professionalism in America was founded within the American university and was from its inception tied to the ideological and technical needs of a rising monopoly capitalism. Furthermore, the early founding fathers of American sociology were themselves men of a class, the new middle class, whose route of upward mobility was no longer a small business, but salaried professional or technical employment. At the turn of the century, they were men whose class was being created by (and was therefore dependant upon) the growth of monopoly capitalism in the United States. It was in the class interests of this rising urban middle class of professionals and technocrats to put themselves at the

---

1. Herman and Julia Schwendinger, *The Sociologists of the Chair,* Basic Books, 1974, p. xxvi. (emphasis added).

service of the trustees and funding agencies of the new universities which were arising to meet the ideological and manpower needs of advanced capitalism.

In this manner during the early, formative years of American sociology as an academic discipline, eminent sociologists increasingly regarded laissez-faire liberals and socialist scholars as beyond the pale of sociological competence. In time, the definition of professional competency became thoroughly positivistic, or more precisely *technocratic*. The professional definitions that arose implied that sociologists were competent only if they were ideologically neutral. Of course, what ideological neutrality *really* means is a commitment to the corporate liberal world-view, theory and standards. Ideological "neutrality" is also, quite obviously, a prime requirement for the self-repression of the discipline. By the late 1930's corporate liberal ideology had permeated almost every facet of the educational process in American colleges and universities. This meant that universities were held to be the repositories of expertise, so that academics had no other function than to teach legitimate (i.e., "ideologically neutral") facts. Consequently, *the personal views of teachers, if they were controversial, had no place* in the institution. This position perpetuated the myth that the university was apolitical, insulated from politics; that the technocratic services provided by the university to political and economic institutions were not determined by essentially political relationships. The mythology of the politically neutral university in turn fostered the conversion of dissident views on political questions into issues of private morality, which were to be kept strictly separated from both the profession and the academy. The final result was that professional competence was to be determined on strictly technocratic definitions (as if those technocratic definitions were themselves ideologically neutral), which in turn provided justification for stripping the principles of academic freedom of any significant meaning.

This has meant that Marxism and socialism — indeed, any impulse toward a fundamental criticism of capitalism and its institutions — has been vigorously repressed to the point of being defined beyond the pale of academic social science professionalism.

The Profession as Policeman

The self-policing function of the corporate liberal professions has always been augmented by overt political repression. Such overt repression has typically involved systematic collusion between external pressures (businessmen, corporations, newspapers, police agencies, various state agencies) and academic administrators operating in concert with tenured faculty members.[2]

In the early 1900's the solution to the problem of direct and overt business and corporate control over universities and university departments was found in the movement to "professionalize" the "ideological" social science disciplines. A claim to professional status conferred the privileges of *expertise* (since an expert can only be judged by a jury of expert peers) which also served to protect the hired faculty of universities from being identified with their wage-earning brethren in the industrial working class.[3] Furthermore, professional associations operated as a substitute for the despised working class trade union. In this respect, the professional association functioned as a guild, organized in response to working conditions that Veblen described as a "species of skilled labor, to be hired at competitive wages and to turn out the largest merchantable output that can be obtained by shrewd bargaining with their employees," and where, in Veblen's opinion "the body of academic employees are as defenceless and unorganized as any class of the wage-earning population.[4]

However, the professional association could substitute for a trade union and assure non-interference in the internal conduct of academic affairs *only so long as it was not necessary for either corporate interest or the State to discipline the liberal professions;* in other words, professional autonomy and academic freedom were contingent upon the profession's ability to be self-policing and the university's ability to be self-repressive.

Thus, the canons of professionalism disguise the self-policing functions of the profession because it is politically expedient to disguise repression as a defense of academic standards. Unlike the so-called "hard" sciences, there exist no single, commonly agreed upon set of standards of excellence or criteria of adequacy in the "ideological" sciences — one man's meat may indeed be another man's poison. The result of professionalization was the creation of interlocking hierarchies of professors and administrators, which established the hegemony of corporate liberalism within the ideological professions as a whole, and the hegemony of the tenured senior faculty within individual departments. However, to admit this sorry state of affairs would, in the first case, threaten claims to expertise, and, in the second case, serve to make the repressive functions of the profession manifestly obvious. It is not surprising, therefore, that the accusation of incompetence has been the chief weapon in the repressive arsenal of professionalism from the earliest days. In the 1914 conference on academic freedom, one participant cited a case in which:

2. For a history of state and police repression, see Schwendinger, op. cit. passim.

3. Which Colfax correctly points to when he says: "Many health, educational and welfare workers, engineers and scientists have come to the realization that the very concept "professionalization" is, to use W.J. Reader's terms, a "sham and hypocrisy." In part, the concept of professionalization results from the increasing proletarianization of the middle class. Partly it comes from recognition that the term arose out of the need for the sons of gentlemen from Oxford and Cambridge to go into formerly despised work without losing status — and thus the needs of capitalism were met through the expansion and elaboration of the notion "professionalism." J. David Colfax, "Repression and Academic Radicalism," *New Politics*, Spring, 1973, pp. 15-16.

4. Max Lerner (ed.), *The Portable Veblen*, Viking Press, 1964, p. 85.

Two professors were hounded by a newspaper for several years and painfully concluded that "it is hard to have one's every utterance examined by hostile eyes, the worst possible interpretation put upon his every act, and harder still to avoid the awkward sentence, the garbled statement, or the misreported utterance that will give his trailers a chance to get rid of him as incompetent.[5]

The same tune accompanied the wave of political repression against radical scholars that began in the late 1960's:

> In subsequent years, the defenders of academic sociology began to question the competency of radical sociologists regardless of the fact that many of these radicals were addressing themselves in an increasingly sophisticated manner to some of the most complex problems . . . By 1971, an unbroken series of articles attacking radical developments in the field began to appear in professional journals such as the *American Journal of Sociology,* the *American Sociological Review,* and the *American Sociologist.*[6]

How is the question of competence so pivotal in the liberal ideology of professionalism? First, as we have outlined, because the profession claims to be expert and this claim to esoteric knowledge is the foundation for the demand to the right of faculty autonomy, on the grounds that only "experts" are competent to judge "expert competence", which in turn supports rights to "academic freedom", i.e., to controls on the power of university trustees to reduce ideological tradesman to the status of hired head. This right is indeed *fragile* since the history of repression shows quite clearly that the right to autonomy will be abrogated at any time that the profession shows itself incapable of satisfactory self-repression and ideological control.[7]

A second reason that competence is of key concern to the profession is that the right to determine competence is also the right to hire, fire and promote: it is the basis of the oligarchic structure of power in the profession. John Kenneth Galbraith was obviously referring to this when he commented on the Sam Bowles case in the Economics Department at Harvard:

> It is established practice in all economics departments to conceal deeply political differences and to say they are not a factor. Anybody who has his general competence, teaching ability, research output, and who had been a good micro-economic model builder would have almost certainly been promoted. The Bowles decision will deeply narrow Harvard's interest in the span of economics. The people whose fame exists in neo-classical model building are embattled and their reaction tends to exclude whoever seems to threaten them . . .[8]

The hegemony of corporate liberal professionals means that men of an ideology and with vested interests hostile to radicalism are in virtual control of a radical scholar's livelihood and academic reputation because it is the corporate liberal hegemony that has the power to judge the competence of these young scholars:

> These repressive relationships, as we have seen, encompass the bureaucratic controls that (as exercised by university administrators and senior academics) have influenced academic working conditions and hiring practices. Furthermore,

5. Schwendinger, *op. cit.,* p. 537.

6. Schwendinger, *op. cit.,* p. 565.

7. For example, the Palmer Raids in the 1920's; the witch-hunts of the 1950's.

8. Lawrence S. Lifshultz, "Could Karl Marx Teach Economics in America?" *Ramparts* April, 1974, p. 28.

because of the identification between the academy and social science disciplines, the effects of these controls have been reinforced by the professional definitions of the domains of these disciplines and the professional criteria for evaluating scholarly competence. In academic life, moreover, both employment practices and professional standards are, to some *extent, formulated, operatively interpreted, and sanctioned by the very same men.* [9] (emphasis added)

What, all considerations of vested interest and power aside, is the competence of these corporate liberal oligarchs? The Schwendingers note that liberal academics deal with Marxist ideas by redefining, vulgarizing or discounting them: "In graduate and undergraduate schools, liberal academics generally provide students with a superficial, biased, and sketchy view of Marxian ideas . . . (A)s a consequence, most sociologists in the United States have neither the time, the education, nor the inclination, to deal with the complexities of Marxian thought in its own terms."

The prejudice that passes for competent judgement among the corporate liberal professionals — an unchallenged prejudice that signals respectability — varies widely in tone and flavor, but is universally condemnatory. A few samples, selected almost at random, should make the point. In economics Lifshultz quotes Harvard's James Duesenberry as "regarding the writings of leading Marxists as "corny" and Yale's Raymond Powell as considering Marxian economics to be "intellectually vacuous and "contentless" by the "canons of (the) British empiricist scientific tradition". Political science, needless to say, is not to be outdone. Professor James Chowning Davies pontificates as follows:

> In his writings Marx left enough food for moral sustenance and self-examination for a very wide variety of people. He has been variously chewed and digested and regurgitated. Like other writers producing new ideas and ideology, he felt inclined to say, about some interpretations of his works, that he could not be a good Marxist. When *Das Kapital* became quickly popular among Russian intelligentsia, in the late 19th century, he commented that Russians always were inclined toward extreme doctrine. [10]

Even if we turn to a political scientist like Robert Tucker, who has in fact taken the trouble to read Marx, we find the following interpretation:

> That the Marxian revolutionary idea has a moral meaning is clear enough. But this dimension would, it seems, be more accurately described as religious than as ethical in nature. Moral teachers desire man to be virtuous according to one or another understanding of virtue; religious ones — Marx among them — want him to be redeemed. In this connection it must be said that there is a close relation between revolution and religion . . . Marx . . . on this account may be characterized as a revolutionist of religious formation. [11]

In a textbook on sociological theory, Don Martindale writes:

> The uniqueness of Marxism does not lie — as its proponents have maintained — in the fact that it is the "only scientific form of socialism." Its claims to scientific standing are usually based on the use of the dialectic and on the thoroughness with which all phenomena in society are explained. The dialectic, which treats scientific method, logic, life growth, physical change, and innumerable other

---

9. Schwendinger, *op. cit.,* p. 279.

10. James Chowning Davies, *When Men Revolt and Why,* Free Press, 1971, p. 108.

11. Robert C. Tucker, "The Marxian Revolutionary Idea" in *Revolution,* NOMOS VIII, Atherton Press, 1967, p. 239.

things as if they were identical, is outright mysticism. Similarly, the claim to be scientific because every phenomenon conceivable is reduced to économics can only be put down to a complete failure to distinguish between metaphysics and scientific theory.[12]

The prejudice, ignorance and stupidity of these kinds of attitudes would be a matter of little concern to Marxists if it were a question of intellectual or scientific debate. It is of great concern to Marxists, when such ignorant prejudice informs those men who formulate, interpret and sanction *competency*. Their intellectual disability does not deter them in their use of arbitrary power as tenured faculty evaluating Marxist scholars; their abysmal ignorance is matched only by their enormous power.

The justification of incompetence cannot always be made to stick, particularly when a scholar's work is widely known to the public at large or when social and political circumstances are such that no one believes that incompetence is the true reason for firing or refusing to promote an academic. While not so popular as it once was, immorality was a favored second line defense against a threatening dissident. It should be understood that "immoral" and "impossible"[13] are two dimensions of the same phenomenon; yesterday's "immoral" is today's "impossible". The utilization of "immoral" and "impossible" as weapons against a difficult opponent are classically presented in the career of Thorstein Veblen:

> The Philistines knew that a giant was among them, but he was the wrong kind of giant, whose strength they feared, and they were glad to see him go packing before he pulled the temple down around their heads. What outraged them in Veblen, one may surmise, was less his unstable ménage than his dangerous thoughts. They got back at him in many ways. He was "not sound", they said; "not scholarly"; and — most damning indictment of all — he was not an "economist", a sociologist perhaps, but not an economist. They made his path hard from the beginning, his salary small, his promotions slow; the range of teaching posts available for him shrank, despite his fame; and he never got a grant of funds for any research project he ever submitted . . . Veblen felt keenly the *cordon sanitaire* that had been thrown around him. He felt it, and understood it. But his understanding it did not make his mood any less bitter. He made no direct answer. But one must take as an indirect answer . . . a book he finished at Missouri . . . It was a book on the American university, *The Higher Learning in America*. When asked, while the book was being written, what the subtitle would be, Veblen answered with more than half seriousness, "A Study in Total Depravity." It eventually became "A Memorandum on the Conduct of Universities by Business Men." No other book like it has ever been written on American education. Veblen's dissection of the governing boards of colleges, the faculty, the faculty wives, the system of promotion, the kind of man who gets along in the university hierarchy, the endowments, the mummery of the big plants, the competition for students, is pitiless. But all of it is mild when compared with his climactic description of the university president as Captain of Education modeled on the Captain of Industry . . . Veblen's friends thought it was too explosive, and he seems to have played with the thought of publishing it only after his death.[14]

Veblen's real "crimes" were his books on political economy, not his "immorality." Veblen's *The Higher Learning in America: A Memorandun on the Conduct*

12. Don Martindale, *The Nature and Types of Sociological Theory*, Houghton Mifflin. 1960, p. 160.

13. "Impossible", means that one's personality, personal style, political convictions and/or cocktail party manners are disapproved by one's colleagues. By some strange chance, most socialists turn out, quite consistently, to be "impossible."

14. Lerner, *op. cit.*, p. 9-10.

of Universities by Businessmen was, needless to say, based upon his experience at the University of Chicago and at Stanford University.

We shall now consider the *impossible*. At the 1914 conference in which Professor Weatherly advocated the principle of the self-policing academy, Frank McVey, president of the University of North Dakota declared:

> . . . that academics must exercise good *judgment* and insisted that the "life of the university depends on its *withdrawal from politics*" . . . In his opinion, "academic freedom involved both *responsibility* and a *privilege*, which can be guarded by only one thing — the *courtesy* and *honor* of a gentleman.[15] (emphasis added)

"Impossible" people, people running the everpresent risk of being stigmatized as irrational, incompetent and unprofessional, without the "courtesy and honor of a gentleman" tended to be of the same political persuasion, as an early socialist sociologist, Lindley M. Keasbey, indignantly pointed out as early as 1907:

> If a sober socialist can be found, let us invite him to share in the discussion — such was someone's suggestion. I trust that I am betraying no confidence; the question is from a letter to our secretary, and the phrase appealed to me particularly: "If a sober socialist can be found!" You all know I am a socialist — professionally of the chair, personally of the floor, a sitting and standing socialist if you choose. So it's only a question of my sobriety. Individualists are never called to account — did you ever think of that? They are expected at all times to be sober, and all that goes therewith safe and sane and sound; it is only the socialists that are suspected of intellectual inebriety, unsoundness, insanity, and so forth.[16]

It was no different in the 1960's when the rebellion of the younger radical sociologists was staged in 1969 beginning with an "impossible" statement from Martin Nicolaus:

> The honored sociologist, the big-status sociologist, the fat-contract sociologist, the book-a-year sociologist, the sociologist who always wears the livery, the suit and tie of his masters — this is the type of sociologist who sets the tone of the profession, and it is this type of sociologist who is nothing more or less than a house servant in the corporate establishment, a white intellectual Uncle Tom not only for this government and ruling class but for any government and ruling class.[17]

The "fat-cat sociologists" with their "eyes down and palms up" responded by deriding the radicals for their "uncouth manners" and their "fascist" assault on the "fragile" university and profession. Alan Wolfe cites an even clearer case when he reviews the firing of John Gerassi:

> This same distinction between political conduct and professional conduct is used in academic departments with much more serious consequences. Because the removal of a member of a department for reasons of his politics is a direct violation of the conventional wisdom of academic freedom (and because it may also lead to censure from the AAUP), the rubric of unprofessional conduct has found a whole new outlet for its use. Surely a person who acts unprofessionally has no recourse to academic freedom, for that is a protection for professionals only. Therefore, firing such an individual, while distasteful, is still defensible . . . Both a departmental committee and a faculty ad hoc committee agreed that Gerassi was guilty of "unprofessional conduct" . . . and he was fired. Here politics is blatantly associated

15. Schwendinger, *op. cit.*, p. 536
16. Schwendinger, *op. cit.*, p. 564.
17. Schwendinger, *op. cit.*, p. 564.

with professionalism. But in defending this action, one of the faculty members instrumental in firing him also said this: " . . . he declined to exercise the normal responsibility of academic authority. For example, he gave all his students A's. In style, dress, associations, and deportment, he made it clear that he regarded the students, and not the faculty, as his peer group." The indictment, if it is meant to be one, is devastating. If you cannot get someone on his politics, get him on his deportment. If it is true that there is a direct correlation between informal dress and left-wing politics, one or the other would do. The possibilities are endless.[18]

The social and political conservatism of the academic guilds derives its justification from the dominant view of the liberal academicians: in a period of political turmoil it is safer to engage in self-repression than to be repressed by the authorities. The conservative guild nature of the professions is manifested very clearly in the norms of professional conduct which assures that a good guild-man threatens neither the professional oligarchs or any other oligarchs:

> Fortunately, professionalism in sociology is better defined by elimination than by enumeration: we can better say what a professional *is not*, rather than what he *is*. The professional does not become *seriously* involved in major controversies; he does not, as a professional, concern himself with major issues; he does not feel compelled to relate his research to practice; he does not let the needs of the oppressed take priority over career opportunities; he is not an intellectual; and he is not a political activist . . . There are subtle and undramatic ways of regulating behavior . . . which eliminates the need to fire (radicals) outright. Perhaps the most obvious, yet most insidious, means is that of withholding the various amenities that come with the attainment of graduate or faculty status in the university. The radical who does not get along with or embarrasses his chairman or the administration may find himself re-thinking his behavior when he discovers that the most obsequious, least controversial graduate student gets the Woodrow Wilson Fellowship, or when his manuscripts take six or eight weeks to get typed, or when he finds himself teaching five days a week, at the hours of eight, one and four. Slowly, impercep-tibly, perhaps unconsciously, he may begin to adapt, to conform and, in short, get along and make himself less noticeable, less controversial . . . He hasn't "sold out;" he has been eroded.[19]

Universities, like all other institutions in our society, are afflicted with internal contradictions. Colfax notes this contradiction when he points out:

> Freedom of ideas — even revolutionary ones — is the primary *raison d'être* of the liberal university; it is the *application* of these ideas that is forbidden. Consistent with liberal ideology, the university is a place where one is forever *searching* for the truth — but god help those who think they have found it, or would use it to bring about revolutionary social change![20]

For the activist, as Colfax points out, the process of successive firings means, to quote an acquaintance: "you end up teaching fifteen hours in every backwater college in America." Colfax concludes:

> As long as radical activists, unreconstructed and incorrigible, manage to survive in any numbers in the American university, repression will grow. It will not wipe out *all* radicals. Rather, like all effective forms of repression, it will be both selec-tive and capricious, disorienting and unpredictable.[21]

18. Marvin Surkin and Alan Wolf, *An End to Political Science,* Basic Books, 1970, p. 295.
19. Colfax, *op. cit.,* p. 16.
20. *Ibid.,* p. 18.
21. Colfax, *op. cit.,*

Purging and Hounding

Most radical and Marxist sociologists who undertake to expose academic repression have chosen to do so as though they were analyzing any other social phenomenon. Sensitive to the constant attacks against them for being "wild" men (or women, as the case may be), they present their evidence meticulously and offer arguments with scholarly decorum and precise detachment. Rarely will it occur to the reader that more often than not under the careful argumentation the radical author is describing his or her own purge. It is often only in personal correspondence that a genuine human voice can be heard. An example is provided by a letter Paul Baran sent to Paul Sweezy in 1964 (the year of Baran's death):

> For the next year I got a teaching load that is about twice as large as that of my "peers," with pay of about 60% of theirs, and all this with a broad grin: "look at us, how democratic and tolerant we are!" The President observed that there are no complaints about my teaching or "scholarship," but my utterances in public are "irresponsible." I asked to be given samples of "irresponsible" statements. If the word means mendacious or incoherent or outside the realm of reasonable discourse, I would like to see any such statements cited with chapter and verse. If the word means "not in agreement with *his* views," I would appreciate having this spelled out . . . But all this is for the birds; he *wants* badly to squeeze me out of here; and I would be delighted to go because my nerves won't stand it much longer but where to go and how? . . . If it weren't for Nicky (Baran's son) I would quit literally tomorrow; I would eke out $100 a week and keep body and soul together and rather do that than have to tolerate those bastards spitting into my face all the time. But how can I leave the little chappy, and how can I take him along into nothingness?[22]

In the opinion of a Stanford University official it is probable that Baran's death was hastened by the brutality of the University's hounding. According to Donald Carlson, the University's alumni relations official: "I doubt if (Baran) enjoyed the harassment he has received because of it (criticizing U.S.A. exploitation of Cuba). Shortly after that speech he had a serious heart attack."

According to Lifshultz it was known around Stanford in 1961 that alumni were complaining about Baran because of his Marxist economics — he was the only Marxist economist holding tenure at a leading American university at that time — and because of his outspokeness on contemporary issues. When Baran returned from a trip to Cuba in 1960 he gave a number of lectures about his trip, in which he said that the rural population in Cuba had been "driven to revolt" by an "increasingly insufferable state of poverty and backwardness." During the Bay of Pigs Invasion, Baran denounced American policy: "American capitalism, cornered, threatened and frightened, may be incapable of leaving the rest of the world alone without so slamming the door that the entire building collapses." Yet even though there were suspicions concerning outside pressures demanding Baran's dismissal, no hard evidence emerged. Most questions about whether Baran had been pressured by the University's administration because of his political views remained unanswered until 1971, when Stanford's confidential "Baran File" was secretly removed from a locked room in the school's archives and released to local newspapers. The "Baran File" contained hard evidence:

---

22. Lifshultz, *op. cit.*, p. 55.

wealthy alumni were demanding that Baran be fired for "treason and subversive statements." The Baran case had been discussed by representatives of the University and Transamerica Corp., Standard Oil of California and California Indemnity Exchange.

However, Stanford had no professional grounds upon which to legitimately dismiss Baran. He had an international reputation, great standing as a Marxist economist, and no real faults could be found with his teaching or his academic performance. The University, under the circumstances, was driven to the last resort: to make life as insufferable as possible. This was explicitly stated by a highly placed university official:

> "We must suffer him," until he proves an incompetent teacher "or does something which would warrant termination of his employment on other grounds." Provost Terman added in another letter: "The evidence to prove that Professor Baran is engaged in unscholarly activities in the classroom is not sufficient for the administration to take punitive action. This is the critical point. To press for such an action on insufficient evidence would risk much greater damage.[23]

The administration and faculty of Stanford University, in order to avoid risking greater damage, chose to hound Paul Baran, to force him to tolerate "those bastards spitting into my face all the time."

Baran's story is a tragedy. It is not unusual. It has been repeated throughout the history of North American universities and throughout the entire period of the 1960's and into the 1970's. Stanford's secret "Baran File" is the prototype for untold numbers of other such files.

It is only the secrecy of those files and the brick wall of academic hypocrisy that leaves so many cases without "hard evidence" to prove the political pressures and motives for the dismissal of political dissenters. In truth, at least in the United States, firing men and women for political dissent became so common and so obvious that administrations (especially in less prestigious schools) no longer troubled to guard their liberal image.

23. Lifshultz, *op. cit.*

Confidentiality and Blacklisting

Veblen wrote in 1918:

So well is the academic blacklist understood, indeed, and so sensitive and trustworthy is the fearsome loyalty of the common run among academic men, that very few among them will venture openly to say a good word for any one of their colleagues who may have fallen under the displeasure of some incumbent of executive office. This work of intimidation and subordination may fairly be said to have acquired the force of an institution, and to need no current surveillance or effort.[24]

Alan Wolfe describes the blacklisting of people affiliated with the Caucus For a New Political Science and comments:

The secrecy and confidentiality which surrounds faculty-hiring procedures permits such informal blacklisting to take place. There are some senior professors who, when they hear of a caucus person being considered for a job in another department where they have a friend, dash off an immediate letter to him dropping the crucial code word, "unprofessional conduct." This is the end of the applicant's chances for a job, for what self-respecting department will hire an unprofessional when they can have a professional? The applicant does not know what happened because he can never see the letter which blackballed him, and in some cases, he may never know that a letter was written. The whole process of confidential letters, which is usually cited as the "professional" way of making new appointments, can easily be turned into a procedure which has no due process, no chance of reply to charges, and no redress.[25]

Paul Baran could ask "to be given samples of "irresponsible" statements" and admirers could wonder for nearly ten years whether or not "outside pressures were brought to compel his dismissal" but all of the ugly proceedings in the Baran case were shielded by "confidentiality" to remain in the "secret Baran file" until 1971.

Confidentiality is justified in terms of defending a prospective candidate, assuring freedom to the evaluator, and protection from the consequences of public knowledge of negative evaluations. In fact, confidentiality functions to deny due process to the powerless in the academic hierarchy, to protect the arbitary exercise of power by senior faculty and machinations on the part of university administrators. Confidentiality alone makes possible the vicious system of persecution and blacklisting which has been characteristic of modern academic life from the earliest days. Confidentiality also serves to hide incompetent (by any standards) evaluations of the work of dissidents as well as out and out prejudice in the evaluation of controversial individuals. Confidentiality has been systematically corcupted to the point where it serves little purpose except to protect the arbitrary and prejudiced exercise of power by professional oligarchs.

---

24. Thorstein Veblen, *The Higher Learning in America*, Hill & Wang, 1969, p. 85.

25. Surkin & Wolfe, *op. cit.*, p. 298.

Proscribed Knowledge

Between the two forces, corporate liberal professionalism and state repression, no authentic North American left-wing academic sociology was ever able to establish itself. When the social turmoil and insurgency of the 1960s erupted throughout the advanced capitalist countries, North American scholars and activists were without any adequate theoretical guidance, true historical knowledge or practical guidelines other than raw and immediate experience itself. Because of the repression of Marxist scholars and scholarship there have been no lasting circles or schools of thought among academic social scientists representing a theoretical structure which has challenged liberalism in all its manifestations. What arose from young graduate students and faculty in the 1960s was "critical sociology", no more than a critique of corporate liberal sociology and its institutional manifestations.

Because all serious study of Marxism was proscribed, guaranteeing the absence of its traditions, creating a complete and deliberately contrived ignorance of and mindless prejudice against it, critical sociology was a debunking exercise, providing no theoretical alternative to corporate liberalism and offering no genuine framework from which to ask the centrally significant questions of modern history. The disintegration of critical sociology as a school (and a basis for organized opposition) was the inevitable consequence of the lack of a coherent theoretical and analytical framework that could create a common universe of discourse, orientation and set of problems. Sociology with its critical opposition was perhaps more fortunate than some disciplines. Wolfe relates, for political science:

> . . . radical organizing cannot take place in professions where there are few radicals . . . Political science is one of those professions in which radical organizing does not make sense . . . Allied disciplines such as sociology and history have recognizable subgroups of scholars whose dissents from the prevailing orthodoxies were well-known . . . Radicals, in a few words, do not really exist in the discipline of political science. At the September 1969 convention of the American Political Science Association, while the leaders of the association and the *New York Times* all waited for the young militants to disrupt the meetings, as was happening at the same time with sociologists in San Francisco and the psychologists in Washington, those of us who knew about these things were laughing. We knew there might be somewhere between five and ten political scientists in the United States willing to challenge the basic notions of pluralistic liberalism[26]

The pitiful state of political science was not so unusual as might be assumed. In a letter refusing to give a special seminar on Marxian economics at Yale, Paul Sweezy had written:

> Every generation of graduate students includes a by-no-means insignificant number of Marxists. But with very few exceptions they are dropped from the academic world before acquiring tenure. And the exceptions for the most part find it prudent to keep their ideology separate from their teaching and research . . . That this situation creates problems for college and university administrators is obvious, and it seems to me that they have no one but themselves to blame.
> Under the circumstances, I have asked myself what my own responsibilities are.

---

26. Surkin & Wolfe, *op. cit.*, p. 305.

Should I stand ready, as far as possible, to lend a helping hand by responding favorably to a growing number of invitations to give lectures and courses in marxian economics? Or should I, by refusing to follow this course do what I can to impress upon the academic authorities that if they want to satisfy their student demands in this area, it is up to them to encourage younger Marxists and to keep them on their faculties?[27]

Sweezy, it is interesting to note, was not granted tenure at Harvard when he was a young scholar (which suggests that we have Harvard, ironically enough, to thank for *Monthly Review.*)

By 1970 ever larger numbers of militants who had been veterans of the various radical caucuses in the social science disciplines turned to the systematic study of Marxism. Yet that study suffers from a number of serious impediments. The first is the absence of any tradition, of any body of native Marxian analysis (although the present revival in books written by communists during the 1930's testifies to the starvation for a native literature) and the consequent dependence upon various European Marxist traditions. The second is the overwhelming number of cases where study has to begin almost from scratch, causing acute bitterness over the years spent in graduate school mastering the intricacies of the corporate liberal world-fantasy. The third is the fact that being purged, black-listed, unemployed or "teaching fifteen hours a week in every backwater college in America" imposes enormous burdens upon the task of mastering one of the largest, most complex and subtle theoretical systems.

The present revival of Marxism is thus being carried on within an acutely repressive and hostile environment. The history of the social sciences in North America should teach us that to the degree that Marxism once again flourishes, to that degree will repression and persecution intensify. The lesson we must draw, and it should be obvious from the very study of Marxism itself, is that knowledge and thought is proscribed when it is dangerous. Marxism is dangerous and for that reason it will remain, until conditions are changed in various ways, a very risky intellectual and practical pursuit.

---

27. Lifshultz, *op. cit.* pp. 53-54.

PART II:

McGill in Quebec

> *The ideas of the ruling class are, in every age, the ruling ideas: i.e., the class which is the dominant material force in society is at the same time its dominant intellectual force . . . The division of labour . . . manifests itself also in the ruling class, as the division of mental and material labour, so that within this class one part appears as the thinkers of the class (its active conceptualizing ideologists, who make it their chief source of livelihood to develop and perfect the illusions of the class about itself). . . . This cleavage within the ruling class may even develop into a certain hostility and opposition between the two parts, but in the event of a practical collision in which the class itself is endangered, it disappears of its own accord and with it also the illusion that the ruling ideas were not the ideas of the ruling class and had a power distinct from the power of this class. The existence of revolutionary ideas in a particular age presupposes the existence of a revolutionary class . . .*
>
> Karl Marx

The documentary evidence that makes up the greater part of this book may seem strange and often hysterical to the "outsider," the non-university person, the student or teacher who may well ask: were democratic reforms so dangerous? After all, we did not set out to revolutionize the university but merely to participate in it. Part I describes how and why democratization is a direct challenge to vested professional interest because it directly challenges professional hegemony over judging professional competence. Democratization is also a direct challenge to the university as a corporate liberal institution. The universal answer to movements for university reform all over North America was minimal co-optation and failing that, overt and blatant repression. Why? Because to democratize a repressive, bureaucratic, elitist and profoundly undemocratic institution *was* to revolutionize it! Only the naive belief in the mythology of the liberal university led young students and young scholars to believe that reform was possible and reasonable.

McGill, like Sir George Williams University and Simon Fraser University and all other Canadian universities, opted for the "American Plan," which was to expel, fire and intimidate the leaders of the student movement and to re-institute political reaction and repressive controls. It is this atmosphere of reaction and repression that sets the stage for this documentary history.

McGill in 1968: Rumours of War

McGill has been in tune with change in Quebec for years. It has been working at it since before 1960 — since before the mailbox bombs. It produced one of the most capable briefs before the B & B Commission. It has established the French Canada Studies Institute which has done wonders on a restricted budget.

The revolutionaries cry out that this is colonialism — 'a study of the natives'. But the truth is that McGill was the first university in Canada to recognize that a new concept of the country was emerging based upon the existence of two linguistic and cultural groups. No university is better placed to study the implications of this new concept than McGill. The creation of the French Canada Studies Programme was an initial step in a process of adapting McGill to the new situation. It implied no derogatory attitudes towards French-Canadians whatever. All McGill's institutes are based on academic and community worth. Our interest in French Canada is not new. James McGill married a French Canadian.

Robert Shaw, Vice-Principal (Administration), March 24, 1969. Reprinted in the *McGill Student Handbook*.

It is a pity that we cannot in this space present an historical analysis of the McGill student movement. We shall have to abstract and emphasize those elements of the battle to democratize McGill that bear most directly on our problem, the repression of dissenting faculty. The repression began with the firing of Stan Gray in the summer of 1969, but the firing of Gray really began in the fall of 1968.

What was known in the 1960's as the Establishment, had not been idle during the summer recess. Kevin Peterson (Canadian University Press) reported from Ottawa:

The summer may have been a holiday for students, but Canadian university administrators used the time to study their own version of the three R's — revolution, reaction and regression.[1]

---

1. Kevin Peterson, "Administration Summer Holiday," *McGill Daily*. September 26, 1968.

Peterson reported that University of Toronto President Claude Bissell, just back from a year's sabbatical leave at Harvard, led the discussion on how to handle Canadian student activists, predicting that Canadian students would not resort to the violence of the Paris or Columbia students, but would use the tactics of sit-ins and marches. Bissell predicted [incorrectly] that Canadian universities had a two-year jump on student power and proceeded to outline plans for increased student "involvement" as a method of avoiding confrontation.

Other administrators were not convinced that token seats on committees, senates and boards would head off trouble. At the Canadian Student Affairs Association conference in Calgary, a meeting of officials involved with student affairs discussed means to pacify student groups. But the problem that most concerned delegates was the question of whether or not city police should be called in when there was "trouble on campus."[2]

The Establishment in Montreal had not been idle during the summer recess either. A boxed feature entitled "Summer Madness" appeared in the *McGill Free Press,* September 19, 1968, reporting that "uptightness about students has not been a purely local phenomenon, in a year when Columbia students halted the operation of their university and French students all but halted France." "Summer Madness" reported:

> that *The Montreal Star's* Mr. Taylor, for instance, has repeatedly divulged the plans of both sides in the coming student-police struggle. He began in late July with the revelation that "major student demonstrations against the administrations of McGill and the University of Montreal are being planned for the fall." Meanwhile Montreal Policeman's Brotherhood President Jean-Paul Picard, "who had earlier warned the unsuspecting public about the "unstable and unhappy youths who are totally without scruples" took up the torch by announcing that "People will die in the streets" when students riot . . . Mayor Drapeau himself appeared worried. He began to deal with unsightly slums by putting fences around them, but the prospect of equally unsightly blood in the streets required stronger action. As Taylor reported on August 23, 'City Police Director Gilbert and Mayor Drapeau were behind closed doors yesterday for a meeting classified as top secret. The secret: discussion of ways to cope with student plans (revealed by this column three weeks ago) for massive anti-administration demonstrations at the University of Montreal and McGill late this month.' Within days, the police department had moved to meet the crisis. '150 hand-picked city cops', Taylor reported the next week, 'began intensive riot training here on Monday. The high level order is that it must be completed by September 23 — in time for the opening of new terms at the Universities of McGill and Montreal.'[3]

Yet the real context for the student movement at McGill was not the preparations for co-optation or repression undertaken by worried administrators or eager policemen. Nor was it the near-revolution in France, the violence at Columbia, the murder of students in Mexico during the Olympics. It was Quebec. Events at McGill tailed the uprising of the Quebec student movement that arose

2. *Ibid.*
3. "Summer Madness" *McGill Free Press,* September 19, 1968.

within the Francophone CEGEPs[4], (community college) which itself was part of the rise of the Quebec independence movement. In October, 1968, students at most of Quebec's CEGEPs occupied their school buildings. At the École des Beaux Arts, students ran their own school for five weeks before yielding to negotiations with their administration. The rebellion of the CEGEP students originated in the colonized position of the Quebec people. As part of the Quiet Revolution, the modernization of Quebec required for the full exploitation of Quebec's resources, educational reforms which had been promised, and which resulted in the CEGEP system. The system, however, reflected the colonial contradictions of Quebec society. CEGEP students were being trained for jobs that didn't exist in the Quebec economy. Those who planned to go on to university — many more than the government had expected — were concerned that French-speaking university places were unlikely to exist. The occupations, which ended in failure and repression, reached their climax on October 21, 1968 when 10,000 CEGEP students massed on the McGill campus and marched through the streets to the University of Montreal. The inexorable logic of colonialism led to a *second* march of 10,000 CEGEP students on March 28, 1969: *Opération McGill.*

About Opération McGill Robert Chodos wrote:

> On March 28, almost exactly four years after the freeze-the-fees rally, 10,000 people marched on McGill demanding its transformation into a French-language university. The demonstration was a peaceful one, and even when police broke it up only minor incidents were provoked — this despite an atmosphere of hysteria that had prevailed in Montreal for the previous two weeks and the alerting of the Canadian Army on the day before. The issue of McGill University had led to the clearest class polarization seen in Quebec in years — on the one side were CEGEP students, workers, radical and nationalist organizations, and a small number of McGill students; on the other were the McGill Administration, the newspapers, the Quebec government, and the cops.[5]

The McGill symbol of Opération McGill, Stan Gray, had written in an article shortly before the demonstration:

> 'Au Québec, le capital parle anglais et le travail parle français . . .' In the Quebec of St. Leonard, of the Domtar strike, of the CEGEP occupations, can McGill remain as it is for much longer? The privileges of Quebec's English minority are particularly evident in the field of education. This minority of 17% occupies 42% of the available university places and receives one third of the government grants for higher education. McGill, the pride of the English community and of Anglo-American capital, is the most flagrant symbol of this privileged position: it receives 22% of the grants going to Quebec universities . . . and its budget for research is equal to those of l'Université de Montréal and Laval combined![6]

Gray's article went on to document the central role McGill plays in the exploitation of the Québécois. McGill's Faculty of Management trains the English

4. In 1964 the Parent report recommended that post-secondary "institutes" be established to equalize the French and English educational systems. Following a series of committee studies and a change in government, there finally emerged the CEGEPs Bill in June, 1967. The first French language CEGEPs were opened in September, 1967. Poor organization and lack of space in the CEGEPs led to massive demonstrations in the streets of Montreal in October, 1968. Examples of the issues protested: 30% in the technical schools looked in vain for jobs; 70% in academics branch could not find places in university

5. Robert Chodos, "A Short History of Student Activism at McGill," *McGill Student Handbook,* 1969, p. 92

6. Stan Gray, "Bienvenue à McGill," reprinted in the *McGill Student Handbook,* 1969, (from a newspaper distributed to Quebec workers and students in preparation for the March 28 demonstration), p. 107.

speaking managers who "will be at the posts of command." McGill used its own placement service (rather than the National Placement Service) to conserve McGill's privileged relations with large corporations. In research, McGill's marriage to English and American corporate interest was clearly demonstrated (if a simple listing of the Board of Governors was insufficient): members of the Financial Research Institute included institutions like the Bank of Montreal, Bell Telephone, the CPR, Montreal Trust . . . and McGill University. McGill also maintains a number of institutes and research centres that serve large Canadian and American corporations directly. One example cited by Gray was the Mining Research Institute with programs tailored to the needs of private industry. The laboratories and research were sponsored by the American-owned Iron Ore Company and other large mining concerns. Moreover, the Ford Foundation and the Rockefeller Foundation had recognized McGill's special status by increasing the amount of money granted to McGill, which were much larger contributions than they made to other Canadian universities. In education, McGill preserves the privileges of the English minority and American Imperialism. Nearly one third of McGill's students (26%) came from outside Quebec. McGill had the largest proportion of foreign students — and on top of that, 51% of McGill's graduates took up careers outside of Quebec. "And all this while thousands of CEGEP students are looking for university places!"[7] Gray summed up the meaning of McGill in Quebec when he wrote:

> It is this which is most striking: McGill, to all intents and purposes, is financed by Quebec society, and yet it remains absolutely inconsistent with the needs of that society. McGill serves only a minority of English students, in a province where 83% of the people speak French, while some 10,000 CEGEP graduates risk finding themselves next autumn condemned to becoming educated unemployed.
>
> In fact, McGill is at the service of the foreign elites that have controlled Quebec for 200 years. American capital has succeeded British capital, appropriating the people and their resources, with the complicity of Quebec's elite and successive governments. Sixty per cent of Quebec's primary industry belongs to American capital, and Quebec workers have the lowest wages and highest rate of unemployment in all of Canada . . .
>
> The two great contradictions in Quebec society are the confrontation between the interests of the working class and the interests of the capitalists, and the conflict between the minority nation and the majority nation. In fact, the two contradictions are inseperable, because they revolve around the same political and social problems: thus, when there is a strike in a large company, one often finds the French on one side and the English on the other. A true liberation for Quebec workers will take the form of independence and socialism . . .
>
> McGill is on the wrong side of both of the two great contradictions of Quebec society.[8]

---

7. *Ibid.*, pp. 109, 107
8. *Ibid.*, p. 108

McGill in Quebec: The Uses of Academic Liberals

To a Reactionary, once a Radical

Admittedly
It was a time of great excitement
Bourgeois assumptions were everywhere
Under attack. If they were not in disarray
They should have been; certainly it was no fault
Of yours. Such sincerity of purpose you had,
One wonders that the millennium wasn't taken
Inchoate from the forge of history.
You cast a jaundiced eye on the moral comfort
Of gentility and advanced upon the drawing-rooms
With fistfulls of mud. If the philistines weren't shaken
They should have been; in any event
It was not you who lacked the resolve
But that was thirty years ago
And now you stand recalcitrant in a cold season
The poet is dead, Louis, and professors don't
Know the meaning of life.

Leslie WAXMAN [9]

Modernization came late to Quebec, and thus came late to McGill. Late-blooming modernity makes of McGill a case study of exceptional clarity in the uses of liberalism, particularly post World War II academic liberalism — the ideology of the technocrats who came to dominate the industrialized world. In other institutions corporate liberalism had sunk its roots deeply and early established its hegemony — but not at McGill, the last bastion of the British Empire in colonial Quebec. At McGill, corporate liberalism had to be imposed over the protestations of colonial conservatives; Americans had to be imported to erase the British stamp and impose MADE IN USA on a needy but reluctant institution. At the end, even the radicals bore the trademark MADE IN USA, as if to complete McGill's theatre of the absurd.

The imposition of corporate liberalism upon a basically conservative institution was captured in a remarkable essay co-authored by Robert Chodos, Stan Gray, Mark Starowicz and Mark Wilson, "The Institutional Imperative", published in November, 1968. The article traces the evolution of McGill beginning with the twenty-three year reign of Frank Cyril James:

> If Principal Emeritus James were to return to the campus from his pastoral reti-
> rement in southern England, he would find its style of institutional leadership
> altered almost beyond recognition. James chose his deans and department chairmen
> with unassailable autocracy, quiet clubhouse racism, and a marked fondness for
> British academics who were willing, like himself, to do a stint of administration
> in the colonies. Not even a token Catholic, Jew or French Canadian disturbed the
> Anglo-Saxon monotony of the Board of Governors . . . The colonial style was
> not unsuited to the McGill of those times. There was no chance anyway of money
> from Quebec or from Ottawa through Quebec; Duplessis was implacably anti-
> Ottawa and anti-education, and no effort of McGill could turn his head.

---

9. From "The World is Ugly and the People are Sad", a *McGill Daily* editorial, November 8, 1968.

Suddenly, in 1959, Duplessis died. The twentieth century began to course through the veins of the Quebecois, and soon after the Lesage Liberals were elected in Quebec, public support of universities became a distinct probability.

And almost as suddenly, James and his kind of lieutenants became a liability to the institution. Their understanding of politics in general and Quebec in particular ranged somewhere between Lord Durham's and Rudyard Kipling's.[10]

By the end of 1962 James had been removed and McGill was beginning to receive grants from the Lesage government. McGill had moved from being the last bastion of the British Empire to an institution required to operate in political terms, whose developing nature interacted with the desires and interests of its different constituencies. Maintaining and increasing grants from the Lesage government rested upon McGill's ability to maintain an acceptable public image, and furthermore raised the problem of public relations — a plebeian consideration which had not troubled Cyril James. McGill's dependence upon funding from the province brought yet another dimension to McGill's public relations: the aggressively awakening French population of Quebec. Finally, after 1965, McGill faced a student movement that, learning from an international movement, grew in militancy, sophistication and intellectual exaction beyond the limits of accomodation that the institution was willing to make. For McGill, this meant that:

> the dominant institutional imperatives of present-day McGill have emerged: (1) to preserve a position of strength in negotiating to maintain its share of financial support from the Quebec taxpayer, and generally maintain the essentials of its position in Quebec education; (2) to present a public face of progress and stability; (3) to contain, repress, and pacify student militancy which called into question the *essentials* of McGill's institutional character.
>
> These imperatives have caused a strain on McGill's resources and historical nature. A private university, an Anglo-Saxon preserve, an institution heavily weighted towards natural science, medicine and engineering, suddenly was greatly in need of social scientists of political understanding, negotiating skill and progressive images; and this at a time when McGill's old-style elite was barely prepared to trust such people, let alone give them administrative control.[11]

McGill had always done so poorly in the humanities and social sciences that the layer of competent people to meet the new imperatives was perilously thin. Between 1962 and 1966 McGill had made Michael Oliver — Vice-Principal (Academic). Oliver presented the image of the new McGill — politically progressive, intellectually competent, a liberal who would act as a bulwark against the hard-liners in the Administration. Labour mediator H.D. Woods presided over the collection of empire-building departments known as the Faculty of Arts and Science. Maxwell Cohen was Dean of Law, and Social Science Vice-Dean Saul Frankel "had become the Administration's key negotiator in dividing up the pie of Quebec government grants among the universities." *Every full Professor of Political Science except one now carried a heavy administrative load.*

We argued before that the essence of academic repression was its secrecy and its mystification — its endless stream of public propaganda to mystify its internal nature. McGill presents an unusually clear picture of why and how secrecy and mystification become essential. Whereas most modern universities have been "modern" since 1900, McGill entered the 20th century only in 1959, previously insulated by Quebec's colonial contradictions: now those very same

---

10. Robert Chodos, Stan Gray, Mark Starowicz and Mark Wilson, "The Institutional Imperative", *McGill Daily*, November 5 and November 7, 1968.

11. *Ibid.*

colonial contradictions force McGill into super-heated "modernization." Internally, McGill is split between the men of the *ancien régime* of Cyril James and the "new men" (most of them from the United States) who are classic examples of what C. Wright Mills called "bureaucratic entrepreneurs." Indeed, this split was to cut deeply into the whole university, but especially into the Political Science and Sociology Departments. McGill was caught in external contradictions as well. On the one hand, it needed to revamp its image to get its cut of the pie in the Quebec Liberal's Quiet Revolution; McGill must try to repaint its image from conservatism to "stable but progressive." This was resisted by the old guard. On the other hand, McGill (whose interests were tightly interlocked with Canadian and American big business) had also to attempt to cajole the Quebecois into acceptance of McGill's mission in French Canada. There is, of course, but one "institutional imperative:" for McGill to "preserve a position of strength in negotiating to maintain its share of financial support from the Quebec taxpayer, and generally maintain the essentials of its position in Quebec education." What unfolds around the PSA (Political Science Association) strike and Stan Gray is a battle of *styles* dictated for and against by the new political situation.

Yet our understanding of these styles is essential, for while we can easily identify the hard-liners, the conservatives and their allies, it is the liberals who best serve the real powers and whose very function is to mystify: to sound progressive with the left hand while the right hand engages in actions designed to "contain, repress and pacify." And all of this in order "to present a public face of progress and stability." The "Institutional Imperative" provided a number of case studies that are gems of stylistic analysis that reveal the functions of the "new men" of McGill. The reader is urged to keep in mind that "radical" often meant opposition to the conservatism of the James era at McGill and the Duplessis era in Quebec. By 1968 the "radicals" are "liberals," most of whom fit into a common mold:

> It's funny how old age makes radicals into reactionaries. Take university professors, for example. Many of them once thought that nothing less than flaming purgatory would make the world habitable. They descended on the known world from hunger, from vague and unwarranted ethnic origins, from the east end of Montreal, intent on shrouding the mountain in a mist of anti-establishment vitriol.
>
> But then something happened. A bizarre sun rose in their previously cheerless world — a sun compounded of academic recognition, tenure, money, status. And the vitriol evaporated, leaving a residue of cynicism, regret, bitterness and political sclerosis.[12]

Needless to say, the actual individuals described in the "Institutional Imperative" are less important than the roles they are assigned: the personnel may change, but the task remains. Let us begin with the Faculty of Arts and Science:

> H.D. Woods brings to the job a different combination of abilities from those of his fellow top administrators. He is the labor mediator, the conciliator, the consummate collective bargainer.
>
> The Faculty of Arts and Science he heads is a curious and sprawling amalgam of several dozen departments of widely varying pursuits and worth. All these departments are encouraged to interpret "academic freedom" in the nineteenth-century spirit of cutthroat competition. They assiduously spend their time hatching schemes for Institutes, Centres, Projects and graduate programs which will attract graduate students and big-name academics (who may also dabble in "teaching" on the side), keep bright young PhDs happy and ambitious between their undergraduate

---

12. "The World is Ugly and the People are Sad," *loc. cit.*

"teaching" hours, bring in money and otherwise jealously preserve and extend the frontiers of those segregated baronies fondly referred to as "disciplines." This is known in the trade as "upgrading."

Woods likes his Deanship to be thought of as a sort of government regulation agency (of limited powers) for the activities of these jungles and swamps. He sees himself as the restrained and diplomatic mediator, occasionally stepping out of line and proposing a radical idea or two at the risk of his job.

Actually, Woods is despotic wherever he can be, and often crude where he shouldn't be. Faculty committees that make plans conflicting with his own find themselves suddenly disbanded, with some letter to the chairman informing him of the "difficulties presented" by the plans, "at least to me in my administrative capacity."[13]

Institutes, Centres and Projects; Baronies; Big-Name Academics; "Upgrading" — these indeed are the jungles and swamps of professionalism and its cutthroat competition, above all characteristic of the parvenu social sciences. The social sciences are indeed afflicted, for while they produce the liberals so necessary to conflict management and image management, government management and student management (in payment for which come the Institutes, Centres and Projects) they also produce the "immoral and impossible" — communists, militants and dope-fiends. At San Francisco State it was Gerassi; at Berkeley it was Lichtman, Schwendinger and a host of others; at Simon Fraser practically an entire department; at McGill Gray, Dixon and Vaillancourt. All that is goodness, truth and beauty (Institutes, Centres, Projects, Big-Names and Upgrading) are menaced by these unprofessional maniacs whose madness brings down the wrath of Administrations and provincial governments and the subsequent spoliation of the best laid plans of academic robber barons. Then, of course, one needs "progressive intellectuals":

In the late fifties a committee of the McGill Association of University Teachers studied and reported on the power structure of McGill, focusing on the Senate. With this report, Maxwell Cohen, chairman of the committee, staked out the topic of university government as almost his private preserve.

"Cohen used to be considered something of a flaming radical around here," said one knowledgeable faculty member looking back at the 1959 Cohen Report. "Now look at him — one of the most powerful Deans at McGill."

For a period during the early "democratization" debates with students, the Administration used Cohen whenever a facade of intellectual respectability was required in dealing with student demands. At one time he spoke often and at length in such debates, with strenuous protestations of his own liberality and progressiveness; but his credibility did not last long . . . His background as a lawyer or "jurist" as he prefers to think of himself and his ability, unique in the Administration, to write passable English prose at lengths of more than one paragraph, made him an indispensable member of a long series of drafting committees: McGill's B and B brief and its Duff-Berdahl report both bear the Cohen imprint; so will the eventual report of the Tripartite Commission.

Cohen also takes care of coping with the hostile environment — Quebec — in such tricky areas for co-ordination as law education. Robertson, in fact, boasted of Cohen's services on a sub-committee composed of Quebec Law Deans when talking to a student leader last year. The Principal said that Dean Cohen has been "leading the sub-committee around by the nose," but added that he was interested to know what might happen when they came to realize this at some future point.[14]

---

13. Chodos, *et. al.*, "The Institutional Imperative," *loc. sit.*
14. *Ibid.*

When Maxwell Cohen could no longer pose as "an old radical," and when exhortations to "bear in mind how fragile order is" fell on deaf ears, an occasional honest statement could be found, such as "the students must be made to realize that they are not the University . . . They must achieve the humility of their age, their status, and their transitory character. This is more humility than I find in them now." (*Daily*, January 23). McGill's real men of power and most of the Faculty were too crude politically and too feeble intellectually to handle the problem of public relations *and* an intellectually vigorous student left. The situation required that Dean Frost's reactionary diatribes be kept within the Faculty and Administration and others of the old guard be muzzled or sent around to Rotary Clubs to assure the bourgeosie that "behind all the student unrest is a power-hungry minority using professional techniques and even imported leadership . . ." which McGill could be trusted to contain. Into the intellectual vacuum at the upper reaches of power at McGill new troops needed to be hurled, squads of liberal social scientists and lawyers who could fulfill the major administrative tasks of McGill in the sixties — getting money from Quebec and pacifying the suddenly obstreperous students, and "it is through the image they provide, the stratagems they devise and the carefully worded reports they write that these tasks are performed:"

> . . . skilled liberal ideologues and professional phrase-mongers are required. Enter the lawyers and political scientists: they can articulate principles and tell the students that they shouldn't be demanding what they are and can justify repressive measures in the right language . . . Enter the legal minds to pontificate on law and order, rights and freedoms.
>
> Students in H. Rocke Robertson's office ask to speak to him about his charges; Maxwell Cohen comes in and lectures them on the virtues of obedience to authority. When the students are tried by the Disciplinary Committee and discuss the issues and the justification for their act of civil disobedience, the one lawyer on the Committee writes a document outlining academic rights and freedoms, a basic one of which is "The Right of University Officers to Carry on their administrative duties without obstruction . . . Senate, at the beginning of the year, approved a report of the Senate sub-committee of the Student Disciplinary Committee, chaired by Maxwell Cohen. The resolution began with a theoretical discussion of freedom in the university and ended with a statement that any student who didn't obey the order of a building director to leave the premises could be disciplined by the committee.
>
> In each of the above instances, liberal language was being used to foster a conservative attitude to university change. As is often the case with statements produced by skilled phrase-mongers, their real meaning has to be extracted from their mystifying appearance.[15]

Rarely is the real political implication of the university liberal ever articulated. Saying anything clearly and unequivocally serves to expose the liberal's true interests and thus to threaten his "image". Reason, rational debate, viable social systems, "mixed political-technical problems," the "fragile surface of order," academic freedom: all serve to erect a wall of words between the rarified atmosphere of liberal phrase-mongering and the all too tangible empires, institutes, centres, projects, grants and the scrabble for tenure that is the real basis of the liberal's interest — self-interest firmly embedded in the jungles and swamps of the academic baronies where the law of the survival of the fittest is paramount (and the devil take the hindmost). Occasionally however, a liberal will be discovered with all of liberalism's banners proudly displayed:

---

15. *Ibid.*

But no institution facing a growing internal political opposition can continue indefinitely to restrict its intellectual responses to rephrasings of Vice President-elect Agnew on law and order (in reference to Maxwell Cohen). If the Administration is to maintain some semblance of respect on campus it needs political ideologues — men who have some understanding of the substantive arguments of the students and who can reply in kind. McGill has no such people. Its history of scientific emphasis and conservative administrators has come back to haunt it. There is no one of the calibre of California's Clerk Kerr, Columbia's David Truman or Toronto's Claude Bissell — men who can present a sophisticated liberal analysis, semi-palatable to the academic community. There is just one man at McGill who occasionally assumes that role, and his calibre indicates just how inadequate McGill's pool of social scientists is.

Saul Frankel is the paradigm Cold-War liberal of the 1950's. Having broken with his earlier Marxist-Zionist affiliations, Frankel rarely misses a chance to warn students about the Marxist Menace. Any attempt at formulating or acting upon an integrated political theory is considered as the first step towards "totalitarianism," either Communist or Nazi. Visions of organic communities are interpreted as logically and historically connected to Robespierre and the Reign of Terror.

Frankel considers himself as an intellectual. And perhaps, compared to his colleagues in the administration, he is. But more accurately, he is a smooth Whittaker Chambers. His intellectual foundations rest upon second-rate books written by second-rate academics whose world-view is essentially that of the CIA.

Totalitarianism is Evil, our system of liberal-democratic pluralism the Good. Constitutional restraints, competing power centres, constant political compromise — these are the only way to achieve the type of freedom we enjoy.[16]

The essence of liberal political practice is compromise but the arguments for reason and compromise never fail to omit the first law of politics: *compromise is directional, the weaker power compromises to the benefit of the stronger.* It is for this reason that another of liberalism's favorite shibboleths, "get the right man in the job", results in the corruption of the man, not in reform of the institution. The case of Michael Oliver is an example. Oliver was obviously uncomfortable with the role into which he was cast by McGill's institutional imperative — but that did not stop him from reading his lines. After Gray's arrest for the *SDU*[17] sit-in against Administration censorship, Gray recounted that "after hearing of the arrests and the beatings, Oliver seemed sickened by the event when he came to visit Gray in his cell at Station 10. At this point, with everything said and done, Oliver could react as a human being, not as vice-principal, to the results of a chain of events he, as vice-principal, had a direct role in creating."[18] Yet, it had been Oliver who, over opposition in the Senate, pushed through the motion passed in a secret emergency session recommending measures and a timetable to recapture the Administration building from the students" including "further and additional action" — calling the police. Oliver's "decency" was in fact exploited by the administration:

Michael Oliver's role in the Administration crystallized during last November's crisis. He was perhaps the most visible administrator, but his job had its invisible aspects as well. When the Administration had to get its version of what happened across the day after the police smashed the student sit-in, it was Michael Oliver who wrote its statement, although it was signed by Principal H. Rocke Robertson and Student's Society President Peter Smith.

16. *Ibid.*

17. SDU: Students for a Democratic University

18. Chodos, et al, *op. cit.*

Some of the details of the Oliver statement were false; it said of the violent arrests — "the single highly unfortunate incident of the entire night" — that "we are informed by police that a constable was struck twice in the face, and that only after this, did he take physical action against those whom he believed were responsible for this action." Meanwhile, the police had been testifying in court that one of them had been kicked to start the incident . . .

The Administration, in a difficult position after police had come onto campus and violence had taken place, has to explain it away while still retaining its credibility with the students and faculty. It decides on the device of a joint statement from the chief executives of the Administration and the Student's Society. And it calls on Michael Oliver to write it.[19]

Such is the establishment that a handful of radical students and faculty will throw it into panic and disarray. These men were forever boasting that the "radicals are but an unrepresentative handful" of McGill students. It must escape their attention that any sensible person would see that if so few could throw so many into such panic and provoke such repression this speaks well only for the radicals.

The McGill Student Center: for Democratization

Now let me tell you, I am an old radical . . . And here you come and you disrupt the fragile surface of order which marks any community. Bear in mind how fragile order is. Don't tamper with order, don't think that because you're in something that is called "passive resistance" this is not disorder. Or course its disorder. It's a very serious kind of disorder and it's very fragile. All systems of order are very fragile and if you have any belief in a viable society, one of the highest things you can do is to protect the order. Revolutions are justified when you have real problems. But where the society itself is socially viable, I suggest that one of your prime obligations is to worry about the fragility of the order wherever you find it.

Dean of Law, Maxwell Cohen
(Radio McGill tape)[20]

In the Fall of 1968 McGill, after a long history of political passivity, began to heat up in the aftermath of the UGEQ[21] debates and the anti-Administration demonstrations over censorship of the *McGill Daily*. Three students had emerged as leaders in the fall of 1967 and the spring of 1968: Bob Hajaly, Mark Wilson and John Fekete. Students for a Democratic University (SDU), a product of the *Daily* crisis, became an increasingly radical organization, especially after Stan Gray — newly returned from Oxford — became its chairman. When the *Daily* published John Fekete's column on November 3, 1967 it contained the infamous political satire from the *Realist*. The next day, Rocke Robertson laid charges of "obscene libel" against Fekete, Pierre Fournier, editor of the supplement

---

19. *Ibid.*

20. Reprinted in *McGill Free Press,* September 19, 1968, "McGill's distinguished Dean of Law, Maxwell Cohen, addressing a group of students sitting-in for a student newspaper free of Administration censorship."

in which the column appeared, and Peter Allnut, editor of the *Daily*. In response, 750 students led by SDU staged a demonstration against Robertson's action while 200 slept in the administration building. The following day SDU following Gray pulled out when the administration made some minor concessions. However, 60 students remained in the building and the next night some of them entered the Principal's office, whereupon the Administration called the police. Stan Gray, having returned to the action, and one other person were arrested. According to Chodos:

> Administration-student relations now resembled a state of open war. The Administration's action against Fekete, Fournier, and Allnutt was a display of naked power, and SDU and its supporters had responded using the only power they had . . . Months later, Fekete, Fournier and Allnutt received reprimands and the sit-in students were put on probation; the damage the Administration had done to its own position — with the aid of a left that knew how to use confrontation politics effectively — was far more serious. One by-product of the new situation (in marked contrast to the situation two years earlier) was the appearance of a bare left-wing majority on campus. In March, 1968, Bob Hajaly was elected president of the Students' Society . . . Ian Hyman and Peter Foster, running with Hajaly as a slate, captured the two vice-presidencies.[22]

The advent of the Hajaly, Hyman and Foster slate was reported by Kitty Hoffman in the Fall of 1968:

> Hajaly-Hyman-Foster ran as a slate last year, they were elected as a slate, and they still work as a tight group . . . Hajaly is the cerebral one of the three . . . It was he who outlined the theoretical basis of the executive's policy: "The most important thing is democratizing the university to change the type of education, given the relation between the university and society, leading to the eventual use of the university as a model for the democratization of society."[23]

In September, the *McGill Free Press* reported that the McGill Board of Governors approved recommendations for a joint Senate-Board committee, and to open these meetings (except for cases involving "confidentiality"), and that "the most drastic changes will be in the composition of the Senate, whose membership will be increased from 38 to 65. Faculty representation will be 32 instead of 9; Arts and Science, the largest faculty, will alone have 14 members[24]." McGill had moved to implement "Plan A," so to speak — student participation in order to avoid confrontation. The student pacification program also increased faculty representation, for which not a speck of gratitude was ever expressed. About the "open meetings" of Senate, Stan Gray was to write:

> The behavior of the individuals in the Senate meeting indicates that most of the members of a deliberative assembly become extremely tight-lipped when confronted with student observers. In debating Professor Frankel's motion on the CEGEPs, the decision-makers were in most instances capable of emitting only incoherent, qualified and brief mutterings. Statements by Vice-Principal Oliver, normally a very articulate and oily waffler, that "I think I deplore the students taking action" and "I feel ashamed remaining neutral in a matter like this" are striking examples of this phenomenon . . . Although there is (sic) no data to confirm this hypothesis, direct observation leads one to believe that most Senate members did not express their real preferences and opinions at this meeting. They only indirectly gave each other signals . . . Some of the less clever participants strongly

21. Union Générale des Étudiants du Québec.
22. Chodos, *op. cit.*, pp. 89-90.
23. Kitty Hoffman, "The Left-Wing Executive," in the *McGill Daily*. September 19, 1968
24. *McGill Free Press*, September 24, 1968

objected, though in cryptic language, to many clauses in Professor Frankel's motion. But our poor motion-formulator was hamstrung: with a howling minority of destructive students present, he couldn't tell his colleagues what was so evident to the observers — that the motion was a carefully-worded evasion of all the issues,, giving the appearance but none of the substance of a progressive stand. But, pushed up against the wall by the Senate cretins, Dr. Frankel emitted a direct stimulus to them: "There is nothing in the resolution that implies, in any way, support of the students' statement."[25]

Student "participation" in Senate and open meetings were to produce sufficient frustration, disillusion and cynicism to significantly contribute to the Political Science Association's vote to strike later in the year. The pattern of *formal* concession without real substance was to remain the norm throughout the brief life of McGill's student movement, to reach an apex of manipulative dishonesty in the Sociology Department's "Student-Faculty Caucus."

Throughout September and October, following the leading force of the Political Science Association, the push for democratization at McGill began to take form. On September 27 the Political Science Association began to present demands for student representation on all departmental committees on a basis of parity with faculty. On October 1 a Manifesto was issued by the PSA. On October 3 sociology students as well as students in the English Department were reported dissatisfied. The *Daily* reported the formation of Le Comite d'Action pour la Participation des Étudiants Français. By October 8 six departments were involved in the mobilization and most others were to follow. On October 3, 1968 a new organization made itself known at McGill, the Socialist Action Committee, with a program for a Critical University:

> that self-consciously develops and teaches radical and critical social theory, as opposed to the present conservative orthodoxy which simply distorts and legitimates the existent structure. The critical university would very concretely and substantively contribute its resources and intellectual productions to the exploited, oppositionist and radical sectors of society, and not to the corporate Establishment and government as it does now . . . Specifically it would establish a Trade Union School rather than a management school, do research for national liberation movements in the Third World rather than for the U.S. Defense department, train slum community organizers rather than government bureaucrats, etc.[26]

Chodos interprets the collapse of SDU and the formation of SAC (Socialist Action Committee) as a sign that the student movement was beginning to split right and left as a consequence of the incorporation of students into the Senate:

> It was precisely at this point, when the liberal battles had been won, when courses were beginning to change, when Hajaly, Hyman, and Foster were instituting long overdue measures . . . that cracks began to show in the student movement. The Hajaly-Hyman-Foster slate's most serious opposition came not from Arnie Aberman-style right-wingers but from liberals, people who had previously been allies. One of that group, Julius Grey, was elected and on Senate continually sided with the Administration against the rest of the students. Meanwhile, SDU had collapsed, leaving only its core, a group of people dedicated to basic change in the university and society who now called themselves the Socialist Action Committee.

25. Stan Gray, "The Greatest Show on Earth, or, On the Historical Experience of Open Meetings: Some Empirical Generalizations," *McGill Daily*. October 24, 1968
26. From the "letters" section of the *McGill Daily*. October 4, 1968

There was at least one thing on which radicals and liberals could still agree — although there were tensions here too — and that was departmental reform.[27]

Meanwhile, by October 10 to 11 more than six French CEGEPs were occupied as was the University of Montreal in support of the CEGEP strikes. The CEGEPs mobilized the support of the McGill left, but in general:

McGill students supported the CEGEP occupations with resolutions [but] there was no sign that they were willing to fight for the transformation of their own university as a partial solution to the CEGEP crisis . . . the show of unity between McGill students and the Quebecois was illusory.[28]

There can be no doubt that the CEGEP strikes and occupations were a stimulous to the McGill student movement. Yet as early as October, 1968 it was also beginning to be evident that McGill students, with the exception of the left, were unwilling to give up or go beyond the parochial privileges of McGill itself. This would be overwhelmingly demonstrated in the lack of McGill student support for Operation McGill in March. Furthermore, while the manifestos, analytical articles and rhetoric of the democratization battle would reflect leftist themes, the majority of the support for departmental democratization was liberal, not radical. McGill was not a French CEGEP. The logic of the colonial situation drove McGill students to stand on the wrong side of Quebec's great contradictions. Perhaps this best explains why co-option was overwhelmingly effective in containing the McGill student movement. The majority of McGill departments faced with demands for student parity ("democratization") quickly moved to containment by proposing various harmless forms of student participation. This included the Sociology Department, which refused the students' parity, but put forward the concept of a "community of scholars" within which elected representatives of the Sociology Students Union would form a caucus and in which decisions would be reached by consensus. The whole system was dependent upon the faculty's "good faith".

The one department that did *not* move to co-opt the "democratization" movement was Political Science — the *one* department, one would think, that would know that ever since 1848, reformism had been the one means to contain rebellious movements! In the open meetings, debates, papers and speeches preceeding the November 18, 1968 rejection by Political Science faculty of a negotiated settlement, the reason for rejecting student demands had been student incompetence — that is, classic professional arguments so thin that students had no difficulty whatsoever in tearing them to shreds. The real combat came down over the hiring committee, just as we would expect, for as we have seen, control over hiring and promotion is the very keystone of professionalism. The situation was one of pure power politics, but nowhere were howls of injury greater than when students pointed out the obvious:

After a full day of discussion between faculty and students in the Political Science section of the Department of Economics and Political Science Friday, it has become obvious that the division between students and faculty is irreconcilable . . . Professor Mallory, Chairman of the Department . . . said that direct student participation in the process is impossible as it is a "professional matter." He admitted that, incorporated into the process of tenure and promotion, there was a "system for mutual protection" which is "naturally prone to resist any intrusions." . . . Lecturer Stan Gray asserted that the only way to avoid a climate of continuous

---

27. Chodos, *op. cit.*, p. 91
28. *Ibid.*, 92

power struggle is to give students parity on all committees . . . Professor Nayar took an opposite view, stating that only the department chairman and administration should make the decision to hire staff, thus excluding not only students but also faculty . . . Professer Shingler, who denied every interpretation of his comments, and at one point indicated the possibility that he wasn't even present, is generally believed to have advocated the communitarian approach. An attempt was made by Professor Brecher to steer the arguments away from what Professor Frankel called the process of "power conquest." He said that the "distrust reflects a breakdown of community," and that "We must recreate this shattered community."[29]

The same arguments, almost word for word, were to be repeated in Sociology.

The Political Science faculty announced on November 18 that it rejected the negotiated settlement produced by its own commission! That was the last straw for the Political Science Association. On November 26, 1968 PSA went on strike and occupied the fourth floor Leacock building. The strike was 100% effective in Political Science and enjoyed wide student support on the campus. Ten days later, the "faculty accepts offer from Poli Sci students." The agreement ending the strike stipulated an eight-man appointments committee including two students, with decisions subject to review by section, on which students would have one-third representation:

> The motion to accept the settlement agreed to, Wednesday, by student and faculty negotiators, passed almost unanimously. Before it was voted upon, speaker after speaker cautioned that the association's original objective, parity, must not be forgotten, and without this equal representation, any talk of "victory would be meaningless.[30]

The Chairman of the PSA, Arnold August, stated:

> The strike had a terrific politicization effect on hundreds of students . . . it has given them the impetus and political experience to carry on the fight for parity next fall by the same type of action carried out in the last few weeks."[31]

Arnold August was wrong. The student movement at McGill died with the PSA strike and the "compromise agreement." The basic agreement had been analysed in an earlier *Daily* editorial in this fashion:

> But even beyond that, this scheme makes it possible to cut out the minority of faculty that would side with the students on appointments questions. This is a scheme which makes no attempt to disguise the basic intent of cutting the students and probably the radical faculty right out of the key appointments area.[32]

The final agreement differed only slightly to the scheme so accurately described above. Later in the year (March, 1969) a student, Mary Johnston, summed up the experience of students "Playing the reform game":

> After three years of organized student agitation and lobbying, and more than a year and a half of Administration PR blurbs and approvals-on-principle, McGill University's progress in improving what goes on in the classroom is still on a treadmill. Every indication is that educational innovation at McGill will remain ineffective for a long time to come. This isn't accidental; behind the facade of "urgent con-

29. Robert Miller, "Everybody Split in Poli Sci," *McGill Daily,* November 4, 1968

30. Robert Miller, "PSA Accepts Compromise," *McGill Daily,* December 6, 1968

31. *Ibid.*

32. "The Power Play," *McGill Daily* editorial, November 18, 1968

cern" and the kind of Senate legislation which lends itself to celebration in press releases, every halting step which McGill has taken has been designed to *ensure* that no real progress whatsoever will result.[33]

It is now 1975 and it still remains that "no real progress whatsoever will result."

The McGill student left: for a Critical University

The actions of student militants are not spontaneous demonstrations of a justified feeling, but operations carefully planned and sometimes aided by quasi-professional agitators who move from campus to campus employing such techniques as walkie-talkie instructions to agitate the crowds for maximum effectiveness . . . Behind all the student unrest is a power-hungry minority using professional techniques and even imported leadership to take over the universities.

McGill University's Dean Mordell, quoted in *McGill Free Press,* September 19, 1968

There are three lines of demarcation between the left of the student movement and its centre and right wing. The right wing, represented at McGill in 1968 by students like Julius Grey, defected to the Administration in return for various plums of office that accrued from student representation in Senate. The centre adopted "democratization" at the department level as its chief concern. The left, on the other hand, stood for, (1) socialism, (2) Quebec independence, and (3) genuinely radical change in the university. The left went through a number of transformations and organizational representations, but it was powerful in its influence in the *McGill Daily.* Student's Council and the Political Science Association. As was true throughout the student movement, the intellectual and practical work was done by the left; relative political sophistication was also a characteristic of the left and was the basis of its militancy — and what made it dangerous. The liberal tricks, the cheating compromises, the fast faculty double talk were unable to baffle and bamboozle the left leadership, which included Stan Gray. The majority of students, on the other hand, were easily led by the nose and repeatedly settled for minor concessions or changes in form without substance.

Analysis of the polemical articles in the *Daily* on students and the student movement demonstrate an inability to move beyond a "student as class" assumption about student activism. The McGill student Left's inability to distinguish the various meanings and concrete situations of student movements probably contributed to their incorrect analysis of McGill. Specifically, there is no indication that the Left leadership understood, for example, that it was not students who had practically halted France, but the French proletariat. Equally, there is no sign that the McGill student leaders understood the interconnections between

---

33. Mary Johnston, *"On Playing the Reform Game,"* McGill Daily, March 14, 1969

racism and imperialism i.e., the draft, upon which the student movement in the U.S.A. was based. Finally, it seems clear that the McGill leadership understood colonialism as a factor in the CEGEP uprisings and in McGill as an institution, but not the implications of colonialism for the McGill student body — who had as big a stake in the Anglophone privileges which McGill represented as did the Administration and Faculty. In short, the McGill student Left was a *student* Left, and manifested the immaturity and simplistic analysis that has plagued most of the international student movement.

The student movements in general suffered from an inability to understand themselves. The general over-estimation of the revolutionary potential of students (and a concomitant inability to see the limits of student agitation) plagued McGill no less than it did the student movement in the U.S.A. This weakness manifested itself in the student left's incapacity to *anticipate* the splits that university liberals were to exploit so successfully. When co-optation pacified the liberal centre of the student movement, the left found itself high and dry, and alone on the barricades. The McGill Administration is forever taking credit for what was historically determined, not by clever machinations and liberal verbiage, but by the class contradictions contained within the student movement itself.

What is of interest at McGill was the Administration's moves to exploit the internal differences within the student movement. Sham reformism proved to be more effective than red-baiting or appeals to reason and order. So long as minimal demands were rejected, as in the Political Science Department, the left leadership continued as the leading force and the students could not be split. But the moment that a long-haul had to be chosen over premature capitulation, the student centre collapsed and moved away from the left. The mass of privileged Anglophone students at McGill pursued within the student movement what they perceived to be their class and status advantages, just as did the faculty and administration. If the left is to be faulted, it is for its own initial incomprehension of the contradictions that class interest imposes upon a student movement.

The maturing of the student left throughout 1968-69 is recorded in its published articles and position papers, and is finally demonstrated in Opération McGill. The action was in Quebec, in the Quebecois independence struggle, and that demarcation, more than any other, was to split the left from the student centre. The split manifested itself very early, but did not become an open split until the PSA strike settlement with its clearly co-optive programme — any hope for a struggle oriented to a "critical university" went out the window after the PSA strike ended. McGill had demonstrated, as had Columbia, Chicago, Berkeley, San Francisco and so many others, that students were not a "class" and as a mass could not be propelled beyond reforms — in fact, usually could not be made to understand that the reforms granted to them were meaningless. The result at McGill was to strip the university of its left, both through repression and through the great bitterness of the leftists themselves who voluntarily departed to do political work with classes and strata that were capable of being revolutionary forces.

The Department of Political Science: Studies in Political Incompetence

"Distrust reflects a breakdown of community . . . We must recreate this shattered community."
Professor Brecher, Political Science, as quoted in the *McGill Daily*

How are we able to understand the apparent anomaly — that Political Science and Economics, a presumably liberal department, should be the department that provoked confrontation? Democratization was demanded in the traditionally conservative departments like Engineering and the Medical School without escalating into a full scale strike and occupation.

Indeed, the exception was the Political Science Department. Indications of intransigence on the part of Political Science and Economics (a joint department at the time) were given as early as October, 1968 when a former ally was pushed into declaring himself:

> The Political Science meeting .vas subjected to a lengthy tirade delivered by one John Shingler, Assistant Professor. Asked to express his opinion on the students' demand for representational parity with the faculty, Professor Shingler began his 15 minute trip by asking the Political Science Association whom they represented and expressing his strong suspicion that they consisted of only a-vociferous minority of all Political Science Students. Professor Shingler then addressed his remarks to the main issue on the floor: the student demand for parity. He was quite clear about what he thought of their position: it was an extremely radical measure that has never been introduced anywhere in North America, it was no solution to the real problems, and anyway this was the first time he had heard of the demand for parity and he had not yet formulated an opinion on it. The kids would be better off, he thought, if they had informal student-faculty discussions and parties. When Professor Shingler had finished, puzzled expressions came over the faces of the PSA leaders. John Shingler (who calls himself an anarchist) had been their political mentor.[34]

It would seem that the key factor was Stan Gray himself. Gray was a Marxist activist, a lecturer in the Political Science Department, but also an articulate and prolific theoretician for the left-wing of the student movement. As a Marxist activist one's enemies are not only the reactionaries — that is obvious. One's enemies are also the liberals, for liberals (like wolves in sheep's clothing) are reactionaries in disguise.

Gray himself set about answering this question, why the Poltical Science Department, in an essay published in November, 1968.[35] The article is astounding, for its description of the "mood of the faculty" would be repeated in the Sociology Department — where it would become not a mood, but a state of mind and a way of life — a permanent state of siege that would last from late 1969 to late 1974. Gray began by tracing the evolution of the "mood of the faculty:"

---

34. Gray, "The Greatest Show on Earth", *op. cit.*

35. Stan Gray, "The Mood of the Faculty: Poli Sci Holds the Line," *McGill Daily,* November 26, 1968. All citations that follow.

When students began to organize the Political Science Association in early Fall, the first faculty reactions were personal and confused. Most recognized the legitimacy or the necessity of limited student participation, but couldn't handle anything that went beyond this. They tended to regard student demands for some representation on the appointments committee as either insane or malicious. Nor could they grasp why the students were protesting the dominance in courses, and in the department as a whole of a particular orientation in political analysis.

More fundamentally, most of them, particularly those insecure about their own competence and privileged faculty status, felt threatened by student criticism and organization.

Gray's next point would become a dominant theme in Sociology, the universal explanation for the disasters that were to befall them:

And some of the more imaginative types began to think that this whole thing was a preconceived plot, perhaps originating in Peking, to destroy the department . . . A senior social science professor in another Department recounted to me the conversations he was having with other political science faculty. Apparently, he said, they conceived of this whole PSA phenomenon as a sinister Marxist plot to seize the Department. They viewed the majority of the PSA as a monolithic bloc of hardline Bolsheviks bent upon destroying the university. As a first step, they were making a test case out of the political science section. If political science fell, no part of the university would be safe. Visions of soviet-type people's courts to try the professors, totalitarian repression, etc., haunted them constantly.

Indeed, the preservation of the status quo becomes the mission of the Political Science Faculty:

Furthermore, he said, the political science faculty saw their own role as one of saving the whole university. The logic of their domino theory led them to view themselves as a vanguard performing a counterinsurgency service for all other departments — defeat the communist thrust here, and all can be saved.

If hordes of Bolshevik students bent on destructive revolution and totalitarian people's courts were not bad enough, the communists were also boring from within:

The faculty was also convinced that an internal fifth column was operating in their midst. The two professors besides myself who differed with the majority were seen as instigating and leading on the students behind their backs, in this plan to produce a Political Science Soviet.

The fact that we three had expressed sharp differences on these issues, in public and in faculty meetings, was said to be a clever ploy to confuse them. Our criticisms of the PSA were similarly interpreted. When asked to provide proofs of their interpretation, the replies were of the following order: "Well, you're all in political philosophy," or "You're for the students, aren't you?"

And deep in their minds, they knew the students couldn't themselves come up with all these clever and sophisticated arguments being used to support their demands — only the faculty, after all, is deemed competent — so it must be originating from those faculty radicals.

If the reader finds this bizarre, one need only turn to the documents section of this book and glance through the "Secret Proceedings from the Department of Sociology." There, such speculations are genteelly termed "international socialist network."

Gray then reviewed the faculty's response to the intellectual challenges presented by the students:

After some paternalistic and ineffective attempts to convince the students that they shouldn't bother with the work involved in running the Political Science section, the faculty's first try at an articulated intellectual position consisted in a collective breast-beating exercise: faculty are more competent than students, therefore they should have more power.

When answered that competence, and judgements about competence, are interconnected with political-intellectual orientation, and that students were able to and had the right to judge orientations, the faculty were confused. This argument didn't fit into any of their preconceived assumptions and intellectual categories.

Nor did they understand the demand for critical courses and professors, and they proceeded to misinterpret and distort, perhaps unconsciously, the student position. They also felt menaced — for people were saying that their theories and their teaching were not the only ones possible in political science.

Towards the end of the article (which it is a pity not to reprint in its entirety) Gray makes a statement which can speak for all of us "Bolsheviks":

I have never ceased to be amazed at how Political Science [and one might add sociology] faculty members, who constantly proclaim their superior competence and scientific understanding in this field, so totally misinterpret and bungle a political situation they themselves are involved in.

Their overall stance applied, for a far more protracted period, in the Sociology Department as well:

At this point, rational and honest discussion with the faculty majority is difficult. They see themselves in a power confrontation with the forces of evil, and, in such a situation, they must not flinch. "Flexibility" and "compromise" are dirty words and even the *appearance* of flexibility and compromise is pornographic.

The last puzzle to be solved is why didn't Political Science fire Stan Gray? Why force the Administration to wield its own ax?

The Administration is the context within which the faculty wages its struggle for individual careers and departmental power and glory. Much is made of the conflicts for "autonomy" between individual departments and the Administration (just as much is made of conflicts for "autonomy" between the Administration and the Trustees and Legislatures). It is, in reality, much ado about nothing. Historically, autonomy has been a function of effective self-policing; that is equally true of the conflict between the Administration and departments. In any case, in 1968, the Political Science Department was interlocked with the Administration, since "every full professor of Political Science except one carried a heavy administrative load". The responsibility for controlling Gray lay with the department which had hired him: Political Science. But the normal firing procedures by which unwanted individuals are dismissed would not work in Gray's case: he had the backing of the student movement and was a leader of the student left. The firing of Gray could not be done in secret and carried the danger of further confrontation. The Department was trapped between the Administration and the students. The Department's liberal image, which it had peddled to new heights of influence in the McGill power structure, was crumbling; expertise in political matters (for were not political "scientists" *experts* in politics?) was noticeably absent; as Chodos dryly notes, "during the strike, faculty members were forced out into the open as administrators had been earlier; political scientists, it turned out, were unable to handle a real political situation. Political Science at McGill was tried and found wanting . . . "[36] To have fired

36. Chodos, "A Short History of Student Activism at McGill", *loc. cit.*

Gray after the PSA strike disaster would have dealt the Department, both within and without McGill, yet another stunning blow to its image. Political Science threw the bomb back into the lap of the Administration.

Opération McGill

For a century and a half this city and this province have had a university on the south side of Mount Royal
"Yes," we say, "it has been one of the world's great universities!"
Yes — we have been proud of it!
Yes — it has produced many great scholars in science, medicine, engineering and the arts!
"But maybe," we have wondered, "It is living in its past — out of step with the present — a creature of the establishment — of Anglo colonialism — a hot-bed of student power."
Gentlemen, you, the public, had better do a thoughtful assessment of McGill right now because its very existence is threatened. It is under attack from some sources and under pressure from others.
From Stanley Gray and his revolutionaries
From Lemieux and his Ligue pour l'Integration Scolaire
From Chartrand and his violent separatists
From the taxpayers who foot the bills
From restless youth who demand change in society — your society
From you who say "let the administration straighten out these kids before you come to me for support"
From a sensitive government which considers pressures as well as need in establishing budgets
The news compound the difficulty when they over-dramatize news and editorials
The time has come for Quebecers — all of us — to decide whether we need an English-speaking university called McGill in Montreal. It cannot remain strong without strong public support and protection
We have reached the point where
The revolutionaries think you will let them smash it — physically
It took 150 years to build
It remains one of the world's great universities
It can be destroyed overnight.
Robert Shaw, Vice-Principal (Administrative) from a speech delivered to the Montreal Bar Association on March 24, 1969, four days before Opération McGill (McGill français; McGill aux Québécois)

The *McGill Daily* of Wednesday, February 12, 1969 carried two big headlines on its front page: "SGWU Bust Hits 94; Computer a Total Loss," and "Administration Out to Fire Gray." The cooptation of the centre and the decline of the student movement had left McGill and Sir George Williams University free to pursue their final solution: the repression and purging of the left. At Sir George Williams University the purge would be violent and brutal for it was against Black students; at McGill the purge would be full of legalistic liberalism until "the white niggers of America", ten thousand strong, would march against McGill. The Administration had underestimated its adversary.

The assault on the Sir George Williams occupation was a clear sign that decisions had been taken in favor of repression over concession. With the blunting of the edge of student militance, Administrations were given a free hand to carry out what they had always intended: repression. Liberal concessions were no more than delaying tactics and pacification programs. The assault on the Sir George occupation lead to retaliation by the black students — the destruction of millions of dollars worth of property, including the sacred symbol of technological society, a *computer!* Hysteria now provided an atmosphere in which repression could not only be justified, it could be demanded — the CEGEP students and now the Black students! The spectre of revolution haunted English Montreal.

The technicality for which Gray was to be fired was his participation in a disruption of the Board of Governors meeting in late January, 1969. The Political Science Department had refused to fire Gray — they had not the grounds to do so without it being obvious that he was being purged; they could not be sure that such an action would not inspire the Political Science Association with new life, thus provoking the spectre of a second strike. The faculty Senate acquitted Gray of the disruption charges. Nonetheless, the Principal continued the campaign to fire Gray. The reason was quite obvious: Gray had successfully established links between the McGill student left and the Quebec independentists. Gray had become the "fifth column" *inside* McGill. As such, Gray and the student left were no longer internal problems; they were now part of the menacing and escalating Quebec revolutionary movement. The McGill left had been deprived of a relatively harmless constituency of McGill students, only to gain allies before whom the entire McGill Establishment trembled. McGill's real vulnerability to a genuine left was now revealed: not its own students, but forces within itself who would act so as to demystify McGill in Quebec, to make its stand on the wrong side of both of the great contradictions of Quebec society glaringly evident. This was to be the real legacy of the McGill student movement.

The technicalities of Gray's firing and the hounding of the student leaders do not concern the main thread of our story which occurs in the aftermath. Little if any attempt was made by the McGill Administration to hide the fact that they considered their actions against Gray and the student left to be counter-revolution, pure and simple. These were dangerous subversives who must be removed at all cost from McGill. The liberals in the Senate might obfuscate, but power speaks to power: Gray and the Administration both understood the situation perfectly.[37] Therefore, what we must understand is Opération McGill, which came *after* the initial moves by the Administration to fire Gray — for it was Opération McGill that they feared and had hoped to head off by Gray's removal. In this they had been foiled by the liberals — and would remain foiled until the summer recess. Well-meaning liberals at McGill will still quack about

37. When the Administration failed to get Political Science to fire Gray, they next tried the Academic Senate, where the proceedings where televised for the benefit of McGill students and faculty. The Senate refused to act against Gray for the Board of Governors disruption, forcing the University Administration to fire him. The appeal against the Administration was delayed until the summer recess. Gray lost the appeal and was thus finally fired from McGill.

the Gray affair to this day; they understand no more now than they did in the winter and spring of 1969.

Yet it was Opération McGill and the Sir George Williams occupation that were to create the repression and the reaction which two women were to stumble into in the fall of 1969, for neither McGill nor Sir George Williams have ever been the same since — anymore than Columbia or Chicago or Berkeley were ever the same again. What was going to happen at McGill (what had happened in the U.S.A.) was the collapse of the liberal facade and the emergence in its most brutal clarity of the real institutional imperatives of the modern multiversity.

The first notice of Opération McGill appeared in the *McGill Daily* on March 14, 1969. However, the notice had been preceeded by a number of articles on Quebec labour, Quebec independence and McGill in Quebec, several authored by Stan Gray. A number of endorsements of Gray and statements of his relevance to the Quebec independence movement had also been published. The "great day" was introduced ordinarily enough:

> A coalition of student, worker, and radical groups is organizing a demonstration March 28 focussed on the role of McGill University in Quebec society.
>
> The demonstrators will protest inequalities in Quebec higher education epitomized by the position of McGill University. Although 83% of the population of Quebec is French-speaking, 42% of the university places are in English universities and English universities receive 30% of government grants to higher education.
>
> Their demands include a three-year program to make McGill a French-language university, the admission of a substantial number of the 10,000 displaced CEGEP graduates in September, the lowering of McGill's fees which would be by $200, bring them into line with l'Université de Montréal's, the abolition of the French Canada Studies Programme, "which studies the Quebec people like vulgar "natives" and "indigènes"," and the opening of McLennan Library to the public.
>
> Groups involved in the demonstration include worker's committees, action committees in the CEGEPS and at l'U de M. le Mouvement d'intégration scolaire, le Front de libération populaire, and le Comité indépendance-socialisme. Some McGill students who hold socialist and independentist views have also participated in its organization.
>
> The demonstration will take the form of a march from St. Louis Square to the McGill campus, beginning at eight on the evening of March 28.[38]

The McGill Administration and the government were planning to defend the University against the criticism it was receiving. McGill hired the public relations firm of Yves Jasmin (who did the publicity for Expo 67) to "improve its image among the French-speaking Québécois." The Administration also planned a French-language edition of its newspaper, the *McGill Reporter,* to be distributed to the French community, but then decided "it would be unwise at this time, on the grounds that the Administration didn't have enough to say to the French community."

The Ministry of Education, in the meantime, was planning a campaign to counter the "impassioned propaganda" of the demonstration organizers with "objective information" on McGill. An editorial in the semi-official Union Nationale paper Montréal-Matin concluded by saying: "If there were to be no more McGill, it would be necessary to create one."

The organizers of Opération McGill were to be subjected to police harassment throughout the previous month, including at least 25 arrests between the 18th and 28th of March and the search and detention of 9 of the leaders (which

---

38. "What Will Happen March 28?" *McGill Daily,* March 14, 1969.

included almost all of these from McGill). The atmosphere of hysteria that was being systematically promoted by McGill, the English press and the Montreal police was interpreted by the organizers as preparing the ground for severe repression. The tone was set by Shaw's famous "Iron Curtain and stop-the-Francos-at-the-Roddick-Gates" speech (part of which introduces this section):

> The revolutionaries use disruption and violence in the name of democracy. We must not permit them to trap us into using such tactics. We must be patient but firm. We must resist violence but not initiate it. We must suffer your accusations that we waited too long — moved too fast — were gutless.
> Believe me, the toughest job in the world today is to be a gutless university administrator.[39]

Shaw's position was eagerly adopted by the English Canadian newspaper advance coverage of the demonstration:

> Turner announces Quebec requested troops on standby. Almost every headline in the country stands to attention: the Globe and Mail blows eight columns on the troops-on-alert story, and discusses when the army is permitted to fire on a crowd, with tear gas or light machine guns.
> The Ottawa Citizen headline. Thursday: "Troops Stand By"
> Toronto Star: "Police set for riot by 5,000 in all-French McGill March"
> Toronto Telegram: "McGill Threat: Mounties move in"
> Edmonton Journal: "Montreal Watches a tense McGill in fear"
> To an English-language reader anywhere outside Montreal, this was the picture: thousands of separatists, anarchists, Marxists and hoods are going to attack one of the greatest institutions in the world. They want to destroy it. Why? Because they're separatists, anarchists, Marxists and hoods. But. The police and army will protect McGill. Now everyone waits in fear.[40]

And, when it was all over Mark Wilson wrote an editorial, "Twilight of the Gods:"

> Whatever else it accomplished, Opération McGill brought to light two important points. First, in spite of the atmosphere of impending carnage and violence which Shaw, Gilbert, and allies took every opportunity to create, the marchers did turn out in strength. This is not quite to say that repression doesn't work: it does. Large numbers who supported Opération McGill stayed home simply because they were afraid of getting their heads smashed by the police. But this time such tactics did not work well enough. Second, it forced into the open the true line-up of forces in Quebec at this time. On the one side, there was the McGill Administration, several police forces, editorial writers, Levesque's Parti Québécois. On the other side: students from CEGEPs and universities, a few sympathetic journalists, workers' groups (including such negligible fringe organizations as the 65,000 member Montreal Council of the CSN).
> As it turned out, the true division of forces was not on lines of language or race; there were English and French on both sides. It was a division between oppressors and oppressed. One side has people, the other has money and guns.
> And the independence movement in Quebec got a clear glimpse of the weapons which will be brought to bear against it as it continues to grow in strength, when the Quebec government made arrangement for federal troops a few days before the march . . . Charles Taylor said last week that the essence of a University is not its buildings but its teaching staff. Perhaps. But those who marched last

39. Robert Shaw (Vice-Principal Academic) "The Time Has Come For Quebecers to Decide Whether We Need an English-speaking University Called McGill in Montreal," speech delivered to Montreal Bar Association, March 24, 1969, reprinted in the *McGill Student Handbook*, 1969.
40. Mark Starowicz, "Terrorism in the Press: An Analysis of the Press Coverage of "Operation McGill," *McGill Daily*, April 2, 1969

Friday are unlikely to forget what they saw as they came to the Roddick Gates — dozens of buildings with every window lighted, separated from them by a thousand policemen equipped like the Huns in Alexander Nevsky.[41]

In October, 1970 Quebec got more than a glimpse of the weapons that would be brought to bear against it. If many were not revolutionaries when they came to McGill, they were when they left it.

McGill in 1969

To anyone who has believed in the basic decency and flexibility of liberal institutions, in the pluralist university, and in the possibility of effecting change from within the system, this should give pause.
Robert Chodos and Mark Starowicz

In the spring of 1969 the left at McGill read the signs and portents of the Sir George Williams repression and the Administration's moves against Gray. In February Peter Foster wrote "The New, Hard Line"[42], an analysis of the shift to repressive policies that was to prove an accurate picture of McGill then and to the present.

Foster begins by reporting on a closed MAUT meeting held during the PSA strike in which Arts and Science Dean Woods referred to the activist elements of the student movement as "dedicated, evil men," and "told the assembled faculty and administrators that the task at hand was essentially one of out-manoeuvering the enemy." Woods continued with a long, emotional tirade in which he said that "the consequences of student participation in the process of hiring and firing of staff, [will be] consequences which are in his considered opinion, horrendous."

Woods' position was in direct contradiction to his public pronouncements on "democratization" in which he had been the Administration's leading advocate of "compromise and dialogue." Woods had "insisted at length in conversations with student leaders" that he had "not reached a personal opinion on the hiring and firing question, that he saw both advantages and disadvantages to a substantial student role."

Principal Rocke Robertson also reflected the "new, hard line." In his welcoming speech to the freshman class Robertson had told them that he was in favour of democratizing the university and that he thought student activism was a healthy phenomenon. On Thursday, February 13 at Gray's hearing on misconduct, Robertson told a "stunned audience of 250 students that he was unqualifiedly opposed to democratization as it has been defined by McGill students for the last two years, that he thought this idea of 'control of decision-making by those affected by it' is not at all the way he wants to see his university run."

41. Mark Wilson, "Twilight of the Gods," McGill Daily, April 2, 1969
42. Peter Foster, "The New, Hard Line," McGill Daily, February 17, 1969

Both Principal Robertson and Vice-Principal Oliver had been proponents of the "compromise and dialogue" policy at McGill. However, in 1967 Robertson had terminated dialogue by calling the cops. In a brief January meeting with the Board of Governors Robertson "displayed his contempt and cynicism for the activists in a remark to a Governor: Don't worry — there'll be no violence — these boys are as yellow as can be.'" Oliver had remarked to a student at the Gray hearing: "If students should occupy our [the Administration] building, we'll be ready for them . . . we'll simply pick 'em up and cart 'em away." Foster comments: "Wham. All at once. Goodby radicals, goodby dissent, goodby demand for change."

Foster sums up the evolution of McGill Administration policy as follows:

> The orientation on the part of the Administration is only now becoming clear to the members of the University. Since early summer, when University bosses from coast-to-coast met to discuss common problems (how to contain the students and maintain the status quo), the liberal elements within the Administration have had control of policy. Their tactic was to grant some token concessions, proclaim flexibility, and never be provoked. In this way, they reasoned, the radical students would be cut off from the moderates, and they could carry on with the business of running the university without being bothered by strikes and occupations and things.
>
> This is why eight students were seated on Senate, why meetings were opened, why Rocke Robertson came out for democracy and said that radicals were good for the university.
>
> Since then the empirical situation has changed. The radicals didn't go away. They grew stronger, in fact. Putting students on Senate proved to be a dysfunctional move: the bastards refused to be 'co-opted' (Max Cohen's word) into the system, and university business slowed to a near halt. The natives got increasingly restless, enough to hold a strike and occupation . . .
>
> The argument offered by liberal members of the Administration began to lose its effect. Some of the liberals themselves began to change their mind . . .

Attempts to close meetings to students on Senate Committees and Arts and Science faculty meetings and the Board of Governors provoked a number of so-called "disruptions" i.e., students coming to the meetings invited or not. Of course, the real business of Senate and Arts and Faculty was going on in the closed meetings. The open meetings were no more than show. The Board of Governors incident precipitated

> the breakdown of the liberal facade. It is one thing to challenge hired administrators. It is another thing entirely to challenge the very men who control Quebec and Canada, let alone McGill.

The Board of Governors meeting "disruption" led to University spokesmen's taking a "law and order" line in the press for the first time. The "administrators, discovering that the radicals would not go away, declared open war on them:"

> The mechanics for this new Administration policy are not hard to decipher. Proponents of the failed strategy used since last summer are discredited, and right-wing administrators are firmly entrenched in the driver's seat of the University . . . The climate is part of the violent repression of student demands which is growing rapidly all over the world . . .
>
> But it should underline certain necessities and certain realities of the student movement. It points out clearly the limited size and potential of students within

society as a whole, and the necessity for alliance with other progressive groups, particularly within the working class.

Foster was very well placed to make such an analysis as part of the Hajaly-Hyman-Foster slate in Students Council. About this time Foster resigned from his student government post with a muted statement indicating that he had come to the conclusion that the limits of student politics made it impossible for him to remain at such a post.

The policy of repression was carried on in the Fall of 1969. Mark Wilson was forced to resign as editor of the *Daily*, making way for a pliable and subservient *Daily* editor acceptable to the Administration. Students were removed from many of the posts which had been given to them in the "compromise and dialogue" period. Student opposition to these moves by the Administration was minimal. McGill had lost its left leadership through repression and through a natural growth process; that is, the activists had learned that the battle for independence and for socialism in Quebec was not going to be fought or won in the McGill Administration building. The leftist students remaining at McGill were embittered by the refusal of the McGill student movement to support Opération McGill and had opted for the "assimilation" line — to assimilate to French language and culture on the grounds that there was no real hope for a progressive movement within the colonizer culture of English Montreal. Furthermore, the role of McGill in Quebec had been clarified, its true function and nature had been exposed. To the leftist, McGill was the enemy: and one does not reform an enemy — one abolishes him.

A last reserve of progressive students still remained in the Sociology Department. These students had not been part of the group close to Gray and had not suffered either the aspirations or the trauma of Opération McGill. They spent months of frustrated struggle to acquire a radical for their Department. To head off a possible strike (which would have joined forces with the PSA on the fourth floor Leacock), Sociology faculty accepted a compromise: candidate for faculty Marlene Dixon from the University of Chicago. One assumes that the faculty must have thought her basically tractable or at least manageable, while the students took what they could get. As for Marlene Dixon, she had left Chicago without a trace of belief in the "basic decency and flexibility of liberal institutions" nor any illusions concerning the possibility "of effecting change within the system". When she came to McGill she was still suffering, much like the McGill veterans of Opération McGill, from the harsh lessons of Chicago, and the Battle for People's Park in Berkeley: the power of University Administrators, no less than big capitalists and the State, grew out of the barrel of a gun.

PART III:

The Anatomy of Repression:
Confidential Documents

SIR, — When Emile Zola wrote his famous "J'accuse," he continued with a statement of the grounds for his accusation . . . If Prof. Vaillancourt has direct evidence to support her claim, it should be presented. If she has no evidence, the course of both intellectual and personal integrity would be to withdraw the charge and to make apologies.

Richard Hamilton, Professor of Sociology, "Prof. Vaillancourt's asser-:r-tions should be backed by evidence," *Gazette*, January 30, 1973

The secrecy and confidentiality which surrounds faculty-hiring procedures permits such informal blacklisting to take place. There are some senior professors who, when they hear of a caucus person being considered for a job in another department where they have a friend, dash off an immediate letter to him dropping the crucial code word "unprofessional conduct." . . . The applicant does not know what happened because he can never see the letter which blackballed him, and in some cases, he may never know that the letter was written. The whole process of confidential letters, which is usually cited as the "professional" way of making new appointments, can easily be turned into a procedure which has no due process, no chance of reply to charges, and no redress.

Surkin and Wolfe

Chronology:

Spring, 1969   Dixon and Vaillancourt interviewed by Sociology and Political Science Departments, offered 3-year contracts, accept.

Repression of McGill student movement begins. Administration begins action that will culminate in firing Gray, *after* Dixon and Vaillancourt had been offered contracts.

June, 1969   Ernst Haas attempts to sabotage Pauline Vaillancourt's McGill appointment.

July, 1969   Special meeting of McGill Political Science decides: "In the circumstances, the risks of not making the appointment were far greater than the risks of going ahead with it.".

Daily reports that Dixon appointment challenged by Board of Governors; appointment confirmed after protests by McGill Faculty Union and Department.

September, 1969   Dixon and Vaillancourt come to McGill to begin their appointments.

The Dixon and Vaillancourt Appointments: Fall, 1969.

The following motion was moved by Ed Horka and seconded by James de Wilde: "Moved that the Department of Political Science officially censure Frank Furedi for breach of confidence in purporting to give an account of the proceedings of the Appointments Committee." After a brief discussion it was passed unanimously. Minutes of the Special Meeting of the Department of Political Science held on Friday, April 13, 1973 at 2:00 p.m. subsequent to the publication of Furedi's "Statement Regarding Appointments Committee Meeting of the Department of Political Science of McGill university on July 31, 1969", McGill *Free Press*, April 10, 1973.

The front page of the *McGill Daily* of September 17, 1969 carried two stories affirming Foster's prediction made the previous spring: reaction was setting in to stay in the upper levels of McGill's Administration. One story informs us that "Student's Council last night fired Mark Wilson, editor-in-chief of the *McGill Daily* . . . ". The firing of the brilliant young Wilson, one of the rather glittering collection of radicals on the 1968-69 Starowicz *Daily* and part of the Gray pro-Quebec left, signalled the effective purge of the student left and the return of the student newspaper and student government to individuals willing to collaborate with McGill's Administration. The policy of collaboration had begun in Senate, when Julius Grey began voting a straight pro-Administration ticket. The infamous character, "Big Julie" (i.e. Julius Grey) of Kopp's 1969-70 satirical cartoons was now Student Council President, and the first "student president in years to address this gathering (the Alma Mater Fund), Vice-Principals Shaw, Frost and Oliver and Principal H. Rocke Robertson" sharing the speaker's platform.[1] It was a sign of things to come. A plaintive editorial on Friday, September 19, 1969 characterized the mood on campus.

> Three years of turbulent change have taken their toll, something in McGill has died, perhaps in the smoke of Sir George. Three years of excess on all sides, shock after shock, anger upon anger.
> Now the numbness is beginning to set in. The vibrancy of the University has been drained, and for many the cost of caring is too high.
> A year ago, the firing of the editor of the *McGill Daily* — for whatever reason — would have unleashed volcanic forces. Protest. Retaliation. Jubilation. Now . . . silence, quiet recognition of the inevitable, because, after all, so what?[2]

On September 18, 1969 the *McGill Daily* staff quit the newspaper in protest, stating:

> We, the presently constituted *Daily* staff, affirm the principles of staff control enunciated in our constitution, our policy statement and the Statement of Principles of Canadian University Press. We regard the Council's move in firing Mark Wilson, our unanimous choice for editor-in-chief, as a political move cloaked in the legalistic positions invented by some Council members. We reaffirm our support for our choice of editor — Mark Wilson — and declare as a collectivity that we will not work for anyone not of our own choosing.[3]

The second story, "B of G trying for renaissance; Robertson memo asserts Board's power in hiring," reports on the continuation of what might be termed the Stan Gray policy against radical faculty:

> The hiring of controversial sociologist Marlene Dixon, whose dismissal from the University of Chicago sparked a week long sit-in there, appears to have led to an attempt by the McGill Board of Governors to reassert its power.
> The attempt comes in the form of a memo issued by Principal Harold R. Robertson August 7 and states that according to the Statutes of the University "all appointments . . . to the teaching staff . . . are made by the Board of Governors," and faculty can only "recommend" prospective teachers.[4]

The *McGill Daily* related that the Administration (represented by Dean Woods) had thoroughly discussed the appointment with the Chairman, the late Howard Roseborough, and that both had decided to go ahead with the appointment. However, trouble started with public reaction and hostility from the Board of Governors:

1. David Ticoll, "New Directions at Old McGill?", *McGill Daily*, September 15, 1969.
2. "Without Even a Whimper?", *McGill Daily* editorial, September 19, 1969.
3. "Statement of the Daily Staff to Council", *McGill Daily*, September 18, 1969.
4. "Bof G Trying for Renaissance," *McGill Daily*, September 17, 1969

The alumni office, radio stations and newspapers were deluged with mail criticizing the decision to hire another radical teacher. As a result, further inquiries were made into Dr. Dixon's credentials by the Department, the Dean, and the Academic Vice-Principal, M.K. Oliver. Again, it was decided to recommend her appointment.

When her contract came before the Board at a closed meeting in June (closed because of the confidentiality of discussing appointments) it was approved. However, informed sources say that several governors disapproved strongly, and that two subsequently resigned over the decision. The Board does not announce resignations, and Secretary J.H. Holton denied the rumor.[5]

Robertson was reported as saying that "further inquiries" and "independent sources of information" referred to "former colleagues and so on" and that the university was concerned "that members of faculty be good citizens."

The Robertson memorandum of August 7, 1969 directed to Vice-Principals, Deans, Heads of Institutes and Schools, Vice-Deans, Associate Deans and Chairmen of Departments explicitly stated that departments do not hire, the Board of Governors hires, and that prospective staff should be sent a letter in the following form:

"I propose to recommend that you be appointed to the rank of _____ for a period of _____ starting _____ at a salary of _____. If this recommendation is accepted, your duties will be _____

The memorandum reminded the addressees that all contracts and appointments are made by the Board of Governors, and any person who offers greater assurance than the form letter quoted above "is acting without authority and contrary to the Statutes of the University. His commitments may not be honoured." If this threat to departmental autonomy was not dire enough, the memorandum concluded darkly:

5. The Department and especially the Chairman is expressly charged with the responsibility of investigating fully the dossier and background of each person it is proposed to recommend for appointment. Chairmen are reminded that it is never sufficient to rely upon references and recommendations supplied by or on behalf of the proposed appointee, and that in addition independent sources of information should be carefully consulted.

This memorandum was so outrageous that it provoked a sharp note from the Interim Executive Committee of the McGill Faculty Union demanding clarification and asking explicitly if the Principal's memorandum signaled "any change in this generally accepted procedure? (hiring *in practice* at the discretion of the department in consultation with the Dean). Does it imply that the board will be exercising active inquiry into the professional qualifications of prospective staff?" At a later meeting between the Principal and representatives of the Faculty Union, Robertson asserted that no change in the appointments procedure was imminent, but reminded the Faculty Union, according to its president, Sidney Ingerman, that the "university was concerned that members of faculty be good citizens." In short, Robertson backed off to avoid a possible faculty rebellion. The warning, nonetheless, had been given; few faculty would miss the point.

The threatening memorandum was obviously linked to the Dixon appointment, attended as it was by a great furor in the mass media in Montreal. What one lone woman might do in the heavily repressive atmosphere of McGill was open to question, and doubtless buttressed the arguments of the Sociology Depart-

---

5. *Ibid.*

ment for whom the appointment was the alternative to a strike. The avoidance of a second departmental confrontation along the lines of Political Science doubtless also served to convince Dean Woods and Vice-Principal Oliver in favour.

What neither the *McGill Daily* nor the McGill Faculty Union could know was that developments in Political Science probably had as much to do with Principal Robertson's memorandum as had the Dixon appointment, for the odds were about (or so it was feared) to be changed: it appeared that Political Science was about to hire a *second* female radical, Pauline Vaillancourt from Berkeley. The stress on "investigating fully the dossier and background of each person" could hardly apply to Dixon, whose dossier had been on the front pages of the newspapers for weeks, nor could the warning that "it is never sufficient to rely upon references and recommendations supplied by or on behalf of the proposed appointee" apply to Dixon who had more than her share of unsolicited and solicited denunciations from an outraged University of Chicago that wondered how McGill *dare* ignore Chicago's anathema against her. In fact, textual analysis of the memorandum would lead one to suspect that it was written in response to the Vaillancourt "catastrophe" in Political Science. Vaillancourt had been offered a position as a product of Berkeley Political Science: empirically-oriented and trained in research methods. How could such an individual have a left-wing political taint? Such people were secure and highly professionalized conservatives!

The documents from the Vaillancourt case, which follow, display the process of black-listing and give a hint as to what probably transpired in the Dixon case, but was successfully hidden behind confidentiality. The appointments were turned into public relations *coups* by McGill liberals, but they were empty victories.

In 1968 Vaillancourt's thesis advisor, Herbert McClosky had written in a letter of recommendation:

> I believe that she has a highly professional attitude and that when she completes her Ph.D., she will go on to a successful academic career. I also think that she will be a conscientious and effective teacher. Her commitment to professional research, as a career, is far above that of most other women graduate students. Even as an undergraduate, she was bent on becoming a technically trained social scientist . . .

Her thesis has subsequently been highly praised as an original and important contribution to the field of political socialization. While graduate students she and Jean-Guy Vaillancourt, a Québécois, had married. It was Vaillancourt's hope to locate an appointment in Montreal so that she and her husband could settle in Quebec.

However, both Jean-Guy (in Sociology) and Pauline (in Political Science) were part of the group of "radical" students engaged in progressive activities around the campus, and particularly around the emergence of what was then called "radical sociology" and "critical" political science. Neither was a Marxist, yet both were part of the general intellectual ferment that had arisen within the social sciences in the late 1960's, in which Berkeley students had always played an important role. By today's standards, neither would be considered extreme. But at the time, they were treading dangerous water. After all, both were in disciplines where, "in the strange logic which imbues these things, supporting this unrepresentative oligarchy and desiring little voice in the associations which made decisions affecting your life was considered responsible and professional, while trying to change it through means considered highly proper in the larger political system (voting, persuasion, organization) was considered demagogic, unprofessional, and generally beneath contempt."[6]

To make matters worse, Pauline Vaillancourt was active in the Political Science Women's Caucus and was the author of a statement detailing discrimination against women in Political Science and demanding amelioration. (See Document #1)

DOCUMENT 1

TO: FACULTY OF THE DEPARTMENT OF POLITICAL SCIENCE

We would like to call attention to a much overlooked area of discrimination. It is clear that women face serious barriers in entering, completing and putting to use professional undergraduate and graduate education. We believe that the political science department can and should act to remedy some of the current problems.

1. Employment and recruitment of women faculty members.

A recent publication of the Department of Labor notes that:

"Although women traditionally have made up a large part of the teacher corps, in recent years only 22% of the faculty and other professional staff in institutions of higher education were women. This is a considerably smaller proportion than they were in 1940 (28%), 1930 (27%) and 1920 (26%) and only slightly above the 20% they were in 1910."

(U.S. Dept. of Labor, Women's Bureau, publication entitled, "Underutilization of Women Workers," (August, 1967), p. 11)

These statistics are particularly relevant to the department of political science, as only 5% of the department's professional teaching staff is female. (See Department of Political Science, Winter Quarter, 1969, Faculty List). Moreover, the actual situation is much worse than the indicated figure of 5%. Although one-third of the department's lecturers are women, the department has no women as instructors, assistant professors or full professors. The table below shows that of the 55 faculty members who hold the rank of assistant professor or above only one is a woman.

Department Position By Sex

POSITION	MEN	WOMEN
Lecturer	6	3
Instructor	5	0
Assistant Professor	20	0
Associate Professor	7	1
Full Professor	27	0

We reject the argument that there is a lack of qualified women for these positions. A random sample of 400 names from the 1968 biographical directory of the American

---

6. Surkin and Wolfe, *op. cit.*, p. 297.

Political Science Association shows that 17% of its members are women. Furthermore, all three women currently employed in the department as lecturers are fully qualified for permanent professional appointments. (It should also be noted that these women received degrees from institutions from which the department has hired men for the higher positions in the past.) Finally, approximately 20% of the graduate students in the department are women. Given that this is not atypical of good graduate schools in political science, there is clearly a sizeable number of women throughout the country who have the necessary professional education for such positions.

2. *Admissions and Graduate Study Policy.*

Women who seek to enter or continue graduate studies while married and/or raising children are frequently stigmatized within the University community as "non-professional," yet men who marry and have families while in graduate school are not considered inferior to single men. Men are also routinely granted 2 year (or more) leaves of absence for military "service," while the needs of women graduate students for interruption or slowing of studies during pregnancy or child care are completely ignored.

We believe that the failure of many mothers to complete studies has a great deal to do with the total lack of practical arrangements and policies directed toward their specific needs and very little to do with "non-professionalism."

There are a number of steps which can be taken to meet these needs:

a. Admissions and recruitment hiring procedures should be absolutely non-discriminatory on any grounds, including sex. (We feel we must point out to the department that given recent civil rights legislation in this area, the department has placed itself in a very precarious position. Because of its latent and overt prejudice against the hiring and advancement of women, it is now leaving itself open to law suits.)

b. A number of full-time positions on the regular faculty should be split into two half-time positions, and qualified women recruited for them.

c. Leaves for pregnancy and child care should be permitted. These leaves should be flexible and adapted to the needs of the individual. Women with children should be permitted to complete studies at a slower pace if they desire.

d. Fellowships, grants, TAships and other stipends, etc., should be fairly allocated without reference to sex or marital status.

3. *Continuing Education.*

We believe that it is important that steps be taken to facilitate the continuing education of all women who desire it. Both faculty wives and the wives of students should be allowed to enter the graduate (and undergraduate) program on a half-time basis. Current University and departmental policies on this point are clearly discriminatory as many graduate students teach or do research work half-time while studying. Some are allowed to take temporary leaves of absence in order to work. Rules against half-time students weigh heavily against qualified students in two categories: women and the poor.

We think that it is very important at this time that the department not interpret our points as being in conflict with increased recruitment of Third World minority group students and faculty. The needs of both groups can be accommodated by the department and the University to the betterment of the academic community as a whole.

We trust the department will do everything possible to immediately rectify the current unhappy situation and will consider it part of the department's overall program to revise past policies in areas where there has been so much misunderstanding and distrust due to long overdue and much needed basic reforms. We appreciate your attention to this problem.

Sincerely,

Women's Caucus   (Signatures continued on attachment)

Pauline Vaillancourt	Judy Van Allen	Tonia Williams
Isabel Marcus Welsh	Judy Mazia	Pamela Emerson
Judy Merkle	Susanne Bodenheimer	Lisbeth Aschenbrenner Meisner
Judy May	Suzanne Pepper	Mary Oppenheimer Fitch
	Julianne Traylor	

In the fall of 1968 Vaillancourt's placement file was sent to the then joint Department of Economics and Political Science at McGill University. In April, 1969, she was contacted by telephone by the Chairman of Political Science, James Mallory, asking if she was interested in a regular three year appointment as an assistant professor. Vaillancourt replied that she was indeed interested. In May of 1969 Chairman Mallory once again telephoned, but informed Vaillancourt that the offer had been down graded to a one-year appointment — but he assured her that this by no means precluded the possibility of being rehired, although he could not guarantee an automatic re-appointment.[7] On the basis of an understanding worked out between Vaillancourt and Professor Mallory, based upon Vaillancourt's insistence that she could *not* afford to come for a closed one-year appointment, in which she was led and to anticipate that she would be renewed for a full three year term, Vaillancourt accepted the one-year offer (although she was puzzled by the whole transaction, which she did not at that time understand).

What had happened between April and May? Later documentation shows that Vaillancourt was being black-listed in precisely the fashion described by Surkin and Wolfe in *An End to Political Science.* What happened was that Professor Michael Brecher (of the Brecher Empire in Political Science) contacted Professor Ernst Hass of the Berkeley Political Science Department in the Spring of 1969. Professor Hass detested Pauline Vaillancourt for organizing the Political Science Women's Caucus in the Berkeley Department (and for her general support for the United Farm Workers and other Bay Area progressive activities). At this point, Vaillancourt had never even met Professor Hass. Nonetheless, at Brecher's request, Hass wrote to Professor Mallory, black-balling her appointment at McGill.

The Hass letter, of June, 1969, lead to "inquiries" into Vaillancourt's political and personal orientations by Vice Principal Oliver and others, leading to the aborted attempt to stop her appointment. (Document #2).

DOCUMENT 2

UNIVERSITY OF CALIFORNIA, BERKELEY

DEPARTMENT OF POLITICAL SCIENCE   BERKELEY, CALIFORNIA, 94720

June 6, 1969

Professor J.R. Mallory
Department of Politics
McGill University
Montreal, Canada

Dear Professor Mallory:

I am taking the unusual step of writing to you about one of our students whom you have engaged for one year even though I had not been involved in the recommenda-

---

7. In 1969 the joint department was split into separate departments of Economics and Political Science. The bulk of the liberal faculty were in the Economics section, leaving the conservatives in control of the Political Science Department. The split resulted in a Department hostile to the 1968 joint-department offer to Pauline Vaillancourt.

tion and have no direct interest in the case. My reason for doing so is connected with my esteem for your department and my concern about the future of the political science profession. You know that in the past I have been very careful about students I have recommended to you and on one or two occasions have advised you against making an offer to people whom I did not consider first-rate, even though not all my colleagues may have shared that opinion.

The present case is similar. I am refering to the appointment offered to Mrs. Pauline Vaillancourt. I think you should know that Mrs. Vaillancourt has impressed several of us as a person much more interested in political agitation than in scholarship. She combines a rather unpleasant personality with a tendency to read political motives into every relationship between herself and the faculty, a tendency which of course contains its own self-fulfilling prophecy. She was a holder of a fellowship from the Institute of International Studies last year, which the Institute declined to renew because Mrs. Vaillancourt had made no progress on her work and thus failed to meet the terms of the original fellowship. Since I have the greatest doubt that she has the makings of an excellent professional, I feel that it is only fair that you should know about this opinion, which is shared by two or three of my colleagues who have worked closely with her. Naturaly I am at your disposal for further discussion.

I have just heard from Miss Barbara Haskell that she will be joining your department in September. I am familiar with Miss Haskell's work and have known her for some time, and I feel that you made an excellent choice. She provides a good example of all the personal and professional qualities which Mrs. Vaillancourt lacks.

Sincerely,

Ernst B. Haas
Professor

EBH:kw
cc: Professor Michael Brecher

DOCUMENT 3

UNIVERSITY OF CALIFORNIA, BERKELEY

INSTITUTE OF
INTERNATIONAL STUDIES

BERKELEY, CALIFORNIA 94720

2538 Channing Way

August 22, 1969

Mrs. Pauline Vaillancourt
1094 — 9th Street
Albany, California 94710

Dear Mrs. Vaillancourt:

I found your letter of August 6 on my return to Berkeley, and should like to clarify the situation regarding your grant application. The Committee on Western European Studies had your report before it in its deliberations and unanimously came to the conclusion that *your project* was not *only not feasible but poorly designed* and unlikely to lead to conclusions valuable for comparative studies. In short, the Committee, in possession of the facts presented, could not support your project further. However, it acknowledged its responsibility to defray expenses you had incurred prior to the date on which you were notified. There is, therefore, no possibility of additional funds being made available.

Yours sincerely,

Ernst B. Haas
Director

The reader will note the operative phrases: "I think you should know that Mrs. Vaillancourt has impressed several of us as a person much more interested in political agitation than in scholarship."

But "impossible" is not left to the imagination: "She combines a rather unpleasant personality with a tendency to read political motives into every relationship between herself and the faculty . . .". A political science graduate student who perceives politics: she *has* to be the re-incarnation of Stan Gray.[8]

Unprofessional and impossible having been established, incompetence is next required: "She was a holder of a fellowship from the Institute of International Studies last year, which the Institute declined to renew . . .". Of course, Professor Haas, who accuses Vaillancourt of reading political motives into every relationship, "a tendency which of course contains its own self-fulfilling prophecy", omits to inform his august colleagues at McGill that he, Haas, saw to it that the Institute declined to renew (see Document #3). The reader will note that Document #2 was written in June, 1969 *before* her grant was "declined". Vaillancourt was informed by Haas, not appointed as Director until August, that her grant was concelled on August 22, 1969, three months after the blackballing letter. Therefore, it is quite obvious that Haas intended to take away her grant long before he was in a position to review her work *or* deny the continuation of her stipend! The work that Haas concluded was "not only not feasible but poorly designed and unlikely to lead to conclusions valuable for comparative studies" was accepted for presentation at the 1970 American Political Science Association Meetings in Los Angeles and later published in the prestigious *Public Opinion Quarterly*.

At this point in our story we must explain how the whole black-listing process against Vaillancourt came to light. It was revealed only because of the student representative who was present during much of the proceedings. Frank Furedi was a member of PSA and elected to be a student representative. What Furedi was observing in the Political Science Department was a nightmare coming true. Such proceedings had been suspected, hinted at, but the reality was surely worse than a student's wildest imaginings. Furedi knew that he was expected to abide by the rules of confidentiality and now he was getting a first-hand knowledge of what the true purpose of confidentiality was. Clearly, Furedi must have been deeply troubled, and wrote to a friend also in Political Science in order that Vaillancourt be given some warning of what was being done against her. Furedi cannot be faulted for requesting that his name not be used "as I

---

8. It should not escape attention that Haas' and Brecher's candidate, Miss Haskell, was appointed without trouble. Is there a relationship between the Haskell appointment and the attempt to stop Vaillancourt's appointment? We shall never know.

would love to get a Canada Council Grant next year".[9] If it were known that he was not collaborating with "things which are done in secret" he would be punished. The Political Science faculty had suffered an extended strike to protest the corruption of their own hiring process; their worst dream was a young graduate student who would choke when exposed to academic realities. It is to Furedi's everlasting credit that he did warn Vaillancourt, and later permitted the publication of his own notes recording one of the infamous meetings of the Appointments Committee for which he was formally censured by the Department and could only expect the same sort of black-balling that so repelled him in the Vaillancourt case. Furedi's exposure served to alert interested parties regarding what sort and where documented evidence might be and eventually was obtained. Furedi's reliability is confirmed by the fact that he *was* censured for "breach of confidentiality" (quoted on the facing page of Part III) by the Political Science Department following the publication of his notes in the *McGill Free press* in 1973.

The next link in the chain of events we have come to know as the Vaillancourt case, was provided when McGill Professor Baldev Nayar returned from a conference in London to circulate rumours acquired from a Haas graduate assistant working in the Institute of which Haas was the Director. Nayar informed McGill professors and administrators that Vaillancourt was some sort of a bomb-throwing Maoist who would destroy the University. Nayar also quoted Haas' graduate assistant as saying "Heaven help the university that hires Vaillancourt."

Nayar's reports in conjunction with the Haas black-balling letter prompted an Administration inquiry into Vaillancourt's dossier which did not "rely on references and recommendations supplied by or on behalf of the proposed candidate". Reports from Berkeley indicate that the inquisitors were particularly interested in Vaillancourt's position on Quebec independence and the role of McGill in Quebec society. Investigations in Berkeley revealed that while many friends and colleagues of the Vaillancourts were contacted, most of the respondents were people who barely knew the couple. Typical of the wild and hysterical allegations made were that she was a Black Panther (?); had been arrested in a demonstration (she hadn't); that she had been expelled from the University and so forth. In many cases the inquiry manifested no interest whatsoever in obtaining information on Vaillancourt's academic work, her research, and particularly her Ph.D. thesis, then in progress. (In fact, by the time of the Department's third "judgment" of Vaillancourt in 1972, no member of the Political Science faculty had yet read the finished thesis).

On July 30, following the Berkeley investigations, Professors Mallory and Charles Taylor attended a meeting on the matter with the Principal, the Academic Vice-Principal and the Dean. Taylor, a right-wing NDP-er and McGill Political Science Professor, voiced his opposition to Vaillancourt's hiring on the basis of her husband Jean-Guy's alleged separatist leanings. The Administrators joined in this opposition and directed the Political Science Department to "reconsider" the offer of an appointment — which had already been accepted.

The July 30 meetings with the Administration precipitated a meeting of the Department's Appointments Committee, in order to conduct the "review" demanded by the Administration. However, certain forces mobilized to support Vaillancourt's rights in the matter. (She, of course, was completely in the dark about events at McGill. She had received a cryptic telegram from Mallory:

---

9. Frank Furedi to David Sanders, November 19, 1969.

"Department is re-examining its recommendation confirming your appointment. Will let you know result as soon as possible." It would not be until much later that the mystery of the telegram would be solved.) From Berkeley, Vaillancourt's thesis advisor, Professor McClosky, phoned McGill to suggest that if the contract was reneged upon legal action would be forthcoming against the University. McClosky noted that if McGill's actions went unchallenged, the careers and personal lives of all would-be academics would be in jeopardy. Other faculty began to respond to a general fear stemming from prior political meddling in departmental affairs by the Administration and Board of Governors. The long and the short of it was that the Appointments Committee reached a compromise: to limit Vaillancourt to a one-year, non-renewable contract while stating that she would be temporarily filling the position of a "senior nomination" to be made the following year.

However, the long and the short of it is most instructive. The official Minutes of the Appointments Committee (Document #4) is disgusting enough. Yet the Minutes, although confidential, are nonetheless *written* and are therefore potentially compromising. While the Minutes echo the Secret Baran File:

> McGill: "In the circumstances, the risks of not making the appointment were far greater than the risks of going ahead with it."

> Stanford: "We must suffer him . . . To press for such an action on insufficient evidence would risk much greater damage."

they are nothing to the actual deliberations of the Appointments Committee as reflected in Furedi's notes (Document #5).

DOCUMENT 4

CONFIDENTIAL

DEPARTMENT OF ECONOMICS
AND POLITICAL SCIENCE
POLITICAL SCIENCE SECTION

APPOINTMENTS COMMITTEE: Notes of Discussion

The Committee met at 3:00 p.m. on July 31, 1969. The following members were present: Mrs. Stein and Messrs. Furedi, Nayar, Waller and Mallory.

The Chairman reported that the meeting had been called because they had been asked to review their recommendation for the appointment of Mrs. Vaillancourt. He had, on the previous day, attended a meeting of the Principal, the Vice-Principal (Academic) and the Dean, with Professor Taylor and himself representing the Section. The reason for the requested review was the further inquiry of referees had raised question about Mrs. Vaillancourt's academic performance, temperament and behaviour during the past year. The information was now before the Committee.

The Committee deliberated on these matters at length and agreed unanimously that it would not alter its previous recommendation that Mrs. Vaillancourt be appointed. The Committee felt that, since Mrs. Vaillancourt had been formally approached more than two months ago, a strong moral obligation now existed which could be broken only on the strongest grounds. It was not felt that the evidence was in this case sufficient for such drastic action, since it had been well understood, both by Mrs. Vaillancourt and by the Political Science Section, that the appointment was only for one year while a more senior appointment in this field was being sought. In the circumstances, the risks of not making the appointment were far greater than the risks of going ahead with it.

J.R.M.

NOTE: — On being advised of this recommendation, the Principal informed me that he would recommend it to the Board for approval next week.

DOCUMENT 5

Statement regarding appointments committee meeting of the dept. of political science of McGill University on July 31/1969.
Free Press, **April 10, 1973**

Present at the meeting were Profs. Mallory, Nayar, J. Stein and Waller and myself (student representative).

At this meeting the appointment of Pauline Vaillancourt was brought up. Prof. Mallory introduced the discussion by stating that there were serious doubts about the viability of Vaillancourt's recent appointment. He stated that a month ago he received a letter from Prof. Haas of the Dept. of Political Science at Berkeley regarding Vaillancourt. Haas stated in his letter that Vaillancourt should not be hired because she was incompetent, had a mean character and that she was a member of such radical organizations as Women's Liberation and the Black Panthers.

Prof. Mallory stated that nothing was done about this letter since it was so emotional and intemperate. Two weeks after this letter, Prof. Nayar was in London for a conference and here he met a graduate student from Berkeley who told him that 'heaven help the university that hires Mrs. Vaillancourt'. When this information was conveyed to Prof. Mallory by Prof. Nayar, a couple of phone calls were made to Berkeley to find out about her from her referees. According to Prof. Mallory, all of her referees (with the exception of Prof. McCloskey) seemed to have changed their minds and had highly negative views about her. This was in sharp contrast to their previous enthusiastic and excellent letters of reference on behalf of Vaillancourt.

Some of the accusations made against Vaillancourt were that she was having problems with her thesis and that she was not devoting sufficient time for her academic work and that she was spending most of her time on radical political activities. Information was also received from these phone calls that Vaillancourt's husband was a French Canadian separatist.

After receiving this information, Prof. Mallory stated that he with Prof. Taylor met with Vice Principal Oliver to discuss this appointment. Prof. Oliver at this meeting asked the Department to reconsider this appointment, as the Administration didn't want a repetition of the Stanley Gray affair. During this meeting, Prof. Taylor stated that Vaillancourt should not be hired. After the meeting Prof. Mallory called up Vaillancourt to state that her appointment is being still considered.

(Please note that all of the above information is based on Prof. Mallory's statement — at the beginning of the meeting.)

During the discussion that followed, most of the talk focused on the political activities of Pauline Vaillancourt and her husband.

Fears were expressed by Profs. Waller and J. Stein that Vaillancourt's appointment might lead to all kinds of problems if for instance she and her husband joined forces and initiated a campaign similar to Operation McGill. Profs. Waller, J. Stein and Nayar stated that Vaillancourt, Stanley Gray and Marlene Dixon were too many radicals for the University to take as they were bound to cause some kind of trouble. Prof. Mallory suggested that the Department might lose credibility with the administration if Vaillancourt was hired and that in any case the administration might reject her appointment. The faculty members on the committee several times reiterated their apprehension that once Vaillancourt was hired it would be impossible to get rid of her, for she could claim that she was being victimized for political reasons.

I expressed the opinion that fears regarding Vaillancourt's possible future political activities and the fact that her husband was supposed to be a French Canadian separatist were not sufficient grounds for the withdrawing of an academic appointment — and furthermore that students would certainly object against such a decision.

After more discussion the meeting decided to hire Vaillancourt for one year with the proviso that notice regarding the non-renewal of her contract would be sent to her in September.

I was personally quite shocked about the proceedings in this meeting for instead of having an academic appointments meeting one had the feeling of being at a political appointment meeting.

signed Frank Furedi

23/11/72

So far the Vaillancourt Case has amply exemplified the processes outlined in Part I: Professionalism and Repression. We have the Profession acting as policeman; covert attempts to carry through political repression; immoral and impossible; purging and hounding; confidentiality and blacklisting. But the richness of these documents are not yet exhausted. In speaking of the liberal ideologues Stan Gray had observed: "As is often the case with statements produced by skilled phrase-mongers, their real meaning has to be extracted from their mystifying appearance." Let us, in this light, examine the text of the Confidential Minutes of the Political Science Section's Appointments Committee (I shall politically translate):

"The Chairman reported that the meeting had been called because they had been asked to review their recommendation for the appointment of Mrs. Vaillancourt." *Translation:* the Administration has asked us to refuse an appointment to Mrs. Vaillancourt. Vice-Principal Oliver, speaking for the Administration, says that the Administration does not want a repetition of the Stanley Gray affair.

"The reason for the requested review was that further inquiry of referees had raised questions about Mrs. Vaillancourt's academic performance, temperament and behavior during the past year." *Translation:* Haas, graduate students of Haas, and Nayar argue that Vaillancourt should not be hired because she was incompetent, had a mean character and that she was a member of such radical organizations as Women's Liberation and the Black Panthers, and "heaven help the university that hires Mrs. Vaillancourt."

"The information was now before the committee." *Translation:* all the gossip and slander collected by Vice-Principal Oliver and Prof. Nayar plus Haas' vendetta is now before the committee. It is possible to summarize this gossip and slander in a fairly palatable way by saying "she was having problems with her thesis and that she was not devoting sufficent time for her academic work and that she was spending most of her time on radical political activities." *Translation:* anyone who spends any time on radical political activities, by definition, is not professional, which is to say spending too much time on political activities. Any time spent on radical political activities is too much time spent; it follows as an absolute law of nature that such a person is incompetent. Not to mention that information was also received from these phone calls that Vaillancourt's husband was a French-Canadian separatist. *Translation:* all wives are tools of their husbands — let her in and we'll have to stop the Francos at the Roddick gates again, not to mention mobilizing the Canadian Armed Forces and deploying one thousand policemen.

"The Committee deliberated on these matters at length . . . ". *Translation:* See Document #5 recording deliberated matters in plain English; however, special note should be taken of deliberations touching upon competence and academic freedom. Chairman Mallory suggests that the department might lose credibility with the administration and in any case the administration might reject her appointment. *Translation:* we are in real trouble boys, and the Administration has been giving it to us — first Gray and now *this!* Heaven help our budget.

"The Committee felt that, since Mrs. Vaillancourt had been formally approached more than two months ago, a strong moral obligation now existed which could be broken only on the strongest grounds." *Translation:* McClosky has decided to go to bat for her and is on the warpath; our reputation is shaky after Gray, can we take this too? Slander is very hard to make stick with a (expletive deleted) like McClosky inciting her to sue us! We don't have the goods on her sufficient to win in court. Are we in the middle of a war between McClosky and Haas? We aren't big enough to take on Berkeley. If the Administration wants her fired, let (expletive deleted) Oliver do his own dirty work — it worked with Stan Gray, didn't it?

"It was not felt that the evidence was in this case sufficient for such drastic action . . . ". *Translation:* we have no grounds any fool would believe for withdrawing our offer; she will claim that she is being victimized for political reasons. This, of course, as we boys well know, is true (since Vaillancourt, Gray, and Dixon together are too many radicals for the university, and are bound to cause some kind of trouble) but it is imperative that no one else know it is true.

"since it had been well understood, both by Mrs. Vaillancourt and by the Political Science section, that the appointment was for one year while a more senior appointment in this field was being sought." *Translation:* it is really clever of us to put in this Big Lie about the "senior appointment" because we will only have to suffer her for a year *and* we preclude it being impossible to get rid of her because she could claim that she was being victimized for political reasons. If the (expletive deleted) says it was not well understood by her, then we will — in unison — say she is a dirty Bolshevik liar, incompetent, mediocre, hated by students, a mother, that she has no trace of integrity, decency, the honor of a gentleman, and so on and so forth.

"In the circumstances, the risks of not making the appointment were far greater than the risks of going ahead with it." *Translation:* We do not get sued;

we do not get attacked by a power like McClosky; we can shed crocodile tears and show how liberal we are like we did with Gray; if the Administration wants to ax her, let them; we wash our hands; our hands are clean; we are good guys; and the truth is, we blew it, made a mess of it, and can't get out of it, Administration or no Administration.

DOCUMENT 6

McGILL UNIVERSITY
MONTREAL

FACULTY OF ARTS AND SCIENCE   October 21st, 1969

Professor P. Vaillancourt,
Department of Political Science.

Dear Professor Vaillancourt:

Professor Waller has assured me that you are aware of the reasons for your appointment for only one year but I want to make certain that you understand the situation and to offer you the opportunity to raise any questions you may have.

You were appointed for one year to help fill the gap created by the resignation of a senior professor at the end of last session, and we are fortunate that you were available to help us in this way. In order to restore the balance of the department, however, it is essential that this position be filled by a senior person again, and we expect that such an appointment will be made for the 1970-71 session. Unfortunately, we cannot look forward to any expansion of the department which would create new positions at the assistant professor level. Because of this, the non-renewal of your appointment will not imply any dissatisfaction on our part with the services you have rendered during your year at McGill, and I would be glad to explain this situation to anyone if it would help to solve any problems you may have in finding another position.

If there are any questions you would like to raise, please do not hesitate to call on me.

Yours sincerely,

E.J. Stansbury,
Dean

EJS/nr
cc: Professor H. Waller

71

McGILL UNIVERSITY
MONTREAL

Professor H. Waller,
Department of Political Science,
McGill University,
Montreal 110.

20 Lennox St.Lane,
Edinburgh 4.
March 8, 1970.

Dear Hal,

I understand from private information that we are not proceeding as well as could have been expected with new appointments for next year.

Some time ago I sent you, at your request, the names of promising prospects for the appointment in comparative politics. I have not heard what happened about these people. One of them in particular, Urwin — who is now at Yale — seemed quite interested and to have just the sort of background we are looking for. I assume that you had him up for interview, since he is so near at hand. Nor have you written to me of your reaction to David Coombes of Reading, who in my judgment is well worth considering in the public administration-international administration field.

If, as I now understand, you are again thinking of a junior appointment only, this is a serious blow to our expectations. But, if that is what we are reduced to, I think it only right that Mrs. Vaillancourt should be considered *on her merits* along with others. I say this with full recollection of all that was said last year, and I do not think it is inconsistent with the position which we then took.

Because of its subject matter, I am sending copies of this letter to Michael Oliver and Charles Taylor, and suggest that its contents be also laid before the Appointments Committee.

Sincerely yours,

J. R. Mallory

CC: M.K. Oliver
C. M. Taylor

It should be noted that the need for a "senior man" in Comparative Politics (at the Associate or Full Professor level only) *first* appears in the Minutes of the July 31 Appointments Committee meeting. Minutes of previous meetings reveal no such constraints on the appointment. Furthermore, Vaillancourt was *first* informed of the newly-discovered priority of a "senior man" upon her arrival in Montreal in early September, 1969. The fact that she would probably not be rehired had never been suggested prior to her conversation with Chairman Harold Waller (replacing Professor Mallory) at that time. The verbal agreement between Vaillancourt and Mallory had been based upon Vaillancourt's clear statement that she could not afford to come to McGill on a closed, one-year appointment. Mallory had replied that he appreciated her position, and that while he could not guarantee re-appointment, the matter was by no means settled. Nonetheless, when her confirmation letter came in October, 1969, the "senior man" line was included in it (see Document #6).

In its usual inept way, the Political Science Department, with its genius for invariably being able to "totally misinterpret and bungle a political situation they find themselves involved in", blew its own cover in February and March, 1970 by interviewing candidates considerably junior to Vaillancourt in terms of professional competence and academic achievement. However, by this time the hounding to which Vaillancourt had been subjected since her arrival had become so blatant that the irregularities in her treatment could not be disguised. She received repeated early warnings that she would not be rehired. Students and faculty reported that concerted efforts were made to avoid any discussion of Vaillancourt's file. Professors favourable to Vaillancourt had privately told her that there is "no use fighting it", as the decision not to rehire her had been made at higher levels. Shabby intrigues were attempted, as when Professor Michael Stein suggested to Vaillancourt that since the Comparative Politics slot was going to a senior man, she might facilitate her chances for reappointment by evincing interest in an area the Department wished to fill. Stein helpfully suggested Urban Politics. Stein's strategy became clear when he informed an Appointments Committee meeting and then a Department meeting on February 26, 1970, that Vaillancourt could no longer be considered for Comparative Politics "because she tells me she is no longer interested in Western Europe, and now wants to do something in Urban Studies." Waller and the other members of the Department, through direct suggestion and innuendo, claimed that her reappointment might be more favourably received if Professor Vaillancourt would come to meetings to "vote against the students" — a not very subtle stratagem to detach her from a growing student support.

The treatment that Vaillancourt received is a standard tactic for assuring that detested people — particularly radicals — are made so miserable that they wish to voluntarily leave. This ugly stratagem backfired in the Political Science Department: first, it was so obvious that it could not be denied, most particularly to students; and second, because it apparently strained Professor Mallory's sense of ethics which, while not too pronounced, were of the British persuasion. The split between the hustling American-identified professionals and the old guard of Cyril James' *ancien regime* erupted at last, and Professor Mallory produced a letter testifying (see Document #7) to his verbal agreements and tearing away the last shred of credibility from the wholly dishonest "senior man" cover for the Political Science Department's desire to conduct a political purge, to escape from an appointment they had trapped themselves into having to honour. And under all of the ugliness, Stan Gray's observation returns:

> I have never ceased to be amazed at how Political Science faculty members, who constantly proclaim their superior competence and scientific understanding in this field, so totally misinterpret and bungle a political situation they themselves are involved in.

In 1970 the combined efforts of the Political Science Student's Association, the *McGill Daily,* and the support of concerned faculty (combined with abundant evidence of procedural irregularities) led to the departmental crisis over the Vaillancourt appointment that was resolved by Professor Mallory's grudging *noblesse oblige* recommendation (Document #7);

> But, if that is what we are reduced to, I think it only right that Mrs. Vaillancourt be considered *on her merits* along with others.

The fact that Professor Mallory felt obligated to write and underline "on her merits" is a direct admission that she had not previously been "considered on her merits" i.e., on her professional qualifications, but had been considered with political and personal prejudice having nothing at all to do with her professional and academic merits and credentials. In 1970 Professor Vaillancourt was finally granted a regular three year appointment as an assistant professor. Between the first contact in 1968 and the regular appointment in 1970 three attempts to get rid of Vaillancourt were made: (1) when the first appointment was withdrawn; (2) when attempts were made to stop the one-year appointment; (3) when the department attempted to back-off the agreement made by Mallory to "consider her on her merits" for a regular three year appointment. In July of 1975 (Professor Vaillancourt to Dean Vogel, Document #35) Vaillancourt states:

> I began teaching at McGill in 1969. In the first four years I was a professor at McGill, as you yourself indicated to me and to another Professor in conversation, four attempts were made to fire me. The attempts failed each time, but only after the facts of the case became known outside of the closed departmental atmosphere.

In conclusion, we know that the Vaillancourt documents presented in this portion of our study would never have seen the light of day within the practiced limits of confidentiality. One of the defenders of "academic standards" at McGill has been Richard Hamilton, Professor of Sociology, self-styled persecuted promoter of excellence against the hordes of radical mediocrities. Professor Hamilton delights in using the press, doubtless under the rubric of fighting fire with fire. He has with impunity slandered Professor Pauline Vaillancourt, Professor Marlene Dixon and Professor Jean-Guy Vaillancourt on numerous occasions (to which we shall return). For now let us examine how such a man depends upon confidentiality in order to get away with personal attacks against the radicals he so detests. A few selections should suffice:

> If Professor Vaillancourt has direct evidence to support her claim, it should be presented. If she has no evidence, the course of both intellectual and personal integrity would be to withdraw the charge and to make apologies.
>> Richard Hamilton, Professor of Sociology, McGill University, "Professor Vaillancourt's Assertions Should be Backed by Evidence", *Gazette,* January 30, 1973.
>
> If the case has to be made with distortion and dishonesty, then maybe it is not as "impeccable" as your reporter-editorialist and judge, Anna Dowdall, would have us believe.
>> Richard Hamilton, "The Vaillancourt Case Revisited", *McGill Daily,* March 13, 1973.
>
> The political refugee of doubtful talent may . . . dramatize him or herself as the victim of a political purge. Newspapers, radio and television, ever eager for hot copy, prove to be willing accomplices in the game and provide free space and time for the self-declared martyr. Departments are restrained from answering through the same channels when a case is under litigation . . . Canadian universities will be denied 30 years of talent because of the decisions being made right now.
>> Richard Hamilton, "Mediocrity in Universities", *Montreal Star,* October 3, 1974.

Mr. Hamilton, of course, feels very smug and very sure of himself, for between his self-righteous calls for "evidence" and the real truth stands confidentiality. Professor Hamilton knows very will that beleaguered radicals, if they wish to remain within the university to carry out their research and teaching, are effectively muzzled. Professor Hamilton, the courageous defender of the *status quo* presents himself as abused by the machinations of stupid, unprincipled and *incompetent* radicals, but nonetheless (even at the expense of exhausting meetings and phone calls and painfully drafted poison pen letters) stands up for goodness, truth, beauty, "standards" and the defeat of the Bolshevik Menace. Of course, Professor Hamilton would like us to believe that he is a progressive: an ex-participant in the now defunct Socialist Scholars Conference, and a man of exemplary courage because he actually insisted that a working class existed in pluralist, equalitarian America.

The evidence that union activity figures, among many other things, in the constant hounding of Pauline Vaillancourt will be forthcoming. This whole section exposes the technique of ugly innuendoes that Professor Hamilton feels so smug and secure in displaying when he says: "The political refugee of doubtful talent may . . . dramatize him or herself as the victim of a political purge" then wringing his hands, declaring — self-proclaimed martyr that he is — that "Departments are restrained from answering . . . " and asserting that "Canadian universities will be denied 30 years of talent because of the decisions being made right now". If Canadian universities are denied 30 years of talent, it is because of the decisions he, and his kind, are making right now.

Chronology: Confrontation and Defeat

November, 1968   Joint Sociology Students Union-Faculty "Caucus" established in Sociology as a measure to avoid a SSU strike against the Sociology Department.

Spring, 1969   In response to SSU pressure for hiring a "radical", Dixon is hired as a compromise candidate acceptable to both Faculty and SSU.

Fall, 1969   David Solomon becomes Chairman of the Sociology Department. He is hostile to SSU. SSU opposition to Solomon is dropped when students are informed that the Department would be placed under the trusteeship of the Administration if any "trouble" were to occur.

Student delegation from SSU asks Dixon to take an active role on their behalf in the Faculty.

SSU continues to demand a second position. Supports progressive Pauline Bart against faculty's choice for a "non-political" or conservative appointment. SSU loses, faculty wins.

January, 1970   Faculty of the Sociology Department expells the SSU from faculty meetings, unilaterally dissolving the "caucus" and leaving the students without a representation in departmental affairs. Dixon was the only dissenting faculty member in the decision to expel students.

Spring, 1970   SSU adopts policy of "intellectual confrontation". Dixon isolated in faculty, continues to support student position demanding rights to democratic participation in departmental governance.

October, 1970   War Measures Act. Teach-ins protesting loss of civil liberties and repression of Quebec independentists held in Dixon's classes.

Spring, 1971   SSU no longer a viable organization. Most of its leaders leave McGill to enter a life of active participation in the Quebec left.

Summer, 1971   Dixon writes the partial portrait of McGill, generalized in "The Failure of the Sociology Liberation Movements".

Fall, 1971   Professor Spector urges Dixon to consider fighting for reappointment.

November, 1971   Sociology Department informs Dixon it is moving to an "unfavourable" decision on her reappointment.

Early 1970:
SSU, Dixon and the Solomon-Westley Coup d'État

"We, the Sociology Students Union, having achieved democratization in the Sociology Department feel that the education of students constitutes the integral role of the university. To this end it is necessary that studen¬s participate in their own education. We do therefore pledge our full moral and physical support to the Political Science Association in their strike action. We condemn the intransigence displayed by the Political Science faculty as an attitude contrary to one which should characterize the progressive and critical role of the university in society. We feel that parity is essential in the Political Science Department so that it may develop to its fullest potential."

    "From SSU and ELA Comes Active Support," *McGill Daily*, November 29, 1968

Of course, the SSU had *not* "achieved parity." What had been given to them by the Sociology faculty was a "caucus committee" made up of thirteen professors and thirteen elected student representatives — *without voting parity*. The method of decision was to consist of *consensus* which gave students veto powers at best.

The marriage between the faculty and students occurred during the fall term in 1968 when the department was under the chairmanship of Dr. Roseborough. The S.S.U. was co-opted and subjugated from the word go; after tens of hours of the S.S.U.'s pressing for a voting parity system, the faculty said that the students would be admitted only if they gave up the idea of a voting system and accepted a "parity-consensus model;" thereby staff and students each sent an equal number of representatives to the Sociology Caucus where decisions were to be unanimous. This model turned out to be a farce; parity and consensus were contradictory. Because there was consensus, there was no parity and in the absence of any new meaningful decisions, the status quo remained . . . .In forcing the students into this parity-consensus model, the faculty accomplished the rare feat of having their cake and eating it too . . . The [Sociology] faculty, frightened by the [PSA strike] proceedings two floors below, had given the S.S.U. a semblance of power in a model which, in and of itself, emasculated this power and robbed the students from engaging in any meaningful action within the system.[10]

What the so-called "parity-consensus" model really created was a situation in which interminable meetings were spent in which the faculty explained at seemingly inexhaustible length why the students should not want what they wanted, and even if they persisted in wanting it, why it was impossible for them to get it. This process was accompanied by frenzied breast-beating by Sociology faculty concerning their sufferings in these proceedings; their martyrdom for the sake of containment and co-optation. Faculty's time was spent not only in caucus meetings (as was that of the students) but also closeted with SSU representatives (on a one-to-one, face-to-face basis) lobbying the students for the faculty position; this charming pastime assured that the students did not form a bloc — for that would have violated the sanctity of the "community of scholars" (which must

---

10. Allen Schwartz, "The Crisis in Sociology," *McGill Daily*, February 4, 1970

be maintained without political taint!) and the "norms" of consensus. What it in fact accomplished was to keep the students confused, divided and intimidated.

It might be argued that the tactical error of the SSU was to have failed to go on strike for parity. However, in an analysis of the PSA system written in December 1968, by students Robert Chodos and Leslie Waxman, [11], both the degeneration of the PSA system and the destruction of the SSU system were almost unerringly anticipated:

> In a sense, the academic department is one of the most hierarchical structures outside of the Roman Catholic Church. There are myriad distinctions of rank: at the top are the full professors . . . then come the associate professors with tenure and then the associate professors without tenure; and so on down to the graduate students, apprentices who are being instructed in the lore of the profession and in ways to get ahead . . .
>
> Power in the department depends above all on whom you know, on what contacts you have at what universities in what fields, on what conferences you attended and who else was at those conferences . . .
>
> The pressures to change this way of doing things have not all come from students. In the Political Science section in the last year there was a move among younger and less powerful faculty to extend decision-making power to a wider faculty base, and this led to the discussion of questions in meetings of the whole section instead of their being decided entirely by the upper echelons. But the basic question, the nitty-gritty — appointments — remained in the hands of a few.[12]

Chodos and Waxman then describe how the PSA students played off the Brecher "empire" against the faculty "moderates" lead by Mallory and Frankel. Very similar moves to capitalize upon student agitation to their own advantage were undertaken by junior faculty in Sociology:

> The position adopted by junior faculty over the past two years can only be defined as vulgar opportunism. To strengthen their own positions junior faculty sided with students at first but have now (except for Marlene Dixon) withdrawn their support. The students were used and then disregarded by the junior staff. The assistant professors refuse to define their position before the students articulate their line. In other words, the junior faculty, whose position by no means coincides with that of the Chairman, have refused to locate themselves in terms of opposing the senior staff. Instead they await anxiously the student position paper which would equip them with an intellectual matrix from which they could refashion their own concepts. . . . Besides being victims of their own discipline, the McGill Sociologists, especially the junior faculty, are captives of their professionalism. Sociology is a business, and one doesn't get ahead in the firm by telling the boss off or by questioning the basic assumptions of the business. One gets ahead by being a yes-man. In their thoughts, some of the junior faculty may be radical, but in their practice, professionalism overcomes good conscience and they slither into the same bag along with the senior faculty.[13]

The alignment in 1970 of all faculty except Dixon, with the senior faculty power bloc not only destroyed the students; it also destroyed the earlier attempts by junior faculty to expand their decision-making powers and participation. One can say about the junior faculty in Sociology that they got exactly what they deserved — to become masters of incompetence and flunkyism in a department

---

11.   Robert Chodos and Leslie Waxman, "The Death of Feudalism," *McGill Daily*, December 13, 1968

12.   Chodos and Waxman, *ibid.*

13.   Schwartz, *ibid.*

where the chairmanship is shared by the two senior faculty right-wingers on a basis of "you appoint me and I'll appoint you."

In 1969, Chodos and Waxman admitted that they were not sure what the effects of the PSA agreement would be (disagreeable and ineffective) but they correctly identified the source of future trouble in both Political Science and Sociology when they wrote, "But there's a catch.".

> The PSA victory was the result of a blatant test of strength on the part of students and faculty. The resolution of issues had absolutely nothing to do with it - and for this reason it is only a matter of time before the conflict between them flares up again. The faculty is still convinced, for the most part, that students have absolutely no part to play in the selection of staff. Until it becomes clear to them that students, who are participants to an equal extent in the productive-consumptive process we call education, are equally entitled to determine the nature of the education that is directed at them, *this conflict will be just below the surface in any activity that involves student-faculty interaction.* (Emphasis added)[14]

In the Sociology Department the conflict did not stay for long "just below the surface" — it blew up in the faces of all concerned in the Winter of 1969 and Spring of 1970, exploding the entire caucus-consensus charade. The process that led to the blow-up is also anticipated:

> Because they still regard the student presence on the governing bodies of the Department as illegitimate, the faculty will try to minimize the effect that students can have. There will be secret faculty meetings, apart from the regular meetings of the section, to determine how best to neutralize the deleterious student presence. A special effort will have to be made, of course, to ensure that aberrant nigger-loving faculty are kept off committees where the chance exists that they might combine arithmetically with student representatives to prevail over the sources of sanity.[15]

In the Sociology Department the perspicacious anticipations of Chodos and Waxman took concrete form:

> Throughout the history of the Caucus, the professors were constantly bitching about the fantastic number of meetings, and finally they forced the student representatives into accepting a cut back in the number of meetings. The business of the Department was to be solved in committees. Thereupon a fantastic number of committees arose. In this stage, students were indeed "lackeys" of this faculty bureaucracy in the real sense of the word. For example, when students suggested at a Directions Committee meeting that any plans for the future of the Department must include a procedure for recruiting more French-speaking Quebec students, faculty, although admitting that the issue was indeed crucial, felt that it was too complex to be dealt with at the time. Their suggestion was to set up another committee. Whenever the students tried to bring up a radical change, they were thwarted by the monster. Over the issue of course content, they were told, "You can't change what's in a man's mind. The only way to effect a change in course content is through hiring." But when it came time to hire, the true nature of the beast emerged. The students were allowed one radical: a token critical sociologist and organizer named Marlene Dixon.[16]

14. Chodos and Waxman, *ibid.*
15. *Ibid.*
16. Schwartz, *ibid.*

As Schwartz points out in "The Crisis in Sociology", the students only allowed themselves to be co-opted into this bizarre system in order that they might have a say in hiring. The compromise that resulted in hiring Dixon gave them hope that if only their endurance could stand the test (at one point a committee was formed in order *to measure a room!*), they might still be able to have some influence in the critical area of hiring — which had always been the object of the SSU just as it had been for the PSA. This last hope was to be dashed, and the caucus repressed, with the return (as Schwartz comments) of "Super Solomon" in the 1969-1970 term:

> When the 1969-70 term began, the S.S.A. found itself co-opted and emasculated once again. During the past summer, Dr. Roseborough had passed away[17] and was succeeded by David Solomon who had been in England on a leave of absence during the year that students had gained a voice. In no uncertain terms, however, Solomon told the executive of the S.S.U. that he was opposed to student participation. Thus, the students among themselves opposed his assuming the chairmanship but said nothing having been informed that the department would be placed under the trusteeship of the administration were any trouble to occur.[18]

Under Chairman Solomon conditions have deteriorated. Many times during the first term the students called for an examination of the Caucus structure but the faculty who maintained that there was a community of interests, objected. That is, they objected until January 12, 1970, when they suddenly reversed their position[19]

The final battle was, of course, a battle over appointments. On Tuesday, January 15, the *McGill Daily* carried a story under the headline "Soc. Caucus Dissolves, Profs Oust Students", by Ed Choueke, reporting that this action was taken by the Sociology faculty following "major conflicts of interest in the appointment of new staff members".

Choueke reports that:

> Faculty chairman, David Solomon, said that the current procedure of agreement by consensus was unworkable. He maintained that the faculty would run the Department by itself until a new arrangement is worked out.[20]

While Solomon is playing "hard cop", William Westley plays "soft cop":

> William Westley, Professor of Sociology, indicated that an organization similar to the Political Science Association, which has one-third student representation on the Department may be acceptable to him and his colleagues as a replacement for the caucus. He said that a tremendous amount of time was being wasted. "Faculty hopes for creating a community to permit the Department to function as it always had were not being realized.[21]

---

17. Dr. Roseborough, like Professor Mallory, belonged to the *ancien regime;* his loss put the American-identified professionals (Solomon & Westley) in full charge of the situation. Solomon is oriented towards the Chicago school, and manifests the same brutality.

18. The threat of the Department being placed in trusteeship will be used again as we shall see.

19. Schwartz, *ibid.*

20. Ed Choueke, "Soc. Caucus Dissolves, Profs Oust Students", *McGill Daily,* January 13, 1970.

21. *Ibid.*

Westley, an expert in "industrial relations", (or how to manage class collaborationist trade unions to the advantage of employers) is a past-master of liberal phrase-mongering. If we are to translate his position, it would read-out in English as follows: Solomon and I have realized that the "caucus" will not permit the "Department to function as it always had", and if possible we will suck the SSU into an arrangement we know is less troublesome — the PSA "solution". For the "tremendous amount of time being wasted", read: the students are refusing to give in to the Faculty, hence obstructing the Department from being permitted to "function as it always had", and this situation is intolerable. In the present atmosphere of repression, a strike is unlikely — a student victory even less likely (no opposition to expulsions from the University) and if we present a liberal facade (the PSA "solution") which we know the students will not accept (c.f. the Chodos and Waxman analysis), we can make the students look like unreasonable maniacs.

David Abbey, spokesman for the SSU, told the Daily:

> that the faculty merely wants dialogue with students but will not tolerate student influence in decisions. "Student representatives assessed candidates for new staff members according to their teaching ability, academic merit and social awareness," said Abbey.[22]

Two members of the SSU, Miyako Okubo and Tybie Trossman, prepared a clarification of the SSU position which was published in the Daily on January 14, 1970:

> Monday, January 12, the faculty of the Department of Sociology chose unilaterally to expel students from the department's decision-making apparatus. Ostensibly, the straw that broke the camel's back was the refusal by students to agree to hiring a certain junior faculty candidate who had been recently interviewed. Faculty portrayed the situation as typical of a general state of affairs in which not enough decisions were being reached with the dispatch necessary for the department to function properly.
> While no one will dispute the fact that there have been real difficulties in the way of student-faculty decision-making over the last year and a half, the record should be kept straight: it was the students who in the first term of this year pushed for procedural reform — testimony to their being equally aware of the pinch of indecision and the maxim that inaction serves only to further entrench the status quo.[23]

This refers to the non-representational role forced upon the SSU student representatives described earlier and which had been exacerbated by the disorganizing tactics undertaken by the faculty, described by student spokesman David Abbey on January 13:

> Abbey, on the other hand, felt that the main reason for the waste of time was the eagerness of faculty to set up committees for the most trivial issues, combined with a refusal of students' requests for more frequent meetings.[24]

In the year and a half that the caucus existed the *only* decision that had been reached was reform of the enormous Sociology 210:

---

22. Ed Choueke, *ibid.*
23. Miyako Okubo and Tybie Trossman, "Things Fall Apart," *McGill Daily,* January 14, 1970
24. Choueke, *ibid.*

Over the issue of Sociology 210, the introductory course, the students were co-opted once again. Pressing all along for a small department-run conference course, the student demands were overruled and the course was put into the hands of Professors William Westley and Louis Goldberg, who were to continue giving mass lectures. The first term passed on as usual and Dr. Westley gave his taped lectures. It was only when Dr. Goldberg fell ill that the panicky faculty decided to accept, at least in part, the suggestions of the students. The course, now reorganized, is more meaningful, more relevant, and more interesting than any 210 course given in the past.[25]

Okubo and Trossman continued by pointing out that while faculty agreed that such reforms were in order, they repeatedly refused to act, because to change the nature of the Sociology "Caucus" would have threatened faculty interests:

And these crucial interests are to maintain control of departmental decision-making so that sociologists of critical or radical perspectives are kept away from McGill.
It was this controversy over hiring of faculty of critical perspective that precipitated the dissolution of caucus. And this on the first day of the second term, when students had no warning that this was in the wind.[26]

The appointments battle that was the beginning of the end of the Sociology Department's system of "parity" is an interesting replay of themes already clear from the Vaillancourt appointment. There were three candidates who had been interviewed for assistant professorships in the fall and winter of 1969. They were Michael Carroll, Gertrude Robinson and Pauline Bart. The fight was over Pauline Bart.

The SSU wanted progressive faculty who were also interested and able teachers. The Sociology faculty wanted non-progressive (preferably conservative) candidates who would not, as Dixon and Vaillancourt had begun to do, "vote with the students." It became very obvious, in the course of the battle, that the Sociology faculty were determined *not* to repeat Political Science's error in hiring Pauline Vaillancourt. The Dixon appointment was absolutely as far as the senior faculty in Sociology were willing to go. The SSU students were painfully slow to realize that their meticulously prepared arguments based on academic research and qualifications carried no weight whatsoever: hiring priorities in Sociology (as with Political Science) had been set in consultation with the Administration. *The criteria were political, they were not academic.* There was no power within reach of the students that would force the Sociology department to place itself in the same position as had befallen Political Science because of the Vaillancourt appointment.

Michael Carroll and Gertrude Robinson[27] were without political taint; both appeared to be the embodiment of academic respectability with the manners of "gentlemen" highly professionalized and therefore politically reliable. They were faculty's choice.

Pauline Bart, from the University of California at Berkeley, was the SSU's choice. The students at Berkeley, where Pauline Bart was an assistant professor, had already communicated with the SSU students at McGill, declaring that SSU would do well if they could get Bart, as she was an excellent teacher, an advisor and participant in the Berkeley Sociology Department's Woman's Caucus, a progressive, and highly responsive to students. Academically, her thesis on the

25. Schwartz, *ibid.*
26. Okubo and Trossman, *loc. cit.*
27. Their political tractability has been well-rewarded. Both have been promoted to the rank of Associate Professor, having qualifications equivalent to assistant professor.

crisis of middle-aged women was already widely recognized as an important contribution to the field of gerontology and sex role research. She was also obviously highly motivated professionally and would be difficult to beat on academic criteria. Neither Robinson nor Carroll came even near Bart's qualifications or seniority. Such were not the faculty's considerations. Bart, from the view of the senior faculty (who like Mallory were keeping well in mind "all that had been said last year") had been a fellow graduate student with none other than Marlene Dixon at UCLA. Like Dixon, Bart was also an activist in Women's Liberation. Unlike Dixon she was not a Marxist, but she was pro-student: the two are synonomous in the lexicon of the profession. In Bart the faculty saw only an alliance: an alliance between Dixon and Bart and the SSU, and who knows? Vaillancourt and the Franco hordes had recently been marching 100,000 strong protesting Bill 63 (as threatening the French language in education). Bart had also been the Subject of an "ambivalent" (which is to say negative, in practice a black-ball) letter from one of her referees, Professor Stinchcombe at Berkeley.[28] Professor Bart's refusal to act the strike-breaker and her general support for student causes were not to be easily forgiven by a battered Berkeley faculty.

The SSU had fought long and hard for Bart — only to lose. Sociology faculty were constantly accusing Dixon of personal and political motivations in order to discredit her support for Bart. The fact that Von Eschen and Pinard had already seen to the hiring of their own friends was ignored; the fact that while Bart was a friend of Dixon's she was also quite obviously the most academically qualified, was denied; another element in the discrediting of both Dixon and the SSU were the constant accusations that support was purely a "politically motivated stratagem to gain control of the department by radicals and students" because it was so obviously a matter of the pot calling the kettle black. Of course the SSU was politically motivated — they had never claimed that they were *not* interested in "the hiring of faculty of critical perspective." They also had the most qualified and "prestigious" candidate, which according to the norms of professional academic judgement ought to have secured the appointment for Bart.[29] The

---

28. When Dixon saw the letter, she told Bart to withdraw Stinchcombe from her list of referees. She did not give Pauline Bart a copy of the letter. This warning on Dixon's part to Bart was interpreted by Maurice Pinard as a heinous act of dishonesty and a breach of confidentiality. Pinard's attack on Dixon had the effect of breaking the last tenuous tie Dixon had to the "norm of confidentiality" — which she hated because of the abuses she had come to know at the University of Chicago. She therefore refused to deny Pinard's charges, although she had done no more than warn a friend and a woman of a damaging letter which ought not come from the candidat's referee.

29. Pauline Bart, whom the faculty insisted was not qualified for McGill, although Robinson and Carroll were, went on to become, in the next four years, an Associate Professor of Sociology and Psychiatry at the Abraham Lincoln School of Medicine at the University of Illinois. Prof. Bart, one of the founders of Sociologists for Women in Society, has published 19 papers on health, sex roles, the sociology of knowledge and done pioneering work in the problems of middle aged women — work that has won her national recognition. Some of the positions she holds or has held reflects this: she is a member of the sub-Committee on Research and Needs of the Mayor's Commission on Child Care for the City of Chicago; a resource scientist on education for the prestigious Illinois Commission on the Status of Women; Chairwoman of the sub-Committee on Hospitals of the Citizen's Advisory Committee on Rape; she is an editor of the Journal of Health and Social Behavior and been Special Editor for one issue of the Journal of Health and Social Behavior and two issues of the Journal of Marriage and the Family; she was a Visiting Scientist in the National Science Foundation and American Sociological Association joint program; a member of the C. Wright Mills award committee; the first chair of the section on sex roles of the American Sociological Association; she taught the first woman's course at the University of California at Berkeley . . . and so forth. Associate Professors Robinson and Carroll are noted for not being noted. So much for academic qualifications and professionalism.

difference between the Sociology faculty and the SSU was that the faculty were unprincipled hypocrites while the SSU was both forthright and principled in their dealings with the "caucus". This was pointed out in the Okubo and Trossman statement:

> It was this controversy over hiring of faculty of critical perspective that precipitated the dissolution of the caucus . . . Thus faculty attempted to force a condition of polarization on the students, despite the students' effort to co-operate with the consensus system of decision-making, doomed to inefficiency from the start.
>
> That polarization did not occur — students did not fly into a rage but remained instead in the meeting with faculty for an extra hour and a half — shows their good faith. They calmly demonstrated that faculty had acted in bad faith [by expelling the students from the caucus]. The students spelled out the dissimilarity of student and faculty interests and the fact that faculty can cope with these differences only by initiating their power in the most naked and gross manner. This action of expulsion by the sociology faculty is further testimony to the inevitable degeneration of a professed liberal position to overt repression when student interests are interpreted by the students themselves . . . And where do students go from here? They should begin by realizing that to trust faculty without reservation contradicts reality and represents a refusal to learn from the lessons of history. [39]

The expulsion of the students from the Sociology caucus had been announced on Monday January 12; on Tuesday, January 13 the "hard line" gave way to the "soft line" and students were "invited back" to the caucus (the faculty feared a strike by the SSU). On January 22 negotiations began between the Sociology faculty and the SSU on the reorganization of the department's government:

> David Solomon, Chairman of Sociology, suggested that an association similar to the Political Science Association may be agreeable to faculty . . . This suggestion was denounced by David Abbey and other student reps who challenged that faculty merely wants to use students as a rubber stamp instead of accepting them as responsible participating members . . . "William Westley, Professor of Sociology, proposed the initiation of several small task forces to direct programs approved by caucus as a method of running the Department. He expressed fears of the destruction of the Department if students were granted equal voting power in the new government structure, since, he said, students voted en bloc.[31]

In this suggestion, William Westley truly put his foot in his mouth, for he now openly admitted his true position, that he feared the "destruction of the Department if students were granted equal voting power" — contrast this with what the SSU had been led to believe at the height of the PSA strike:

> We, the Sociology Students Union, having achieved democratization in the Sociology Department . . . it is necessary that students participate in their own education . . . (the attitude which should) characterize the progressive and critical role of the university in society. We feel that parity is essential . . . (November 29, 1968)[32]

"We, the Sociology Students Union, having achieved democratization . . ." The students had "believed in" their faculty; in Westley with his smooth proposals; in Von Eschen playing Shingler's "Student mentor" role; in Pinard, the crypto-progressive continentalist. Yet, the 1968 SSU statement highlights another important aspect of the SSU battle. Gray, about Political Science, had written:

---

30. Okubo and Trossman, *loc. cit.*

31. Choueke, *loc. cit.*

32. "From SSU and ELA Comes Active Support." *loc. cit.*

And deep in their minds, they knew the students couldn't themselves come up with all these clever and sophisticated arguments being used to support their demands — only the faculty, after all, is deemed competent — so it must be originating from those faculty radicals.[33]

The line of the Sociology faculty was precisely the same: all the trouble with the SSU and the Caucus was due to the agitating and inciting activities of Dixon. In this way the Sociology faculty attempted to excuse, to rationalize and to disguise the blatant and dishonest manipulation they had employed to keep the SSU in check. The SSU principles so clearly stated in 1968, echoing the calls for a Critical University supported by the McGill left and articulated by Stan Gray in the *McGill Daily* (issues which had also been important later in January, 1969 during the Administration Building occupation at the University of Chicago which Dixon had supported[34] clearly stated the SSU's stand in favour of real as against token student participation in *order to create a critical university.* Leading the students to believe that they had real parity set the stage for the bitterness and frustrated rage that was to come in the aftermath, when the entire con-game collapsed with its first test: "when student interests are interpreted by students themselves . . . ." In short, the SSU was not being manipulated by an evil woman, but was in fact carrying out in a principled way the founding principles of its own organization. Dixon supported them because she also believed in those principles.

The end-game of the Sociology Caucus was to set the tone for the coming years. In the course of the expulsion of the students from the caucus:

> Solomon reported a near-unanimous proposal (Marlene Dixon voted nay) to form an interim committee to consider vital department business while the caucus was negotiating.

> Student reps were furious since the proposal called for a 4-man committee with only one student. Roger Rashi, BA 4, charged that "the proposal is outrageous and it reveals that the faculty is acting in bad faith.".[35]

A token gesture, a committee to talk with students, was rejected by the SSU because it was staffed by David Solomon and Roger Krohn, both hostile to students, and Larry Felt, an assistant professor who most resembled Professor Shingler when he "denied every interpretation of his comments, and at one point indicated the possibility that he wasn't even present" during a faculty-student confrontation. The interim committee also contained a faculty executive committee, made up of the core senior faculty and their trusted allies. The end of democratization for the students also signaled the end of democracy for the faculty, although the process would take somewhat longer.

The Department's next move was a replay of events in Political Science a year earlier, with the difference that the Sociology Department, thanks to the Administration-orchestrated repression, had no student movement that would support the SSU. There is no doubt that Sociology deserves higher marks for counter-insurgency effectiveness than does Political Science:

> The faculty of the Sociology Department reneged on an earlier agreement to negotiate with the students . . . According to David Abbey, Chairman of the So-

33. Gray, "The Mood of the Faculty" *loc. cit.*

34. See Immanuel Wallerstein and Paul Starr, *The University Crisis Reader,* Vol. One, Chapter 15, "Participation and Power: should the university be restructured," pp. 479-518, esp. "Student Participation in Faculty Hiring: the Marlene Dixon Case," pp. 510-518.

35. Ed Choueke, "SSU Faces Struggle for New Government", *McGill Daily,* January 22, 1970.

ciology Students' Union, an Interim Committee was to have been established by both students and faculty to run the department. "They went ahead and unilaterally set up everything by themselves, leaving the students with no voice in the department", Abbey charged.[36]

Schwartz summarised the outcome of the Solomon-Westley *coup d'état* as follows:

Students and faculty have not met since [the expulsion of January 12] and the Department of Sociology is run by committees without students. Dr. Dixon was not placed on any committee at first, and Solomon initially claimed that this was because she had not requested an appointment. Professor Westley and others, however, freely admit that they were put on committees without a request. When questioned further Solomon admitted to Barbara Berger that some people felt that Dr. Dixon shouldn't be placed on a committee because she had been "uncooperative". He admits that arguments may have been made in favor of Professor Dixon's inclusion but that he was the victim of "selective perception", a typical example of jargon sociology meaning that he heard only what he wanted to hear. Professor Solomon sits on each committee in an ex-officio capacity and, it can be said, runs the department almost single-handedly.

The department has thus taken a radical turn to the right. The junior faculty dare not oppose the senior faculty, expecially with students off caucus, for promotion and tenure decisions ultimately rest in the hands of the full professors. The few assistant professors who did support the students have given up the struggle leaving Solomon unchallenged. Hemming and hawing, they have apologized and evaded confronting issues directly. The contradiction in their position, given their previous left-liberal stance has been ignored. In a word, they have retreated.[37]

The fears of the SSU in regards to the form of faculty governance was to become the nightmare of the entire department by 1972-73:

The SSU spokesmen are particularly disturbed by the new Executive Committee, which now assumes full control of the department. As Chairman of the Executive Committee, Professor Solomon becomes and ex-officio member of all the other committees.

SSU Chairman Abbey pointed out that only two members of the Sociology Department were not placed on Committees. One is Professor Aileen Ross, professor of sociology, who is retiring, and the other is Marlene Dixon, assistant professor of sociology, who has been helping the students all through the year. The SSU Executive charged yesterday that this is a negation of her rights as a faculty member and that Professor Solomon purposely did this so that Professor Dixon would not be able to help the students.[38]

The crushing of the SSU and the ostracism of Dixon were the goals of the Solomon and Westley strategy: what had happened was not the reorganization of the Sociology Department, but a *coup d'état* by Solomon and Westley (still playing hard cop and soft cop) with the support of Van Eschen, Pinard and Krohn. In January, 1970 faculty democracy died in the Sociology Department as the price of defeating the students. The SSU could now echo the cynical anger of Robert Chodos and Mark Starowicz:

To anyone who has believed in the basic decency and flexibility of liberal institutions, in the pluralist university, and in the possibility of effecting change from within the system, this should give pause.

---

36. Evelyn Schusheim, "Solomon Reneges: SSU Protests", *McGill Daily*, January 29, 1970.

37. Schwartz, *ibid*.

38. *Ibid*.

Just how much "pause" it was going to give was indicated in a statement for the SSU Executive by Mike Fulop and David Abbey entitled "Democratization:"

What little power has been granted students in the university resulted firstly out of the fear that students would tear it down and secondly from the belief that students would be unable to accomplish anything of consequence in any case, i.e., they could easily be co-opted into playing the games of the power structure.

And while the students persisted in believing they could effect change from within the system, the object lessons learned in the department of Sociology, Political Science and English dictated otherwise.

And look at (or perhaps, look for) motions that the "moderates" on Senate have been able to push through.[39]

Administrators expected, and succeeded in forcing students to play by the rules, thus defusing the threat of student power. The proliferation of committees is one brilliant tactic to paralyze a structure and forestall change. In the Sociology caucus the situation had reached such absurd proportions that a committee had to be formed to measure a room — but the principles of democracy and tripartite representation were not to be ignored: the committee was composed of one professor, one graduate student, and one undergraduate.

The next step — the smashing of even tokenistic student participation — was both logical and inevitable, especially when administrators drop the liberal pretense and embrace the dictum that totalitarianism is easier to administer than democracy. On January 16, the sociology faculty decided that it had had enough of the students and kicked them out of the department's decision-making body.

Students must realize now that the road to significant change in the university and society as a whole lies outside the existing structures. If we desire to change the established order of things, we must act to educate ourselves through our own liberated classes, through actions taken to point out the oppressiveness and total vacuity of the system.

Specifically, we must challenge the authority of the professors in the classroom by questioning their fundamental assumptions — and they do have many, many which are indeed questionable.

This counter-education can be effected not only through rational, academic debate, but also through the mocking guerilla theatre such as now is being performed by Sociology's Red Star Chicken Shit Brigade.[40] For professors may often be inconsistent in their own terms and laughable when they would persist in their self delusion that they are rational creatures cognizant of the true operations of a society.[41]

The "Democratizion" statement by Executive members Fulop and Abbey signaled the strategy that the SSU had adopted in the face of repression:

the SSU is now going out and organizing the bulk of students. They are in the process of instituting radical seminars and teach-ins. Truth squads will be drilling professors in class, putting their basic assumptions up to rigorous and thorough-

39. A student would resign from Senate while others had resigned from Student's Council to protest the repression being practised by the Administration and the sell-out being conducted by "Big Julie" Grey — the student resignations were also designed to show their refusal to collaborate with the system of tokenism that had been established in 1968.

40. The Red Star "Chicken Shit" Brigade adopted that name to indicate the student's contempt for the sociology faculty; it was also adopted from the University of Chicago, where a "Chicken Shit Brigade" (of students, who because of previous political arrests, could not occupy the administration building) engaged in some of the most daring and militant actions of the occupation: it also referred to the decision of the SSU not to go on strike, since a strike could not have been won and would only have resulted in the the arrest and expulsion of students occupying Leacock.

41. Mike Fulop and David Abbey, "Demockratizion, "McGill Daily, January 30, 1970

going investigation and interrogation. Periodic one hour sit-ins on the seventh floor will disrupt the normal functioning of the classes and inject an air of uncertainty into the atmosphere.[42]

The new policy of intellectual confrontation was adopted by the SSU in a general meeting January 30, 1970 and the first action involving 100 students in a hour long "seminar" (a de facto occupation of seventh floor Leacock) took place on Monday, February 2, 1970. The students would continue to carry out actions designed to present critical sociology to sociology students in direct confrontation with the sociology faculty throughout the spring term of 1970. It is hard to imagine the atmosphere in the department at that time unless one were a participant. The students had been stripped of power, humiliated, defeated: but they had refused, in the words of Fulop and Abbey, to accept the role of "undutiful children" who have been banished. One member of the Sociology faculty, a young assistant professor, suffered a nervous breakdown during this period and wrote a letter to the *McGill Daily* which indicated, with tormented frankness, the consequences in human terms of the Westley-Solomon-Administration strategy:

> If I have seemed angry at times and caused old friends of mine in the university community anguish over the past several months, it has not been because of a destructive intent, but because of a sincere desire to see my values, Jewish values, realized within the context of your culture. There is obviously a conflict between the way of life of Jewish people and English people, although this is not irreconcilable if people are willing to compromise and go half-way toward respecting and understanding different points of view . . . I owe much to Stanley Gray and to all my wonderful students who taught me as much about myself and where I was, as I taught them and where I have been and what I had learned. I hope at some point that old grudges can be forgotten, the shields and spears put down, and the conflict between my generation and yours ended. But as I told Principal Robertson in my lunch meetings with him last year, this will take a greater courage for communication and change than the "old Guard" at McGill has thus far shown. A real act of courage which would demonstrate to me that you have regained your faith in the future would be to invite Stanley Gray to return to the University . . .[43]

The SSU, while presenting its own position paper, took its ideological orientation towards critical sociology from the stunning address made by Martin Nicolaus to The American Sociological Association's convention in Boston, September, 1968 when the Sociology Liberation Movement demanded and won (in a hall lined with policemen) the right to state an SLM keynote address. Nicolaus' address was reprinted in the *McGill Daily* on January 14, 1970.

Of the many SSU actions, class-room interventions, "flying-sit-ins",[44] alternative class notes and guerilla theatre actions of the Red Stars (who became

---

42. Schwartz, *loc. cit.*

43. "letters," *McGill Daily,* January 28, 1970

44. A complete history of the SSU's activities during this period is not to be found in this *McGill Daily,* for the Krauthammer *Daily* reflects the same conservative, pro-administration line that "Big Julie" Grey had brought to Student's Council. Krauthammer was a Grey appointee to replace the fired, and politically unacceptable, Mark Wilson. The Krauthammer *Daily* stresses Administration sponsored "educational innovation" programs, the drug culture, rock music and sex. Little if any coverage of political activity (except anti-war protests in the U.S.A. or support actions in Canada, is even made. The SSU engaged in a constant struggle with Krauthammer in order to get *minimal* coverage of the situation in the Sociology Department.

noted throughout the campus for the eerie whistles that preceeded their assault on a political science or sociology professor's class) one, reported in the *McGill Daily*, may be taken as representative. On March 6, 1970, the *McGill Daily* reported that:

> The Worker-Student alliance in conjunction with the Sociology Student's Union effectively disrupted a conference on labor-management relations yesterday. The two-day conference, sponsored by the Industrial Relations Center, was terminated by the Chairman, Sociology professor William A. Westley, after it became apparent that he could not go on with the normal agenda.
>
> Preceding his decision were two hours of "dialogue" between the "establishment" and its challengers. The discussion was basically very rational, unlike other meetings which have been disrupted this year.
>
> Professor Westley greeted the approximately 120 students at the door of the Leacock Council room. "Let's be clear you are forcing your way in. I am not stopping you."
>
> The students and some workers [the "some workers" were the Gars de Lapalme that were to become central during the "October Days"] carrying placards denouncing the conference, capitalism, and the University, then took their seats among the flabbergasted conference participants.
>
> "This is university life," Professor Westley, smiling desperately, informed his co-chairman.
>
> At the beginning of the meeting, the general feeling was one of nonchalance, and one participant even suggested making coffee for the new arrivals. However, the atmosphere deteriorated during the intense dialogue when WSA members and students challenged the right and willingness of conference participants to represent the "true" interests of workers . . . The protesters charged that conference participants did not deal with the basic problem in labour-management relations, which, according to them is capitalism . . . A female sociology graduate student was particularly explicit in accusing union leaders of lack of concern for women workers who have no contract and are underpaid. "I hate you guys, I'll hate your guts until you do something for me," she shouted at the stunned managers.
>
> Professor Westley explained to his neighbours that they were observing a "liberated woman."
>
> Attempts by Professor Westley to return to the agenda were in vain. "Justify your presence; then you will have the right to go on," students challenged.
>
> John Huberman, a consulting psychologist, replied that there is no world without bosses, and agreed with the student conclusion that the "human race might be doomed forever."
>
> Professor Westley finally closed the meeting and apologized for what had happened . . ." I am quite disturbed by this," he apologized.[45]

What the *McGill Daily* reporter did not (and perhaps could not) convey about this disruption was its intellectual motivation and its intellectual content. The SSU, like the PSA, was often devastating in its critique. The action against Westley and his "Industrial Relations" empire was a manifestation of the general SSU strategy, outlined in their "Position Paper of the SSU:"

> The content of the manifesto can be divided into three related parts: 1) demand for reform in teaching methods, 2) an articulation of the ways in which sociology is linked to the university and society, and 3) demands for change in course content. All of this was based on two assumptions. Firstly, that creative thinking and critical sociology might emerge out of a pluralist intellectual community in which all views were represented and debated. Secondly, the students could gain control over their lives through student power and could thus effectively direct the course of change.

---

45. Barbara Halsig, "WSA and SSU Hit Conference," *McGill Daily*, March 6, 1970

After a year and a half of participation in the Sociology Department the position of students has changed substantially and experience has reshaped theory, policy and strategy. It has now become evident that pluralism is a myth — a false conception of how society, university and the Sociology Department operate. Just as in the wider society where it is evident by the experience of North American Indians, the French population in Quebec, the black and Latin peoples that there is no pluralism of power, so it is evident in the Sociology Department that "pluralism" tolerates viewpoints within certain well-defined parameters — that pluralism extends the right of legal expression of grievances to all but denies to the majority of every population the power to affect history.[46]

The SSU position paper had included emphasis upon the importance of Quebec:

> We want to emphasise the role of action in sociology. Any honest leftist movement which wishes to struggle with the people must face the issues which are most immediate. For McGill and for this department, the issue is Quebec. At this stage, we believe that McGill is not irrelevant to Quebec. McGill is the bastion of the English establishment. It represents a colonial power and trains colonisers instilling in the minority a majority mentality. As such, McGill is a reactionary institution, the Department of Sociology shares its fate . . .[47]

Thus, it was no accident that the "some workers" in the Industrial Relations confrontation were the *Gars de Lapalme* that were later to be a symbol and a focus of the struggle of Quebec labour. Following the action at Westley's conference:

> The worker representatives also went to a Sociology 211 class trying to muster support for their cause. They alleged that the truck drivers involved in the recent mail showdown will lose their job after April 1, and will not have the seniority or job security even if some individuals succeed in finding new employment.[48]

The SSU had brought Quebec to McGill, and workers with profound grievances to the "Industrial Relations" conference (which cost $80.00 per person to attend: the Lapalme drivers, not having jobs, certainly did not have $80.00 each to talk to labour and management leaders!). What was Professor Westley's reaction?

> The *Daily* of March 6th reports that "The Worker-Student Alliance in conjunction with the Sociology Student's Union effectively disrupted a conference on Labour Management Relations." Effectively disrupted, indeed! It sounds as though they had won some kind of a battle. But just what did they overcome? There was no resistance. A gathering of labour leaders, managers, government officials, professors and *McGill students* listened politely to and debated with them for almost two hours, after which the meeting had to be adjourned because their disruption would not allow it to continue.
> What was the basis of the protest? The handout said that blue collar workers and students had been excluded from the meeting. Neither is true. The conference was open to anyone who registered and students and teachers were admitted free of charge. Both labour and students were present at the conference. Sure, the fees were high for the ordinary working man, but not for the purpose of excluding him, but because the costs of the Conference were high.

---

46. "Action in Sociology: The Position Paper of the S.S.U.," *McGill Daily,* February 18, 1970 (this was one of the few such stories covered).

47. Ibid.

48. Halsig, *ibid.*

The student protestors accused the participants of colluding to exploit the worker. Did they really think that two of the union speakers: Robert Sauve, Deputy Minister of Labour who spoke very strongly in favor of greatly increased worker participation and control and Andy Andras of the Canadian Labour Congress, a long time and doughty champion of workers' rights were there to exploit the worker? . . . Then what did they accomplish with this disruption? This is what they did. They damaged a meeting that had taken months of work to arrange, to which distinguished speakers had been brought from great distance and at great expense, for which we had hired simultaneous translations system at great expense, for which we had hired a court reporter to make a transcript so we could publish the proceedings, and to which men and women from all over Canada . . . had come with a sacrifice of time and money to learn about innovations which included ways of obtaining greater rights and better working conditions for workers. They interrupted the speech of a gentle and brilliant industrial psychologist, a man who has fled from persecution in Europe to make his career in Canada . . .[49]

Court reporters and simultaneous translation and distinguished speakers from great distances, all at great expense — who could not listen to nor understand a group of "blue collar workers" who would come to symbolize the colonization of the Quebec working class? What sort of "fighters for workers' rights" were these? A "gentle and brilliant industrial psychologist" who had "fled persecution" but who agreed that "there is no world without bosses?"

What did they gain? Who will praise them for it? I felt only shame and embarrassment, and then later deep anger. I was incredulous at this wanton destruction, this obliviousness to the rights of fellow citizens. I had refused to keep them out of the meeting by force for I felt them to be deeply honest people and I was confident that after they had made their protest, they would certainly leave or allow the meeting to continue.[50]

What had the SSU tried to accomplish in the last months of its existence in the Spring term of 1970? They had outlined their purpose in their position paper in February:

At this point, let us clarify the meaning of radical sociology. In addition to the above mentioned concerns, it is important that one realize that radical sociology need not be an "import" — that students at McGill envisage a striving for a "new radical sociology" with a sence of problem relevant to the issues of our time and our situation. That this sociology should work consistently to develop a sense of history, addressing itself to the people and their problems as they are related to the larger structure, recognizing no "disciplinary" boundaries in the social sciences and abandoning the status and privilege of the academic in order to bring theory and its concomitant practice (hence struggle) into an intimate relationship with a radically changed and changing world. This involves praxis — a sense of past and a radical vision of the future, united through thought and action in the present.[51]

The defeat and destruction of the SSU terminates the "progressive" period in the McGill Sociology Department. Reaction, guided by Solomon and Westley, set in swiftly as every gain won by the SSU was dismantled and the stage was set for the removal of the "compromise," Professor Dixon. Reaction in the Sociology Department was coordinated with reaction in the Political Science Department so that the same actors Solomon, Westley, Von Eschen and Pinard et al. along with Waller, Taylor et al. appear in the attempted purges of *both* Professors Vaillancourt and Dixon.

49. William A. Westley, Director, McGill Industrial Relations Center, "Effective Disruption' As Wanton Destruction," *McGill Daily*, March 13, 1970.

50. *Ibid.*

51. "Action in Sociology," *Ibid.*

McGill in Quebec, Fall 1970: State of Siege

"Tell me," said one of the interrogating detectives, "do you think it is possible to impose an ideal division of society on that society?" No, said Lasko, but you have to have an ideal to work towards. "Have you ever been to Cuba?" he was asked. "No," he answered. "Why," the policeman asked, "are sociology students always the first ones involved in campus political activity?"

The police weren't even bothering to write down the results of this aimless political questioning. They took him back to his apartment, searched it, and then let him go. Lasko was one of three or four engaged in the same survey who were picked up as they made their rounds, obviously on the complaints of suspicious householders. McGill Professor Pauline Vaillancourt received a phone call from a ranking Quebec police officer after some of her students engaged in the survey had been detained. "He asked me," she reported, "if we had permission to do a survey and I said I didn't think you had to have permission under the War Measures Act. And he said you have to have permission to do anything."

Rumours of War, Ron Haggart and Aubrey E. Golden

The first F.L.Q. manifesto, translated by Canadian University Press was published in the *McGill Daily* of October 9, 1970. The Later F.L.Q. manifesto would not be published by the *McGill Daily*, but would circulate illegally in smudged, dittoed copies. The *McGill Daily* of October 13 reported that "Security intensified in wake of kidnappings," and "FLQ demands release of political prisoners." On October 13 the *McGill Daily* reported that Le Front d'Action Politique, F.R.A.P. President Paul Cliche said, "No worker, I am sure, feels menaced by the FLQ."

The *McGill Daily* reported on October 15 that "Lawyer Robert Lemieux, FLQ appointed mediator in the negotiations for the release of James Cross and Pierre Laporte . . . stated that the 'Front's patience is frayed' . . .'The government is playing a dangerous game in taking a lot of time in negotiations'. On Friday, October 16, the *McGill Daily* announced "Support for FLQ Mounting", reporting on the meeting held at Paul Sauvé Arena attended by 5,000 sympathisers. The *Daily* also reported that "students and faculty of the University of Quebec voted yesterday to shut down the university until the government meets all the demands of the FLQ". In a small box on the front page of the *Daily*, it was announced: "Rally at 1 p.m. on the steps of the Arts Building to support the FLQ and to oppose political repression." Another story related: "FLQ's Chenier Cell believed discovered.". What it did *not* report is that at 4 a.m. Quebec was put into a state of siege with the imposition of Public Order Regulations — the War Measures Act:

> And whereas the government of Canada desires to ensure that lawful and effective measures can be taken against those who thus seek to destroy the basis of our democratic governmental system, on which the enjoyment of our human rights and fundamental freedoms is founded, and to ensure the continued protection of those rights and freedoms in Canada . . .[52]

---

52. From "Text of Emergency Regulations under the War Measures Act", *McGill Daily*, October 19, 1970.

The "enjoyment of our human rights and fundamental freedoms" necessitated the occupation of the city of Montreal by heavily armed units from the Canadian Armed Forces and the suspension of all civil rights and massive numbers of arrests and indeterminate detention of every Francophone who had ever said anything political at any time recorded (or suspected) in police dossiers.

The big headline of the October 19 *Daily* was the announcement that Pierre Laporte had been executed. There was now to be no limit to the repressive activities of the government (a government which was willing to give M. Laporte a state funeral, but was unwilling to negotiate his release alive and well). *Daily* coverage of events at University of Montreal and the University of Quebec announced the cancellation of Operation Debrayage in support of the FLQ manifesto — the Quebec left not yet imprisoned was going underground:

> However, as some movement leaders at the Montreal campus of the University of Quebec pointed out, further action will not be brought on by a strike but rather by the canvassing of clandestine and semi-autonomous groups at the local level. They explained that fear of police reprisals will force the situation to go underground.[53]

The *Daily* also reported on October 19 that a rally held to protest the War Measures Act at McGill had attracted 300 people, although only ten were willing to undertake a temporary occupation of the Administration Building. Since such an occupation would have resulted in the internment of the participants and organizers, it did not seem unreasonable that people thought better of it. They did, however, make their feelings known:

> This was in contrast to the students' enthusiastic approval of his [the speakers] earlier comments on the present tense situation in Quebec. "There is a state of martial law in Quebec," he declared amid cheers. "We all know about it. What are we going to do about it?" At this point, Stanley Frost, Vice-Principal (Professional Affairs), shouldered his way onto the stairs with a megaphone to declare the meeting illegal. He was greeted with boos and cries of "you bloody fascist". "The University disclaims all responsibility for the consequences of your actions," he warned the assembled students. "I therefore urge you to disperse at once." The students elected to stay and listen to the speakers.

McGill became the safest spot in all Quebec, with the possible exception of Westmount, because the government terror during the October Days was based upon the judicious use of selective repression. It would not do to arrest Anglophones: that might stir a tiny echo in favour of civil liberties in the otherwise stony hearts of the majority of the English professional and managerial class.

The October 16 *Daily* reported:

> The McGill Faculty Union came out solidly behind the aims and actions of the Front de la Liberation du Quebec at their meeting yesterday. Their support came in the form of ratification of the resolutions of the Montreal Central Council of the Confederation of National Trade Unions, of which the MFU is a member. The resolutions include:
> — unequivocal support of the FLQ manifesto
> — support for the position taken by the Front de l'Action Politique permanent council (that the violent methods of the FLQ were forced upon them)
> — condemnation of the arrest of FLQ lawyer Robert Lemieux and of the government for losing control of the police forces in Quebec

---

53. Jean-Michel Joffe, "Students Reject Operation Debrayage", *McGill Daily*, October 19, 1970.

— reaffirmation of their belief that the FLQ will confine their attacks to the dominant minority in Quebec and not harm the general populace
— an expression of faith in democracy as practiced by the labour unions, but not in democracy dominated by an economic dictatorship

The meeting attracted about one third of the Union's 35 card-carrying members, which was sufficient for a quorum. [54]

It is possible that some MFU members have not recovered to this day from the effects of being "card-carrying members" of such a subversive organization! [55]

The *McGill Daily*, in this story, is reflecting the witch-hunting hysteria typical of the October Days, for the MFU had *not* "come out solidly behind the aims and actions of the Front de la Liberation du Quebec . . ." The MFU had ratified the resolutions of their parent union, the C.N.T.U., supporting the grievances contained in the FLQ manifesto, supporting Front de l'Action Politique (FRAP) *not* the FLQ, and protesting the arbitrary arrest of lawyer Robert Lemieux. The actions of both the C.N.T.U. and the MFU (along with many other Quebec organizations) reflected the growing mass support for the FLQ manifesto (which did not include, in most cases, support for the tactics of armed propaganda). Indeed, it is almost a certainty that the state of siege imposed upon Quebec was a direct result of the growing popular support for the FLQ manifesto, since the manifesto brilliantly expressed popular frustration and discontent.

The Administration could not have failed to ascertain that the moving force in the MFU ratification of the CNTU position had been none other than Professor Pauline Vaillancourt, nor that Professor Marlene Dixon had been the moving force in drafting an even more radical statement from the SSU. The spectre of Gray and the "enemy within" was once again haunting Old McGill.

Events were proceeding at McGill, but since the *Daily* had received a personal warning from the Quebec police to observe the restrictions in the War Measures Act the news was sparse and far from complete; no analysis of the situation was printed. Public activity was generally paralyzed. To some it seemed a pity to waste an opportunity to use English McGill against English Montreal. For by now it was obvious to all that the War Measures Act was invoked for the defense of the English Compradors, to deal a devastating blow to the Quebec independence movement. One suspects that U.S. Government advisors were busily engaged in providing the usual blood-thirsty American advice on proper counter-insurgency, having had so much experience in Vietnam, Brazil, Greece, the Congo, Chile, and countless other colonies, near and far, where "insurrection" needs to be "apprehended".

On Friday, October 23, 1970 the *McGill Daily* reported "400 At WMA Teach-In:"

Close to 400 students crowded into Leacock 26 yesterday to participate in a civil liberties teach-in inspired by the War Measures Act. The discussion, led by four McGill professors, concluded with the organization of the McGill branch of the newly formed United Front. [56]

Since political assemblies were illegal, and since McGill had banned all political activities, the "teach-in" was technically Prof. Dixon's Sociology of

54. Robert Mackenzie, "MFU Supports FLQ Goals", *McGill Daily*, October 16, 1970.

55. MFU retracted its ratification the following day.

56. Linda Farthing, Ross Baker and Julian Sher, "400 At WMA Teach-in," *McGill Daily*, October 23, 1970.

Oppression course. An attempt to find a larger meeting space (Leacock 26 was too small for the number of people who wanted to attend) was thwarted when the University locked up all the other available rooms. They would have locked Leacock 26, except that a large force of students was left behind to secure it.

> The front has been organized to aid those arrested since the invocation of the War Measures Act, and to work for the recision of the Act. Three McGill professors, Michel Pelletier from the School of Social Work, Marlene Dixon of the Department of Sociology, and Daniel LaTouche of the French Canada Studies Programme, all condemned the government for its implementation of the War Measures Act . . . All three professors concurred that the declaration of the War Measures Act was for reasons other than those offerred officially. LaTouche saw the Act as proof that the Federal government will never allow Quebec to separate, and Dixon described the Act as an excuse to remove the separatist threat from Quebec and to undermine the politics of le Front d'Action Politique. "The government, "said Professor Dixon, "had no real reason to invoke the War Measures Act, because there was no sign of an immediate and imminent insurrection in Quebec. Although the topic of the teach-in was civil liberties, much discussion revolved around the need for social reform rather than police power to meet the crisis in Quebec.[57]

So far, the teach-in had been quite tame, all participants mindful of the fact that freedom of speech was at the pleasure of the Montreal Police Department. Newsmen and television crews had come to the teach-in, possibly anticipating that the speakers would be snatched from under their very eyes. However, the day was to have its hour of real drama. In the midst of the discussion, a breathless man arrived in a state of agitation:

> Robert Keaton, a FRAP delegate from CAP St. Louis, made a plea for support against the charges of Regional Expansion Minister Jean Marchand and others. The allegations were that FRAP was a front organization for the FLQ.
> Keaton discussed FRAP plans for a newspaper campaign to counter these claims, which he characterized as untrue and an effort to discredit the FRAP electoral campaign [against Mayor Drapeau]. The FRAP organization is apparently severely handicapped by lack of funds and is therefore unable to answer the charges of Marchand through the daily media.[58]

The move against FRAP was obviously a cynical ploy by Mayor Drapeau to use the War Measures Act to destroy his only political opposition. The organizers of the teach-in, (which did result in the formation of a defense organization), were perhaps most pleased that they had, unwittingly, been able to provide FRAP with at least one vehicle to the mass media in its attempts to defend itself against the despicable tactics of the Mayor.

To appreciate the outrage that such goings-on inspired at McGill one must recall *Opération McGill* and that the Board of Governors had arranged the firing of Stan Gray on grounds that he was the "enemy within" spearheading an attack upon McGill's power and privilege.

During the period of the War Measures Act both MFU and Dixon were *again* playing the role of the "enemy within" using McGill's protected and privileged grounds to attack the Government's repression of the Quebec independence movement. This was all the more galling as Mc Gill's Establishment wanted nothing more dearly than the repression of a movement that it had considered, since *Opération McGill,* to be a direct and constant threat not only to McGill but to English Canadian hegemony in Quebec.

---

57. *Ibid.*
58. *Ibid.*

PART 4: Plots and Conspiracies

Chronology: The Dixon Case

January, 1970

Expulsion of SSU isolates Dixon within the Sociology faculty. January 1970 to November 1971 period of the anti-student-anti-Dixon United Front of Sociology faculty.

November, 1971

Spector defects from the faculty's anti-Dixon United Front. Wallerstein and Ehrensaft represent Dixon during appeal of faculty's "moving to an unfavourable decision" joined by Spector.

September, 1972

Wallerstein elected Chairman of McGill Faculty Union.

January, 1973

Wallerstein, as President of MFU, agrees to represent Pauline Vaillancourt's case against the Political Science Department's decision to terminate her employment. Professors Hamilton, Pinard and Von Eschen of Sociology collaborate with the Political Science faculty's attempts to purge Vaillancourt.

November, 1971:

The chief danger to academic freedom in the United States today comes not from student disruption but from the self-deceptions of the professoriate itself, because of its reluctance to take moral risks, and the resulting tendencies toward mandarinism, discrimination, and collegial pressure. I do not, however, condemn my colleagues but rather appeal to them to rethink their actions in the light of their ideals.

The chief safeguard of academic freedom would be the transformation of the liberal university into the critical university. Asserting the legitimacy of collective expressions of opinion would be the first step on an arduous path to making our quest for freedom relate to the power realities of contemporary American society.

Immanuel Wallerstein, "Academic Freedom and Collective Expressions of Opinion," Journal of Higher Education, *Vol. XLII, Number 9, December 1971*

One of the cohort of progressive graduate students who dropped out of McGill after the Dixon re-appointment battle said, three years later: "There were so many casualties that year; it is as if the place is poisoned, that it taints whatever it touches." Dixon would later say, in the letter of resignation given to Dean Vogel in October, 1974:

It was once my belief, which I must now think to have been hopelessly naive, that universities were places in which one furthered intellectual work in a supportive and collegial atmosphere. But what I have experienced at McGill in the Department of Sociology has been an ever increasing atmosphere of repression, vindictiveness and distrust, which leads in turn to such bitterness, anger and disgust, that one's whole life becomes corroded by it . . . for me, to accept reappointment in that department would be to continue to try to survive an oppressive, reactionary and vengeful atmosphere. That would be analogous to accepting a prison sentence, to serve time in a prison of the mind and spirit. That is what they have made of "their" department.

In May, 1974 Professor Prudence Rains would say in a memo inserted into the Departmental Minutes:

More generally, I find it distressing that as a department we have become so hardened to conflict and so adapted to subtle forms of violence that we simply sit and hope that it will pass quickly and that we can forget about it as soon as possible.

The atmosphere described began with the expulsion of the SSU. When Wallerstein was recruited to the Department, he was given the same rosy picture that had been painted for Dixon in 1969: a progressive department, with radical faculty, student participation, and space for competing streams of thought. Even after the re-appointment battle, Wallerstein obviously still had hope for the department, reflected in his paper on academic freedom, "I do not, however, condemn my colleagues but rather appeal to them to rethink their actions in the light of their ideals." However, when Wallerstein expressed these hopeful sentiments, he did so without true knowledge of the history of the student movement at McGill, of the purging of Stan Gray, the defeat of the PSA and the expulsion of the SSU. This history would not be clear to him until 1975. In 1971 the reappointment fight did not mean the same thing to the "scholar" and the "activist." Wallerstein believed in the protection of professional rights, and he believed in the crucial function of "competing streams of thought." That is, he defended Dixon's professional and intellectual rights on principle, not out of political expedience.

97

It was Professor Wallerstein's fate to arrive in the Department at the very moment that the programmed purge of Marlene Dixon was about to be implemented. Yet, in fact, the long process of Dixon's purge from the McGill Department of Sociology actually began in January, 1970 before Hamilton and Wallerstein had come to the Sociology Department. Her re-appointment, however, was to focus and center the contending forces within the Department, to serve as the starting point of the new political polarization of the Department and to redefine the struggle for pluralism from the realm of the student movement into the faculty itself.

Document #8 informs Professor Dixon, according to the new departmental regulations, that her re-appointment committee is moving to an "unfavourable" decision on the renewal of her contract. It will be noted that a few redeeming features actually appear in the general indictment of Professor Dixon. The redeeming features stem from arguments made by Professor Malcolm Spector. Professor Spector, after being badly mauled during his own renewal hearing not long before, had encouraged Professor Dixon to resist her long anticipated expulsion — unfortunately delayed after SSU by the legal niceties of holding a contract. Professor Spector had encouraged Professor Dixon purely and simply on the grounds that it was outrageously unfair to fire her after Spector himself had been renewed — for Professor Spector at that time had not published (and thus did not have academic credentials anywhere equivalent to those already possessed by Professor Dixon).

DOCUMENT 8

McGILL UNIVERSITY
MONTREAL

Department of Sociology,
McGill University,
P.O. Box 6070,
Montreal 101, Quebec,
November 3, 1971.

Dear Professor Dixon:

Enclosed please find a copy of the document which sets forth the Department's agreed upon procedures for considering renewals of contract for assistant professors.

Following these procedures I have convened a committee consisting of Professors Hamilton, Hanigsberg, Ehrensaft, Krohn, Pinard, Von Eschen, Westley, Wallerstein, Spector and Solomon, Professors Ehrensaft and Wallerstein being your nominees. The committee has met 3 times: on Oct. 28th from 2 to 5:30 p.m., on Nov. 2 from 2:00 to 5:30, and 7:45 to 9:00 p.m., all members being present, except for the absence of Professors Krohn and Von Eschen from the last evening session.

Since the committee feels that it may be moving towards a doubtful or unfavourable decision, i.e., that it may recommend something other than a 3-year renewal, in accordance with the agreed procedures, I am prepared to discuss with you the state of the committee's thinking to date, and also to invite you to attend the committee's next meeting, which I hope to be able to hold early next week, the week of Nov. 8th.

In anticipation that you might wish the committee to summarize the state of its thinking to date, a short document was prepared, and I attach this also. As is indicated in the document, I and other members of the committee are prepared to discuss and elaborate. Please let me know when you would like to meet with me.

Yours sincerely,

David N. Solomon,
Chairman,

DNS:lp

In accordance with the Procedures of the Department of Sociology for Renewal of Contract for Assistant Professors, Article Ie, the Committee herewith presents the state of its thinking and invites the candidate's comments in person prior to making a final decision in the case of Professor Marlene Dixon.

The Committee discussed the candidate's teaching, writing, and contributions to the administrative work of the department.

Though no systematic survey was made of student opinion, the Committee received mixed accounts of performance in this area, ranging widely. One major complaint was that classes were characterized as harangues. Other students, by contrast, felt that she offered fresh analytical insights. Some felt she was very responsive to students and some felt quite the opposite. There were some complaints of arbitrary or biased grading. Some faculty members asserted they had seen substandard work given high grades. It was reported that some students expressed fears they would be penalized for expressing certain views in their papers. It was not possible to reach a definitive judgment on teaching performance, given the range and variety of reports received.

The majority of the Committee felt that the published work was lacking. They characterized the work as adding very little, if anything, to knowledge, even judging the work within the frame of reference explicitly adopted by the candidate. At the other end of the spectrum, some members felt that the candidate's recent work combined with her active participation in social movements gave her original insights and offered the potential for important intellectual contributions. How far she has realized thus far this potential was a matter of debate and doubt.

There was a substantial and widespread sense that the administrative contribution was inadequate, some even expressing the sense that it was negative. There was minimum involvement in departmental meetings and committee work and even that some asserted to be largely self-serving. It was argued, on the other hand, that the rest of the department, by their attitudes and behavior may have contributed to the genesis of this behavior, and that the social conditions which gave rise to such behavior may no longer exist. There was question as to what this portends for the future.

The committee authorizes the individual committee members, in particular the chairman of the department and the two committee members chosen by Professor Dixon, to further specify the substance of the committee's deliberations, the identity of sources not being revealed.

(The original draft of this document has been initialled by all members of the committee)

The accusations of incompetence of such degree as to justify a refusal to renew Professor Dixon's contract as an *assistant professor* must also be judged within the prevalent norms of the McGill Sociology Department. The previous year three assistant professors had been awarded renewals of their contracts; of the three, two did not have their Ph.D.'s (Professor Dixon completed her doctorate in 1966) and *none* had ever been published! According to the last *Graduate Student Handbook* (McGill Sociology Department, 1975) the last paper published by Chairman Solomon appeared in 1970 and no book is listed; the last paper published by Associate Professor Donald Von Eschen appeared in 1969 (a version of a paper presented orally in 1966) out of a grand total of three articles; two published with himself as author and a third with two co-authors (one of whom is Maurice Pinard). In 1971, Professor Dixon had published six articles with three more in process, while her work on the women's movement was among the most widely reprinted in the literature.

Nonetheless, in the normal course of things Dixon would have been dismissed, or at best, given a terminal one year contract. She knew and the Department knew that the real decision had been made in January, 1970. Dixon did not believe that there was even a trace of hope for winning reappointment at McGill. She had spent the summer writing and resigning herself to departure from academia. Her mood was bitter, angry and cynical when she decided, on principle, to put up a fight for renewal. The polarization in the Department was so complete and her isolation so effective that she turned to two new members of the Sociology faculty to represent her within the appeal procedures that had been instituted within the Department. Dixon first asked Professor Ehrensaft to stand as her representative, since both were veterans of the student movement and had begun to form a tentative basis of trust and friendship. But Ehrensaft had only just been hired as an assistant professor — he felt he had no chance alone against the whole Department and the bloc of senior professors headed by Hamilton. At Ehrensaft's urging, a very reluctant Dixon approached Wallerstein. Wallerstein agreed to a reading of Dixon's publications file and papers in process and subsequently, on the basis of his evaluation of her written materials, agreed to be the other representative for her within the Renewal Committee. Many "secret agreements" have been alleged to account for Wallerstein's representation of Dixon to the committee. The agreements alleged to have been made as part of political conspiracies or for reasons of political expedience never existed. The only agreement struck between them was that Wallerstein should proceed as he saw fit in the Renewal Committee and Dixon should proceed according to her own strategies outside of it.

Having only just come to McGill, there was no way that Professor Wallerstein could have anticipated what the *political* consequences would be of defending her in the Renewal Committee. While there arose many speculations, on both the Left and the Right to explain Professor Wallerstein's decision the truth was that, in the first place, he did not believe that there existed professional grounds upon which to decently terminate Dixon. In the second place, as the closed, confidential hearings dragged on, Professor Wallerstein received an education in the political actualities of the Sociology Department. The more the Sociology Department argued for Professor Dixon's termination, the more their arguments strengthened Professor Wallerstein's defense — for it became glaringly obvious that she was being purged for political activism and for her support of student demands for democratization — and because she was a Marxist-Leninist who, it was alleged, desired the "destruction of McGill University" — and thereby all the nice things the McGill Faculty enjoyed. In the 72 hours of deliberations the case clearly fell into the arena of political struggle, in which Professor Wallerstein held very strong opinions. For example:

> There is much hard intellectual work to be done by the left. This intellectual work will never be done well if it is isolated from praxis, from involvement in a political movement and political action.[1]

In another context, he had written:

> The measure of the existence of freedom, which nowhere is absolute, is whether or not those who fundamentally dissent from the most basic assumptions of the social order are, in fact, free to act in those ways which are most likely to persuade others of the wisdom of their views. In short, there is freedom only if social transformation is possible.[2]

Documents 9 through 12 will reveal that Professors Ehrensaft, Spector and Wallerstein were not alone in their judgement of Professor Dixon's qualifications for re-appointment. Professor Dixon's strategy was to carry the re-appointment struggle *outside* of the McGill Sociology Department *and* outside of McGill University because she did not believe for one moment that McGill — at any level, faculty or administration — could be trusted to treat the question of her re-appointment according to the normal canons of professional judgement. Her strategy, in essence, was to mobilize external pressure from the larger academic community and from general public opinion against what was obviously a political purge. The first step was to contest the Sociology Faculty's allegations that "the published work was lacking" and "adding very little, if anything, to knowledge." Professor Dixon had a double advantage in combating allegations of incompetence: first, the academic recognition that the *Ramparts* article, "The Rise of Women's Liberation" had already achieved; secondly, the public recognition of her role in the women's movement in the United States and Canada. Professor Dixon was confident that if the judgement of the Sociology faculty was made public the Sociology faculty would be fully exposed as exercising arbitrary and biased judgement in the evaluation of her work. The letters from outside referees tore the Sociology faculty's judgement to shreds — and exposed as false the accusations that Professor Wallerstein was "soft on standards" where "radicals" were concerned.

---

1. Immanuel Wallerstein, "Radical Intellectuals in a Liberal Society," in Starr and Wallerstein, *The University Crisis Reader,* (p. 477).

2. Wallerstein, "Academic Freedom and Collective Expressions of Opinion." *op. cit.*

DOCUMENT 9

UNIVERSITY OF CALIFORNIA, BERKELEY

DEPARTMENT OF SOCIOLOGY
BERKELEY, CALIFORNIA 94720

November 10, 1971

Immanuel Wallerstein
Phillip Ehrensaft
Department of Sociology
McGill University
Montréal, Québec

Dear Manny and Phil:

Jim Hawley called me the other day and told me about the situation Marlene Dixon was in. I suppose he did so because of my involvement in a similar case, that of Dave Colfax and the Sociology Department of Washington University, St. Louis. He asked me whether I would agree to read Marlene Dixon's writings and offer an opinion. I agreed and the materials were sent to me, whence this letter.

I am not very familiar with Marlene Dixon's case, but from the material I have received, I am struck by the similarity. Both Colfax and Dixon are activists. Both are amazingly prolific, articulate, and insightful writers. Both have done some superb critiques of radical intellectuals (Colfax vis-à-vis Alvin Gouldner; Dixon vis-à-vis Kettler). Both are in strong opposition to predominant trends in professional sociology. Both have stepped on lots of toes and have violated a basic if unmentioned rule in academic life that first be a member of the team, then say and do what you like. Both are facing dismissal from departments which are not per se hostile to radical sociology.

In the St. Louis case, the reasons ostensibly cited are that Colfax does not contribute to intellectual excellence such as one would expect from a tenured faculty member. I suspect that similar grounds may be advanced in Dixon's case. Naturally, Colfax's supporters maintain that the real grounds are his activism, particularly in St. Louis' black community. Dixon too has been active regarding the French Canadian community, bringing the concerns of that community into McGill classrooms. But let me argue the case on the grounds used by the two departments in question, which are also used by the Berkeley Sociology Department in tenure cases. During the 14 years I have been in the Berkeley Sociology Department, generally two criteria of intellectual excellence have been applied: [1] that the candidate produced outstanding work in terms of standards accepted by professional sociology; and [2] that the intellectual quality of the work he did was so clear-cut that it did not matter whether it was strictly sociological or not.

Active involvement in the mid-1950's was a very different thing from what it is now. Then people pretty much assumed that society would remain as it was, that, as Daniel Bell argued, the problems were mainly ones of adaptation, reform, and personal adjustment. Now, that which was once taken for granted in society no longer is. That applies to the university as well as to other social institutions. Active involvement has always been a major source of Western sociology, and not just in the "Chicago school." Just think of how many established sociologists now, such as Lipset and Selznick came out of activist Socialist and Marxist traditions. Max Weber was actively involved in German politics, albeit on an establishment side.

Western sociology has had two origins. One, more purely theoretical, derives from men like Pareto, Durkheim, Weber. Another, more activist and practice-oriented, derives from social reformers like the Chicago School and from Marxists of one kind or another.

102

The problem that contemporary American sociology, like economics, faces is that professionalization has led to such excessive weight being given "theory", "concepts", "research designs" that much of the life has gone out of it. This is quite evident from the professional journals. Many of the professional sociologists are rather defensive about their work, often because they are not sure of its validity or relevance. This has led to expectation of conformity and a disinclination to take risks. Add to this the political and budgetary pressures a university faces, one can easily understand this predilection for conformity. But sociologists continue to insist they really would welcome true intellectual excellence. But they must recognize that such excellence comes from the turbulence of involvement, and an involvement refined by thought.

I have read Dixon's pieces on women's liberation and her critique of Kettler. The former told me more about women's liberation than anything else I had read, and the piece on Kettler, along with Colfax's critique of Gouldner, also told me a lot as to what was wrong with a certain radical intellectual sociology. Women's liberation certainly is one of the major social phenomena in the modern industrial world at the present time. How else can one write about it except by being in it, except by praxis? I doubt that a questionnaire handed out at a women's meeting would get very much in the way of meaningful responses, even if the people filled them out. If sociology takes itself seriously as a monitor of society as it is and is becoming, then its practicants, or at least some of them, must remain within it. And there is no way of being in the real world except through real commitment.

I certainly sense commitment in Dixon's work, and at times there is obvious stress on certain facts, silence or omission on others. But that is what we all do all the time. Our minds are all structured in certain ways to see certain things and not others. It is only such structuring which makes it possible for us to do analysis. The correctives come from other people whose minds are structured in different ways.

I think the Colfax and Dixon cases are symptoms of a basic choice which the field of sociology must make: either it takes the risk of retaining people who are deeply involved in social problems, write and think articulately about them, but may cause turbulence where many would prefer serenity, or it takes the easier road with the greater danger that sociology become a sterile, academic field as has happened to much of Classical Studies in the Western academic world.

With best wishes,

Franz Schurmann
Professor of Sociology and
History

DOCUMENT 10

Sociological
Resources for
Secondary
Schools
A project of the AMERICAN SOCIOLOGICAL ASSOCIATION

ROBERT C. ANGELL
Executive Director

27 Shepard St
Cambridge, Mass. 02138, USA.

November 11, 1971.

Professors Emmanuel Wallerstein and Philip Ehrensaft.
McGill University,
Montreal, P.Q., Canada.

Dear Sirs,
I am writing to give my judgment of Professor Marlene Dixon's article, "The Rise of Women's Liberation", *Ramparts*, December, 1969.

In connection with a project of the American Sociological Association, financed by the National Science Foundation, I have been getting out a series of compilations of scholarly articles in sociology, adapted for use in high schools and junior colleges. For one of the compilations, *Crowd and Mass Behavior*, I needed a good piece on the women's liberation movement, to go with articles on student protest, black nationalism, white militancy, the hippie movement and the counter-culture in general. I found it in Professor Dixon's article.

Her piece differs from most of the literature on the new feminism, which is either a rallying cry to the cause or a catalogue of wrongs. It is sound scholarship, tracing the membership to working women, middle-class housewives and students and connecting the movement with changes in the labor force and the family cycle, the growth of the civil rights movement and differentials in remuneration and hierarchical position. Her article stands out as a seriously worthwhile contribution to the literature of a field that is highly controversial.

Very sincerely yours,

Helen MacGill Hughes, Ph.D.

DOCUMENT 11

THE UNIVERSITY OF MICHIGAN
DEPARTMENT OF PSYCHOLOGY
ANN ARBOR, MICHIGAN 48104

November 15, 1971

Professor Immanuel Wallerstein
Department of Sociology
McGill University
Montreal, Quebec
CANADA

Dear Professor Wallerstein:

Professor Marlene Dixon has informed me that there is a dispute within your department about the quality of her professional contributions. I cannot comment about her teaching effectiveness or anything on the personal level because we have never met and I do not know her personally. Perhaps you would be interested in my evaluation of her published work. It is not irrelevant to mention that I am not a radical. I am an academician whose research work has dealt largely with psychological theory about women and psychosomatic gynecology. I have taught a graduate seminar in the psychology of women since 1964, am a co-author of "Feminine Personality and Conflict," author of, "Psychology of Women," and the editor of "Readings in the Psychology of Women." I am mentioning these qualifications in order to underline the fact that I am professionally responsible for knowing and evaluating the literature on the subject of women.

The book of readings will be published this spring and will include one section about the Womens Liberation Movement. It seemed important to include different points of view about this controversial topic and especially because I had included a harsh critique I wanted a powerful, logical, academic, pro-feminist paper. That turned out to be the most difficult paper of all to find. Obviously there are many current publications that are pro-feminist, but they do not stand up to an academic critique. I chose Dixon's paper, "Why Women's Liberation," and this is my comment about the paper in the introduction:

"The intellectual simplification characteristic of most of the radical polemic distorts the complex truth. Though exhilarating to its adherents, false simplification presents no answers. Dixon's model combines sociology, psychology and economics in an analysis and justification for political revolution. Dixon denounces not only female subordination but the presumptions of the movement itself.

"Dixon's 1969 paper is a tightly reasoned argument for women's liberation and the end of male chauvinism; in 1971 the arguments have a familiarity about them because the movement came to dominate the media. Dixon's 1971 paper is very different. That paper puts the women's movement in a context less of male arrogance than of national imperialism, racism and classism. That the movement deludes itself by not recognizing that it is characterized by its middle-class, white, liberal, American values and perpetuates the race and class destructiveness of the country, fills Dixon with contempt and fury. For Dixon, significant change in the position of women will require a supra-national political revolution. It isn't, for Dixon, that women are not exploited — they are. But the enemy is less men than an imperialistic form of economic exploitation that requires the subordination of races, women and classes in order to prosper.

"Dixon challenges what she sees as an existential insanity: the rejection and loathing of the privileged, white, educated, middle-class woman of her privileged life. It is a unique phenomenon this vast unhappiness of those lucky enough not to confront a hollow-bellied, war-riven, poverty-dominated search for existence. Asking, "who am I?," or, "what am I doing?," or "where is my identity?" is itself a symbol of the privileged.

Those who struggle for survival do not ask these questions. Dixon's paper challenges not only familiar male chauvinistic ideas but hallowed litanies within the movement."

Embedded in the passion which is what initially impresses one, is a tight, data-based, academic argument. Similarly, there are sociological insights which are Dixon's own, and which form an important contribution towards an understanding of the sociological ecology of womens' roles.

I hope that this opinion will be useful in your assessment of Professor Dixon's work.

Sincerely yours,

Judith M. Bardwick, Ph.D.
Associate Professor

JMB:csg

cc: Marlene Dixon

DOCUMENT 12

Documentation & evaluation
of experimental projects in schools

a division of
Scientific Analysis Corporation

November 8, 1971

TO: Professors Immanuel Wallerstein and
Phillip Ehrensaft

FROM: Professor John R. Seeley (California Institute of the Arts and Union of Experimental Colleges and Universities)

RE: Professor Marlene Dixon, McGill University

Professor Marlene Dixon, who is known to me personnaly and professionally, is important and of high merit, in my opinion and that of many others, as a Professor of Sociology, as a member of any faculty (presently McGill), as a member of the sociology profession, as a citizen of North America, and as a fount of original ideas closely related to ever-better-defined praxis: praxis inside as well as outside the University.

As such, it becomes of more-than-normal interest and more-than-local consequence what McGill does with reference to the renewal of her contract. It is almost impossible to believe, in the face of her importance and early fame, that refusal to renew (if she desires to stay) can rest finally on any consideration but her holding of "unpopular" views.

I have access only to a similar unsystematic sample of people who have learned from her, but more than the usual proportion have spoken warmly of their experience of her as a teacher and themselves as learners learning.

As for her writing, I think it is sufficient, that it fills gaps in sociological thought and thought about sociology that would otherwise go long unfilled, and that both in conventional terms *and* in the terms that many share as to what sociology ought to be, it is fresh, important, indeed irreplaceable. Of those trying to revivify social thought by sacrificial immersion of themselves in the agonies of their times, she has gone further than most in realizing her potential and the as-yet-unknown full potential of that way of being and doing. Unless we intend to preclude the rebirth of sociology (i.e., unless we are unscientifically and dogmatically counter-"Marxist" and pro-American-convention on this point), I should think any adequate department would want to have an advanced practitioner of Dr. Dixon's kind, indeed, Dr. Dixon herself, if possible, around.

That an administration might — almost must — view with less favor someone deeply committed to "outside" causes for her strength and renewal and the development of her thought, than someone wedded to working precisely with what one has to distance oneself from in order to be properly critical, is almost a foregone conclusion. But then that is what one has colleagues for: to protect one against the improper uses of administration. The most sinister, because quietest, such use is the demand for participation (or, from another viewpoint, complicity). Just as one must be a participant-observer to gain one perspective, one must be a principled non-participant in order to gain and preserve another. If we do not defend that right, we cripple our science — and perhaps move toward totalism in the University.

I would welcome Dr. Dixon to any faculty I could influence.

Sincerely,

John R. Seeley
Co-Director

JRS/cw

The procedures for the Renewal Committee permitted the individual being considered to meet with the committee in the case of unfavorable decision. Dixon requested such a meeting. In the usual course the individual comes before the Committee for degradation rituals, to defend her/himself and argue with the hostile faculty. However for Professor Dixon the meeting was an opportunity to clearly define what the political battle meant, what the issues really were, why the purge was attempted. Dixon was not so naive or disarmed that she intended to walk into the Renewal Committee hearing alone, or to inform Chairman Solomon, the military master of the Colonels Coup[3] in the sociology department, that she intended to have witnesses on her behalf during the proceedings of her hearing. Her witnesses were Jean-Guy Vaillancourt and Sidney Ingerman, President of the McGill Faculty Union. After a 45-minute debate that could be hear through the doors and down the hall, the voices saying "but what will it look like in the *Star* if we don't let her in" prevailed.

It was at the hearing before the Renewal Committee that Professor Dixon presented fifteen letters testifying to her academic competence from scholars outside of McGill. Professor Dixon then proceeded to read aloud *Academic Roles and Functions* — the only manifesto to which she ever put her name stating her reasons for having found herself in confrontation with the university.

---

3. Professor Solomon, an "expert" in military sociology, has long term relationships with the military and Defense apparatus. In 1974, along with Professor Westley, Professor Solomon acted as consultant to the Defense Research Board. Professor Solomon is also a member of the Defense Research Board's Advisory Committee on Social Aspects of Defense Research.

Academic roles and functions

1. *The political context of the question of activism within the Academy*

For twenty years in North America the witch hunts of the Cold War banished dissenting thought. Only a handful of men and women within universities continued to keep the ideas of socialism and revolutionary Marxism alive. It was during this long period of ideological repression and virtual thought control that the social sciences rose to prominence, supported by government and foundation money. The social sciences in North America, dominated by an American elite of Cold War anti-communist intellectuals, developed its theory and methodology based upon the ideological premise that American Capitalism and the American form of political democracy were the present apex of human civilization and the only system which guaranteed human liberty. The social sciences justified the socio-political system, gathered information necessary to the government, and became deeply involved in the counter-insurgency establishment created by the world-wide counter-revolutionary policies of the U.S. government. The result was a social science which was in reality an applied technique for efficient information-gathering. No dissenting tradition emerged within the social sciences beyond a mild debunking reformism. The social sciences, notably sociology and political science, were explicitly anti-Marxist. Behind a "scientific" rhetoric of "value free social science" the completely ideological nature of American social science was hidden, even while the attack against the Marxist tradition of social science as "ideological" was carried forward.

During the long repression intellectuals who maintained their socialist analysis existed in isolation from their colleagues and without any viable social movements among the people. As a result, there grew up a tradition of defensiveness and withdrawal. The role of the dissenting intellectual was held to be "detached," cautious, divorced from action. In those years, the role requirements reflected the real conditions of existence in isolation and the equally real and pervasive fear of repression. The courage of those who refused to abandon their commitment during these years must be respected by all. Yet, the repression had been successful, for "liberty" had become limited to "civil liberties."

So it was understandable that during the 50's radical intellectuals would withdraw into a "life of the mind" for no other mode of organized action was viable at the time. It is also understandable that intellectuals, especially those sequestered in universities, would lose faith in the possibility of a revolutionary transformation of the west, reconciling themselves to be observers of the revolutionary energy of the third world. Yet the objective basis for pessimism and withdrawal represented by the passive role of detached university intellectuals without hope and embittered by the passivity of the masses of the people no longer exists.

With the opening of the decade of the 1960's social conditions were changed completely. The fundamental contradictions inherent in American society revealed themselves in the rise of Black insurgency, anti-war movement, student movement, the New Left. The Cold War myth of America the defender of liberty and justice against the evil tide of "communist aggression" was finally smashed as the truth of American aggression, subversion and brutality was revealed by the genocidal war in Vietnam. In Quebec, the same period is marked by the rise of the Quebecois independence movement, student unrest, and the formation of revolutionary organizations. The long passivity of the people was at last broken, the dissenting intellectuals were no longer working in isolation from popular insurgent movements. The objective basis for a withdrawn and defensive role no longer existed. Indeed the times cried out for action.

The tragedy was that in many cases radical intellectuals repudiated the new social movements, refused the obligation to translate theory into practice, and sometimes became the objective and ideological enemies of social movements they ought to have embraced. This was above all true in the case of the student movement: The students turned upon their own society, striking out at what they knew best, the schools. In every advanced country, Germany, France, Italy, Britain, Quebec, U.S.A. and Japan the left student movement attacked the complicity and subservience of universities and their faculties to the Establishment: Corporate international capitalism and the governments which acted in its interest. The rise of the student New Left and the consequent student movement brought the struggle into the university itself, into the classroom, onto the campus. The students demanded that academic rhetoric be translated into reality, that liberty embrace liberty of action, the right to participate in the institution, and that the university be "relevant," that is, serve the interests of the community and of the people. In the U.S.A., consciousness among students of racism and militarism, exploitation, aggression, and poverty replaced the patrioteering jingoisms of the Cold War. In Quebec, consciousness of U.S. and English Canadian exploitation of the Quebecois and the injustice of an enormously privileged English minority was growing stronger. In the University struggles which followed, the empty rhetoric of academic detachment and university autonomy was revealed for the fraud it was.

The effect of the student movement was to directly challenge the faculties and administration of the university. That confrontation shattered forever the pretentions of "detachment" in the role of the professor. It became clear that no professor was "detached" from a central institution in society; no social science was without ideology and application. Professors were faced with the same demand to serve the interests of the community and of the people that students demanded of themselves and of the university at large.

Civil liberty, the freedom to write dissenting articles in obscure journals, was no longer sufficient. Now it became necessary to demand freedom of action as well. It became necessary to burst apart the system of professional norms developed in the 40's and 50's which defined the academic role in narrowly "professional" terms and which operated to maximize conformity and ideological passivity. It became necessary to demystify "tokenism" — the lone Black Man or House Marxist — used to perpetuate the mythology of "freedom of thought." Liberty is not defined by thought, which divorced from action becomes impotent: liberty is defined by the ability to determine one's own life, to exercise real power in the daily round of life; liberty is ultimately defined as the right to revolution.

In response to the times a new professor emerged who rejected the narrow bounds of academic life, who plunged into active participation within insurgent movements. In that process, the role of professor, writer, researcher, teacher and colleague by necessity became defined in new ways, governed by new expectations, which in turn brought all of the turmoil of conflict and change home to' the faculty itself.

Academics who had become entrenched in power during the long years of repression became the vanguard of the purges to rid themselves of the students and professors — the activists — who challenged their power and influence. Lesser academics whose privilege and recognition was dependent upon the system of professional norms, whose careers were based upon being recognized by those who held power, joined as willing allies, purging their own ranks of trouble-makers. All over North America a new witch hunt was in progress. Whole faculties were purged at Simon Fraser and NYU, while hundreds of individuals (in sociology numbering over 200 by the S.L.M. count) were fired and often blacklisted. The use of "professional criteria" — attacks against the person and his work — to mask the political nature of these firings has become so transparent, its hypocrisy and cruelty so repellent, that the very notion of professionalism is becoming synonymous with reaction.

Everywhere, the new insurgent movements of the 60's and 70's have been answered by reaction and violent repression. The social system of Capitalism has not even demonstrated its well known powers of co-optation. Reactionary repression has been the overwhelming response within universities, and the complicity of faculties in that repression has turned professors into the hatchet men of the ruling interests.

Many students and intellectuals have turned away from the university, seeing in it only the same cynical lies, the same repression, the same hypocrisy that is found in every major institution of modern society. Yet the reality remains that universities which have turned to repression begin to die: conformity replaces creativity; the "team spirit" replaces the long traditions of standing alone, if need be, to speak the truth; self-interest replaces idealism; passivity replaces action. Thought divorces from action and commitment dies in the endless repetition of form without significant content. Why? Because to think is to act, and to act is to struggle. For the physicist that struggle might be contained in the laboratory. For the social scientist, above all for the Marxist, the laboratory is society itself, the experiment living insurgent movements. Through repression, the social sciences condemn themselves to decay, to obsolescence, to monumental irrelevance.

There is truth in the great traditions of western thought which marks the rebel and rebellious thought and action as the very measure of the vitality of intellectual life. Now when new thought and action arises to confront the failures of the old, we are not witnessing a renaissance, but a deeper twilight than we knew before. The questions of activism and of activists is a profoundly political question, one that directly confronts the crisis of the university: will the university remain a knowledge factory, bureaucratically organized and infused with the Corporate spirit, or will the university keep alive its ancient commitment to liberty, to freedom of thought and action? If it remains possible to follow the latter course, then the faculties of universities must reconcile themselves to the turbulence of the world, for its conflicts of power, idea and aspiration must be reflected within, as without, the academy.

II Academic Roles

a) *The role of revolutionary intellectuals within the Academy*

Each person accepting the demands of praxis and embracing commitments to direct participation in insurgent movements evolves his own form of integration of the role of professor and activist; therefore, I speak primarily from my own experience.

b) *General Commitments of Marxist Professors* — I believe that there are two primary obligations which intellectuals, particularly in the arts and social sciences, must fulfill. The first is to be a critic of the established order, to confront its injustices, inequalities and corruption and to provide explanations for the origins of such injustice, inequity and corruption. The second is to act, to translate theory into practice, to be a direct, personal participant in the historical process of social transformation and political and economic revolution which has marked our century.

Furthermore, I believe that intellectuals who have been trained in universities, and who work in universities carry the heaviest burden of obligation because the privilege of education, especially advanced education, is denied to the majority of the people. Yet it is the majority of the people who pay for the education of the privileged few. Governments obtain their funds from taxation, and we all know that the heaviest burden of taxation falls upon the very working classes who cannot afford to send their children to the universities which are paid for by their labour. Grants or money from foundations and corporations are only possible because those economic institutions appropriate profits from the mass of the people. The universities and their teaching staff ought not, in my view, to serve the special interests of government nor the private interests of large-scale capitalists. Universities and their teaching staffs ought to be directly obligated to those who in fact support them, the majority of the population, the working people. The primary obligation of the university intellectual is to serve the people, directly.

For a Marxist intellectual, the very nature and basis of social analysis is praxis, the integration of theory and practice. A Marxist cannot escape the logic of an analytical system whose very roots are founded in theoretical study and practical action; whose methodology demands praxis; whose ethics and historical vision has been a demand for active participation in revolutionary change for 120 years.

A Marxist, by the very nature of Marxist analysis stands in opposition to a capitalist system of production; to Imperialism and its colonization and exploitation of whole peoples; in opposition to governments of special interests — Corporate interests — in opposition to all prevailing social practices and institutions which serve to implement and perpetuate the exploitation of the majority of the people.

Battles may be large or small; they may range from the struggle for an independent, socialist Quebec, to massive opposition to American Imperialism, to the organized activities of poor people against a system which dehumanizes them, to strikes, to the university itself as a major institution supporting and serving monopoly Capitalism, to the microcosm of a university department. In some ways, the small battles are as important as the great movements for popular confrontation, for it is impossible to separate daily life and round of work from intellectual ethical commitments, from an analytical vision of the world which demands that the educator be educated, that self-transformation is the first step towards social transformation.

111

III. *Specific academic functions*

a) *Students* — The role of learning and teaching, which ought to be a reciprocal role, is the axis around which academic activities should be organized. It is through the teaching function that a professor shares skill and knowledge with students; it is through the mutual confrontation of ideas that students and professors alike develop ideas and analysis; it is the process of learning from students that professors are kept continually aware that all people are students, that learning is continuous throughout life.

The present university structure is hostile to learning and teaching. The medieval role of master and student with its encrustations of faculty privilege and power over students creates almost insurmountable barriers to true learning and the free human development of creativity, boldness and originality in students. The abyss of rank and privilege alienates students from teachers and contributes to the alienation of students from the very act of learning itself.

Learning ought to be an act of mastery, of developing powers of self understanding and self-determination. Instead, learning in the present university is an act of subservience and submission. Learning ought to be intrinsically rewarding, marked by a passionate engagement between student and knowledge. In the present university, learning is competitive, the student is constantly forced to rank himself against all others, to become obsessed not with a thirst for knowledge and self mastery, but to become obsessed with grades. This means that the grading system becomes an end-in-itself. Students are driven to cheating and plagiarism at worst; to compulsive, sterile and cautious work most typically. The traditional system of University education creates technicians and obedient professionals, working against the development of a disciplined and challenging perspective.

Under the present system teachers and learners are driven into forming a conspiracy to short-circuit the impediments to learning represented by the traditional role of professor, the powerlessness of students and the competitive grading system. In the name of a conspiracy to commit relevant and meaningful learning I have experimented with democracy in the classroom; neutralizing competitive grading; complete freedom in the definition of work by students; highly disciplined but collective learning situations; to name but a few. Some experiments worked, others did not. I have no formula for critical and significant learning in an environment hostile to such development, but I am committed to the search. To protect the autonomy of my classroom and my right to teach according to my own best judgment, in consultation with my students, I have conspired against university regulations and sometimes been extremely uncommunicative about my methods. Since I am committed to learning and teaching and not to bureaucratic regulations, I fully intend to continue to pursue a conspiratorial course. Any other course would be a betrayal of the learning and teaching process itself.

It is true that some students are fearful and resentful of learning situations which are not rigidly programmed according to standard procedures. I regret that I cannot reach such students, but I will not sacrifice the creativity which can be stimulated in so many students to calm the anxieties of a few. Meaningful teaching will always be controversial, and should be controversial. Teaching is neither a popularity contest nor a sterile routine of examinations and marks, but a process of struggle and engagement. It is my pleasure to have been denounced in every institution at which I have ever taught. Were I not to be denounced, I should consider that I was indeed failing my obligations.

b) *The Rights of Students* — I believe that people should have the power to determine their own lives within the communities and institutions within which they live. This is one aspect of the cry "power to the people." In the present university system, students are powerless and that powerlessness is the root of their alienation from learning itself. I have always supported student struggles for self-determination, and I will continue to support the aspirations of students for liberty in schools. I supported the Sociology Students Union in their struggle for the right to participate in departmental decision-making, and watched them go down in total defeat, before the intransigent determination of the faculty to retain its power and privilege. Even though the position I took resulted in my virtual ostracism from faculty life, I would give the same support to student aspirations if the struggle were renewed. I cannot be committed to true democratic principles of self-determination and not support those principles for students. I deplore the present powerless position of students, and submit that the present repudiation of all student rights has caused great harm to students and faculty alike. Were I a student under these conditions, I would be inclined towards rebellion. Indeed, were any of the faculty in the position they force students into, they might discover in themselves a clearer sense of justice. In my classroom I reserve the right not to play tyrant insofar as that is possible under the present system.

c) *Politics in the Classroom* — I believe it is my primary obligation to speak the truth, as I understand truth, in my classroom. I am a Marxist. I teach Marxist scholarship, theory and practice. I engage in revolutionary movements as a participant. I take political positions on current political events. I state all of these truths to my students. Furthermore, because I represent a dissenting analysis of the world, I am obligated to be more scrupulously unbiased toward my students than those who proclaim their objectivity and disguise their ideology under the cult of scientism.

In every class which I have taught at this University I have made my own position clear from the first day of class. I have also clearly stated to the students what I expect of them: that they also present their position clearly and cogently. I have never to my knowledge in all the years that I have taught ever penalized a student whose political views differed from my own. I have however, more than once, warned students against a false presentation of radical views in hopes of a higher mark because I detest such forms of intellectual dishonesty.

I believe, furthermore, that politics above all, belongs in the classroom. Education should indeed prepare the student to participate actively in his own community and his own history. The political events of the world are what is relevant and immediate. Education ought to prepare the student to face his world, to analyze its processes, and to actively and critically weigh his role in the events of his time. Indeed, politics is a part of every classroom, but complaints are voiced about political positions which are radical, which are informed by the power of negative thinking, which stands in opposition to the ruling ideologies.

I have taken highly controversial positions in my classrooms. I have supported the rights of students to rebellion and of the right of oppressed people to revolution; I have stood for the self-determination of black people; I have supported the movement for an independent socialist Quebec; I have denounced the War Measures Act and the government that invoked it and abused it; I have stated my opposition to the capitalist socio-economic system, to U.S. imperialism in general and its plunder of Quebec and of Canada in particular. I have stated my views on occasion with passion and conviction, but in so doing, I have not neglected to present either reasoned argument or empirical fact. The allegation that the Marxist tradition is mere "ideology" or "opinion" must be ignorant of 100 years of Marxist scholarship and of the example set by Marx himself.

Commitment and passion may be termed a "harangue" by those in violent opposition to my views. Yet those who have been participants in even the most impassioned hours during the early days of last October, before and after the War Measures Act, also know that the classroom had become a forum for debate, which raged on the floor in support and rejection of arguments which I had presented. No one was denied the right to make his views and his understanding of the situation known. Indeed, I believe that the most significant learning of which I have ever been a part while at McGill was provoked by the passion and relevance of the crisis in Quebec as class hour after class hour two hundred, and often more, students struggled to understand Quebec and the Quebecois as they never had before.

In the end, the degree to which I may have influenced students has not resulted from any abuse of faculty position, but from the spark of idealism and the strong sense of justice which students bring with them into the learning situation. I have only sought to make the alternatives clear, and to aid students in their quest for self-understanding, for commitment and relevance in their own lives. The final decision about what commitment they will choose, and what they will consider relevant, is always theirs.

d) *Students and Activism* — Marxists stand in a special relationship to radical students because of the commitment to praxis. Students who are actively engaged in political action within and without the University are engaged in activism, which is itself a process of action-learning-analysis more significant than any classroom situation. The University itself does not make provision for the recognition of praxis as a learning experience. The professionalism of the department demands that such activity be recognized only if some form of "research" is involved. Yet I know from my own life that the most valuable learning which I absorbed was in the process of activism itself, therefore I see no reason why an artificial set of "professional" criteria should be forced upon activist students. For radical students (and in some cases students who were not radicals) I have recognized activism as a learning experience and given marks commensurate with that learning experience. It is part of the conspiracy to learn one must wage against the present system. I have, in a sense, "protected" these students from those who would deny any recognition of the learning value of their practice and from those who oppose the very practice in which these students are engaged. It may not appear that the same grading standards are applied to radical students, but such a claim ignores the weekly discussions and consultations that were in fact the substance of the students' work. Furthermore, in many cases I am required to respect the confidentiality that exists between professor and student, in which the substance of the learning is by its nature confidential. As I am in my own life and work committed to praxis, I will support the praxis of my students as central to their lives and to their education.

One of the primary obligations of radicals, whether they work in universities or not, is education. Discipline, rigor and respect for truth are essential elements in any scholarship. Yet true discipline and complete commitment to truth are characteristics which cannot be fostered mechanically, or forced upon students through oppressive and alienating learning conditions. Students must learn to embrace the search for truth and commitment out of the joy, the intrinsic satisfaction that comes from intellectual and self-understanding. It may be true that one fails to see this happen more often than one sees success; but success when achieved is worth all the effort. To achieve that success I remain willing to use any means necessary.

e) *Research and Publication* — During the 1940's and 1950's the growth of sociology was dominated by liberal ideology which based its claims to be "scientific" on an imitation of a natural science model. The natural sciences were endowed with a prestige and acceptability that the sociologist wished to win for himself and his profession. This was the era in which sociology, claiming to be an "objective" science, asserted that its research was "value free" and sought only "objective" empirical fact.

Time has proved the "scientific" claims of sociology have been illusory. Sociology is not "value free." On the contrary, it is often so biased with the values of liberal anti-communism as to render its "objective empirical data" irrelevant or absurd. Yet, the attitudes of "scientism" with all of its pretensions remains predominant in mainstream sociology. The demand is made of everyone to go through the motions of "empirical research" regardless of the utility of such procedures to one's theory or problem.

Adherence to a Marxist tradition must lead one to reject the claim that the only acceptable form of research is "empirical research" accomplished through the traditional methods. The traditions of Marxist scholarship, while often scholastic, are in their most vital forms based upon a methodology of praxis, of active engagement in insurgent social movements, in which theory and practice are integrated into a living whole.

Certainly Marxists differ in the extent of their engagement in a turbulent world of social change. Some people, by inclination or by their particular histories and commitments are plunged almost overwhelmingly into a life of activism; others are less absorbed, and enjoy greater freedom for contemplation and purely theoretical work. The two types of intellectual workers ought to complement one another; to exchange information and analyses, integrating the different virtues of the emphases of their practice. But this is not to say that the activist role is in any way free from the obligation of analysis and criticism, for otherwise the experience of participation becomes useless to others.

The scholastic role of Marxist theoreticians not engaged in praxis is amenable to the mainstream definition of the professional role and is consequently widely accepted in the Academy, but this is not true of the activist role. Activism, while as old as Marxism itself, is still new and unwelcome in the post-World War II university. The role of the activist, however, is essential to Marxist scholarship, for it is only in the crucible of practice that theories may be tested and new theory generated which reflects real social conditions.

No Marxist ought to publish for the sake of publishing; no Marxist ought to pursue his studies as a "career." If this is the ideal of the scholarly role, it is a necessity for the activist role. The demands of the immediate struggle become the primary focus of the activists' analysis and publication. Publication occurs when errors need to be corrected, when a fuller education of participants becomes mandatory, when changes are demanded in strategy and tactics, or when theoretical and practical debates within social movements are the most urgent and immediate struggle. The demands of activism. particularly for those in significant leadership positions, require constant judgment, based on theory and practical knowledge, and those judgments and their consequences are all part of the analytic process. Yet one may never communicate this knowledge in written form, but transmit it only orally through consultation, speeches, seminars, study sessions and planning groups. Since one does not struggle in order to publish, but publishes in order to struggle, the activist role is in contradiction to the "publish or perish" expectations of mainstream sociology. Furthermore, the activist explicitly recognizes the legitimacy of the oral tradition and the value of collective analysis and decision making. If theory and practical experience can best be transmitted verbally in face to face situations, there is no need to publish it.

Activists recognize the need for contemplation, for periodic withdrawal from immediate social action in order to further theoretical mastery and to systematize and integrate practical knowledge with the existing body of theory. Such "stolen moments" are very precious, and a university position is one of the chief means by which activists are able to accomplish much study and writing. It is one of the chief reasons why Marxist activists seek to remain within universities. Yet the cycles of intense involvement and contemplative withdrawal are not provided for, nor is their importance recognized by mainstream "empirical" sociology.

In my own case it has been my fate to have been absorbed in active participation since my graduate studies. Events at the University of Chicago threw me into an even more demanding activist role. My first year at McGill was one of intense practical activity; my second year has been one of relative seclusion and devotion to study, the course of which I have not yet completed. Part of my concern has been drawn precisely to the problem of a closer and more fruitful integration of the scholarly and activist roles, for it seems clear to me that scholastic analysis has been weakened by its isolation from practical action and practical action weakened by its isolation from theoretical analysis. My studies and my problem have led me to sharply criticize the profession, the academy, and the role of the academic "radical." This has meant that I have ruffled the feathers of numerous sociologists and radicals. So be it.

In those articles which I have published to date all have been analyses demanded by the immediate tactical and strategic needs of a particular social movement, the women's struggle, although my work as an activist has not been limited to the women's movement. My aims were not to impress professional colleagues, but to influence the direction and goals of the women's movement. my "data" is practical experience itself, which includes work in every region and in every major city of the United States and Canada. The men and women for whom I am writing are themselves participants and have no need for footnotes — they need only check what I say against their own experience. Participants are also constrained by the discipline of their activism; there are issues, events and sources that we do not reveal and do not write about. An activist is engaged in a revolutionary process; the first commitment is to serve the furthering of that revolutionary process to the best of one's ability.

In the end, the true evaluation of my work is revealed in its usefulness to the movement itself. Its value consists not only in education, but also in the accuracy of my prediction and the success of the strategies I propose. I submit that this is a harder test of merit than is ever demanded of an article published in the *American Sociological Review*. It has been my reward to see the realization of my work represented in the direction and actions of the movement itself. Nonetheless, my present concerns remain the problem of praxis, the integration of theory and practice, and a clarification and extension of a Marxist methodology. The only ways in which the problems of praxis can be truly solved is by creating the role itself, and this I am presently, in company with many others, endeavouring to do.

f) *Collegiality.* — The informal norms of any workplace arise to smooth human interaction, to ease the stress and strains of the demands of one's job, and to facilitate the collective work of the group. This "team spirit," defined by codes of etiquette and norms against "rocking the boat" are as prevalent in university departments as they are in offices or factories. The system works well and facilitates work and social interaction so long as there exists a general consensus as to the goals of work and the most desirable means and organization of work. When there exists conflict over basic goals and means of work the "boat is rocked" and the "team spirit" impaired. In periods of conflict, the basic power structure of the group rises clearly to the surface, cliques and coalitions are formed, polarization occurs along lines of disagreement, and the more powerful seek to contain or to expel the contending faction.

Of course it is no accident that radical activists are frequently the source of conflict and as frequently in the weaker faction that finds itself purged. The reason that radicals and Marxists are so often at the root of departmental conflict is not difficult to locate: the reason stems from the whole of the foregoing discussion, from the profound differences in modes of work, perspectives on the world and fundamental life commitments between radicals and non-radicals in the academy.

If the radicals in question happen to be women, the initial situation is greatly compounded by the prejudice to which women in a thousand subtle ways are subject. Entrenched power dislikes any challenge to its supremacy, and when the entrenched powers are men, and one of the challengers a woman, their fury surpasses understanding, as I have witnessed on more than one occasion.

A commitment to praxis makes head-on collision almost inevitable, for the radical or the Marxist will seek to realize his conceptions of teaching, departmental governance and style of work. The undemocratic organization of university departments, the meritocracy based on professionalism and the privileges of rank, the pressures of the "team spirit" all work to force the radical to accept conditions of work which are not only repugnant to a radical consciousness, but which also effectively impede his intellectual participation. Prior to the great university rebellions most radicals were obliged to come to terms with their powerlessness to effectively challenge or change the professionalism and norms of the workplace as defined by mainstream sociologists. The result was often profound alienation and sometimes a complete erosion of any meaningful radical commitment.

Many radicals and Marxists, however, persisted in challenging their entrenched opposition, primarily by asking how it came to be that in an institution in which departments were supposed to be democratic there was so little democracy; in sciences which were said to be autonomous there was so little autonomy; in institutions which were said to be the guardians of freedom of thought there was so little dissent; in institutions which were said to protect liberty there were so many purges; and in educational institutions there was so little education.

With the rise of the student movement and its challenge to entrenched university life, with an increase in the number of rebellious professors engaging in activism, conflict within departments, as well as within the university itself, reached unprecedented levels of tension. More often than not, students and activist professors shared many of the same aspirations for change, and joined together in a common alliance for reform and fundamental changes in university life. The unforgivable sin in any professor, needless to say, was to engage in a confron-

117

tation which not only rocked, but often upset, the boat. Equally unforgivable, it would seem, was the pollution of the professional mystique and claim to special privileges by fraternizing unduly with students.

Whatever form the struggle may take, it is a struggle for freedom: for the freedom of thought and action which a dissenting tradition needs if it is to grow and prosper. The corporate ethos of "team spirit" with its norms of submission and compromise, its implicitly alienating demand that conviction and action, work and practice, must be separated, is not conducive to vigorous and meaningful debate. The "team spirit" stultifies thought and works towards intellectual sterility and passivity. It became clear in the course of successive university rebellions that entrenched faculty power was almost universally opposed to any significant reform which they saw as treatening their own rank and privilege. The most common answer to the activist professor who sought freedom to pursue his own style of work and teaching was: get out of *our* university if you cannot submit to our departmental organization. The activist was rejected as a colleague and treated as an outsider, often as an enemy — a practice which almost guarantees creating an enemy where none might have existed before.

A university department is a web of human relationships characterized by relatively close inter-personal interaction. It is because of the personal nature of the workplace that political conflicts become so easily expressed as personal conflicts. Overt political discrimination, which is morally unacceptable to many, may become disguised by sole emphasis upon strained personal relationships. Once this occurs it is possible to ignore or even forget the nature of a personal conflict which grew out of a political confrontation. Yet such interpersonal strains are clearly political in their origin and perpetuation. A famous case of this sort was Staughton Lynd's dismissal from Roosevelt University in Chicago for "ad hominem" reasons. It was clear to any outsider that political conflict was at the heart of the matter, and in the end the Roosevelt department made itself absurd by claiming that the problem was Lynd's personality.

When the dissenting activist is isolated from a department it is a common tactic to make life so miserable that the individual is literally driven by desperation to leave the department. Such procedures disguise the fundamental political conflict which is the real issue. Furthermore it is often the isolated and frustrating position in which the activist finds himself which leads him to retreat into a defiant and angry posture — a result which is then used to justify purging the individual on the "personal" grounds that the activist was a "bad" colleague.

In answer to allegations that I have been a "bad" colleague, or made "negative" contributions, I reply quite simply that what I have presented in this response I have learned in this department. Charges that I am "self-serving" are simply absurd when one recalls that it was by a deliberate act of principle (which I was perfectly well aware worked against my self-interest) that got me into this position in the first place. I made every attempt to contribute to the department in those areas in which I felt I had most to contribute — matters concerning students. I was explicitly informed that I was too politically unreliable to be permitted work on committees relating to graduate and undergraduate students, just as I had been explicitly told that never again would an activist be hired by the McGill Department.

The point is not to belabor the past, but point directly to the political origin of the charges that my "administrative contribution was inadequate" as under the circumstances it could hardly have been otherwise. Nor is my situation unique, on the contrary it is a common experience of many radicals.

Conclusion. — Activists by their nature are prone to take action; they are equally prone to resist taking the easy course of conformity; finally, they are committed to resist injustice and pretension when they are confronted with it.

Political discrimination against activists is an injustice. Political discrimination may be a predictable response, but that does not mean that one should passively yield to its commission. The purge of radical activists from North American Universities is part of an overall repression by which a system threatened by rebellion attempts to crush all efforts of the people on their own behalf. My whole life has been committed to resistance. I have no intention whatsoever of betraying that commitment. Therefore, Gentlemen, I submit that you have no legitimate grounds whatsoever for denying a full renewal of my contract.

The *McGill Daily* of November 17, 1971 reports that:

When Dixon had finished her presentation, the committee was absolutely silent. "No responses, no questions — nothing," reported Ingerman. One committee member stated bluntly, "Confidentiality has been broken and I don't feel like talking." As it became clear that the committee was not going to cooperate at the open meeting, Dixon decided to make the first move. She demanded that the committee justify its reluctance to renew her contract, in view of the fact of the lesser academic credentials of the three professors whose contracts have been renewed. Dr. David Solomon, Chairman of Sociology, answered, "Well, procedures have changed over the years."[4]

Dixon asked him to clarify his statement . . . At that point, several members of the committee burst into a defense of their decisions, but, according to the two observers, they failed to clarify the issue.

Both Ingerman and Vaillancourt were highly critical of the whole procedure. 'It is hard for me to understand on what grounds her contract was not renewed,' said Ingerman. 'I have read appraisals from leading sociologists who evaluated her work as being an outstanding contribution to her field. In addition, there has been no clear evidence that her teaching ability is seriously in question.' . . . Vaillancourt felt that Dixon should have been judged on her involvement in the 'wider community' rather than on her administrative contribution. 'She's one of McGill's only sociologists that has taken a position in the Quebecois situation in favor of the Quebec people.'[4]

The anti-Dixon majority in the Renewal Committee had indeed been outraged when Dixon had demanded that observers be present at the hearing. In fact, everything that Professor Dixon did contributed to the increasing rage and distress of the Sociology faculty as they found their every action and word repeated the following day in the *McGill Daily*. While the *Daily* was an annoyance, the *Montreal Star* was a far more formidable threat to a quiet, efficient political purge. The daily calls from reporters from the *Star* put Chairman Solomon into a visible panic. Clearly, things were not being kept under control. Professor Dixon was taking care to short-circuit confidentiality. She felt she had nothing to hide (contrary to the Sociology Department, which had everything to hide);

---

4. "Dixon Rebuts Charges of Academic Incompetence," *McGill Daily*, November 17, 1971

her strategy in this instance was based on the conclusion that her only real protection lay in making everything public.

On November 24, 1971 the *McGill Daily* ran a headline, "Dixon's Contract is Renewed." The *Daily* reported:

> The renewal committee of the sociology department decided last night to grant Marlene Dixon a new three-year contract. There is speculation that this sudden change of heart was prompted by the university administration in order to avoid campus unrest. The department apparently has realized that it failed miserably in its attempt to disguise the political motives behind Dixon's possible dismissal.[5]

The *Daily*, being a student newspaper, cannot really be faulted for speculating that the University and the Department were motivated by a desire to "avoid campus unrest". But the truth of the matter was that it was neither the students nor last moment faculty remorse that lead to the midnight reversal in the Renewal Committee. What accounted for the second-thoughts of the key senior faculty opposing Dixon's re-appointment was growing concern for the professional image of the Department and a feeling that if the proceedings continued, Wallerstein might turn toward a larger forum and thus broaden awareness of the conflict. He had refused to budge an inch from his position in favor of a regular three-year contract renewal. The majority faculty favouring the purge were caught in a pincers made up of Professor Dixon's public celebrity and open, political defense in the press and Professor Wallerstein's professional defense within the Renewal Committee itself. It is most probable that both Professors Solomon and Westley had finally realized that a purge of Professor Dixon was going to be on the front pages of the city newspapers *as a purge* and that, furthermore, it would be perceived within the North American academic community as a purge: the Sociology Department had no case that would stand up to the light of publicity.

On November 24, 1971 the victors were rejoicing. It seemed that the purge had been defeated, justice had prevailed, and that progressive forces still had a future in the McGill Sociology Department. All the celebrations, however, were premature, for the battle had only been redefined along new lines of demarcation: anti-Dixon vs. pro-Dixon. The group of faculty who were united around their hatred for Professor Dixon — lead by Hamilton, Pinard and Von Eschen — were now united in their hatred for Professors Dixon *and* Wallerstein. The first taste of things to come took the form of Professor Hamilton's attempted punishment of Professor Jean-Guy Vaillancourt for his presumption in interfering in the private purging activities of McGill University (see Document #13).

5. Julian Sher, "Dixon's Contract is Renewed," *McGill Daily*, November 24, 1971

DOCUMENT 13

McGILL UNIVERSITY P.O. BOX 6070, MONTREAL, P.Q., CANADA

Department of Sociology,
March 6, 1972.

Professor Michael M. Ames,
Chairman, Professional Ethics Committee,
Canadian Sociology-Anthropology Association,
Department of Anthropology and Sociology,
University of British Columbia,
Vancouver, British Columbia.

Dear Professor Ames:

A member of your committee has engaged in behaviour which is of a very doubtful ethical character. The member in question is Jean-Guy Vaillancourt.

Professor Vaillancourt made an appearance as "an observer" before the renewal committee which was considering Professor Marlene Dixon. He was introduced by Professor Dixon as a member of the Ethics Committee of the Canadian Sociological Association. That affiliation was the only identification, other than his name, which was made at the time.

The following day, the *McGill Daily* (November 17, 1971) carried an account of the proceedings and again Vaillancourt was presented as a "member of the Ethics Committee" of the Association. It was also noted that he was a professor at the Université de Montréal. This account carried the following statements:

Vaillancourt felt that Dixon should have been judged on her involvement in the "wider community" rather than on her administrative contribution.

She's one of McGill's only sociologists that has taken a position in the Quebecois situation in favour of the Quebec people.

The final sentence of the article reads:

"The McGill sociologists are setting a very bad precedent by doing a hatchet job on one of their professors," Vaillancourt concluded. "It's not the first time and it won't be the last."

A story in the *McGill Daily* of November 23, 1971 repeats this account. The relevant paragraph reads:

A second observer, Jean-Guy Vaillancourt, professor at Université de Montréal, and member of the Ethics Committee of the Canadian Sociology Association, condemned the whole procedure as a sloppy "hatchet job" done on "one of McGill's only sociologists that has taken a position in the Québécois situation in favour of the Quebec people."

All of this public comment appeared prior to the final committee decision. The decision, which was to renew Professor Dixon's contract, was taken on the evening of the 23rd.

On the 24th of November the *Daily* reported the renewal of the contract. This account contains the following quotation:

> One observer, Jean-Guy Vaillancourt, a member of the Ethics Committee of the Canadian Sociological Association, warned that this political "hatchet job", as he called it, would not go unpunished.

Some days later, on November 30th, a letter from Professor Vaillancourt appeared in the *Daily*. He indicated his wish to make correction of two slight errors that had slipped into two of the *excellents articles* that the *Daily* had published about Professor Dixon's case. One of the errors involved the "hatchet job" quotation. At that late point he chose to make disavowal. It should be noted that he chose to disclaim only the statement appearing in the November 24th issue of the *Daily,* that is, the issue appearing the day after the decision. It is not clear whether he was denying the "hatchet hob" quotation or the "would not go unpunished" statement or both. (His actual words: "Je n'ai jamais dit que 'this political "hatchet job" . . . would not go unpunished.'") In his letter of correction he made mention of the "hatchet job" quotation which appeared in the *Daily* on November 17th but this was only for the purpose of correcting an obvious difficulty in the logic. That statement was not disavowed nor was the statement of November 23rd. If Professor Vaillancourt is only denying the threat of punishment, then his declaration of judgment still stands. As such it is a peculiar judgment especially for a member of an Ethics Committee, since judgment ordinarily follows a consideration of the evidence. Professor Vaillancourt also used his letter of the 30th of November to indicate that he did not appear at the meeting of the renewal committee as a representative of the Canadian Sociological Association's Ethics Committee.

Vaillancourt's statements in the *Daily* have recently been reprinted in a publication called *The Insurgent Sociologist*. The "hatchet job" quotation appears there once again together with the mention of the Ethics Committee affiliation. There is no mention made of his subsequent corrections.

I met Professor Vaillancourt for the first time a few days prior to his appearance at the renewal committee meeting. At that time he enquired as to how the "firing of Marlene Dixon" was progressing. I indicated that his judgment was unwarranted since no decision had been made. He pressed for more information on the subject. I informed him that I did not consider it proper to discuss the matter with outsiders while the discussions were still continuing. I have since asked the other nine members of the committee whether Vaillancourt had approached them or whether he had had any discussion of the matter with them prior to the decision. All nine persons have replied in the negative. It is difficult to see how any responsible observer could make judgment in such a matter without having undertaken even the most rudimentary inquiry. It is, to be more specific, difficult to see how he would be in a position to judge the *Daily's* contributions to be "excellent".

There is reason to believe that Professor Vaillancourt was aware of the contents of the *Daily* articles as they appeared and was in a position to make denial of the statements attributed to him at some earlier point. In a conversation with a member of the Department which occurred on the 21st of November, Professor Vaillancourt denounced the behavior of the renewal committee and, when asked for his source, referred to the articles appearing in the *Daily*. The only articles that had appeared to that point were those of the 17th and one on the 16th. (A statement presented to the committee by Professor Dixon was reprinted in two parts on the 18th and 19th).

It strikes me as unethical for a member of the Ethics Committee to suggest that he is appearing in an official capacity on behalf of that Committee or to allow himself to be so represented. It strikes me as a highly dubious behavior for a member to make use of this affiliation in an effort to influence a pending decision and then disclaim any official connection once that decision has been reached.

The members of an Ethics Committee, it seems to me, ought to be, like Caesar's wife, above reproach. Professor Vaillancourt's behaviour, again in my judgment, does not meet that standard.

Sincerely yours,

Richard F. Hamilton,
Professor of Sociology.

RFH:rg
cc: Hubert Guindon

Professor Dixon had asked Professor Vaillancourt to be an observer because he was familiar with the case, but principally because he came from *outside* of McGill, and from a French-speaking Quebec university. Ingerman could not be attacked, because as President of MFU he was clearly exercising his mandate to act in the interests of a member of the union — but being a McGill insider, and a member of MFU, left him open to various attacks of bias and "Unionism." Dixon wanted to be sure that Prof. Ingerman had some protection as well. When Professor Vaillancourt was introduced to the Renewal Committee, he was *not* introduced as an observer *from* the Ethics Committee of the Canadian Sociological Association. It was clear to all participants that Vaillancourt was acting as an academic observer for Professor Dixon in an individual capacity. It was the *McGill Daily's* story that gave the ever-eager Hamilton his opening, since the *Daily* inadvertently implied that Vaillancourt attended as a member of the Ethics Committee, rather than as a personal advisor.

Document #13 is nothing more than an attempt to discredit, professionally, a man who had presumed to interfere in McGill politics. It is a classic example of the academic poison pen letter used to undermine an individual's professional reputation. The two documents, one may note happily, show that every attempted "hatchet job" does not succeed, as Professor Ames rebuffs Hamilton's poison pen letter with exemplary good sense and dignity. (Document #14)

It should also be noted in Professor Hamilton's letter that Professor Vaillancourt is alleged to have asked only Hamilton (of all the other members of the Renewal Committee) how the "firing of Marlene Dixon was progressing." If such an exchange actually ocurred it would have been prompted by Vaillancourt's belief that Richard Hamilton was a genuine socialist — and it was common knowledge in the Montreal academic community that Dixon was up to be purged, if on no other grounds than her positions and activities during the period of the War Measures Act.

123

DOCUMENT 14

THE UNIVERSITY OF BRITISH COLUMBIA
VANCOUVER 8, CANADA

DEPARTMENT OF
ANTHROPOLOGY AND SOCIOLOGY

29th November 1972

Professor Richard Hamilton,
Department of Sociology,
McGill University,
P.O. Box 6070,
Montreal 101, P. Q.

Dear Professor Hamilton:

My sincere apologies for the long delay in responding to your request for information about a matter brought before the C.S.A.A. Ethics Sub-committee. I mislaid my notes and then got engaged in other duties. The fault thus lies with me and not with either the Sub-committee or with the C.S.A.A.

Originally you wrote to me suggesting that a member of the C.S.A.A. Ethics Sub-committee may have acted improperly during a dispute in Montreal. I can report that the Sub-committee discussed this matter and issues arising out of it for some time. Your original letter served a most useful purpose of focusing debate on a number of crucial issues.

You presumably also expected some "action" by the committee in response to your complaint. The committee has not been empowered to judge the ethical behaviour of individuals, however. The terms of reference (published in an earlier issue of the Bulletin) specify that this committee should "begin a process of developing a code of professional ethics" and should "promote and encourage" debate about the ethical implications of our professional activities. It would be difficult to judge the ethics of professional conduct without first having an agreed upon code of conduct.

One issue that your letter raised was the necessity of maintaining a clear distinction between being a *member* of an ethics committee (or of any other association committee) and being a *representative* of said committee. It appears from the information you provided that certain newspapers might have conveyed the impression that Professor Vaillancourt was representing an ethics committee. But I discover no evidence that he made such a claim, not do I believe that an individual should be held responsible for errors of interpretation or fact expressed by newspapers over which one has no control. These are my views and probably also represent the views of other members of the Ethics Sub-committee.

The task of the Ethics Sub-committee as it is presently constituted, if I may now return to an earlier point, is not to adjudicate such issues as these but to encourage their open discussion. (I must stress here, however, that the focus is on issues, not individuals. The C.S.A.A. at present has no institutional mechanism for the adjudication of the ethical conduct of individual members.)

You may wish to explore these matters further with the Ethics Sub-committee. The new chairperson is Professor Tom Philbrook, 12 Poplar Plains Crescent, Toronto 7.

the MFU is a splinter group which broke with the MAUT in the wak
roversy surrounding Stanley Gray, a political science professor, dismisse
'69 for participating in a number of student sit-ins and protests. Dis-
the MAUT's overwhelming vote of support for Administration action
Gray joined in the ensuing months with other faculty members unhapp
JT policies to create the MFU.
major point of contention between MFU and MAUT partisans lies i
belief that McGill should be more fully involved in the concerns o
iety. To this end the MFU has involved itself on a number of occasion
cal issues reaching beyond the confines of the University.[7]

es included opposition to the Montreal Municipal By-Law agains
a statement in favour of the FLQ manifesto objectives (late
nvolvement with an urban development protest group in the com
ding McGill (the Milton Park Citizens' Committee against th
Project). The MFU joined the CNTU because it hoped to ge
larger society, and CNTU is noted for its outspoken capacity t

n's affiliation with the MFU was no joking matter to top level
Administration. If we recall the analysis of McGill as a fortres
ec context; if we recall the interconnection between the CNTU
McGill; if we understand that the anti-union activities at McGil
(not in 1972) then we may begin to understand how seriousl
ion would take the role of a man of Wallerstein's rank and pres
the then tiny MFU. Their worst fears would be realized durin
of the Service Employees Union — the first strike in the 17
McGill! During the strike, Hamilton crossed the picket lines bu
striking workers; Dixon (normally a rank and file MFU membe
with the Student Strike Support Committee, while other MFU
d energetically and effectively among the teachers until entir
o go out in support of the Service Employees. The combine
f unions, students and faculty resulted in victory for the servic
a precedent for how more strikes can be won at McGill.
re, Wallerstein provided effective leadership, and the member
grew steadily during his presidency. This growth was directl
ct that of every grievance brought to MFU during the tim
President, he lost not a single battle! It got to the point wher
department would approach Wallerstein, attempting to see if h
d with one or the other. In this light, we way begin to gai
tanding of the virulent campaign against Wallerstein personall
J. The attack against MFU was worthy of the machinatior
A. for the official line that was taken was that the Universit
ith MFU and its membership.
st indication of the Administration's concern with the "new
n a "Personal View" statement circulated in February, 197
of the MAUT, Professor Stanley J. Shapiro (who, the followin
be appointed Dean of the School of Management). We mu
T was the body addressed by Arts and Science Dean Wood
trike to whip up the faculty troops in opposition to Stan Gra

Again, I apologize for the long delay in replying to you. I have no better excuse
than the distraction of other work.

Yours sincerely,

M. M. Ames,
Professor and Acting Head.

MMA/pa

cc: T. Philbrook.

cc: Members of the Ethics Sub-committee.

The attack against Professor Vaillancourt was the opening gun in a war
that began with the Dixon re-appointment, but a war that would spread to attacks
against Professor Pauline Vaillancourt, Professor Spector, Professor Ehrensaft
and eventually to Professor Wallerstein.

The most fascinating development from the Dixon re-appointment was,
perhaps, the witch-hunt that would become the major tactic in the Right's
attempt to "control" (and eventually to remove) Professor Wallerstein. The witch-
hunt took the form of accusations that Wallerstein was unprofessional when it
came to the evaluation of "radicals;" that he was operating, in alliance with Dixon,
as a member of an international network of socialism; or that he pursued "outside
political interests." The "cold war" witch-hunt in the Sociology Department
would not become public knowledge until the publication of the purloined
(by whom is still unknown) document from the Chairmanship Search Committee
in the *McGill Free Press* (reprinted here in Part VI: *The Purge*).

Chronology: The Vaillancourt Case

November, 1971
The Dixon Re-appointment Battle. Immanuel Wallerstein serves with Philip Ehrensaft as Dixon's representatives on the Renewal Committee.

May, 1972
Pauline Vaillancourt is informed that Political Science will delay in considering the question of her re-appointment.

September, 1972
Wallerstein President of the McGill Faculty Union.

October, 1972
Pauline Vaillancourt is informed by the Department of Political Science that she will not be re-appointed as Assistant Professor of Political Science.

November, 1972
Letters from Sociology attacking Vaillancourt; real target is Wallerstein.

January 16, 1973
Vaillancourt's statement to Political Science Committee On Promotions, Rehiring and Tenure. Immanuel Wallerstein serves as her academic advisor to the appeal hearing.

January 16, 1973
The Grievance Committee of the McGill Faculty Union sends a memorandum to Dean R. Vogel "in support of the appeal against the recommendation of the Dept. of Political Science not to reappoint Pauline Vaillancourt".

January 29, 30, 1973
Professors Pinard and Hamilton attack Vaillancourt and the McGill Faculty Union (i.e., Immanuel Wallerstein).

March 20, 1973
Pauline Vaillancourt requests the C.A.U.T. to review the Political Science Department's refusal to renew her appointment.

March 30, 1973
C.A.U.T. agrees to arbitrate the Vaillancourt case.

April 10, 1973
The Report of the Chairman's Search Committee prepared by F. Henry is published in the *McGill Free Press* as "The Secret Proceedings from the Department of Sociology". Wallerstein refuses Chairmanship.

June 26, 1973
David Solomon and William Westley are "appointed" as Co-Chairmen of the Sociology Department, having the power to unilaterally decide any issue that cannot be resolved unanimously. Second *coup d'etat* à la 1970.

August 20, 1973
C.A.U.T. decides in favor of Vaillancourt against Political Science.

June, 1975
Pauline Vaillancourt resigns from McGill. She accepts an appointment at U.Q.A.M. She is elected, in the same month, to the Board of Directors of the Canadian Political Science Association.

1972-1973:
Wallerstein and the McG

There is conflict of interest with
he will defend anybody including
committee he sits. There is a clea
Defense of Vaillancourt and gene
faction in order to increase potent
Anonymous members of the
to the Chairman's Search C

In the fall of 1972, following
unionized (as stated in *University in*
intellectual work of the left cannot be
in a political movement and political
a university department), Immanuel
Faculty Union with an executive com
rer), Pauline Vaillancourt (Secretary
and Laurier Lapierre.

A prestigious scholar belonged i
sity Teachers); it was *indecent* to rul
Who could any longer doubt that a na
to wreck all and any hopes of up-gr
To grasp the full scandal of the situa
of the MFU. According to the *McGi*

> Since 1969, the MFU has counte
> in the MAUT with the collective
> sees university teachers as *workers*
> their employers, the university adm
> the universities.
> According to MFU spokes
> teacher as worker by including
> members. Far from acting as an
> the MAUT is accused of promot
> happy family" devoid of conflict.

McGill was furiously attempting
clerical workers with another version
top administrators in command, the
in terror of unionization at McGill,
major Quebec institutions of "higher
are increasingly becoming politicize
fear the C.N.T.U. the most, for it
independence that had participated i
writing up socialist "manifestos". Tl
Menace:

6. Ralph Seliger, "MFU: the Professor as W

In a sen
of the co
in Augu
sidents
regardin
with M,
A
the MFI
Quebec
with po

These i
demonstration
retracted), and
munity surrou
Cité Concordi
involved in th
politicize issue
Wallers
of the McGill
within the Qu
and Operation
belong in 189
the Administr
tige within eve
the 1974 strik
year history of
MFU backed t
acted as liaiso
members work
faculties voted
"united front"
workers, settin
Furthern
ship of the uni
related to the
Wallerstein wa
factions within
would be aligr
a political unde
and against M
of a M15 or C.
was *unconcerned*
The clea
MFU is found
by then Preside
Autumn, was
recall that MA
during the PSA

7. *Ibid.*

PSA and student participation in the hiring and firing of staff. (Part II, McGill in 1969). MAUT also, it must be remembered, voted confidence in the Administration's summer firing of Gray, even after the Academic Senate had refused to wield the ax: that is, had made the decision that Gray could not be fired on grounds of academic misconduct. MAUT is, for the faculty, the equivalent of a "company union" as MUNASA was for the clerical and technical workers, until the formation of a C.N.T.U. local for clerical, technical and library workers.[8] Thus, it is well known at McGill that when a major policy statement is produced by MAUT, it is a statement made with the full consent, or at the command of, the McGill top administration.

The memorandum from Shapiro, "Some Issues that *must* be faced — A Personal View," laid out a series of proposed policies that were obviously intended to co-opt major points of the MFU program under Wallerstein. The real give-away came, however, with Shapiro's comments on the question of salaries:

> The membership must also decide whether MAUT should more aggressively move to improve salary levels at McGill. The enclosed statement prepared by the salary committee reveals that McGill salaries are continuing to fall behind those of comparable Canadian universities . . . Do these developments suggest that MAUT must become a professional syndicate? Should binding arbitration of salary disputes be demanded by MAUT representatives?[9]

Shapiro then went on to explain that the Salary Policy Committee of MAUT would begin meeting with Administration representatives. The challenge presented to MAUT in its role of pacifier and company union is quite clear in the concluding paragraphs of Shapiro's memorandum:

> Many would argue that MAUT's refusal to adopt a classic collective bargaining stance is appropriate. However, different attitudes prevail on other campuses, *and a stronger position on salary matters is being advocated by some McGill professors* . . . (emphasis added)[10]

Of course, "some McGill professors" refers to the program of the MFU. Shapiro's memorandum also refers to issues concerning the "promotion and tenure sphere" comprising, in fact, three out of five items in the entire "Personal View." MFU was obviously making inroads into the traditional repressive and arbitrary promotion and tenure procedures at McGill. Central to this issue was, of course, the Vaillancourt case. A glance at the Chronology that prefaces this section will show that on January 16, 1973 Wallerstein served as academic advisor at Pauline Vaillancourt's appeal hearing to Political Science's Committee on Promotions, Rehiring and Tenure. Then, dated the same day, the Grievance Committee of the McGill Faculty Union sent a memorandum to Dean R. Vogel "in support of the appeal against the recommendation of the Dept. of Political Science not to reappoint Pauline Vaillancourt." It is quite obvious that the top levels of McGill's Administration were growing increasingly disturbed by the MFU under Wallerstein's leadership. MAUT President Shapiro in February would hardly call for an "essential" MAUT "period of self-examination during which

8. MUNASA's company union activities lead to a split, similar to the MAUT/MFU split, in 1975 with the formation of NUMOTLE — National Union of McGill Office, to Technical and Library Employees.

9. Stanley J. Shapiro, President, McGill Association of University Teachers, McGill University, to all members of the McGill teaching staff, "Some Issues that *must* be faced — A Personal View," February 22, 1973.

10. *Ibid.*

present negotiating policies are subject to critical review and alternate approaches are openly and honestly explored" if MFU were not proving far more formidable than various sources of McGill Administration propaganda are willing to admit. Indeed, the attack against Wallerstein, hidden in the attack on Vaillancourt, began in November of 1972, prior to the MAUT campaign attempting to co-opt the MFU program and MFU's defense of aggrieved professors on questions of rehiring, promotion and tenure.

From the point of view of the McGill Administration, the real danger was not MFU — but MFU *and* Wallerstein. While previous leaders of MFU had been courageous and determined, they did not have the academic power nor the prestigious weight that Wallerstein brought to the job. Wallerstein had as well the advantage of nearly 20 years of operating within bureaucratic and repressive settings in various battles for progressive causes — this meant that he was a highly sophisticated and skilled combatant. Wallerstein was perfectly prepared to beat them at their own game — thus the overt repression that had proved so efficacious in the Gray and student movement challenges was useless against Wallerstein. More cunning and roundabout methods were required in the new situation. Consequently, the attacks against Wallerstein/MFU were not direct, since that would backfire, but indirect: by attacking the individuals that Wallerstein and the MFU defended, claiming them to be incompetent or dishonest or unscrupulous. In this way it could be implied that Wallerstein was, at least, dishonest and unscrupulous (if not incompetent). If dishonest and unscrupulous could not be made to stick, being "soft" on standards was the other line of defense.

The first assault upon Wallerstein, indirectly through Dixon and Vaillancourt, came in November, just prior to Vaillancourt's appearance — with Wallerstein as her Academic Advisor — before the Political Science Department's Committee on Promotions, Rehiring and Tenure. While these attacks from members of the Sociology Faculty were obviously aimed at assisting Political Science, they were also attempts to discredit Wallerstein by discrediting the two radical women he had or was defending — and to discredit Wallerstein was also to discredit the MFU. (Documents #15 & 16)

DOCUMENT 15

McGILL UNIVERSITY P.O. BOX 6070, MONTREAL 101, QUE.,

McGILL UNIVERSITY
P.O. BOX 6070, MONTREAL 101, QUE., CANADA

Department of Sociology,
November 29, 1972.

Professor H. Waller,
Chairman,
Department of Political Science,
McGill University.

Dear Professor Waller:

It has been suggested that it might be helpful if I were to write to you with respect to the teaching of Professor Pauline Vaillancourt in this Department during the 1970-71 session.

Perhaps I could first review the circumstances of Professor Vaillancourt's appointment, which as you know, was for half-time. Due to an unexpected leave or our being unable to fill a vacant position, it became apparent in April or May of 1969 that the Department would have sufficient funds to make a one-year half-time appointment, and also that certain courses might not otherwise be taught. The Department was persuaded to appoint Professor Vaillancourt for this purpose. I say persuaded, because, as I recall it there was uncertainty as to what the Department wanted to do about this half-position, and it was as a result of very strong sponsorship by one or two people that Professor Vaillancourt was appointed.

Professor Vaillancourt taught two one-semester courses during that session — one an undergraduate course, the other a graduate seminar. More complaints came to me either directly from students who approached me, or indirectly through other students or colleagues who passed complaints on, than has been the case of any other course in this Department since I became chairman. As I recall it, students felt that they were not being taught anything and that they were not learning anything. The courses were generally regarded as failures.

The Department's evaluation of Professor Vaillancourt's teaching is indicated by the fact that when the question of a similar reappointment for her came up the following year, none of her previous sponsors was willing to support any further appointment.

I hope these comments will be helpful to you.

Sincerely yours,

David N. Solomon,
Chairman.

DNS/cbs

131

DOCUMENT 16

McGILL UNIVERSITY
P.O. BOX 6070, MONTREAL 101, QUE., CANADA

Department of Sociology,
November 23, 1972.

Professor Hal Waller,
Chairman,
Department of Political Science,
McGill University.

Dear Professor Waller:

I understand that Professor Vaillancourt is contesting your decision not to renew her contract. I understand that she is basing her argument partly on letters submitted by students praising her teaching. It is with respect to a letter from one of these students, Jerry Spiegel, that I am writing you.

I know Mr. Spiegel fairly well. He took a course from me in which he received one of the few A's I gave and I encouraged him to enter our graduate program. In an informal conversation at the end of the school year two years ago, he told me that Professor Vaillancourt's course on critical political theory was extraordinarily bad. In particular, he was quite angry about her exam in that course, which was a particularly indiscriminating multiple choice rather than essay test. He seemed, in fact, to regard the course as a dead loss. I was very surprised, therefore, to find he had submitted a favorable letter to you.

I suspect that this change of opinion was made on political grounds. Mr. Spiegel is, as I am, a political radical. It may be that he fears that Professor Vaillancourt is being terminated for political reasons, and thus wanted to support her in spite of his previously unfavorable judgement of her teaching. Or, it may be that he wants diversity of opinion in your department and is supporting her for this reason. If so, his letter should be discounted, for it apparently does not reflect his real views.

That his letter is politically motivated is supported by an incident that occured in our department when we were considering whether to renew Professor Dixon's contract. Here again, Mr. Spiegel had told me in private conversation that the course he had taken from Professor Dixon was bad. Specifically, he told me that the only thing he had learned from her course was that for every stupid conservative idea, (which he felt made up the content of most courses taught by political conservatives) there was an equally idiotic radical idea. (i.e., the ideas propounded by Professor Dixon). But, in this case, too, he sent in a letter praising her teaching; again, I suspect, on the grounds that she was a political radical.

The issue this raises goes beyond the question of Mr. Spiegel's true beliefs. *The question it raises is whether one can trust letters from students when the professor they are defending is seen as upholding their political views.* I am inclined to think not. The first clue to this is that most of the letters written in such cases seem to be from political radicals, not from a cross section of students with all political beliefs. The second clue is cases of reversals of opinion by students such as seems to have occurred in Mr. Spiegel's case. I have reason to believe in the case of Professor Dixon at least, that Mr. Spiegel was not alone in saying one thing in conversation and another in a letter.

If student views are going to be used, and they should be, the opinions of a *cross section* of students should be solicited and this should be done *prior* to renewal consideration time when students become pressured by those soliciting letters to change their views.

It is as important that political consideration not be used to force retention of an incompetent person as it is important that they not be involved in firing a competent one. Justice should be even-handed.

Sincerely,

Donald Von Eschen,
Associate Professor,
Department of Sociology,
McGill University

DVE/dd

For the investigator, the real question is this: what is Sociology doing in the business of the Political Science Department? First, we note that it is Solomon, Von Eschen, Hamilton and Pinard engaged in the double attack upon Vaillancourt and Wallerstein. Solomon and Von Eschen are used against Vaillancourt, while the Department's two reactionary "heavies" with some claim to professional reputations, Hamilton and Pinard, are used directly against Wallerstein (not by name, but in attacking MFU and Vaillancourt the target *has* to include Professor Wallerstein).

Further, a short exercise in documentary translation may begin to reveal the motivations of the authors of Documents 15 and 16. In 15, the reader will note that Solomon makes much of the fact that there was support for Vaillancourt when she was appointed, but no support at the termination of the half-time appointment, indicating her lack of competence. This argument is subject to question when we recall the history of the SSU and of the original Vaillancourt appointment. In 1969 Pinard and Von Eschen were members of MFU and were playing at being "political radicals". The membership of MFU overlapped between Sociology and Economics and MFU was involved in combating the politically motivated attempts to deny appointments to both Vaillancourt and, earlier, Dixon. Hence, the initial support. But in 1969-1970 McGill undertook the repression of the student left, Sociology expelled the SSU from departmental decision-making and the honeymoon with radicalism was over. Meanwhile, Vaillancourt was proving herself to be more than a fair-weather radical and was displaying many of the personal characteristics that the Sociology faculty found so hateful in Marlene Dixon (that is, being a woman with lower class origins and being pro-student as well as politically unreliable).

In the meantime the fair-weather "political radicals" departed the MFU and began their shift to the right. By 1971 Vaillancourt was no longer acceptable, either politically or personally. Therefore, it became expedient for the Sociology Department to repudiate Vaillancourt, hence Document #15.

Document #16 is a trifle more complicated. Von Eschen, unlike Chairman Solomon felt compelled to assure his colleagues in Sociology and Political Science that while he is a "political radical" (his past cannot be denied) he is not pro-

133

student (hence the attacks on the integrity and judgement of radical students) and he does not support the politics of such people as Vaillancourt and Dixon, i.e., "that for every stupid conservative idea . . . there was an equally idiotic radical idea (i.e., the ideas propounded by Professor Dixon)." Von Eschen seems oblivious to the contradiction of hiding his own opinion behind what he alleges a student to have said, while asserting at the same time that student recommendations about professors "should be discounted" for not reflecting "real" views. He is certainly eager to transmit the juicy gossip he claims to have heard but at the same time asserts that one cannot trust letters from students "when the professor they are defending is seen as upholding" student political views. One wonders how it follows that (1) conservative students can be trusted to make objective evaluations of professors who are seen as opposed to their political views and (2) why gossip alleged to have been communicated in private by a student to a faculty member about another professor — whom the student knows is hated, particularly by his interlocutor — can be taken as "true" while written and public statements are said to be untrue? *Ergo,* no student can be trusted, for they will make politically motivated, dishonest public and written statements (from which it follows, obviously, that students should have no voice in faculty hiring and firing!)

The interesting thing about both letters is that it would seem that complaints and second-or even third-hand gossip about teaching is the best that these two can come up with in their efforts to discredit Vaillancourt. It should be noted that there is not one word about her professional or academic competence.

The attack on Wallerstein and the MFU from Hamilton, and Pinard, which was much more serious than Solomon and Von Eschen's malicious sniping, was symptomatic of the fact that Professor Wallerstein and the MFU were now embroiled in a larger war. The brush fire in Political Science had escalated into a MFU vs. McGill confrontation. In January the Political Science Renewal Committee had refused to re-consider their decision to fire Professor Vaillancourt. Departmental procedures having been exhausted, the case now became fully MFU's responsibility. In the following set of documents we shall see a display of tactical skill and boldness that McGill Administrators, all the way up to Principal Bell, were beginning to fear. At some point a decision was made (when, where and by whom we do not know) to counter-attack, using the persons of Professors Pinard and Hamilton. The counter-attack took the form of public and intra-university attempts to damage Professor Wallerstein's professional reputation. (The reader must realize that MFU, Professor Wallerstein and Professor Vaillancourt would be completely vindicated — when the letters from Pinard and Hamilton are read in that light, they can be seen for what they are).

However, let us proceed in the order of events. Once the Political Science Department rejected Professor Vaillancourt's appeal, the MFU position asserted that the firing was academically unjustified. Accordingly, it followed that there must exist reasons *other* than academic and professional concerns to explain why she was fired. The conceivable reasons for her dismissal (i.e., points requiring investigation) could be assumed under three headings: (1) Vaillancourt's union activity, (2) the faculty's anti-woman bias, (3) Political Science faculty's fear of Vaillancourt's radicalism.

The burden of proof as to which one, or in what measure all, of these factors contributed to the Political Science Department's decision did not rest

Again, I apologize for the long delay in replying to you. I have no better excuse than the distraction of other work.

Yours sincerely,

M. M. Ames,
Professor and Acting Head.

MMA/pa

cc: T. Philbrook.

cc: Members of the Ethics Sub-committee.

The attack against Professor Vaillancourt was the opening gun in a war that began with the Dixon re-appointment, but a war that would spread to attacks against Professor Pauline Vaillancourt, Professor Spector, Professor Ehrensaft and eventually to Professor Wallerstein.

The most fascinating development from the Dixon re-appointment was, perhaps, the witch-hunt that would become the major tactic in the Right's attempt to "control" (and eventually to remove) Professor Wallerstein. The witch-hunt took the form of accusations that Wallerstein was unprofessional when it came to the evaluation of "radicals;" that he was operating, in alliance with Dixon, as a member of an international network of socialism; or that he pursued "outside political interests." The "cold war" witch-hunt in the Sociology Department would not become public knowledge until the publication of the purloined (by whom is still unknown) document from the Chairmanship Search Committee in the *McGill Free Press* (reprinted here in Part VI: *The Purge*).

Chronology: The Vaillancourt Case

November, 1971	The Dixon Re-appointment Battle. Immanuel Wallerstein serves with Philip Ehrensaft as Dixon's representatives on the Renewal Committee.
May, 1972	Pauline Vaillancourt is informed that Political Science will delay in considering the question of her re-appointment.
September, 1972	Wallerstein President of the McGill Faculty Union.
October, 1972	Pauline Vaillancourt is informed by the Department of Political Science that she will not be re-appointed as Assistant Professor of Political Science.
November, 1972	Letters from Sociology attacking Vaillancourt; real target is Wallerstein.
January 16, 1973	Vaillancourt's statement to Political Science Committee On Promotions, Rehiring and Tenure. Immanuel Wallerstein serves as her academic advisor to the appeal hearing.
January 16, 1973	The Grievance Committee of the McGill Faculty Union sends a memorandum to Dean R. Vogel "in support of the appeal against the recommendation of the Dept. of Political Science not to reappoint Pauline Vaillancourt".
January 29, 30, 1973	Professors Pinard and Hamilton attack Vaillancourt and the McGill Faculty Union (i. e., Immanuel Wallerstein).
March 20, 1973	Pauline Vaillancourt requests the C. A. U. T. to review the Political Science Department's refusal to renew her appointment.
March 30, 1973	C. A. U. T. agrees to arbitrate the Vaillancourt case.
April 10, 1973	The Report of the Chairman's Search Committee prepared by F. Henry is published in the *McGill Free Press* as "The Secret Proceedings from the Department of Sociology". Wallerstein refuses Chairmanship.
June 26, 1973	David Solomon and William Westley are "appointed" as-Co-Chairmen of the Sociology Department, having the power to unilaterally decide any issue that cannot be resolved unanimously. Second *coup d'etat* à la 1970.
August 20, 1973	C. A. U. T. decides in favor of Vaillancourt against Political Science.
June, 1975	Pauline Vaillancourt resigns from McGill. She accepts an appointment at U. Q. A. M. She is elected, in the same month, to the Board of Directors of the Canadian Political Science Association.

1972-1973:
Wallerstein and the McGill Faculty Union

There is conflict of interest with his union activities. As president of the union, he will defend anybody including members of his own department on whose review committee he sits. There is a clear conflict of interest here.

Defense of Vaillancourt and general union activities suggest creation of a radical faction in order to increase potential power of the left in the Department.

Anonymous members of the sociology faculty, as quoted in F. Henry's report to the Chairman's Search Committee (Document #45)

In the fall of 1972, following his conclusion that professors ought to be unionized (as stated in *University in Turmoil*) and to the position that the hard intellectual work of the left cannot be properly done in isolation from involvement in a political movement and political action (by which Wallerstein never meant a university department), Immanuel Wallerstein was elected president of *McGill Faculty Union* with an executive commitee made up of Phil Ehrensaft (Treasurer), Pauline Vaillancourt (Secretary) and Members-at-Large Sidney Ingerman and Laurier Lapierre.

A prestigious scholar belonged in the MAUT (McGill Association of University Teachers); it was *indecent* to rub shoulders with the scruffy MFU bunch! Who could any longer doubt that a nascent Red Menace had surfaced, determined to wreck all and any hopes of up-grading the battered Sociology Department. To grasp the full scandal of the situation, one must know a little of the history of the MFU. According to the *McGill Daily:*

Since 1969, the MFU has counterposed the philosophy of professionalism prevalent in the MAUT with the collective-bargaining approach of trade unionism. MFU sees university teachers as *workers* inherently engaged in a conflict of interests with their employers, the university administration and the government agencies funding the universities.

According to MFU spokesmen, the MAUT undermines the view of the teacher as worker by including deans and other administrators as prominent members. Far from acting as an interest group on behalf of faculty, therefore, the MAUT is accused of promoting the notion that the university if "one big happy family" devoid of conflict.[6]

McGill was furiously attempting to combat the unionization of technical and clerical workers with another version of MAUT, the university "association" with top administrators in command, the MUNASA. McGill top administrators live in terror of unionization at McGill, (which remains the least unionized of all major Quebec institutions of "higher learning") because the Quebec trade unions are increasingly becoming politicized. Of all the unions McGill Administrators fear the C.N.T.U. the most, for it is the political union supporting Quebec independence that had participated in *Operation McGill*, and which spent time writing up socialist "manifestos". The very founding of the MFU reeks of Red Menace:

---

6. Ralph Seliger, "MFU: the Professor as Worker," *McGill Daily,* September 22, 1972.

In a sense the MFU is a splinter group which broke with the MAUT in the wake of the controversy surrounding Stanley Gray, a political science professor, dismissed in August '69 for participating in a number of student sit-ins and protests. Dissidents to the MAUT's overwhelming vote of support for Administration actions regarding Gray joined in the ensuing months with other faculty members unhappy with MAUT policies to create the MFU.

A major point of contention between MFU and MAUT partisans lies in the MFU belief that McGill should be more fully involved in the concerns of Quebec society. To this end the MFU has involved itself on a number of occasions with political issues reaching beyond the confines of the University.[7]

These issues included opposition to the Montreal Municipal By-Law against demonstration, a statement in favour of the FLQ manifesto objectives (later retracted), and involvement with an urban development protest group in the community surrounding McGill (the Milton Park Citizens' Committee against the Cité Concordia Project). The MFU joined the CNTU because it hoped to get involved in the larger society, and CNTU is noted for its outspoken capacity to politicize issues.

Wallerstein's affiliation with the MFU was no joking matter to top levels of the McGill Administration. If we recall the analysis of McGill as a fortress within the Quebec context; if we recall the interconnection between the CNTU and Operation McGill; if we understand that the anti-union activities at McGill belong in 1890 (not in 1972) then we may begin to understand how seriously the Administration would take the role of a man of Wallerstein's rank and prestige within even the then tiny MFU. Their worst fears would be realized during the 1974 strike of the Service Employees Union — the first strike in the 175 year history of McGill! During the strike, Hamilton crossed the picket lines but MFU backed the striking workers; Dixon (normally a rank and file MFU member) acted as liaison with the Student Strike Support Committee, while other MFU members worked energetically and effectively among the teachers until entire faculties voted to go out in support of the Service Employees. The combined "united front" of unions, students and faculty resulted in victory for the service workers, setting a precedent for how more strikes can be won at McGill.

Furthermore, Wallerstein provided effective leadership, and the membership of the union grew steadily during his presidency. This growth was directly related to the fact that of every grievance brought to MFU during the time Wallerstein was President, he lost not a single battle! It got to the point where factions within a department would approach Wallerstein, attempting to see if he would be aligned with one or the other. In this light, we way begin to gain a political understanding of the virulent campaign against Wallerstein personally, and against MFU. The attack against MFU was worthy of the machinations of a MI5 or C.I.A. for the official line that was taken was that the University was *unconcerned* with MFU and its membership.

The clearest indication of the Administration's concern with the "new" MFU is found in a "Personal View" statement circulated in February, 1973 by then President of the MAUT, Professor Stanley J. Shapiro (who, the following Autumn, was to be appointed Dean of the School of Management). We must recall that MAUT was the body addressed by Arts and Science Dean Woods during the PSA strike to whip up the faculty troops in opposition to Stan Gray,

---

7. *Ibid.*

PSA and student participation in the hiring and firing of staff. (Part II, McGill in 1969). MAUT also, it must be remembered, voted confidence in the Administration's summer firing of Gray, even after the Academic Senate had refused to wield the ax: that is, had made the decision that Gray could not be fired on grounds of academic misconduct. MAUT is, for the faculty, the equivalent of a "company union" as MUNASA was for the clerical and technical workers, until the formation of a C.N.T.U. local for clerical, technical and library workers.[8] Thus, it is well known at McGill that when a major policy statement is produced by MAUT, it is a statement made with the full consent, or at the command of, the McGill top administration.

The memorandum from Shapiro, "Some Issues that *must* be faced — A Personal View," laid out a series of proposed policies that were obviously intended to co-opt major points of the MFU program under Wallerstein. The real give-away came, however, with Shapiro's comments on the question of salaries:

> The membership must also decide whether MAUT should more aggressively move to improve salary levels at McGill. The enclosed statement prepared by the salary committee reveals that McGill salaries are continuing to fall behind those of comparable Canadian universities . . . Do these developments suggest that MAUT must become a professional syndicate? Should binding arbitration of salary disputes be demanded by MAUT representatives?[9]

Shapiro then went on to explain that the Salary Policy Committee of MAUT would begin meeting with Administration representatives. The challenge presented to MAUT in its role of pacifier and company union is quite clear in the concluding paragraphs of Shapiro's memorandum:

> Many would argue that MAUT's refusal to adopt a classic collective bargaining stance is appropriate. However, different attitudes prevail on other campuses, *and a stronger position on salary matters is being advocated by some McGill professors* . . . (emphasis added)[10]

Of course, "some McGill professors" refers to the program of the MFU. Shapiro's memorandum also refers to issues concerning the "promotion and tenure sphere" comprising, in fact, three out of five items in the entire "Personal View." MFU was obviously making inroads into the traditional repressive and arbitrary promotion and tenure procedures at McGill. Central to this issue was, of course, the Vaillancourt case. A glance at the Chronology that prefaces this section will show that on January 16, 1973 Wallerstein served as academic advisor at Pauline Vaillancourt's appeal hearing to Political Science's Committee on Promotions, Rehiring and Tenure. Then, dated the same day, the Grievance Committee of the McGill Faculty Union sent a memorandum to Dean R. Vogel "in support of the appeal against the recommendation of the Dept. of Political Science not to reappoint Pauline Vaillancourt." It is quite obvious that the top levels of McGill's Administration were growing increasingly disturbed by the MFU under Wallerstein's leadership. MAUT President Shapiro in February would hardly call for an "essential" MAUT "period of self-examination during which

---

8. MUNASA's company union activities lead to a split, similar to the MAUT/MFU split, in 1975 with the formation of NUMOTLE — National Union of McGill Office, to Technical and Library Employees.

9. Stanley J. Shapiro, President, McGill Association of University Teachers, McGill University, to all members of the McGill teaching staff, "Some Issues that *must* be faced — A Personal View," February 22, 1973.

10. *Ibid.*

present negotiating policies are subject to critical review and alternate approaches are openly and honestly explored" if MFU were not proving far more formidable than various sources of McGill Administration propaganda are willing to admit. Indeed, the attack against Wallerstein, hidden in the attack on Vaillancourt, began in November of 1972, prior to the MAUT campaign attempting to co-opt the MFU program and MFU's defense of aggrieved professors on questions of rehiring, promotion and tenure.

From the point of view of the McGill Administration, the real danger was not MFU — but MFU *and* Wallerstein. While previous leaders of MFU had been courageous and determined, they did not have the academic power nor the prestigious weight that Wallerstein brought to the job. Wallerstein had as well the advantage of nearly 20 years of operating within bureaucratic and repressive settings in various battles for progressive causes — this meant that he was a highly sophisticated and skilled combatant. Wallerstein was perfectly prepared to beat them at their own game — thus the overt repression that had proved so efficacious in the Gray and student movement challenges was useless against Wallerstein. More cunning and roundabout methods were required in the new situation. Consequently, the attacks against Wallerstein/MFU were not direct, since that would backfire, but indirect: by attacking the individuals that Wallerstein and the MFU defended, claiming them to be incompetent or dishonest or unscrupulous. In this way it could be implied that Wallerstein was, at least, dishonest and unscrupulous (if not incompetent). If dishonest and unscrupulous could not be made to stick, being "soft" on standards was the other line of defense.

The first assault upon Wallerstein, indirectly through Dixon and Vaillancourt, came in November, just prior to Vaillancourt's appearance — with Wallerstein as her Academic Advisor — before the Political Science Department's Committee on Promotions, Rehiring and Tenure. While these attacks from members of the Sociology Faculty were obviously aimed at assisting Political Science, they were also attempts to discredit Wallerstein by discrediting the two radical women he had or was defending — and to discredit Wallerstein was also to discredit the MFU. (Documents #15 & 16)

DOCUMENT 15

McGILL UNIVERSITY P.O. BOX 6070, MONTREAL 101, QUE.,

McGILL UNIVERSITY
P.O. BOX 6070, MONTREAL 101, QUE., CANADA

Department of Sociology,
November 29, 1972.

Professor H. Waller,
Chairman,
Department of Political Science,
McGill University.

Dear Professor Waller:

It has been suggested that it might be helpful if I were to write to you with respect to the teaching of Professor Pauline Vaillancourt in this Department during the 1970-71 session.

Perhaps I could first review the circumstances of Professor Vaillancourt's appointment, which as you know, was for half-time. Due to an unexpected leave or our being unable to fill a vacant position, it became apparent in April or May of 1969 that the Department would have sufficient funds to make a one-year half-time appointment, and also that certain courses might not otherwise be taught. The Department was persuaded to appoint Professor Vaillancourt for this purpose. I say persuaded, because, as I recall it there was uncertainty as to what the Department wanted to do about this half-position,, and it was as a result of very strong sponsorship by one or two people that Professor Vaillancourt was appointed.

Professor Vaillancourt taught two one-semester courses during that session — one an undergraduate course, the other a graduate seminar. More complaints came to me either directly from students who approached me, or indirectly through other students or colleagues who passed complaints on, than has been the case of any other course in this Department since I became chairman. As I recall it, students felt that they were not being taught anything and that they were not learning anything. The courses were generally regarded as failures.

The Department's evaluation of Professor Vaillancourt's teaching is indicated by the fact that when the question of a similar reappointment for her came up the following year, none of her previous sponsors was willing to support any further appointment.

I hope these comments will be helpful to you.

Sincerely yours,

David N. Solomon,
Chairman.

DNS/cbs

DOCUMENT 16

McGILL UNIVERSITY
P.O. BOX 6070, MONTREAL 101, QUE., CANADA

Department of Sociology,
November 23, 1972.

Professor Hal Waller,
Chairman,
Department of Political Science,
McGill University.

Dear Professor Waller:

I understand that Professor Vaillancourt is contesting your decision not to renew her contract. I understand that she is basing her argument partly on letters submitted by students praising her teaching. It is with respect to a letter from one of these students, Jerry Spiegel, that I am writing you.

I know Mr. Spiegel fairly well. He took a course from me in which he received one of the few A's I gave and I encouraged him to enter our graduate program. In an informal conversation at the end of the school year two years ago, he told me that Professor Vaillancourt's course on critical political theory was extraordinarily bad. In particular, he was quite angry about her exam in that course, which was a particularly indiscriminating multiple choice rather than essay test. He seemed, in fact, to regard the course as a dead loss. I was very surprised, therefore, to find he had submitted a favorable letter to you.

I suspect that this change of opinion was made on political grounds. Mr. Spiegel is, as I am, a political radical. It may be that he fears that Professor Vaillancourt is being terminated for political reasons, and thus wanted to support her in spite of his previously unfavorable judgement of her teaching. Or, it may be that he wants diversity of opinion in your department and is supporting her for this reason. If so, his letter should be discounted, for it apparently does not reflect his real views.

That his letter is politically motivated is supported by an incident that occured in our department when we were considering whether to renew Professor Dixon's contract. Here again, Mr. Spiegel had told me in private conversation that the course he had taken from Professor Dixon was bad. Specifically, he told me that the only thing he had learned from her course was that for every stupid conservative idea, (which he felt made up the content of most courses taught by political conservatives) there was an equally idiotic radical idea. (i.e., the ideas propounded by Professor Dixon). But, in this case, too, he sent in a letter praising her teaching; again, I suspect, on the grounds that she was a political radical.

The issue this raises goes beyond the question of Mr. Spiegel's true beliefs. *The question it raises is whether one can trust letters from students when the professor they are defending is seen as upholding their political views.* I am inclined to think not. The first clue to this is that most of the letters written in such cases seem to be from political radicals, not from a cross section of students with all political beliefs. The second clue is cases of reversals of opinion by students such as seems to have occurred in Mr. Spiegel's case. I have reason to believe in the case of Professor Dixon at least, that Mr. Spiegel was not alone in saying one thing in conversation and another in a letter.

If student views are going to be used, and they should be, the opinions of a *cross section* of students should be solicited and this should be done *prior* to renewal consideration time when students become pressured by those soliciting letters to change their views.

It is as important that political consideration not be used to force retention of an incompetent person as it is important that they not be involved in firing a competent one. Justice should be even-handed.

Sincerely,

Donald Von Eschen,
Associate Professor,
Department of Sociology,
McGill University

DVE/dd

For the investigator, the real question is this: what is Sociology doing in the business of the Political Science Department? First, we note that it is Solomon, Von Eschen, Hamilton and Pinard engaged in the double attack upon Vaillancourt and Wallerstein. Solomon and Von Eschen are used against Vaillancourt, while the Department's two reactionary "heavies" with some claim to professional reputations, Hamilton and Pinard, are used directly against Wallerstein (not by name, but in attacking MFU and Vaillancourt the target *has* to include Professor Wallerstein).

Further, a short exercise in documentary translation may begin to reveal the motivations of the authors of Documents 15 and 16. In 15, the reader will note that Solomon makes much of the fact that there was support for Vaillancourt when she was appointed, but no support at the termination of the half-time appointment, indicating her lack of competence. This argument is subject to question when we recall the history of the SSU and of the original Vaillancourt appointment. In 1969 Pinard and Von Eschen were members of MFU and were playing at being "political radicals". The membership of MFU overlapped between Sociology and Economics and MFU was involved in combating the politically motivated attempts to deny appointments to both Vaillancourt and, earlier, Dixon. Hence, the initial support. But in 1969-1970 McGill undertook the repression of the student left, Sociology expelled the SSU from departmental decision-making and the honeymoon with radicalism was over. Meanwhile, Vaillancourt was proving herself to be more than a fair-weather radical and was displaying many of the personal characteristics that the Sociology faculty found so hateful in Marlene Dixon (that is, being a woman with lower class origins and being pro-student as well as politically unreliable).

In the meantime the fair-weather "political radicals" departed the MFU and began their shift to the right. By 1971 Vaillancourt was no longer acceptable, either politically or personally. Therefore, it became expedient for the Sociology Department to repudiate Vaillancourt, hence Document #15.

Document #16 is a trifle more complicated. Von Eschen, unlike Chairman Solomon felt compelled to assure his colleagues in Sociology and Political Science that while he is a "political radical" (his past cannot be denied) he is not pro-student (hence the attacks on the integrity and judgement of radical students) and he does not support the politics of such people as Vaillancourt and Dixon, i.e., "that for every stupid conservative idea . . . there was an equally idiotic radical idea (i.e., the ideas propounded by Professor Dixon)." Von Eschen seems oblivious to the contradiction of hiding his own opinion behind what he alleges a student to have said, while asserting at the same time that student recommendations about professors "should be discounted" for not reflecting "real" views. He is certainly eager to transmit the juicy gossip he claims to have heard but at the same time asserts that one cannot trust letters from students "when the professor they are defending is seen as upholding" student political views. One wonders how it follows that (1) conservative students can be trusted to make objective evaluations of professors who are seen as opposed to their political views and (2) why gossip alleged to have been communicated in private by a student to a faculty member about another professor — whom the student knows is hated, particularly by his interlocutor — can be taken as "true" while written and public statements are said to be untrue? *Ergo,* no student can be trusted, for they will make politically motivated, dishonest public and written statements (from which it follows, obviously, that students should have no voice in faculty hiring and firing!)

The interesting thing about both letters is that it would seem that complaints and second-or even third-hand gossip about teaching is the best that these two can come up with in their efforts to discredit Vaillancourt. It should be noted that there is not one word about her professional or academic competence.

The attack on Wallerstein and the MFU from Hamilton, and Pinard, which was much more serious than Solomon and Von Eschen's malicious sniping, was symptomatic of the fact that Professor Wallerstein and the MFU were now embroiled in a larger war. The brush fire in Political Science had escalated into a MFU vs. McGill confrontation. In January the Political Science Renewal Committee had refused to re-consider their decision to fire Professor Vaillancourt. Departmental procedures having been exhausted, the case now became fully MFU's responsibility. In the following set of documents we shall see a display of tactical skill and boldness that McGill Administrators, all the way up to Principal Bell, were beginning to fear. At some point a decision was made (when, where and by whom we do not know) to counter-attack, using the persons of Professors Pinard and Hamilton. The counter-attack took the form of public and intra-university attempts to damage Professor Wallerstein's professional reputation. (The reader must realize that MFU, Professor Wallerstein and Professor Vaillancourt would be completely vindicated — when the letters from Pinard and Hamilton are read in that light, they can be seen for what they are).

However, let us proceed in the order of events. Once the Political Science Department rejected Professor Vaillancourt's appeal, the MFU position asserted that the firing was academically unjustified. Accordingly, it followed that there must exist reasons *other* than academic and professional concerns to explain why she was fired. The conceivable reasons for her dismissal (i.e., points requiring investigation) could be assumed under three headings: (1) Vaillancourt's union activity, (2) the faculty's anti-woman bias, (3) Political Science faculty's fear of Vaillancourt's radicalism.

The burden of proof as to which one, or in what measure all, of these factors contributed to the Political Science Department's decision did not rest with the MFU. All that MFU had to prove was that Vaillancourt was academically qualified, which they were completely confident of doing at any fair appeal procedure. Furthermore, it was the MFUs duty to pursue *all* available options for redress of Vaillancourt's grievance. It was, after all, *not* MAUT, but the McGill Faculty *Union,* and unions do *not* assume that employers have "the honour of gentlemen"!

One of the options open to the MFU was the Quebec Labour Code. However, the law requires that a complaint must be filed immediately after a suspect firing has occured. MFU, as a CNTU affiliate, had every right to utilize the protective laws in the Labour Code. Accordingly, when the McGill Board of Governors informed Professor Vaillancourt that her contract was to expire in August, 1973:

> CNTU lawyer Jacques Desmarais said yesterday he has filed a complaint on Prof. Vaillancourt's behalf with the labour department's chief investigation commissioner. He cited articles of the Labor Code which state that if an investigation commissioner finds that a dismissed employee has exercised a right accorded her of him under the code, there shall be a presumption she or he was dismissed for exercising such a right.[11]

The MFU Executive had certainly learned the lessons of the Stan Gray purge, which was that internal McGill procedures for the redress of a radical faculty's dismissal were, at the very least, suspect. As for MAUT, the Stan Gray case had shown that where radicals were concerned, MAUT acted as an agent of the McGill Administration.

It was also considered that Professor Vaillancourt had been subjected to one procedural irregularity after another, one delay after another, to the point where considerations of humanity alone called for a speedy resolution to her case.

Therefore, on January 23, 1973 McGill University was summoned to present itself before the Chief investigation commissioner of the Quebec labour Department.

Let us now turn to Documents #17, 18, 19 and 20. These letters comprise an attack against Professor Wallerstein. In part, the Sociology Department may have been using the Solomon-Von Eschen tactic to disassociate themselves from him; but the greater import of their efforts was aimed at discrediting him and the MFU under his leadership. Why these tactics? We may venture a guess (since we have no direct proof) that the motives were (1) to attempt to punish him for his defense of the two hated women, Vaillancourt and Dixon; (2) to propagandize against him in order to block his chances of being elected Chairman of the Sociology Department; and (3) to serve the ends of the Administration by discrediting him and thereby discourage additional faculty from joining MFU. Indeed, all of these motives may have been called into play, plus others we cannot imagine. But the objective effect was to link the integrity of Professor Wallerstein's professional and intellectual motives and behavior to the outcome of the Vaillancourt case.

The *Montreal Star* story on the complaint to the Quebec Labour Department appeared on January 20; McGill University was summoned to present itself in a letter dated January 23; on January 29 McGill requested a postponement; on the same Day, January 29, Professor Maurice Pinard wrote to Dean Robert Vogel (Document #17). This sequence could not have been a coincidence. As to the text itself, Professor Pinard claims that "to pretend that the decision may have been taken because of Professor Vaillancourt's union activities is pure

---

11. "Probe Asked in McGill Firing," *Montreal Star,* January 20, 1972.

foolishness and simply dishonest.". Who is Pinard claiming is "pretending" and "dishonest"? Professor Vaillancourt, to be sure, but also the architect of Vaillancourt's strategy, Professor Wallerstein. Professor Pinard asserts that union activities could not possibly have influenced Political Science's Promotions, Rehiring and Tenure Committee. But how does he know this? Does he mean to imply that he, Maurice Pinard, the champion of "confidentiality" has violated confidentiality in collaboration with members of the Political Science Department? That they have been privately discussing the Vaillancourt case? Further, does he wish us to believe, on his word alone and without investigation, that as an *ex*-member of the MFU he has absolute knowledge that union activities played no role?

Professor Pinard continues his indictment, accusing both Professors not only of dishonesty, but for using "political manoeuvres" as well, and "questions the intellectual integrity of the members of the McGill Faculty Union who so easily accept to play this game". In the first case, what game? MFU has done no more than file a complaint under the Quebec Labour Code, a complaint that does no more than initiate an investigation. Is it dishonest for a union to file a complaint to the Quebec Department of Labour when a member of its executive, the secretary of the union to be precise, is fired? Who is playing what game here?

Then Professor Pinard claims that he feels "the politicization which is developing (sic) once more of a strictly academic decision is most regrettable." In this he can only be referring to the Dixon re-appointment and possibly Stan Gray. However, as Committee of Enquiry will affirm, the Vaillancourt dismissal was *not* a "strictly academic decision". A strictly academic decision would require that Pauline Vaillancourt's contract be renewed. Whom does Professor Pinard think he is fooling this time? In both cases the politicization that developed and the "political manoeuvres" are on the part of the respective renewal committees, and are not the responsibility of Dixon, Vaillancourt or Wallerstein. Dixon did no more than point out the political motives behind the attempt to fire her — she did not invent them. The same is true for Pauline Vaillancourt.

Professor Pinard then claimed that he knew of no one who had questioned the intellectual and professional integrity of the members of the "Political Science Committee" that reached the decision. How odd! It must be that Professor Pinard does not read the press, for we can think of people who have: Stan Gray for one, Pauline Vaillancourt for another, many members of the PSA as well. Then, we remind readers (lest they be unwilling to accept the word of those listed above) that the proof is in the Political Science faculty's own words, to be found in Part III concerning the original Vaillancourt appointment. Does Professor Pinard wish us to regard that behaviour as a model of "intellectual and professional integrity"?

The real sore point, however, does not come until the last paragraph: "Let me add that I also think that it should be left to such Departmental Committees to make decisions of this nature . . . " It would seem that Professor Pinard is opposed to the existence of procedural appeal, even to the right of professors to appeal an injustice beyond the Star Chamber that committed it. Pinard is, in effect, saying that Departments are to be given absolute powers to hire and fire, promote and purge just as they please without being troubled by rights to appeal.

We must conclude, in the last analysis, that Professor Pinard's letter is indeed a superb reflection of the reactionary mentality in both the political science and sociology departments.

DOCUMENT 17

McGILL UNIVERSITY
MONTREAL
DEPARTMENT OF SOCIOLOGY

January 29, 1973

Dean Robert Vogel
Faculty of Arts
McGill University
Montreal

Dear Dean Vogel.

The case of the dismissal of Professor Pauline Vaillancourt from the Department of Political Science is taking such an unhappy course that I feel obliged to let you know some of my reactions to it.

I feel that the politicization which is developing once more of a strictly academic decision is most regrettable. Let me state clearly that I know very well most of the members of the Political Science Committee that reached that decision, that I have the utmost respect both for their competence — which is well established beyond the confines of this University and for some of them, particularly in French Canada — and for their intellectual and professional integrity, which has never to my knowledge been questioned before. To pretend that the decision may have been taken because of Professor Vaillancourt's union activities is pure foolishness and simply dishonest, and as an ex-member of the McGill Faculty Union, I deeply resent the use of the Union for such political manoeuvres. It places me in a position, in turn, where I have to question the intellectual integrity of the members of the McGill Faculty Union who so easily accept to play this game.

Let me add that I also think that it should be left to such Departmental Committees to make decisions of this nature, except under unusual circumstances. And in this case, the efforts to attract media attention in French Canada should not be any more relevant than in any other similar case.

Yours sincerely,

Maurice Pinard
Professor

Copy to Professor H. Waller
MP:msp

DOCUMENT 18

(

PROF. PAULINE VAILLANCOURT'S ASSERTIONS SHOULD BE BACKED BY EVIDENCE

SIR, — When Emile Zola wrote his famous letter that began with the words "J'accuse," he continued with a statement of the grounds for his accusation. Prof. Pauline

Vaillancourt has accused four of her colleagues of recommending termination of her employment at McGill University because of her union activities. This accusation has been made in representations to the Quebec Department of Labor and has been disseminated by her and her spokesmen in the press (The Gazette, Jan. 23 and 24, 1973).

Her claims, it will be noted, constitute an attack on the intellectual integrity of the professors making that decision. It is clearly no trivial matter when someone makes claims affecting the integrity of colleagues, and, as in this case, asserts that they are biased and that their judgments are corrupt.

Unlike Zola's statement, however, her assertion is presented without one shred of direct supporting evidence.

One of the rules of scholarship is that major claims must be backed up and supported. Quite apart from the requirements in academic circles, ordinary human decency requires it in the present case.

Does she (or her spokesmen) have any direct evidence to justify this flagrant assertion? Has she or her spokesmen heard any of the members of the committee express sentiments condemning her union activities? Has she any evidence that her union activities were a factor in their decision?

If Prof. Vaillancourt has direct evidence to support her claim, it should be presented.

If she has no evidence, the course of both intellectual and personal integrity would be to withdraw the charge and to make apologies.

RICHARD HAMILTON
Professor of Sociology
McGill University

Gazette Jan. 30, 1973.

We may now turn to the revealing exchange of public letters between Professors Vaillancourt and Hamilton. It began with Professor Richard Hamilton's letter to the *Gazette*. (Document # 18) Our comments on this will be very brief. First, note the references to "her spokesmen", who are, of course, Professor Wallerstein and the MFU. Second, note that he admits that "it is clearly no trivial matter when someone makes claims affecting the integrity of his colleagues.". Indeed, it is not. "If she has no evidence, the course of both intellectual and personal integrity would be to withdraw the charge and to make apologies." If such a course would be correct for Professor Vaillancourt, would it not also be correct for Professor Richard Hamilton? Then why have we not heard from him? Why has he not exercised the "ordinary human decency" to withdraw his charges (made in this letter and others and by word of mouth) and make his apologies to both Professors Vaillancourt and Wallerstein?

Hamilton writes a second letter (Document # 19), this to the *McGill Daily* which allows Professor Vaillancourt to respond. (Document #20) These letters appeared in print at the very time that C.A.U.T. was considering the Vaillancourt case (i.e., whether to arbitrate it or not). The only point that Professor Vaillancourt does not touch upon in her reply is the parade of "radical credentials" for certain members of the Political Science Department (and by implication, for Professor Hamilton himself). We think it is not necessary to comment at length. Suffice it to say that it is "old radicals" with "credentials" like these who gave *all* university radicals a bad name on the authentic left in North America.

DOCUMENT 19

THE VAILLANCOURT CASE REVISITED.

Tuesday, March 13, 1973

Editor:

Over the course of the last few weeks a number of Daily writers have made the claim that Professor Pauline Vaillancourt's contract has not been renewed because of her union activities. Some rather obvious questions need to be raised about this allegation.

Who were the members of the commitee making that decision? Is it not the case that the committee in question — the "clique of senior professors with narrow conformity of view" — contained the following persons?
— Professor Charles Taylor, a person who for years has been active in and a leader of the New Democratic Party?
— And did it not contain Professor James Mallory, a founder of the McGill Association of University Teachers and a long-time defender of academic freedom?
— And what about Professor Henry Ehrmann? Is it not true that Professor Ehrmann spent time in Hitler's jails and concentration camps — for his political activities, among which were the defence of union rights?

Does this sound like a committee that would require "a narrow conformity of views"? And does that sound like a committee that would refuse further employment because of a person's union activity?

Why has your reporter-editorialist, Anna Dowdall, been silent about these facts? Why has she chosen to withhold all information about the committee itself? And why have Professor Vaillancourt and her spokesmen hidden this information? Is it because the claim of retaliation for union activity could not stand up for one instant in the face of this information?

And those "unsolicited" letters of support? How many of them were unsolicited? Is the letter sent out by the "Save Pauline Committee" somehow or other not a letter of solicitation? Was the letter from Professor Leon Dion unsolicited?

Professor Vaillancourt's statement in the January 26th issue of the Daily refers to a "pilfered exam". Is it not the case that Professor Vaillancourt herself gave a copy of her examination to Professor Ehrmann in order to permit him and other members of the Department to evaluate a student's performance? Why does Professor Vaillancourt make public accusation of theft when she personally, of her own free will and volition, put that examination into the hands of her colleagues?

If the case has to be made with distortion and dishonesty, then maybe it is not as "impeccable" as your reporter-editorialist and judge, Anna Dowdall, would have us believe.

Richard Hamilton

Ed. Note: Mr. Hamilton's letter was forwarded to Pauline Vaillancourt. What follows is her reply.

DOCUMENT 20

It has been of continuing interest to me that Richard Hamilton of the Sociology Department has such a deep concern in McGill University's decision not to renew my contract. Mr. Hamilton has called on me to make public the legal case that would be presented in court (should the legal case be taken up) in advance of the Labour Board Inquiry itself. Why Does Mr. Hamilton maintain that I have the duty and even the obligation to make my case available, in detail, beforehand to McGill University and McGill's lawyers but he did not contend that the Department of Political Science had a similar duty and obligation to make available to me in detail (1) the reasons for recommending that I be fired and (2) the evidence on which said decision was based? I have made the point repeatedly that in the absence of any other just and sufficient reason for my being fired, I must assume, that among other reasons, my union activities was one of the most important factors motivating the University Administration to take this action.

My recent experience with justice in the academic community (my appeal to the Dean and to the Political Science Department's Promotion, Rehiring and Tenure Committee) demonstrates that due process is lacking in this University. While I have been compelled to present testimony and evidence against charges that the Department has refused to make explicit, I have never been presented with such specifics of the case against me. I have been cross-examined at great length on both occasions but I have never had the right of cross-examination in either instance. I was not allowed to be present when the Department made its case to the Dean, though the Department had available to it in advance, all the details of my defense. While the Dean assured me that should new evidence be introduced by the Department I would have the right to return to defend myself, I was not given this right, even though it is clear from the Dean's letter to me (January 16) that the Department introduced such new arguments. Why does this lack of due process not equally upset Professor Hamilton?

Mr Hamilton suggests that the letters of support of my academic qualifications were solicited. Some were, many were not. I clearly pointed out the distinction between these two types of evidence at both of my appeals. Does Mr. Hamilton question the legitimacy of my asking for outside, expert evaluations of my academic writings and publications in a situation where the Department first neglected to read my writings and then refused to do so by insisting that any further information I presented at my appeal was to be limited to oral evidence only. (Waller's letter of November 1, 1972.)

As concerns students, I have avoided soliciting students to write letters to the Dean on my behalf, largely because I realized that to do so was to jeopardize possibilities of an appeal to the C.A.U.T. Does Mr. Hamilton consider it inappropriate that the Chairman of the Political Science Department telephoned students requesting them to write negative letters to the Dean concerning my renewal? Does Professor Hamilton consider letters written by these students as "unsolicited"? I have also been informed that Professor Waller solicited signatures amongst Assistant Professors of the Political Science Department for an editorial that was to have been sent to the Gazette. Does such behavior on the part of the Chairman of the Political Science Department not strike Professor Hamilton as unprofessional?

On the subject of the examination that was considered by both the Department and the Dean with respect to my renewal, I can only say that I have no proof that the examination was stolen. However, I did not provide it to the Department as evidence of any student's performance. I arrived at a Department meeting last June where a copy of an examination from one of my courses, which Professor Waller himself had provided to the meeting, was being considered with respect to a student's performance. It was my assumption that

Professor Waller took it off my secretary's desk as this was where I had deposited all the corrected exams to be returned to students in my classes. I did indeed pass the exam to Professor Ehrmann during the course of the meeting, as the person next to me requested that I do so.

The Promotion, Rehiring and Tenure Committee never asked me to provide them with copies of the nearly two dozen examinations I have given in the past four years at McGill. The transcript of my appeal at the Department level indicates that some members of the Promotions, Rehiring and Tenure Committee even acknowledged that the consideration of this one examination was unrepresentative. Probably, even more importantly, in the cases of the several other members of the Political Science Department up for renewal this year, none to my knowledge was asked to submit copies of examinations as part of the renewal process.

I am surprised that Professor Hamilton is not shocked and offended at the injustice of the decision not to renew my contract here at McGill. It is clearly a decision that rests heavily on "distortion and dishonesty".

Yours sincerely,
Pauline Vaillancourt
Assistant Professor

McGill's lawyers, the firm of Laing, Courtois, Clarkson, Parsons, Gonthier, and Tetrault responded by petitioning for a delay "until university procedures have been exhausted." We can well imagine the panic in the Top Administration given the fact that:

> The burden of proof, Mr. Desmarais said, is on McGill to show that there was "good and sufficient reason" for failure to renew Prof. Vaillancourt's contract. [12]

Since McGill could not possibly show "good and sufficient reason" for its failure to renew her contract, all tactics of delay, tricky kangaroo courts and similar ploys had to go out the window. And therein lay the boldness of the correct tactical utilization of *all* available options open to an aggrieved party! It was the correct and logical conception of the employee vs. employer relationship as fundamental within the university that gave the MFU the power to resist the war of attrition which the university as employer uses to exhaust and demoralize and usually defeat a purged professor.

At no time, however, did MFU or Professor Wallerstein or Professor Vaillancourt assert that union activities alone were the cause of her dismissal. They asserted only the truth: that there was sufficient doubt to merit an investigation under the Quebec labour code. Neither MFU nor Professor Vaillancourt can be held responsible for the content of stories in newspapers, as Professor Ames of the CSAA Ethics Sub-Committee had pointed out on an earlier occasion to Professor Richard Hamilton.

---

12. *Montreal Star, loc. cit.*

The MFU's inspired use of its rights under the Quebec Labour Code propelled McGill's Principal Bell into rapid capitulation. On March 13, 1973 Bell wrote to Wallerstein:

> . . . I can only recommend that Professor Vaillancourt, advised by you, should decide whether or not she wishes to enter further proceedings in this case, and if so, should elect either to continue with the legal proceedings under the Quebec Labour Code, or to request the AFT Committee of C.A.U.T. to investigate her case, or pursue further steps within the university. This is a choice which in any case is hers and hers alone, and I simply propose that she should exercise it. Presumably a choice of more than one of these procedures is also open, *but I think we all agree that only one of them ought to be actively pursued at any one time.* (Document #30)

"Presumably" and "I think we all agree . . . " indeed! Bell was prepared to do almost anything to keep McGill out of court, not to mention wheeling and dealing to avoid simultaneous attack on three fronts! Under the circumstances McGill was forced to admit the futility of appeal procedures for radicals within McGill:

> However, it is an unusual feature of this case that the faculty member appealing and the University, whatever their differences over the details of the case, are both agreed that there remains a need for further inquiry. (Document #22).

The Canadian Association of University Teachers (CAUT) recognized as well that internal appeal procedures are sometimes suspect:

> It is our experience that there is a limit to the number of successive appeals that can be usefully pursued within a university, as well as a limit on the duration of time that can be usefully expended on internal prodecures. (Document #22).

MAUT's letter to CAUT (Document #21) is McGill's last feeble gasp of outrage at the MFU's pre-emption of the tractable MAUT's previous monopoly on faculty representation. MAUT's protest demonstrates that MFU, born out of the Stan Gray purge, had now proved itself to be a dangerous adversary, a sharp thorn in Old McGill's hide. The Hamilton-Pinard assertion that "the claim of retaliation for union activity could not stand up for one instant" or that "to pretend that the decision may have been taken because of . . . union activities is pure foolishness" is disproved by McGill's capitulation to Vaillancourt's and MFU's rejection of "internal procedures" and demands for a disinterested CAUT arbitration. Persons with experience in dealing with university purges know that a university will move heaven and earth to keep appeals within its own jurisdiction, or when forced to an accommodation will move heaven and earth once again to assure procedures unfavourable to the purged professor.

Vaillancourt's preference for CAUT arbitration was based upon her determination to foil the Political Science Department's attempted professional character assassination. Her decision was also in recognition that MAUT is infamous for its servility to the McGill Administration and its utter unwillingness to defend professors' interests, be it for pension funds, salaries, or tenure guarantees. Pauline Vaillancourt is not only a radical, she is also a highly motivated research political scientist. The next section of this book will present Professor Vaillancourt's professional defense, showing the dishonest and vile "political manoeuvres" of the Political Science (and Sociology) faculties.

DOCUMENT 21

McGILL ASSOCIATION OF UNIVERSITY TEACHERS
McGILL UNIVERSITY   P.O. BOX 6070, MONTREAL 101, QUEBEC

April 25, 1973.

Mr. Donald Savage,
Executive Secretary,
C.A.U.T.,
66 Lisgar,
Ottawa, Ontario.   K2P 0C1.

Dear Dr. Savage:

I am writing you this letter to express the views and concerns of the MAUT Council as to the proposed involvement of CAUT in the dispute surrounding the non-renewal of Professor Vaillancourt's contract. Of course, MAUT supports strongly the right of an individual to make an appeal to CAUT.

The MAUT Council has carefully reviewed what it understands to be the procedures recommended both by Dean Vogel and by you. We have the following questions which we would like to raise at this time:

1. Do you consider the course of action spelled out in your letter to Dean Vogel of March 30th, 1973 as primarily in response to Dean Vogel's earlier request for advice from CAUT to him, or, alternatively, is it designed primarily to deal with the subsequent appeal of Professor Vaillancourt to CAUT?

2. Page 18 of the CAUT handbook spells out in its first paragraph a careful three-stage process of academic freedom and tenure committee involvement. We understand the following to constitute these three separate and distinct steps:

   (a) An informal investigation sufficient to enable CAUT to establish whether an appeal has an appropriate basis in fact.

   (b) If in CAUT's opinion an injustice has been done, make an appropriate effort to mitigate this injustice.

   (c) If such informal attempts are unsuccessful, initiate an effort to deal with the case formally by such steps as an "ad hoc" informal investigating committee.

The MAUT Council is concerned about the fact that you have apparently moved to stage (c) of this procedure without proceeding through stages (a) and (b). More specifically, we have some real reservations as to whether the exercise in fact finding has been carried out.

The MAUT Council would also like to call two other matters to your attention:

1. Professor Vaillancourt has not, to the best of our knowledge, exhausted all appeal procedures within McGill University. Specifically, she has not appealed to the Staff Relations Committee of the McGill Senate. Is it appropriate for CAUT procedures to begin before all internal stages of appeal at McGill have been exhausted?

2. MAUT Council recalls that it approved, at least by default, the fact that Professor Vogel appealed directly to you for assistance to her. Nevertheless, there is some concern in retrospect as to the precedent this might set for CAUT involvement in internal procedures before their completion at the University level.

We look forward to hearing from you on the above matter before arrangements are finalized concerning the nature and extent of CAUT involvement in the Vaillancourt controversy.

Yours sincerely,

Stanley J. Shapiro,
President.

SJS/ht
cc: Principal R. Bell
    Dean Vogel
    Professor Vaillancourt
    Professor Waller
    Vice-Principal Pedersen
    MAUT Council

Document #22 is Dr. Savage's reply for CAUT to MAUT's protest letter. Document #22 is both revealing and illuminating on two counts: first, on the evaluation of McGill; secondly, on Dean Vogel's role in the initiation of the last stage of the Vaillancourt case. Dr. Savage rather huffily replies to Professor Shapiro's innuendo, "More specifically, we have some real reservations as to whether the exercise of fact finding has been carried out.", by noting "In the case of Professor Vaillancourt we have in fact examined a very large body of documentation, and would be in a position to make a judgement as to whether the appeal has an appropriate basis in fact . . .". To Professor Shapiro's obvious attempt to exploit further possibilities for a war of attrition against Professor Vaillancourt, ("Is it appropriate for CAUT procedures to begin before all internal stages of appeal at McGill have been exhausted?"), Dr. Savage tartly notes that "It is not a CAUT position that all internal procedures in a university must have been exhausted before CAUT can act. It is our experience that there is a limit to the number of successive appeals that can be usefully pursued within a university, as well as a limit on the duration of time that can be usefully expended . . .".

As interesting as the dismissal of MAUT's last ditch attempt to keep the Vaillancourt case within McGill may be, the more interesting revelation, by far, concerns Dean of Arts, Robert Vogel. On January 16, 1973 Professor Wallerstein had submitted, from the Grievance Committee of the McGill Faculty Union, a memorandum to Dean Vogel on behalf of Professor Vaillancourt requesting that the Dean recommend appointment for three years. (Document #27) The MFU's demand would have required the Dean to have over-ruled a departmental decision. Such an action might have set a very dangerous precedent permitting Administrators to over-ride departmental decisions, which threatens departmental independence in questions of hiring and firing. The Dean was thus placed in a most difficult position: how to secure equity for Vaillancourt while not setting an undesirable precedent for Administration interference in departmental rights to self-government. It would appear from both the Savage letter (Document #22) and the Bell letter (Document #30) that Dean Vogel hit upon the admirable solution of a Committee of Enquiry acceptable to CAUT (on behalf of the professor) and to Dean Vogel (on behalf of the University).

Dean Vogel certainly had a number of options open to him, one of them being a rubber stamp of the Political Science faculty's decision against Vaillancourt. Dr. Savage's letter seems to make it plain that Dean Vogel was unwilling to play Political Science's game.

DOCUMENT 22

CANADIAN ASSOCIATION OF UNIVERSITY TEACHERS
ASSOCIATION CANADIENNE DES PROFESSEURS D'UNIVERSITÉ

Professor S.J. Shapiro, President
McGill Association of University Teachers
McGill University
C.P. 6070
Montreal, Quebec

Dear Professor Shapiro:

Thank you for your letter of 25 April in which you expressed the views and concerns of the MAUT Council as to the proposed involvement of CAUT in the dispute surrounding the non-renewal of Professor Vaillancourt's contract.

I shall try to answer the specific questions you put to me.

1. The proposal I made to Dean Vogel in my letter of 30 March was in response to the appeal of Professor Vaillancourt addressed to CAUT in a letter of 20 March. In making the proposal I took account of the views of Dean Vogel and of his Advisory Committee as these were expressed in his letter of 14 February addressed to Professor Waller.

2. In many cases appealed to us, the faculty member will claim that the appeal has an appropriate basis in fact, whereas the University administration will reply that there is nothing to appeal, that in fact there is no problem to be resolved. In such situations we undertake the informal investigation mentioned in paragraph I.1 of the Policy Statement on Academic Appointments and Tenure. This investigation involves examining the documentation and often engaging in correspondence, and sometimes will involve the use of an ad hoc investigating committee. If as a result of such investigations CAUT decides that the appeal has a basis in fact — that there is a problem to be resolved, or even that an injustice has apparently been done — it then proceeds to suggest modes of settlement. In the case of Professor Vaillancourt we have in fact examined a very large body of documentation, and would be in a position to make a judgment as to whether the appeal has an appropriate basis in fact, if that judgment were necessary. However, it is an unusual feature of this case that the faculty member appealing and the University, whatever their differences over the details of the case, are both agreed that there remains a need for further enquiry. That is the request made to us by Professor Vaillancourt in the last paragraph of her letter of 20 March and that apparently is the conclusion of Dean Vogel and his Advisory Committee as recorded in his letter of 14 February

to Professor Waller (see especially pages 5 and 6). It is because there is apparently agreement between the appealing faculty member and the Dean of Arts on the need for further enquiry that I made proposals contained in my letter to Dean Vogel of 30 March. CAUT has not taken a position on whether justice or injustice has been done in this case, and therefore has not made the efforts referred to in Section B of your question 2. My proposals derive generally from the fundamental CAUT position that academic disputes should be solved by equitable means within the academic community. The details of my proposals are designed to establish a committee of enquiry that can resolve the problem that exists, and to provide both the Department of Political Science and Professor Vaillancourt with the fullest possible opportunity to be heard. I would like to point out that the Committee of Enquiry I have proposed is not a CAUT enquiry as such, but rather an enquiry conducted by three academics mutually acceptable to Dean Vogel and to the CAUT. CAUT in addition has proposed certain basic procedures for the committee, but once established the committee would operate on its own authority and would not be subject to direction either by the Dean of Arts or by CAUT.

I note the other matter which you called to my attention on page 2 of your letter. I should point out that on 13 March 1973 Principal Bell wrote to Professor Wallerstein:

> In view of all the above, I can only recommend that Professor Vaillancourt, advised by you, should decide whether or not she wishes to enter further proceedings in this case, and if so, should elect either to continue with the legal proceedings under the Quebec Labour Code, or to request the AFT Committee of CAUT to investigate her case, or pursue further steps within the university. This is a choice which in any case is hers and hers alone, and I simply propose that she should exercise it. Presumably a choice of more than one of these procedures is also open, but I think we all agree that only one of them ought to be actively pursued at any one time.

This seems to me to recognize that Professor Vaillancourt had three courses open to her and chose the option of appealing to the CAUT.

Furthermore, it is not a CAUT position that all internal procedures in a university must have been exhausted before CAUT can act. It is our experience that there is a limit to the number of successive appeals that can be usefully pursued within a university, as well as a limit on the duration of time that can be usefully expended on internal procedures. This is even more the case when both the administration and the professor concerned wish to have a final enquiry involving outside assessors rather than to continue with internal procedures.

I have discussed your letter and my proposals with the Academic Freedom and Tenure Committee and they concur with my view that these offer a reasonable promise for a full, fair and conclusive enquiry into the matter.

Yours sincerely,

Donald C. Savage
Executive Secretary

cc: Academic Freedom and Tenure Committee
Principal R.E. Bell
Vice Principal Pedersen
Professor P. Vaillancourt
Professor H. M. Waller
Dean R. Vogel

146

PART 5:
The Vaillancourt Papers

The real importance of the Vaillancourt case at McGill was the clarification that it demanded of the rights of professors on probationary appointments for Canadian professors in general, and for McGill professors in particular — for McGill has traditionally exercised the most arbitrary and non-professional criteria in hiring, renewals and promotions. The arbitrary procedures at McGill have persisted past its "modernization," and essentially reflects its "old boy" past, in which norms of academic judgement are no more than a thin veneer, and in most cases, ignored in practice, if invoked in word.

The Vaillancourt case also raised the key questions of *how* is competence judged? what are the *major* criteria that ought to be used in making professional judgements? how is consistency applied? what are the rights within a department of a non-conformist or dissenting professor? While a number of these issues are reviewed in the CAUT report included in this section the full discussion of such key questions was lost when the tape-recorded transcript of the hearing was first "lost" and then "erased."

The author debated at length, given the Committee of Enquiry's decision, whether or not to include the Vaillancourt Papers in this book. The reason that they are included is that while the Committee of Enquiry's final report was a *procedural* victory, the case remains that both Professors Vaillancourt and Dixon have been driven out of McGill by constant hounding and persecution to which there is no procedural appeal or redress. The repression of dissenting thought in North American, and particularly Canadian universities, is a complex process, which cannot be understood in procedural terms or discerned within reports outlining procedural irregularities.

The Vaillancourt case is but another instance where confidentiality has served to cover-up the real nature of an attempted purge. Only the audio-tape recordings of the testimony before the Committee of Enquiry could answer (beyond any capacity for denial, plausible or otherwise) *WHY*? If there were so many procedural irregularities, of such a gross and blatant nature, how and why did they occur? That is the heart of the question of academic freedom which no amount of procedural niceties can address — procedure can only permit the circumvention of a cure for the basic disease that presently infects the academic body politic. The present realities cry out for a clean-up, not a cover-up!

At the time that the author submitted her letter of resignation to Dean Robert Vogel at McGill, she also wrote to the Academic Freedom and Tenure Committee of the CAUT, attempting to raise the issue of the circumvention of procedures and the failure of procedural appeal to secure redress of unjustifiable dismissals or to guarantee academic freedom. The AFT Committee of the CAUT wrote a letter in reply informing the author that the matter was under discussion. Meanwhile the purge at McGill continued unabated. It is not the author's desire to impede the activity of the CAUT in the defence of professors' rights;

but neither will she submit without protest to the injustices and brutalities to which she has for so long been the object and witness.

The Vaillancourt Papers are invaluable as a documentation of how and why an absolutely unjustified, and completely politically motivated purge, was undertaken. The motives of the political science and sociology faculties were *not* those of "good men and able scholars." Yet, we shall let the reader judge from what follows.

The Due Process Game

If Stan Gray is to attempt to have his view of the University and of society realized, there are certain things he must do. He must ally himself with the students, the only group in the University not firmly committed to the preservation of the status quo. He must participate in movements on campus organizing for the expression of radical views and action on radical issues. When the administrative rulers of the University consistently and systematically ignore the issues, he must confront them directly with those issues . . .

The Administration, confronted with demands that it deal with pressing social issues, can reply only with discipline. Given an issue, it answers "due process." That is a smokescreen that cloaks the fundamental refusal of the university to consider its basic position. Robertson will cling feverishly to his phrase "due process" . . . But the process does not transcend the issues; the process is a total circumvention of them . . .

Robert Chodos and Mark Starowicz, "Don't Put Out the Fire — Stop the Fire Alarm," *McGill Daily,* February 13, 1969

The documents that follow need very little in the way of introduction. The chronological order is slightly altered in the interests of clarity, where an earlier document is explained or interpreted by a later document. By now even non-university readers should be able to engage in the "art of translation." Some notes and short introductions are provided as little "maps" to help guide the reader through the "due process maze." Hopefully the reader, by this time, has been provided with all the necessary elements for understanding the story as it unfolds in the Vaillancourt Papers.

Documents #24 through 26 introduce the Due Process Game. Document #24 spells out the Political Science Department's "reasons" for denying Professor Vaillancourt reappointment. Document #25 is so outrageous that Vaillancourt responds in Document #26 protesting the arbitrary and unfair "terms" being imposed upon her. The whole exchange could be titled from Vaillancourt's telling phrase in that document : "I am not appealing for clemency but justice."

DOCUMENT 24

McGILL UNIVERSITY
DEPARTMENT OF POLITICAL SCIENCE

October 25, 1972

Professor Pauline Vaillancourt
Department of Political Science
McGill University

Dear Pauline:

In response to your request, I wish to inform you of the reasons upon which the Committee on Promotions, Rehiring and Tenure based its decision to recommend that your contract not be renewed. I want to stress the fact that your position was considered in the light of the needs of the Department within the context of the long-run objectives determined by the Department, as well as an assessment of your qualifications. Furthermore, the Committee took the view that fulfillment of certain minimal requirements may not be sufficient grounds for renewal. Thus it based its decision in part on a judgment of how much your teaching, stimulation of post-graduate research, and scholarship contribute to the improvement of our resources in a strong and balanced Department. In addition, your administrative contribution was taken into account.

With the above considerations as background, I can now list the more specific points that affected the Committee's decision. The members of the Committee took into account the following:

1) The Committee's careful evaluation of the writings which you submitted leads the members to doubt whether by interest and inclination you could furnish the scholarly contribution that they wish to see strengthened in the offerings of our Department. In addition, I should stress that the members of the Committee believe that the person in your fields of empirical methods, political behaviour and socialization is inevitably closely involved with the research needs of others, both staff and students. Therefore, anyone in this position must possess exceptional qualities of leadership and cooperation. In the judgment of the Committee, you do not meet these criteria. Consequently, the Committee thinks that you are not really the right person to develop these fields in this Department.

2) The Committee's greatest reservation concerns your classroom performance. The members are well aware of some favourable student reports about your teaching. They did not base the unfavourable judgment merely on the very numerous complaints and course evaluations that have been received from both graduate and undergraduate students. They sought to obtain an impression of the actual content of the courses given by you, of the examinations, an example of which they have inspected, and of the classroom atmosphere. All this conveys an impression which the Committee clarified as unsatisfactory.

3) Your contribution to the general administration of the Department and the University has not been outstanding. However, your service as Official Representative of the ICPR was taken into account.

In conclusion, I wish to emphasize that the Committee has taken all possible factors into consideration and has arrived at a decision based upon an overall assessment of your qualifications and the manner in which you fill the needs of the Department.

Again, I regret the outcome of these deliberations. I hope that the above information has served to clarify the situation.

Yours sincerely,

Harold M. Waller
Chairman

HMW/ilw

DOCUMENT 25

DEPARTMENT OF POLITICAL SCIENCE
McGILL UNIVERSITY

November 1, 1972

Professor Pauline Vaillancourt
Department of Political Science
McGill University

Dear Pauline:

I note your letter of October 31st and shall be happy to speak to you to try to arrange a time for your appearance that would be convenient to all concerned. However, it is necessary to clarify a few misunderstandings. First of all, if you will read my letter of October 27th carefully, I indicated that you could be accompanied to the meeting by *an* academic advisor. That means one and only one academic advisor. Therefore please indicate to me who your academic advisor for that meeting will be. Secondly, the purpose of the meeting is to enable you to present oral evidence to the Committee, which is in addition to any other evidence that you have already presented. The terms of reference of this meeting do not include any response from the Committee to you. The members of the Committee may ask questions about the evidence that you present, but they are not required to provide you with any explanation other than that which has already been communicated to you in writing. If they have any further communication to make to you after this appearance, that will also be done in writing.

You might seek further information from Dean Vogel, who has suggested this procedure as being both fair and sufficient before he takes a departmental recommendation under consideration.

Sincerely yours,

Harold M. Waller
Chairman

HMW/ilw

150

DEPARTMENT OF POLITICAL SCIENCE
McGILL UNIVERSITY

November 6, 1972

Professor Waller
Chairman
Department of Political Science
McGill University

Dear Professor Waller:

Apparently there are some rules governing procedures within the Department of Political Science of which I was unaware. When and by whom were such procedures established, and by what authority?

Since, to my knowledge, no such appeal procedures are established in the Political Science Department, I was assuming that we were functioning on a sort of common law definition of administrative appeal, and that there would be no objection to my bringing more than one advisor. In fact other departments at McGill have raised no objections to aggrieved professors bringing three advisors.

As for the form of the interaction at the meeting, I am not appealing for clemency but justice, in which case there is scarcely any possibility of rational discussion without an interchange in which each side justifies its arguments. It is hard to refute unspoken rebuttals of my views.

I also find your own views of the appeal form inconsistent. Your October 6 letter to me does not specify the form of evidence I will be allowed to present at the appeal.

I should like to point out to you that you have the right to appear before the Committee to present any information in addition to that which has already been presented in writing.

However it is clear from your October 27 and November 1 letters that the Committee will now consider only oral evidence. Must I read my PhD. dissertation and the majority of my writings to the Committee before they will take them into account.

I have consulted a high level National C.A.U.T. representative whose advice surprised me. He recommended that I not accept the Committee's offer of an appeal at the Department level. He based this advice largely on the spirit in which the appeal was being offered as communicated in your October 6 letter to me. He suggested that it was unusual that the Committee did not indicate any willingness to change its recommendation to the Dean if new evidence so warranted and that the recommendation of non-renewal was forwarded to the Dean before the appeal was held.

By refusing to allow me the advisors I have requested and an open form for the appeal (a precedent in many McGill Departments) you are setting undue limitations on my actions and clearly violating my legal rights. You are certainly deviating far from the practice accepted by those institutions that respect the civil rights of its members.

Nonetheless I shall come to the meeting with the intention of indicating the ways in which the explanations of the Committee are inadequate, specious, and fallacious. I shall bring Immanuel Wallerstein as advisor and I shall bring copies of my writings which the Committee has not considered, including my PhD. dissertation. I do this under protest as to the form.

Finally, I must point out that the membership of the Committee which considered my case has thus far not been revealed to me. I should appreciate it if you could give me a list of the members of this Committee.

I await your indications about a possible meeting time.

Sincerely,

Pauline Vaillancourt
Assistant Professor

PV/hs

Document #27 is the product of the meeting of November 22, 1972 between Professor Vaillancourt, Professor Wallerstein (Academic Advisor) and the Political Science Department's Committee on Promotions, Rehiring and Tenure, and was prepared for the appeal from the Department's decision to the Dean's Advisory Committee (DAC). DAC eventually refused to decide and suggested involving the CAUT. Document #27 is very precise concerning the conclusions drawn from the deportment and argumentation of the "extremely good men and able scholars" of political science, summarizing the procedural irregularities and denial of due process and consistency in the Political Science Department's treatment of Professor Vaillancourt. The Committee of Enquiry will agree.

DOCUMENT 27

McGILL UNIVERSITY

January 16, 1973

MEMORANDUM

TO: Dean R. Vogel

FROM: Grievance Committee, McGill Faculty Union

RE: In support of the appeal against the recommendation of the Dept. of Political Science not to reappoint Pauline Vaillancourt

We feel that the recommendation of the Department that Pauline Vaillancourt, now completing her second appointment at McGill as an Assistant Professor, not be reappointed is arbitrary and a travesty of due process, and cannot be justified on any legitimate academic grounds. We shall argue successively that procedural irregularities are gross, that her academic achievements are superior, and that the recommendation violates principles of equity.

1. Procedural irregularities

We pass over minor disagreements about procedure to concentrate on the two central issues: failure of the Department of Political Science to give fair and careful attention to her record prior to arriving at a judgment, and failure of the Department to give adequate reason for their final recommendation.

It is clearly evident from a reading of the transcript of the meeting on Nov. 22, 1972 between Professor Vaillancourt and the Committee on Promotions, Rehiring and Tenure that the Committee, when making their initial recommendation, had not read the two principal writings of Professor Vaillancourt: her dissertation and her important paper on "The Stability of Children's Political Orientations". One member of the Committee indicated he did not even know the name of the sponsor of her dissertation (see transcript, p. 12), which scarcely indicates careful consideration. Since Professor Waller has refused to elaborate on the reaffirmation of the Department's position after the meeting of Nov. 22 there is no evidence that the Committee as a whole subsequently read these materials. If they have, there is nowhere indicated their evaluation of them. This is not an unsubstantial point to which we shall return in discussing her academic achievements.

Nor did the Committee make adequate efforts to assess her teaching competence. They used formal student evaluations, but did not reveal, if it was ever assessed, how these evaluations stand in comparison to others in the Department. They used only one examination to judge the kind of examinations she offered, and one that Prof. Vaillancourt never offered to them as a representative sample of her work. The item was, for the purposes of the Committee, randomly chosen. The Committee questioned graduate students *after* their initial recommendation.

Secondly, Professor Waller has repeatedly refused to give a statement of reasons "other than that contained in (the) letter of October 25, 1972" (letter from Prof. Waller, 30 Nov. 1972). We can draw one of two conclusions from this refusal. Either the Department gave no careful attention to the material presented, in which case Professor Vaillancourt's due process was violated. Or they did at that point give careful attention to the writings they previously neglected, and gave more careful attention to the teaching evidence, in which case they cannot simply reaffirm their previous judgment, since the new evidence directly challenged this judgment. They must now tell us whether or not they reject the validity or weight of academic support for Professor Vaillancourt's excellence. They must tell us whether or not they still stand by Prof. Waller's statement of Oct. 25, 1972 that "the Committee's greatest reservation concerns (the) classroom performance." If so, how does that square with the views of the chairman of the Committee, Prof. Mallory, that "most of us will also agree with Mr. Wallerstein's (negative) observations about how reliable (student evaluations) are really." (transcript, p. 14). Perhaps this is no longer their "greatest" reservation. But how may Prof. Vaillancourt know? And if she does not know, how meaningful is it to appeal against an assessment, whose coordinates are unclear?

In her letter of Nov. 6, Prof. Vaillancourt stated that "[T]here is scarcely any possibility of rational discussion without an interchange in which each side justifies its arguments. It is hard to refute unspoken rebuttals of my views." Prof. Vaillancourt appeared before the Committee nonetheless. However, her point remains well-taken, and by refusing to explicate the case, either orally or in writing, the Department has denied her due process. Is it possible that the reason that the Department is so reluctant at this time to spell out their arguments is that they have no valid ones capable of bearing the scrutiny of disinterested parties? It might appear so, as we shall now see from a consideration of Prof. Vaillancourt's substantive achievements.

II. *Academic performance*

The usual grounds on which overall academic assessment is made are scholarly achievement, teaching efforts, and administrative contribution. What are the facts with regard to each of these?

a) *Scholarly achievement*

Prof. Vaillancourt has presented evidence that her paper on childhood political socialization drew unsolicited comments of praise from a long list of scholars in the field of socialization. Listed in alphabetical order, they include Paul Abramson, Paul Beck, R.W. Connell, Fred I. Greenstein, Richard Merelman, Michael Riccards, Rodney P. Stiefbold. They represent an impressive galaxy of those *most competent to judge her work.* The most prominent among them, Fred I. Greenstein said that her article was "unquestionably an important contribution". This article has since been accepted for publication in the *Public Opinion Quarterly*, probably the most prestigious journal publishing articles on this topic.

Prof. Léon Dion, perhaps Quebec's leading political scientist, writes: "Madame Vaillancourt, tout en pouvant utiliser de façon fort compétente toutes les techniques quantitatives de recherche empiriques, manifeste à l'endroit de leur utilisation une sagacité que je voudrais bien voir plus répandue ... . Pour (toutes) ces raisons, je recommande fortement que le contrat de madame Vaillancourt soit renouvelé ou, selon les normes prévalent à McGill, que la permanence lui soit accordée."

How many members of the Department of Political Science at McGill can present similar testimony of scholarly recognition? Does the Department not agree with Prof. Greenstein that Prof. Vaillancourt's article was "unquestionably an important contribution" or with Prof. Dion that she shows "une sagacité que (l'on) voudrai(t) bien voir plus répandue?" They are not obliged to agree, but in the light of testimony of this degree of strength from persons of this reputation in the field, are they not obliged at least to defend their judgment?

Prof. Vaillancourt's article is assigned regularly in graduate courses in other universities. Of how many members of the Department of Political Science at McGill can that be said? Prof. Vaillancourt's article is recommended from scholar to scholar. Of how many members of the Department of Political Science at McGill can that be said? Prof. Vaillancourt has just been awarded a grant of $21,000 for a six-month period for scholarly research. Is there any other member of the Department of Political Science of which this can be said?

One would think that with such a record the Department would feel honored by her presence. She contributes importantly to the Department's reputation and thereby to McGill's. Is the Department or McGill so rich it can afford so lightly to cast away precisely the kind of person that comparable universities normally seek to obtain for their staff? Why is the Department, instead of rewarding academic excellence, dismissing it?

b) *Teaching efforts*

Considering the fact that Prof. Waller placed greatest emphasis on class-room performance, the Department has failed to present any negative evidence. Asked to demons-

154

trate that student evaluations were lower than the norm, the Department took refuge behind the promise of confidentiality to the students. But Professor Wallerstein pointed out to them on Nov. 22 that all that was required was to list other professors as a, b, c, d, etc. and thereby make a comparison without violating confidentiality (see transcript, p. 14). Has the Department done this? If so, have they ever presented their results to Prof. Vaillancourt and to the Dean?

Beside the Department's assertions without concrete evidence, Prof. Vaillancourt has presented statements by students at McGill and at the Université de Québec of her diligence, devotion, and inspiring competence. Even more impressively, she has offered a letter from Prof. Gaboury of the University of Ottawa, where she has also taught, which indicates that the Department there is "pleinement satisfait" with her teaching. Prof. Gaboury reports that students there have spoken to him of her only "en terme élogieux."

We contend that teaching skills are hard to evaluate, and should be taken into account only when a person's skills are said to be extremely good or extremely poor. The Department has offered nothing significantly negative, certainly nothing substantiated. Against this, Prof. Vaillancourt has offered specific, affirmative evidence. The Department has no case on these grounds.

c) *Administrative contribution*

The contribution of Prof. Vaillancourt has been exceptional, and a model to emulate. Even Prof. Waller was forced to make a bow in this direction (letter of 25 Oct. 1972).

a) She has served as a consultant in methodology to undergraduate and graduate students working with other professors;
b) She has served as a consultant to faculty and students at the Université de Montréal (letter of Helene David);
c) She has represented McGill on the Interuniversity Consortium of Political Research;
d) She has been very active in the McGill Faculty Union, and is presently both its Secretary and its representative to the Conseil Centrale des Syndicats de Montréal;
e) She has been active in the creation and ongoing activity of the Centre Coopératif de Recherche en Politique Sociale;
f) She has served actively as a referee in French and English for the Canadian Journal of Political Science (letter of Prof. Dion).

There cannot be many assistant professors at McGill who can match this record, one achieved while completing a Ph.D. dissertation, be it noted.

She has responded to both of Prof. Waller's pleas to the department (made in 1969), that members engage in research on Quebec politics, and that they engage in public policy-oriented research about Montreal or the Province of Quebec. Has any other member of the department, including Prof. Waller himself, done as much?

III. *Equity*

At the same time as the Department recommended against the reappointment of Prof. Vaillancourt, three other assistant professors were reappointed: one for three years, one for two, one for one. The two latter had already served six years.

No doubt all are worthy of reappointment. But none has completed a dissertation and none has a record of scholarly achievement comparable to Prof. Vaillancourt. If they are worthy of renewal, so is Prof. Vaillancourt.

155

IV. *Conclusions*

There are no valid academic grounds for not reappointing Prof. Vaillancourt. Quite the contrary. One would have thought her dossier to present one of those obvious cases about which there should be little doubt and no hesitation. One might have expected enthusiasm at the prospect of keeping her in the Department. Why truly is this enthusiasm absent?

We request that the Dean recommend reappointment for three years as assistant professor. We request further that the Dean ask the Department to commence immediately consideration, by their normal procedures, of promotion of Prof. Vaillancourt to the rank of associate professor.

Document #28 comprises one of the many outside scholarly evaluations of Professor Vaillancourt's work. The reader will recall from previous documents (particularly from Professor Hamilton's attacks on Professor Vaillancourt) in which the motives and integrity of persons writing "solicited" letters was constantly impugned, often insinuating that the outside evaluation was "politically" or "personally" motivated. This tactic was utilized later in the proceedings before the Committee of Enquiry, which provoked the indignant statement (Document #28) from Professor Leon Dion, one of Quebec's leading political scientists. Professor Dion was at that very moment giving a course jointly with Chairman of Political Science at McGill, Harold Waller. Is it necessary to mention that Professor Dion was not a member of the Parti Québécois? "Political motivations" could hardly be alleged in his case — although neither this fact nor Professor Dion's scholarly reputation deterred Political Science zealots.

The statement in Document #29 was a result of Professor Dion's anger at the insinuations proferred by professors of Political Science in their testimony before the CAUT-appointed arbitration commitee that Professor Dion had "not really meant" his previous recommendation for Pauline Vaillancourt.

DOCUMENT 28

UNIVERSITÉ LAVAL
FACULTÉ DES SCIENCES SOCIALES
CITÉ UNIVERSITAIRE
QUÉBEC 10, CANADA

Le 6 novembre 1972

SUJET: *Renouvellement du contrat de madame Pauline Vaillancourt*

A qui de droit,

Madame Vaillancourt me demande une brève appréciation de ses capacités académiques et scientifiques. Je ne connais malheureusement pas madame Vaillancourt aussi bien que je le devrais, étant donné la proche parenté de ses intérêts intellectuels et des miens. Néanmoins, il m'a été donné de prendre connaissance d'un certain nombre de ses écrits de même que, à titre de co-directeur de la Revue canadienne de science politique, de bon nombre de commentaires qu'elle a bien voulu faire sur des projets d'articles soumis pour publication à la Revue. Ce qui me frappe surtout chez madame Vaillancourt, c'est sa façon d'aborder les questions de participation et de socialisation politique. Madame Vaillancourt, tout en pouvant utiliser de façon fort compétente toutes les techniques quantitatives de recherches empiriques, manifeste à l'endroit de leur utilisation une sagacité que je voudrais bien voir plus répandue. C'est ainsi, par exemple, que dans son texte "The Stability of Children's Political Orientations", elle montre avec beaucoup de maîtrise qu'il importe tout autant de se soucier de ce qu'on mesure que des instruments de mesure utilisés! Son analyse aiguë explicite bien des malaises que professeurs et étudiants ont ressentis à la lecture des travaux récents sur la socialisation politique des enfants.

Je ne peux malheureusement pas me prononcer sur les aptitudes pédagogiques de madame Vaillancourt; me basant toutefois sur ses travaux, il me paraît qu'elle est exceptionnellement douée pour la recherche et qu'on doit s'attendre à des contributions majeures de sa part dans les années qui viennent. Par les contributions nombreuses et empressées qu'elle a apportées à la Revue canadienne de science politique, il me paraît également certain que madame Vaillancourt participera activement aux activités de la communauté académique canadienne et québécoise. Pour ces raisons, je recommande fortement que le contrat de madame Vaillancourt soit renouvelé ou, selon les normes prévalant à McGill, que la permanence lui soit accordée.

Je demeure à votre ample disposition pour toutes les informations supplémentaires que vous pourriez désirer à ce sujet.

Sincèrement,

Léon Dion, professeur
Département de science politique

LD/pm

DOCUMENT 29

STATEMENT CONCERNING TELEPHONE CONVERSATIONS
WITH LEON DION, JUNE 28, 1973

1. I called Professor Dion on the morning of June 28 to ask him to appear as a witness before the Commitee of Enquiry on the complaint of Professor Vaillancourt.

2. He explained that he could not come for two reasons. First, he has a prior engagement tomorrow at Rimouski. Secondly, he would wish to come only on the invitation of the Commitee of Enquiry itself and not as a witness for one side.

3. Professor Dion wishes to state that his original letter was not written in order to take sides in a dispute. Indeed, he had not known at the time that a dispute existed. He wrote the letter in the spirit of "to whom it may concern." It represents an impartial assessment of Professor Vaillancourt and may be used by whomever finds it useful.

4. Professor Dion emphasizes that the letter is in no way a matter of academic politeness, as he does not believe in giving recommendations in which he does not fully believe. His recommendation was meant to be taken seriously.

5. Professor Dion asserts that his original letter speaks exclusively to the academic competence of Professor Vaillancourt, of which alone he has some knowledge.

6. Professor Dion bases his evaluation of Professor Vaillancourt on the reading of various of her writings.

7. The most important of these is the paper on "The Stability of Children's Political Orientations" which he takes to be extremely new and provocative. It places in serious doubt what has been heretofore almost a postulate of those working in the field of the political socialization of children: that the political attitudes of adults is somehow formed in childhood.

   Her paper finds recent further confirmation in the lead article of the most recent issue of the *American Political Science Review* (CLXIV, 2, 1973, 413-433): Donald Searing, Joel Schwab and Allen E. Lind, "Structuring Principles, Political Socialization, and Belief Systems." Professor Vaillancourt's article was of course written well before this article appeared, but such an article in such a journal comes as opportune confirmation of the validity and importance of her work.

8. Professor Dion has read the two reviews in *Études Internationales* and the *American Political Science Review*. He found them both very well done.

9. Professor Dion has read the project for which Professor Vaillancourt has received a grant from the Ministry of Social Affairs of Quebec. He has also read the abstract of her thesis and read rapidly the whole of it. While he has not read these with the care that would allow definitive judgments, they seemed very, very good on first glance.

10. In addition Professor Dion had solicited her evaluations of articles for the *Canadian Journal of Political Science/Revue Canadienne de Science Politique* in his capacity as co-editor. Such acts in themselves demonstrate the respect Professor Dion has for Professor Vaillancourt's scholarly judgment.

11. Professor Vaillancourt is at the beginning of her academic career. It might well be that she will not fulfill the hopes she now inspires. But it seems clear that she has performed at a level of competence that would justify a renewal of appointment, insofar as one were evaluating her scholarly achievements.

12. Professor Dion emphasizes once again that he does not wish to take sides in an academic dispute, but he has been provoked into reaffirming his position because some persons who appeared before the Committee of Enquiry have questioned the degree to which he was fully committed to what he previously said and the degree to which it was based on knowledge of her writings.

13. Professor Wallerstein has read this written version of the oral conversation to Professor Dion on the evening of June 28, and Professor Dion authorized him to say it was accurate.

14. Professor Dion is at the disposition of the Committee of Enquiry should they wish to have further clarification or confirmation of this declaration, either orally or in writing.

Immanuel Wallerstein
June 28, 1973

Document 30 is the famous capitulation of McGill before the MFU strategy outlined in Part 4: Plots and Conspiracies. Document 31 is the text of Professor Vaillancourt's request for an appeal to the Academic Freedom and Tenure Committee of CAUT; Document 31 also recounts the rapidly changing stories generated by Political Science to justify its refusal to re-new her contract.

DOCUMENT 30

PRINCIPAL AND VICE-CHANCELLOR
ROBERT E. BELL
McGILL UNIVERSITY

March 13, 1973.

Professor Immanuel Wallerstein,
Department of Sociology,
Leacock Building.

Dear Professor Wallerstein,

Last Thursday morning, you called on me in your capacity as advocate for Professor Vaillancourt, and we had a long conversation. Your message on that occasion, if I understand it correctly, was that you and Professor Vaillancourt would like us ("us" presumably means Dean Vogel, at least initially) to make a proposal to you about some further stage of adjudication of this case. You mentioned, for example, a reinstatement of Dean Vogel's proposal that the CAUT Academic Freedom and Tenure Committee examine the case.

Since our conversation, I have consulted with Dean Vogel and Vice-Principal Pedersen, and have seen some of the recent correspondence that I had not seen last Thursday. In the process, I cleared up one point that our conversation had left in an uncertain state. You will remember that I thought that I thought that Dean Vogel had in mind as an initial step an Ad Hoc, informal investigation by the AFT Committee. This might or might not be followed by more formal procedures, depending on the outcome. You said that you thought that he was asking for the CAUT to set up an arbitration. I have now verified with Dean Vogel that he was indeed thinking what I thought he was thinking.

The following facts and statements seem to me of importance.

1. The informal procedure just referred to is "normally done at the request of the professor" (Dr. Savage, February 20), and "the CAUT is reluctant to become involved . . . if legal proceedings are going forward in the courts" (same source).

2. Professor Vaillancourt's proceedings under the Quebec Labour Code are still going forward, and "I am unable at this point to accept any form of arbitration that would prejudice the legal case" (Professor Vaillancourt, February 14).

159

3. It seemed clear that the Department of Political Science is ready to participate in an AFT Committee inquiry instituted by Professor Vaillancourt, but is reluctant to be, in effect, a petitioner to CAUT for such an inquiry.

4. There are still university procedures that Professor Vaillancourt could elect, for example, an inquiry by the Senate Staff Relations Committee.

In view of all the above, I can only recommend that Professor Vaillancourt, advised by you, should decide whether or not she wishes to enter further proceedings in this case, and if so, should elect either to continue with the legal proceedings under the Quebec Labour Code, or to request the AFT Committee of CAUT to investigate her case, or pursue further steps within the university. This is a choice which in any case is hers and hers alone, and I simply propose that she should exercise it. Presumably a choice of more than one of these procedures is also open, but I think we all agree that only one of them ought to be actively pursued at any one time.

I believe that Dean Vogel and Vice-Principal Pedersen will agree with the above recommendation, though they will not see the text of this letter in advance.

Yours truly,

R.E. Bell

cc: Professor Pauline Vaillancourt
Dean R. Vogel
Vice-Principal E. Pedersen

DOCUMENT 31

March 20, 1973

Dr. Don Savage
President
Canadian Association of University
Teachers
66 Lisgar Street
Ottawa, Ontario K2P 0C1

Dear Dr. Savage:

I would like to appeal to the Academic Freedom and Tenure Committee of the CAUT. My rights have been violated by McGill University in its failure to renew my contract which terminates August 31, 1973. The violations include the following:

a)   Failure to follow proper procedures:

1)   The Department of Political Science's Promotions, Rehiring and Tenure Committee did not read the majority of my written work prior to making its decision and did not properly evaluate my teaching record.

2)   Following my appeal to the Department of Political Science, after its initial decision, the Department refused to specify the grounds on which they based the refusal of my appeal, despite specific repeated efforts to get them to do so.

3)   The Dean refused to adjudicate my appeal, alleging that he was "confronted with a Departmental judgement which . . . it was not within (his) competence to question . . . " Subsequently following my refusal to accept an appeal to the CAUT on the terms proposed (final adjudication of the appeal was still pending), Dean Vogel wrote

that he had now "explained to the Principal that Faculty deliberations in this matter (had) now ended, (that he had) no basis on which to change the (previous) recommendation made (to the Principal) on 7 December 1972."

b)   The decision of the Department was blatantly inconsistent with decisions made at the same time concerning other assistant professors in the department.

c)   The grounds of the decision by the Department were inconsequential. In Professor Waller's letter of 25 October 1972 and in the Dean's report of Waller's testimony to the Dean's Advisory Committee (letter of Vogel, 14 February, 1973, p. 3), the Department rested its case primarily on my "inadequacy" as a teacher. There are two remarks to be made about this. First of all, the Department has refused to make available either to me or to the Dean (Vogel's letter, 14 February, 1973, p. 3) the primary objective evidence on which such an allegation could possibly be made. Secondly, this is a notoriously weak ground on which to base such a decision for non-renewal. Professor Mallory, the chairman of the Department's Committee, himself agreed at the Departmental appeal that a collection of student evaluations, that is not overwhelmingly positive or negative, is not "reliable" as a means of distinguishing gradation of teaching ability (Transcipt, p. 14). My scholarly competence or my contribution to the administrative work of the university, has never been called into question.

Furthermore, it seems that the Political Science Department, (See Dean Vogel's letter of 14 February, 1973, p. 2) is now arguing that my case is that of a professor on a first, probationary appointment and that the Department is not therefore required to give reasons for its decision. I was not previously aware of this argument, but I disagree strongly with this interpretation. In fact, I am now on my second contract at McGill and it is therefore my third appointment that is in question. I enclose a xerox copy of the letter I received from the Board of Governors of McGill confirming my *reappointment* in 1970.

You now have in your possession the following documents that I have sent to your office over the last several months:

a)   The transcript of my appeal to the Promotions, Rehiring and Tenure Committee which includes copies of all the early correspondence on my case.

b)   My original statement on banda "To whom it may concern", prepared for the Dean and his Advisory Committee (with corrections and additions).

c)   The McGill Faculty Union's statement to the Dean.

d)   The correspondence on my case with all parties concerned since my appeal to the Dean, except for the letter from Principal Bell to Professor Wallerstein (a copy is enclosed).

I believe this is all the necessary documentation, but I shall be willing to send any other that seems necessary.

I request that the Academic Freedom and Tenure Committee enquire into this matter.

PV/hs
Enclosures

cc: Principal Robert Bell
    Dean Robert Vogel
    Professor Immanuel Wallerstein

Sincerely,

Pauline Vaillancourt
Assistant Professor

Document #32 signifies CAUT's acceptance of Professor Vaillancourt's request for CAUT intervention. The reader is invited to exercise her or his imagination in re-creating the negotiations and considerations that reach their conclusion in this document. Once CAUT agreed to arbitrate the case, it disappeared from public view and proceedings in the Quebec Labour Court were suspended: the "price" of the University's "audacity" (see CAUT *Newsletter*, November, 1973) in accepting CAUT's proposal for a Committee of Enquiry. A number of important specifications should be noted:

(1) "The CAUT would not insist that such a judgment be binding on the parties"

(2) That the agreement between CAUT and McGill University is *not* for a CAUT ad hoc investigating committee, indeed, "not a CAUT committee at all," but a "committee authorized by both McGill and CAUT to conduct an independent hearing and bring down a decision" (Savage to Vaillancourt, March 18, 1974 Document #38)

(3) Note that Dean Vogel granted to the Political Science Department a special budget to meet expenses for the hearings, but granted *no* such budget to Professor Vaillancourt, who was forced to meet all the expenses personally. This is why there is no written record of Professor Wallerstein's summing up to the Committee of Inquiry (for the portent of this, see: The Battle for the Tapes). (Also see: Vaillancourt to Savage, September 26, 1973).

DOCUMENT 32

CANADIAN ASSOCIATION OF UNIVERSITY TEACHERS
ASSOCIATION CANADIENNE DES PROFESSEURS D'UNIVERSITÉ

30 March 1973

Professor Robert Vogel
Dean of Arts
McGill University
Post Office Box 6070
Montréal 101, Québec

Dear Professor Vogel:

Professor Pauline Vaillancourt has appealed to the CAUT concerning the non-renewal of her contract in the Department of Political Science. I believe that she has sent you a copy of her letter.

I understand from your letter of 14 February 1973 to Professor Waller that you considered that one possible solution to the problem might have been for you, with the approval of your Advisory Committee, to approach the CAUT with the suggestion that the Academic

Freedom and Tenure Committee might be asked to hear the case or possibly name the members of an arbitration that would be binding on you and that you would have been prepared to extend Professor Vaillancourt's contract for up to eight months if that became necessary in terms of the length of the enquiry. I further understand that Professor Vaillancourt rejected this and that the offer was withdrawn by you.

Now that Professor Vaillancourt has appealed herself to the CAUT in the normal way, I would recommend to you that you and the CAUT agree to the creation of a jointly named committee of enquiry. Normally we would first create an *ad hoc* investigation committee of our own. But two matters persuade me that it would be useful to proceed immediately to such a committee of enquiry. First, you have stated in your letter to Professor Waller: "This can surely be done without the assumption or conviction that Professor Vaillancourt's allegations have been proven, but precisely on the grounds that sufficient questions have been raised by her and by her academic advisors to make it imperative that the Department be given the opportunity to make its case before an impartial body outside the Faculty". The latter part of your sentence establishes what an *ad hoc* investigation would normally be asked to do, namely to decide whether or not there were grounds for further proceedings. Secondly, the academic year is about to close. I do not want to debate who may or may not be responsible for the timing of the proceedings, but I think that it would be in the interest of both parties to settle the matter before the end of the academic year, particularly since your offer to extend the contract has been withdrawn. For both of these reasons I would, therefore, suggest a jointly named committee of enquiry. If you were to refuse this, I would then consult the Academic Freedom and Tenure Committee on the advisability of creating a CAUT committee of enquiry.

I would suggest that such a committee be composed of three academics named by you and by the CAUT. I would, however, suggest that the parties be defined as Professor Vaillancourt and the Department of Political Science. In other words I think that this committee would fit into the recommending structure at McGill in a manner similar to your proposal of 14 February 1973 but that for the purposes of establishing procedures it would be simpler to define the parties to the dispute in the manner I have suggested,

I would further suggest:

a) that the committee meet at McGill and *in camera* unless the parties agree otherwise;

b) that both parties be permitted to introduce written or oral evidence;

c) that Professor Vaillancourt and her academic advisor plus two representatives of the Department be permitted to attend all sessions of the committee when evidence is being given;

d) that the Dean or his representative be present as an observer;

e) that examination and cross-examination be allowed;

f) that the committee be empowered to require each party to indicate the nature of the evidence it intends to rely on, in order to enable the other party to make a fair and full answer;

g) that no formal transcript of the proceedings shall be kept; however, the committee shall have the authority to require that a logged audio tape of all or part of the proceedings be kept for its own use;

h) that the parties would be requested to make a final summary, if they so wish, which would be presented simultaneously in writing at the close of all testimony;

i) that the committee be required to issue a written decision which contains findings of fact, reasons, and conclusions as to adequacy of cause and that this decision be sent to you with copies to the Department of Political Science, Professor Vaillancourt and to the CAUT.

Finally I think that the committee should be charged to investigate the circumstances surrounding the non-renewal of the contract of Professor Pauline Vaillancourt and to make such recommendations as it sees fit. It should be responsible for its own procedures consistent with any specific terms agreed in advance and with basic fairness and it should have the authority to make its own procedural rulings.

The CAUT would not insist that such a judgment be binding on the parties. We would anticipate that if the decision were favourable to Professor Vaillancourt that you would in the normal course of events support that recommendation when it was sent on to the Principal. We would assume that you would only reject the findings of the committee for gross procedural errors and that you would then offer detailed reasons. If the committee decides against Professor Vaillancourt, we would assume that your original decision in the case would stand, namely to forward the Department's recommendation.

I have written Professor Vaillancourt to ask her to assure us that she has withdrawn her case before the Labour Court. As the Principal pointed out in his letter of 13 March 1973 to Professor Wallerstein, Professor Vaillancourt has three options open to her which she can take but that if she wishes to pursue all three, she should do so sequentially and not simultaneously. I take it, therefore, that the Principal agrees that, once such a CAUT/McGill Committee has completed its task, she can appeal to the Labour Court if she so desires.

I hope that you will see this as a reasonable means of settling the case of Professor Vaillancourt. We are, of course, open to other suggestions. If you have any questions, please do not hesitate to write or to phone.

Yours sincerely,

Donald C. Savage
Executive Secretary

cc: Profs. P. Vaillancourt
A.E. Malloch
Chairman, MAUT

slm

Document 33 consists of responses respectively from Professor Vaillancourt and Professor Waller (on behalf of the Political Science Department) to a request for a statement of issues from each party made by Professor D.L. Johnston, Chairman of the Committee of Enquiry, prior to the time the committee went into formal session.

DOCUMENT 33

McGILL UNIVERSITY

June 10, 1973

Prof. D.L. Johnston
Chairman

Dear Prof. Johnston,

The issues before the Committee as I see them are as follows:

a)   *Whether or not non-renewal of my contract was justified.*

I contend that my record, on the traditional academic criteria of research, teaching, and administration, is a superior one, and that therefore the decision not to renew my appointment was totally unreasonable. I contend that the grounds offered by the Department were inconsequential, as I have elaborated already in my letter to Dr. Savage of 20 March 1973.

b)   *Whether or not the procedures followed in making these decisions were proper.*

I allege that the Committee on Promotions, Rehiring, and Tenure of the Department of Political Science failed to read the majority of my written work prior to making their decision, and did not properly evaluate my teaching record. In addition, the Department refused to give me adequate reasons in writing for their denial of appeal, despite repeated attempts to get them to do so. In addition, I contend that the appeal procedure itself within the Department was deficient.

c)   *Whether or not the Department's decision was consistent and equitable in the light of other decisions on renewals made in recent years.*

Sincerely yours,

Pauline Vaillancourt

June 8, 1973

STATEMENT OF ISSUES

1)   In the Department's handling of Professor Vaillancourt's case, did it use improper procedure or act in a biased manner?

2)   If there were any faults in the procedures are they sufficiently substantial to require voiding the recommendation?

3)   What relief may the Committee recommend?

HAROLD M. WALLER
Chairman

165

Document #34 is the Report of the Committee of Enquiry. It was this report which vindicated both Professors Vaillancourt and Wallerstein, and upon which Professor Wallerstein would base his discussion of the Vaillancourt Precedents. The heart of the final report begins with Item #14. Items #36 through #37 of the Report (Document #34) summarize the conclusions of the committee:

> We conclude that an accumulation of irregularities and improprieties in procedure, and an inadvertent inconsistent creation and application of standards produced a decision sufficiently lacking in due process that it should not be allowed to stand.

The *Report of a Committee of Inquiry into the decision not to renew the contract of professor Pauline Vaillancourt* is reprinted here in its entirety. The reader will learn from the survey of the "Vaillancourt Precedents" presented at the conclusion that the Report of the Committee of Enquiry is potentially the most significant decision pertaining to the definition and protection of the rights of junior staff on probationary appointments. Most repression occurs early, before the dissenting scholar has had the opportunity to establish a professional reputation or gain promotion or tenure. Therefore, the protection of junior staff must be the first priority in any strategy to oppose academic repression. Indeed, the Report of the Committee of Enquiry is so "hot" that its distribution has not been encouraged by CAUT. If one wished to read the report (prior to this book) one would have to travel to the CAUT headquarters in Ottawa in order to gain access to it. Professor Wallerstein was unsuccessful in persuading the CAUT *Newsletter* to publish all or parts of it. It is a landmark decision, and should be studied by *all* junior staff for their own protection; its precedents can be used by all faculty concerned with defending academic freedom and resisting academic repression. It is hoped that its publication here will serve to increase general knowledge of the Committee of Enquiry's decision and the *implications* of the decision.

DOCUMENT 34

REPORT OF A COMMITTEE OF INQUIRY INTO THE DECISION NOT TO RENEW THE CONTRACT OF PROFESSOR PAULINE VAILLANCOURT DEPARTMENT OF POLITICAL SCIENCE, McGILL UNIVERSITY, MONTREAL, CANADA

Representing McGill Department of Political Science:

Professor H. Waller, Department Chairman
Professor J. Mallory, Chairman, Department Promotions, Rehiring and Tenure Committee

Representing Professor Vaillancourt:

Professor I. Wallerstein, President, McGill Faculty Union
Professor Pauline Vaillancourt

166

Observer:

Professor R. Vogel, Dean, McGill Faculty of Arts

Inquiry Committee:

Professor L. Balthazar, Political Science Department, Laval University
Professor C.B. MacPherson, Political Science Department, University of Toronto
Professor D.L. Johnston, Faculty of Law, University of Toronto, Committee Chairman

Hearings:

McGill University, June 11, 17, 20, 27, 29, 1973.

Committee Meetings:

University of Toronto, July 4, 13, 1973.

I.   *Brief History:*

1.   Professor Pauline Vaillancourt was appointed as an Assistant Professor for one year in the Political Science Department (the Department) of McGill University (the University) effective September 1, 1969. In March, 1970, she was renewed for three years as an Assistant Professor effective September 1, 1970. In September, 1972 the Department Chairman (the Chairman) notified her that the Department's Committee on Promotion, Rehiring and Tenure (the DC) had recommended that her contract not be renewed at its expiration on August 31, 1973 and that he had communicated this recommendation to the Dean of the Faculty of Arts (the Dean). She requested and was given reasons for the decision (appended hereto as appendix A). She requested and was given an opportunity to appear before the DC in November, 1972 to present additional evidence. The Chairman subsequently informed her that the DC's decision remained unchanged. She requested and was given an opportunity to appear *ex parte* before the Dean's Advisory Committee on Promotion, Rehiring and Tenure (the DAC) in February, 1973. The Department also appeared *ex parte* before the DAC. The DAC did not make any decision but recommended an outside inquiry committee be jointly appointed by the University and the Canadian Association of University Teachers (the CAUT) according to terms of reference set out in a letter of the CAUT Executive Secretary and a letter of the Dean (appended hereto as appendices B-1 and B-2 respectively). On May 28, 1973 the three member inquiry committee (the Committee) was appointed. It requested the Department and Professor Vaillancourt to meet and forward to the Committee an agreed statement of facts and non-contested documents and each to produce and forward to the Committee a statement of the issues (appended hereto as appendices C-1 and C-2) to be determined by the Committee.

2.   The Committee met with Professor Vaillancourt and her adviser, Professor Wallerstein, the Chairman and the DC Chairman, with the Dean present as an observer, on June 11 (for procedural matters only), June 17, 20, 27 and 29, 1973 to hear and receive evidence and argument. The Committee met on July 4 and 13, 1973 and now renders its report.

II.   *Issues:*

3.   The Department and Professor Vaillancourt were in disagreement as to the issues to be determined (as will be seen in appendices C-1 and C-2.) The Committee was asked to rule. Its ruling is as follows:

Procedural Ruling re Statement of Issues

11 June 1973

i)   We have concluded that some statement from the Committee with respect to the issues before it is appropriate at this stage of the proceedings. However, the Committee reserves the right to add to the statement of issues to be considered as further evidence is adduced and argument made.

ii) We found our statement of issues in the CAUT Policy Statement on Academic Appointments and Tenure, III, Section A, 2(b), and in particular the statement "Normally an appeal from a recommendation of non-renewal should be based either on a failure to follow proper procedures or on evidence of bias or inconsistency in the grounds for the recommendation."

iii) We agree with the position put forward by both Professor Waller and Professor Wallerstein, that in a non-renewal case the onus is on the person who is not renewed to challenge the grounds for and method of arriving at the decision.

iv) In our view it would not be possible for the Committee to make an adequate inquiry or to make recommendations as we are charged to do without asking more than whether or not the prescribed McGill University procedures were formally adhered to. Professors Vaillancourt and Wallerstein have argued that the decision of the departmental committee was improper on all three counts set out in the CAUT Policy Statement referred to above. We cannot satisfy ourselves about those allegations without inquiring and asking for more evidence on all three counts.

v) All three of these counts can be brought under items (i) and (ii) of Professor Waller's written statement of issues or under items (b) and (c) of Professor Vaillancourt's written statement of issues. However, we prefer to deal with them under the three heads stated in the CAUT Policy Statement referred to.

vi) On the matter of the head dealing with procedure, there should be objective evidence of departmental policy. On the head of bias, some evidence as to how and why the departmental committee's decision was reached is necessary. On the head of inconsistency, we cannot accept the interpretation that would rule out a comparison between persons renewed and not renewed, for example by way of a comparative assessment of publications.

vii) With respect to the matter of recommendations by the Committee and the remedy that might be requested, we prefer not to deal with the matter at this time.

4. The relevant portions of the CAUT Policy Statement on Academic Appointments and Tenure are as follows:

III A 1 The purpose of a probationary appointment is to provide a period of mutual appraisal for the university and the candidate. Probation does not imply inevitable appointment with tenure. It should imply that the university will give very serious consideration to such an appointment.

A2. (b) The length and conditions of initial and subsequent probationary appointments should be clearly stated in writing. Proper consideration of the renewal of a probationary appointment should be assured through clearly defined and well-publicized procedures. The decision of a department on renewal should be made with proper consultation on a systematic basis, preferably through an elected departmental committee. The faculty member should be advised when a review of his appointment is to take place, and he should be given the opportunity to present written and oral evidence. The candidate should be given reasons in writing for non-renewal if he requests them. It should be understood that such reasons might include consideration of budgetary and departmental needs as well as of the specific qualifications of the individual concerned. Suitable provisions for appeal should be available. Normally an appeal from a recommendation of non-renewal should be based either on a failure to follow procedures or on evidence of bias or inconsistency in the grounds for the recommendation.

III. *Committee's Approach:*

5. In this report we consider only the most pertinent items among an overwhelming volume of evidence and argument. This report considers in turn each of the issues of procedural irregularity, inconsistency, and bias, and where relevant within those heads uses the three traditional academic criteria of scholarship, teaching and administrative or university community contribution. Since the onus of establishing to the Committee's satisfaction that substantial breaches of the guidelines relating to fair procedure, consistency and impartiality had taken place was on Professor Vaillancourt we proceed here chiefly by considering allegations made by her.

168

IV. *Alleged Procedural Improprieties:*

6. We proceed under this heading by considering what are the appropriate principles to govern procedure in academic renewal cases. We then consider in paragraphs 8 through 13 some of the general allegations of procedural improprieties. Finally we consider in paragraphs 14 through 19 alleged procedural irregularities within the three traditional academic criteria for renewal decisions: scholarship, teaching and administrative or university community contribution, these being the criteria which the DC applied in reaching its decision.

7. There are two questions to be considered under the head of alleged failure to follow proper procedures in university non-renewal decisions. The first is whether the currently established procedures in the university in question have been faithfully followed by the persons charged with decision making responsibility. The second is whether those procedures and any others created by the DC for its own use, are adequate, that is, are fair, appropriate to the particular case and capable of commanding the confidence of the university community to which they apply and the academic community in Canada generally.

8. Professor Vaillancourt alleged a number of irregularities in the procedures relating to the non-renewal decision up to and including the deliberations of the DAC. She alleged that the constitution of the DC was improper in that it was entirely composed of senior members of the Department. Its composition was the five full professors with tenure, its Chairman being the senior member. While the CAUT guidelines indicate a preference for elected committee, we conclude that this DC was not improper. The composition of the DC was a well established and well known practice of the Department, to which no one had objected prior to the time of the decision in question. While other departments within the University have used other models which involved junior faculty members and/or students, and/or elections to the DC, we are not persuaded that the composition of the DC taken by itself would result in unfairness or partiality.

9. It was alleged that the Department and in particular the DC committed procedural improprieties in failing to warn Professor Vaillancourt at an earlier date of inadequate teaching or to advise her with respect to alleged deficiencies in her teaching. On the one hand, the counsel of perfection suggests that senior members of the Department and the Chairman in particular should advise Faculty members on probationary contracts with respect to matters of pedagogy particularly when complaints are registered. On the other hand the Chairman and members of the DC pointed out that Professor Vaillancourt's attitude did not lend itself to advice of this kind and they apprehended that it would be rejected, resented, or misunderstood. On balance we find some minor impropriety in that some attempt should have been made to communicate the nature and scope of the complaints to Professor Vaillancourt in the spirit of constructive criticism and in the hope that she could make the necessary adjustments and improvements, with an onus on the Department to take the chance of a rebuff at least once.

10. It was alleged that the Department had failed to provide reasons for its decision at an early stage following its decision and that when it did produce reasons they lacked sufficient detail and in particular should have been cast in the form of a "bill of particulars" by way of identifying deficiencies. While approximately nineteen days elapsed before the reasons were given following the initial decision we do not conclude that that was an unwarranted delay in the circumstances. The reasons would first have to be formulated and written by the DC Chairman, circulated and amended and approved by the other members of the DC, then communicated to the Chairman, and then communicated by him in writing to Professor Vaillancourt following her request for a statement of reasons. The matter of the detail which is required in these reasons is more difficult. While greater detail might have been advisable in the initial statement of reasons, we conclude that the statement in fact provided here does not depart greatly from the norm in non-renewal decisions and we do not find that it fails to meet the minimum procedural requirements.

169

11. It was alleged that it was improper for the Department to communicate its non-renewal recommendation to the Dean before or at the same time as Professor Vaillancourt was informed for the first time of the non-renewal decision, and before giving her a statement of reasons or meeting with her to permit her to produce additional evidence. A decision to reverse the previous decision would not only involve a change of mind at the first level but the sending of an opposite signal up to the next stage of the appeal procedure. A second important factor to be considered here is that the role of the DAC was not entirely clear. It functioned as a review tribunal rather than a true appeal tribunal. Thus, while apparently it would intervene in a non-renewal decision if the procedures followed by the department were inadequate, it was not prepared to hear the case on its merits with repeated and new evidence from each side and the opportunity for the parties in front of one another to state opposing cases. Thus the first and only decision substantially on the merits was that of the DC. Thus, we conclude that the DC should have provided full appeal remedies. These would include the statement of reasons, the opportunity to introduce new evidence and argument to attempt to meet those reasons and the obligation of the DC to reply to the new evidence and argument. This should all have been done before the decision left the Department and was taken to the next step, the level of the Dean.

12. Professor Vaillancourt alleged a breach of fair procedure in the failure by the DC to enter into dialogue in some detail with her and to communicate its decision to her following this dialogue. What in fact happened following the initial decision was this. The reasons were communicated in a one and one half page letter; Professor Vaillancourt was initially told that she could appear before the DC with an adviser to introduce whatever additional oral evidence she wished. That meeting took place, and some time after she was advised that the DC had considered the additional evidence advanced by her and had concluded there was no reason to change its initial decision. Our conclusions are these. First the limitation of oral evidence only was unduly narrow. In fact the DC did at the meeting permit written testimonials to be placed on the record and by the time of the meeting assured Professor Vaillancourt it was prepared to read whatever additional research and publications she wished to produce. However, we conclude it should have been made clear at the outset that she was entitled to produce for and have considered by the DC additional written material as well as oral evidence. Furthermore given the rather limited written material considered by the DC in the first instance (as described below), given the substantial volume of additional written material Professor Vaillancourt produced at the appeal meeting and given the fact that this appeal to the DC which deliberated and concluded in the first instance was the only substantial appeal, there was an obligation on the DC to provide a more detailed reply than simply to say the additional evidence was not sufficient to produce any change.

13. Finally Professor Vaillancourt alleged an impropriety in the DC placing pressure on students to support the Department's position on the non-renewal recommendation. The two specific allegations in this general claim were a notice by the Chairman on a departmental bulletin board several years prior to this non-renewal decision to the effect that students asking professors for letters of reference should not conclude the letters would always be favourable. The second, more substantial, allegation was that the Chairman had solicited letters from students to be written to the Dean supporting the Department's position by substantiating complaints of inadequate teaching that the students had earlier made with regard to Professor Vaillancourt. On the first specific allegation we find no direct link between the notice on the departmental bulletin board and the letters from students and conclude there was no impropriety here. On the second matter, of soliciting letters, we conclude that the better procedure would have been for the Department to avoid solicitation of letters. The Department might better have taken the position before any review committee that it did not attempt to produce rebuttal evidence of this kind. On the other hand, it is apparent that Professor Vaillancourt and her supporters made strenuous efforts to solicit letters in her support resulting in approximately forty favourable letters being forwarded to the Dean and consequently the Chairman felt he had to make a

rebuttal case. In the circumstances, while we conclude a more advisable course would have been for the Chairman to avoid solicitation of letters, we do not find that his decision to do so with regard to students who had already registered strong concern and complaint about Professor Vaillancourt's teaching was manifestly irregular.

(a) *Scholarship*

14. The DC met in May, 1972 to consider the renewal of five members of the Department. It decided to postpone the decisions for all until September and communicated its request for evidence of Professor Vaillancourt's scholarship as follows:

McGILL UNIVERSITY, DEPARTMENT OF POLITICAL SCIENCE

May 25, 1972

CONFIDENTIAL

Professor Pauline Vaillancourt
Department of Political Science
McGill University

Dear Pauline:

The Department's Committee on Promotions, Rehiring and Tenure met on May 15th to consider your contract, which expires on August 31, 1973. After careful deliberation, the Committee came to the conclusion that it would be best to defer a decision on your case until September. Obviously, the Committee was reluctant to make a definite decision at this time. The members of the Committee feel that they need further information from you before they can make a decision.

The information that the Committee requires is confirmation of the completion of your Ph.D. degree. Furthermore, the members of the Committee would like to be able to look at some of your published work, particularly the study with Guy Lord and others on the elections on Montreal, and the paper which you presented to the ISA on **Methodological** Problems in Socialization Studies. Please give copies of these two studies to Professor Mallory at your earliest convenience. If any further information is required, I shall be in touch with you.

Sincerely yours,

HAROLD M. WALLER
Chairman

15. The clear impression from this letter is that the DC wished to have only the jointly authored article and the ISA paper, although the letter did not foreclose Professor Vaillancourt from taking the initiative and placing additional evidence of her scholarly work before the DC. In fact the DC already had her curriculum vita (the c.v.) which listed the following items of scholarly work:

Areas of   Social Science Methodology, Political Behaviour, Political Socialization,
Specialization: American Government, Comparative Government (emphasis West Europe),
                  Social Movements, Critical Political Science

Theses, Publications
and Papers Read:

1. "Non-attitudes in Political Socialization Studies", submitted for publication.

2. "Problems in Political Socialization Studies; a consideration of the subfield and its raison d'être", submitted for publication.

3. Guy Lord, Pauline Vaillancourt, Jean-Guy Vaillancourt, Pierre Fournier, "Les Élections du 30 Avril 1970 à Montréal: *Cahiers de l'Université du Québec,* 1972, forthcoming.

4. "Review of Strategy for Revolution, de Regis Debray, *Études Internationales,* 1972, forthcoming.

5.   "Review of Political Socialization and Educational Climates by Robert M. Merelman, in *American Political Science Review*, March, 1972.

6.   *The Political Socialization of Young People A Panel Survey Of Young People in the San Francisco Bay Area,* U.C. Berkeley, 1972, unpublished Doctoral thesis.

7.   Pauline Vaillancourt, "Methodological Problems in Political Socialization Studies", paper presented to the Annual Meeting of the International Studies Association, March 1972.

8.   Discussant, Comparative West European Panel, Annual Meeting, St. John's, Newfoundland.

9.   Pauline Vaillancourt, "Stability of Children's Political Orientations; A Panel Survey", paper presented to the Annual Meeting of the American Political Science Association, September 1970.

10.   Jean-Guy and Pauline Vaillancourt, "Ideologie religieuse et politique d'une elite internationale de laics catholiques", Communication présentee au Congres annuel de la Society for the Scientific Study of Religion, October, 1968.

11.   *Community Power Studies: A Critical Analysis of the literature,* U.C. Berkeley, 1966, (unpublished Master's thesis).

16.   We conclude that it was improper for the DC not to invite either a larger sample of her scholarly work, or to invite her to choose several items which represented the best of her scholarly work, or to encourage her to produce for the DC all the evidence of her scholarly work she wished, in a situation where her case was one of doubt and where very considerable importance would be attached to scholarship.

17.   The four members of the DC gave extensive testimony as to the methods of arriving at and the rationale for the non-renewal decision. There was considerable uncertainty as to why the two articles — the jointly authored paper and the ISA paper — were selected as the basis for evaluating scholarship. The evidence of the DC members made it clear that the greatest reliance for assessing scholarship was placed on Professor Henry Ehrmann whose subfields of interest were more closely related than those of any of the other members of the DC to Professor Vaillancourt's main interests, Political Behaviour and Socialization. He concluded that the jointly authored article was useless for the purpose of evaluating scholarship because it was impossible to tell how large or small a role Professor Vaillancourt played in it. Thus the DC was left with only one article upon which to base its evaluation of scholarship for its initial decision in September, although one member of the DC testified he had heard her read another paper at an earlier time. Professor Vaillancourt indicated that several other articles and her doctoral dissertation represented her best work.

18.   We conclude that the DC acted improperly in choosing as one of the two articles for its sample of scholarship an item which it conceded was useless for the purpose. We conclude that it was improper for the DC to deprive itself of a full and fair opportunity to assess scholarship by placing reliance on one of the less important items listed on the c.v. Finally we conclude that it was inaccurate for the DC to make the statement through the Chairman's letter in its statement of reasons that "The Committee's careful evaluation of the writings which you submitted leads the members to doubt whether . . . you could furnish the scholarly contribution" desired. In fact one of the two writings requested by the DC was not evaluated at all. Furthermore the initial position that oral evidence alone would be permitted in the appeal to the DC (referred to above), though corrected by the time of the appeal, was improper in view of the DC's extremely limited sample of evidence of scholarship for its initial decision.

(b) *Teaching*

(c) *Administration*

19.　The main issue of alleged irregularity in assessing teaching and administration or contribution to the university community were also raised as alleged inconsistent application of standards. We deal with them later under Part V Consistency.

V.　*Consistency:*

20.　Consistency in developing and applying standards has a range of interpretations. For present purposes we conclude it means first applying the same standards in the same way to each individual being considered. It also means applying standards that have been previously enunciated, since a person may have directed his efforts to meet those standards. It means that new standards which reverse previous understanding and customs may not be created midstream in the judgement process during which the individual's competence is being measured. We now consider consistency in each of the three traditional academic criteria areas.

(a) *Scholarship*

21.　.No evidence of a comprehensive statement or plan of policy directives or priority areas enunciated by the Department was produced before this Committee. However in September, 1969 shortly after becoming Chairman, Professor Waller circulated "Some Suggestions for the New Year" in which he stated that Quebec politics was a research area to which the Department should direct greater emphasis, that there should be more problem-oriented research on public policy questions in Montreal and Quebec and that the Department should become more innovative in educational techniques. In fact Professor Vaillancourt was heavily involved in the two types of research stressed by the Chairman and was cited favourably by him in a subsequent annual report for innovative teaching. She had been involved in a four member study sponsored by a Canada Council grant of the April, 1970 provincial election. One of the four participants, Professor Guy Lord from the University of Quebec was a man for whom Professor Ehrmann evidenced a great deal of respect. Professor Lord's prestige would normally be expected to characterize the project as a prestigious one to the credit of all its participants. Professor Vaillancourt had received from the provincial government's Department of Social Affairs a grant larger than any other member of the Department had ever received to undertake a research project on a specific phenomenon of Quebec political life. She had taught as a visiting professor at the University of Ottawa and at the University of Quebec and had highly enthusiastic testimonials from members of the political science departments in those institutions and the University of Montreal which attested to her constructive assistance in the research work of their students and faculty and her significant collaboration in inter university study of Quebec politics. For several years she had been actively involved as a director of and adviser to several projects on Quebec politics in the Centre de Recherche en Politique Sociale in Montreal. In spite of the Department's stated policy emphasis no explicit attempt was made prior to the initial DC decision to seek detailed evidence of Professor Vaillancourt's performance in these areas. Finally, she produced for the DC at the November, 1972, appeal meeting a number of testimonials from scholars of Quebec politics who assessed her past performance and potential in laudatory terms, including one from Professor Leon Dion, willingly acknowledged by the members of the DC to be a seminal intellectual figure in Quebec political science, reinforced by his detailed affidavit in support of Professor Vaillancourt submitted to the Committee. We conclude that there is evidence of a contribution to research oriented to Quebec and local politics and that the DC has not applied the criterion in a manner consistent with the emphasis on this area as a priority for the Department.

22.　Professor Vaillancourt was initially hired, after efforts to find a more senior person had failed, with research interests primarily in political science methodology, political behaviour and socialization. She taught at least one course each year in that area. In the statement of reasons (attached as appendix A) it was stressed that:

> "the members of the Committee believe that the person in your fields of empirical methods, political behaviour and socialization is inevitably closely involved with the research needs of

others, both staff and students. Therefore anyone in this position *must possess exceptional qualities of leadership and cooperation.* In the judgement of the Committee, you do not meet these criteria. Consequently, the Committee thinks that you are not really the right person to develop these fields in this Department. **(emphasis added)**

This was the first occasion on which Professor Vaillancourt's fields were singled out as ones requiring such exceptional qualities. We conclude it was inconsistent for the Department to establish several other priority areas without mentioning this one and then to declare an unusually high standard for this one for the first time after the evaluation process had been applied and after Professor Vaillancourt had lost the opportunity to adjust her effort in the attempt to meet this higher standard.

23.   The DC evaluated five members of the Department for renewal including Professor Vaillancourt. It decided to renew three of them with various conditions for the completion of their Ph.Ds by a given date and not to renew Professor Vaillancourt and one other on the judgement in the latter's case that it was unlikely he would complete his Ph.D. In making the judgement positively for the first three, the DC assessed the *potential* for scholarship of the three and attempted to forecast because there was not a great deal of concrete evidence at this stage in their careers. The same type of assessment of potential and forecasting without thorough evaluation of present concrete attainments was done in the case of Professor Vaillancourt. But in her case there was a good deal of concrete evidence of scholarship. The DC's statement:

> The Committee's careful evaluation of the writings which you submitted leads the members to doubt whether by interest and inclination you could furnish the scholarly contribution that they wish to see strengthened in the offerings of our Department

implies that this future assessment was being made. But in making such an assessment there was at least a minimal obligation to test it against present and past evidence when that evidence was greater at least in quantity than the evidence for the others who were being evaluated. The existing evidence was this. Unlike the other four considered at the same time Professor Vaillancourt had completed her Ph.D.. This was tangible evidence of her interest and inclination to scholarship up to that time. Aside from her masters and doctoral dissertations, her c.v. listed eight items of scholarly work, one of which had been published, two of which were about to be published, and two of which had recently been submitted for publication. The remaining two items were papers read at the annual meeting of the International Studies Association and the annual meeting of the American Political Science Association. Unsolicited and solicited letters of appraisal on her scholarly work from approximately fifteen different scholars in the field assessed her existing work with substantial enthusiasm. Professor Dion had engaged her to appraise articles submitted for publication in the *Canadian Journal of Political Science* and valued her scholarly standards highly. The provincial government and the Canada Council had made substantial grants for her research referred to earlier. All of this information had been placed before the November, 1972 DC appeal meeting. It would appear to demonstrate a very tangible interest in and inclination towards scholarship, marked by the fact that much of it was done while the Ph.D. was being completed, at an early stage in her career. If the DC had doubts as to her *future* scholarly productivity ("interest and inclination") expecting that it would diminish over the next few years, it would have been more consistent with the DC's conditional Ph.D. treatment of the successful three to have resolved any future doubt in Professor Vaillancourt's favour by giving her a one, two or three year renewal to see what would happen, knowing that there was ample time to test the doubt before she would be considered for promotion or tenure.

(b) *Teaching*

24.   The DC's "greatest reservation" concerned Professor Vaillancourt's "classroom performance". It stated:

> The Committee's greatest reservation concerns your classroom performance. The members are well aware of some favourable student reports about your teaching. They did not base the

unfavourable judgment merely on the very numerous complaints and course evaluations that have been received from both graduate and undergraduate students. They sought to obtain an impression of the actual content of the courses given by you, of the examinations, an example of which they have inspected, and of the classroom atmosphere. All this conveys an impression which the Committee classified as unsatisfactory.

The individual members of the DC who testified ranked her fourth or fifth among the five candidates being assessed. One graduate student whom the Department called as a witness on teaching ranked her very low, although higher than one member of approximately similar seniority in the Department who had been renewed in the previous year. From the student witnesses called either by the Department or Professor Vaillancourt the clear conclusion that emerged was that she produced strong reactions. Some of her witnesses classified her teaching as the most stimulating and inspiring they had ever experienced while a number of the Department's witnesses classified her classroom performance as the most repelling or irrelevant they had encountered, though this direct criticism was based primarily on her 1969-70 and 1970-71 years and there was no direct assessment of her 1971-72 year.

25. The DC did have in its possession student questionnaires for the years 1970-71 and 1971-72. The DC Chairman indicated that the DC considered these questionnaires by looking through them and noting the narrative or additional comments that students were invited to add on the reverse of the questionnaire, and had noted that a number of them were adverse. They did not, however, quantify the questionnaire scores and compare Professor Vaillancourt's overall scores with those of the others being considered for renewal or other teachers in the Department. Had they done so, they would have found that for the last complete year for which she could be tested, 1971-72, there were almost no ratings of "poor", the rating of "excellent" continued to be given by some students, and the average score placed her in or above the middle range for the Department as a whole. At our request the Department did produce comparative evaluations for our perusal but since the evaluations were not identified by professors' names except for Professor Vaillancourt, it was not possible to determine how she rated on a quantifiable analysis with the other four persons being considered for non-renewal.

26. The concern the DC expressed for the extreme adverse reactions and a classroom atmosphere which, for some students discouraged views which dissented from the Professor's own or were less radical, was an important one. But consistency required that the DC determine whether these views were widely held or might be determined in a quantitative analysis and whether they were lasting or likely to continue. In this regard, we conclude the DC's testing procedures were irregular and inconsistent.

27. On the matter of continuing or prevailing teaching competence the facts were these. The 1970-71 questionnaires showed scores which were considerably lower than 1971-72. The Sociology Department, in which Professor Vaillancourt had taught two half courses in 1970-71, chose not to continue her in these courses due to student complaints and the Sociology Department's judgement that her performance was unsatisfactory. On the other hand the adverse criticism centred on the first year and to some extent on the second, and not to any substantial extent on the third. The student evaluations were, overall, positive in the third year compared with the Department as a whole. The evidence from the two other universities where Professor Vaillancourt held visiting positions attested to a noteworthy teaching contribution there. Professor Vaillancourt was teaching courses in several instances which were experimental and novel and had been cited in one of the Department's annual reports as making a creative contribution in innovative teaching. Innovation in teaching methods had been one of the Department's stated objectives. The DC had made some allowance for reports and evidence of inferior teaching by a professor renewed in the previous year on the grounds of an expected improvement with experience. A similar flexibility should have been extented to Professor Vaillancourt especially when she was encouraged to employ innovative methods. When questioned about recognition of an upward curve in teaching evaluation forms the DC discounted this evidence on the principle of self selection, viz. as a teacher's reputation became known in a department only students

specially interested in his courses and his methods would enroll and this would produce an artificial inflation of evaluation scores. We reject this argument. First, if it applies to one teacher, it applies to all, so long as non-compulsory courses are involved at least, and the effect will disappear in a comparison involving all teachers in the system. Second, if the self-selection discount argument were accepted it would be impossible for any teacher to show an improved performance in a later year by showing an improved evaluation score.

28.   The DC indicated that it sought to obtain an impression of the actual content of Professor Vaillancourt's courses and examinations. However, it seems it did not request or consider samples of course reading lists or syllabi or give particular attention to the responses on the student questionnaire which related to course content and examinations. It did form a judgement of her examining methods on the basis of one exam produced by Professor Vaillancourt in another context which the DC Chairman characterized as so bad that evidence of other exams could scarcely compensate for it. We conclude that a consistent application of standards as to course content would require a broader sampling of evidence, particularly when Professor Vaillancourt was encouraged to experiment with different teaching methods. We also conclude that a consistent application of standards would give greater recognition to an upward curve or marked improvement in teaching competence with maturity.

29.   While the DC was appropriately concerned over strong complaints about Professor Vaillancourt's teaching, a consistent application of its standards required a more comprehensive evaluation before it concluded it was unsatisfactory, particularly when the complaints were matched by eulogies.

(c) *Administration*

30.   In the DC's statement of reasons and in the testimony of its members before the Committee it appeared that the evaluation of administrative contribution was of little importance in the case of any of the five persons being considered for renewal. It stated in Professor Vaillancourt's case:

> Your contribution to the general administration of the Department and the University has not been outstanding. However, your service as Official Representative of the ICPR was taken into account.

Given the limited significance of administrative contribution in the DC's evaluation of all five members being evaluated we do not consider it further here.

VI.   *Bias:*

31.   The allegations of bias were the most difficult for us to assess, since the definition of bias is quite unclear. We were somewhat helped by the statement made by the Executive Secretary of CAUT who was called as a witness at the first hearing where he gave the following explanation of bias or inconsistency:

> The CAUT position on probationary appointments can be put in these general terms, that a faculty member on a probationary appointment does not have a right to renewal, but has a right to a proper consideration for renewal. A proper consideration concludes in a reasonable judgement — which is not the same thing as a judgement that will necessarily be acceptable to the faculty member concerned. The right to a reasonable judgement means that a department cannot decide a matter of renewal in a biased or arbitrary manner. It cannot ground its judgement in non-academic considerations, or give one form of consideration to one faculty member and a different form to another. A department must make a judgement which follows reasonably from the relevant information in the case. A department is not free to make just any judgement, nor is a judgement validated by the mere assertion that it was made in good faith, since good faith alone does not exclude the possibility of inadvertence or negligence. What constitutes a reasonable judgement is the most commonly disputed issue in cases of non-renewal. CAUT has compiled a series of examples from its casework to indicate what it regards as unreasonable judgements. A department cannot decide against renewal on the grounds that the faculty member's scholarly interest does not coincide with the academic priorities of his department, if it transpires that his department has never established a set of academic priorities; it cannot decide against renewal on the grounds of ineffective teaching if there

176

existed no data on which to base a judgement of effectiveness; it cannot decide against renewal on grounds of an absence of scholarly publications, if the faculty member's scholarly publications outnumber those of most of his colleagues. On the other hand a mere dissent from the judgement of the department, by the faculty member, does not argue inconsistency or bias in the judgement itself. A faculty member is rarely willing to concur with a judgement that has led to the non-renewal of his appointment.

While the statement was extremely helpful it still leaves the meaning of bias in some doubt.

32.   We are clear that bias is not the opposite of integrity or good faith, and that recognition of integrity and good faith does not establish lack of bias. We are fully persuaded of the integrity and good faith of the DC, but find this irrelevant to the question of bias.

33.   We considered an affirmative theory of bias put forward by Professor Vaillancourt. She alleged that shortly after she was initially invited to consider joining the McGill Department, reports from Berkeley where she studied suggested that she was a political activist and a non-conformist; that a climate of opinion developed over her time at McGill with her association with dissenting causes in several discernible stages; that it culminated in a desire on the part of more traditional oriented members of the Department to eliminate from the Department someone who was not congenial, who challenged many of the customs that had developed in the Department over the years and whose own political views were associated with minority causes; that the desire to sever crystallized in the quiet and polite decision to let Professor Vaillancourt go at the first convenient opportunity, the termination of the three year probationary appointment. We found no sufficient evidence to support this affirmative theory of bias.

34.   We note however that the Chairman in his submission of the Department's case put the question whether it was not proper for a department to use a probationary period to decide not to renew a member "who seems to create so many problems and difficulties" in the department?

This depends on the kind of problems and difficulties. Scholarship often makes problems. A new style of scholarship introduced into a department where a different style has prevailed is very likely to disturb the smooth congeniality of the department. But the claims of congeniality must not be allowed to outweigh the claims of scholarship, and a problem of this kind is an entirely improper reason for non-renewal.

35.   None of the considerations in the previous four paragraphs can be held to be decisive as to the charge of bias. We find, however, that our decision can be sufficiently made on considerations under the other two heads of procedure and consistency.

VII. *Conclusion:*

36.   *We conclude that an accumulation of irregularities and improprieties in procedure, and an inadvertent inconsistent creation and application of standards produced a decision sufficiently lacking in due process that it should not be allowed to stand.*

VIII. *Recommendations:*

37.   We recommend that Professor Vaillancourt be offered a three year renewal of her contract commencing August 31, 1973.

38.   A second recommendation is also necessary. During the course of the hearings Professor Vaillancourt reported to the Department and the Committee that she had been offered a teaching position at the University of Quebec in Montreal. Since it was not known what this Committee's recommendation would be and since she wished to be sure of an academic position for 1973-74 we agreed that she should accept the offer and that if our recommendation were that her appointment at McGill be renewed we would add the recommendation that she be granted leave without pay from McGill for the academic year 1973-74. We accordingly make this recommendation also.

L. Balthazar   C.B. Macpherson   D.L. Johnston   August 20, 1973

The next document and chapter, titled *The Vaillancourt Precedents,* was a communication from Professor Wallerstein, as President of MFU, to the membership interpreting the "rights of faculty members on probationary appointments, as confirmed by the McGill-CAUT Committee of Enquiry. It is included in order to give the clearest possible summary of the implications and uses of the precedents established by the Vaillancourt case.

The Vaillancourt Precedents

From: Immanuel Wallerstein,
      President, McGill Faculty
      Union to the general membership.

Sept. 17, 1973

Dear Colleague,

You have probably heard that recently a committee of enquiry jointly appointed by McGill and the Canadian Association of University Teachers recommended that McGill overturn the recommendation of the Dept. of Political Science not to rehire Prof. Pauline Vaillancourt. The Committee so recommended on the grounds of improper procedure and lack of consistency.

Thus ends a long and painful process for Prof. Vaillancourt, the Department, and the University. We are of course pleased that the Committee of Enquiry has upheld the contentions made throughout the year by the McGill Faculty Union. We write you now not in order to discuss once more the Vaillancourt case, which is closed, but to call to your attention the wider implications of the Committee's report. For the Committee's interpretation of university norms, natural justice, and CAUT guidelines has spelled out in important ways the rights of probationary professors. The MFU believes it is now time for all the departments of the university to establish procedures that will fully protect these rights.

We would like to spell out the rights of faculty members on probationary appointments, as confirmed by the McGill-CAUT Committee of Enquiry.

1)   *The right to proper consideration for renewal*

Dr. Donald Savage, Executive Secretary of the CAUT, asserted in expert testimony the following:
   "The CAUT position on probationary appointments can be put in these general terms, that a faculty member on a probationary appointment does not have a right to renewal, but has a right to a proper consideration for renewal. A proper consideration concludes in a reasonable judgement — which is not the same thing as a judgement that will necessarily be acceptable to the faculty member concerned. The right to a reasonable judgement means that a department cannot decide a matter of renewal in a biased or arbitrary manner. It cannot ground its judgement in non-academic considerations, or give one form of consideration to one faculty member and a different form to another. A department must make a judgement which follows reasonably from the relevant information in the case."

The Committee of Enquiry used Dr. Savage's testimony as part of the basis of their own decision.

2)   *Procedural rights*

a) *Judgement about scholarship should be based on an adequate sample of a professor's work*

In the Vaillancourt case, one of the points of contention was that the decisions of the Committee were based on a small and improper sampling of her scholarship. The Committee said:*

"We conclude that it was improper for the DC not to invite either a larger sample of her scholarly work, or to invite her to choose several items which represented the best of her scholarly work, or to encourage her to produce for the DC all the evidence of her scholarly work she wished, in a situation where her case was one of doubt and where very considerable importance would be attached to scholarship."

In addition, Dr. Savage testified:

"[A Department] cannot decide against renewal on grounds of an absence of scholarly publications, if the faculty member's scholarly publications outnumber those of most of his colleagues."

b) *Evaluation of teaching effectiveness must be careful and comparative.*

There was much controversy about the teaching atmosphere of Prof. Vaillancourt's classes. The Committee had the following to say:

"The concern the DC expressed for the extreme adverse reactions and a classroom atmosphere which, for some students discouraged views which dissented from the Professor's own or were less radical, was an important one. But consistency required that the DC determine whether these views were widely held or might be determined in a quantitative analysis and whether they were lasting or likely to continue. In this regard, we conclude the DC's testing procedures were irregular and inconsistent . . . While the DC was appropriately concerned over strong complaints about Professor Vaillancourt's teaching, a consistent application of its standards required a more comprehensive evaluation before it concluded it was unsatisfactory, particularly when the complaints were matched by eulogies."

In addition, Dr. Savage testified:

"[A Department] cannot decide against renewal on the grounds of ineffective teaching if there existed no data on which to base a judgement of effectiveness"

c) *The Department must hear the case of the professor against whom they may be rendering adverse judgement, and must discuss this case with the professor.*

This is a crucial procedural right, and the one most frequently disregarded. The absence of such a discussion about substantive matters is in itself a denial of due process. In the Vaillancourt case, the Committee asserted:

"Thus, we conclude that the DC should have provided full appeal remedies. These would include the statement of reasons, the opportunity to introduce new evidence and argument to attempt to meet those reasons and the obligation of the DC to reply to the new evidence and argument. This should all have been done before the decision left the Department and was taken to the next step, the level of the Dean."

3)   *The Meaning of Consistency*

In the Vaillancourt case, the Department argued that it should not be obliged to present comparative assessments of Prof. Vaillancourt and others of similar status in the Department, as each case presents a particular complex whole, and that such comparisons would vitiate the possibilities of constructing a balanced Department. The Committee ruled at the outset that such comparisons were not merely legitimate, but were called for by the CAUT guidelines which require "consistency."

---

* Departmental Committee

In its report, the Committee spelled out what it believed consistency to involve: "Consistency in developing and applying standards has a range of interpretations. For present purposes we conclude it means first applying the same standards in the same way to each individual being considered. It also means applying standards that have been previously enunciated, since a person may have directed his efforts to meet those standards. It means that new standards which reverse previous understanding and customs may not be created midstream in the judgement process during which the individual's competence is being measured."

4) *Illegitimate practices of Departments*

a) *The "priorities" of the Department cannot be taken into account unless they are explicit, formulated by the appropriate departmental body, and existed during the prior employment of the professor.*

Dr. Savage testified that as a general rule:
"A department cannot decide against renewal on the grounds that the faculty member's scholarly interest does not coincide with the academic priorities of his department, if it transpires that his department has never established a set of academic priorities . . ."

In applying this principle to the Vaillancourt case, the Committee argued:
"Professor Vaillancourt was initially hired, after efforts to find a more senior person had failed, with research interests primarily in political science methodology, political behavior and socialization. She taught at least one course each year in that area. In the statement of reasons (attached as appendix A) it was stressed that:

> 'the members of the Committee believe that the person in your fields of empirical methods, political behavior and socialization is inevitably closely involved with the research needs of others, both staff and students. Therefore anyone in this position *must possess exceptional qualities of leadership and cooperation*. In the judgement of the Committee, you do not meet these criteria. Consequently, the Committee thinks that you are not really **the right person to develop these fields in this Department**.' (emphasis added)

This was the first occasion on which Professor Vaillancourt's fields were singled out as ones requiring such exceptional qualities. We conclude it was inconsistent for the Department to establish several other priority areas without mentioning this one and then to declare an unusually high standard for this one for the first time after the evaluation process had been applied and after Professor Vaillancourt had lost the opportunity to adjust her effort in the attempt to meet this higher standard."

b) *The Department cannot invalidate improved teaching reports on the grounds of self-selection by students.*

A key issue in the Vaillancourt case, the Committee judged: "When questioned about recognition of an upward curve in teaching evaluation forms the DC discounted this evidence on the principle of self selection, viz. as a teacher's reputation became known in a department only students specially interested in his courses and his methods would enroll and this would produce an artificial inflation of evaluation scores. We reject this argument. First, if it applies to one teacher, it applies to all, so long as non-compulsory courses are involved at least, and the effect will disappear in a comparison involving all teachers in the system. Second, if the self-selection discount argument were accepted it would be impossible for any teacher to show an improved performance in a later year by showing an improved evaluation score."

c) *The Department cannot use the probationary period to weed out "troublesome" professors.*

See the Committee's views:
"We note however that the Chairman in his submission of the Department's case put the question whether it was not proper for a department to use a probationary period to decide not to renew a member "who seems to create so many problems and difficulties" in the department?
This depends on the kind of problems and difficulties. Scholarship often makes problems. A new style of scholarship introduced into a department where a different style has prevailed is very likely to disturb the smooth congeniality of the department. But the claims of congeniality must not be allowed to outweigh the claims of scholarship, and a problem of this kind is an entirely improper reason for non-renewal."

d) *It is no defense for the Department to justify its decision on the grounds of the good faith or integrity of its departmental committee.*

See Dr. Savage:
"A department is not free to make just any judgement, nor is a judgement validated by the mere assertion that it was made in good faith, since good faith alone does not exclude the possibility of inadvertence or negligence."

And see the argument of the Committee of Enquiry:
"We are clear that bias is not the opposite of integrity or good faith, and that recognition of integrity and good faith does not establish lack of bias. We are fully persuaded of the integrity and good faith of the DC, but find this irrelevant to the question of bias."

The Battle for the Tapes

The battle for the tapes forms a curious and disturbing post-script to the Committee of Enquiry. The tapes in question are the logged audio-tape of the proceedings of the Committee of Enquiry inclusive of all testimony before the Committee and Professor Wallerstein's final summation of Pauline Vaillancourt's case. The testimony given before the Committee of Enquiry is considered confidential, but not Professor Wallerstein's summing up which, it had been agreed, he could present in either oral or written form. It was given in oral form because of time and financial limitations. A promise had been made by Professor D.L. Johnston, Chairman of the Committee of Enquiry, that a transcript of the final summation would be given to Professor Vaillancourt. The saga of the tapes begins very innocently, when Professor Vaillancourt (who had requested the transcript on June 29, at which time Professor Johnston had readily agreed) wrote to Professor Johnston in August to remind him of his promise.

On September 5 Professor Johnston replied that he regretted that he had forgotten his promise and that he had no objection to the request for a transcript of the final summation — however, the tapes had been returned to Dean Vogel. Following Professor Johnston's letter Professor Vaillancourt telephoned Dean Vogel — at which point the plot thickens! Dean Vogel informed Professor Vaillancourt that he "refuses her request on principle". (Cf., Document #32, Savage to Vogel, "no formal transcript of the proceedings shall be kept, however, the committee shall have the authority to require that a logged audio tape of all or part of the proceedings be kept for its own use".) She also discovered for the first time that it was intended to *erase* the tapes.

Note that authority over the tapes appeared to reside with the Committee of Enquiry (so that as Chairman, Professor Johnston had every right to promise a transcript of the final summation). Dr. Savage (Document #40) wrote in March that it "is of capital importance [to realize that] the real authority of the Committee that was chaired by Professor Johnston lay in the fact that it was neither a committee of the University which had decided not to renew your appointment, nor a committee of the Association . . .". In other words, neither CAUT, Dr. Savage, Dean Vogel, nor McGill University had the right or the authority to refuse to honour Professor Johnston's promise *nor* to erase the tapes. Why then were Dr. Savage and Dean Vogel so determined to destroy the "logged audio tape of all or part of the proceedings", *including* Professor Wallerstein's final summation?

On September 26 Professor Vaillancourt wrote a sharp protest, raising a number of pertinent issues, while quite properly requesting that the tapes be returned to Professor Johnston for safe-keeping. (Document #35)

DOCUMENT 35

DEPARTMENT OF POLITICAL SCIENCE

McGILL UNIVERSITY

September 26, 1973

Dean Vogel
Faculty of Arts
McGill University

Dr. Savage
Executive Secretary
CAUT
66 Lisgar Street
Ottawa, K2P 0C1
Ontario

Dear Dean Vogel and Dr. Savage:

I am writing you concerning 1) the disposition of the tape recordings that were made of the C.A.U.T. Inquiry into the decision not to renew my contract here at McGill, and 2) the refusal to allow me to have a typed copy made from the tapes of Professor Wallerstein's summary arguments.

The eventual disposition of the tapes was discussed at the first meeting of the inquiry, June 11, 1973. Professor Wallerstein asked if it was Professor Johnston's (the chairman's) intention to eventually deposit them with the C.A.U.T. The Chairman responded that he had no such intention and that as far as he was concerned they would remain in his personal possession. I was very surprised when I was informed recently that the chairman had sent the tapes to Dean Vogel because "he had acted as depository of materials to date." It seems to me that the Dean is an inappropriate choice as he has functioned as the Department's representative during the jointly initiated (CAUT and Dean Vogel) inquiry. You will recall that he consulted the Department while the CAUT consulted me during the negotiations over the composition of the inquiry committee. In addition, the Dean allocated to the Department a special budget to cover their expenses incurred as a result of the inquiry.

I would like to request that the tapes be returned to Professor Johnston and that you jointly mandate him to retain the tapes until the statutes of legal limitations has passed. My lawyer has advised me that it would be appropriate for me to ask that the tapes not be destroyed or held by McGill. I am requesting that they be retained by Professor Johnston, or at least jointly by the CAUT and Dean Vogel because of the remote possibility that they may be relevant in legal proceedings related to my employment at McGill University in the future.

I must also question the somewhat arbitrary decision made by yourselves in consultation with Professor Malloch* that I not be allowed to make a typed copy of Professor Wallerstein's final arguments during the inquiry. I am most surprised about your decision

---

* Chairman of the Academic Freedom & Tenure Committee of the CAUT, and also Professor of English at McGill.

183

since when I discussed this matter with Professor Johnston, in Professor Waller's office the evening of June 29, 1973, no objections were raised by Professors Waller and Mallory, and Professor Johnston agreed to send me a copy in the near future. I agreed to pay the expenses involved in having a typed version. I believe his decision (and the department's acquiescence) was based in part on his understanding that Professor Wallerstein and I were functioning under severe restraints of time and staff, since we had no special budget at our disposal for this. While we had the option of presenting final arguments in either written or oral form (or both), we were constrained by these factors to present final arguments orally.

I must reject your suggestion that my having this text typed from the tapes would set a precedent for making other portions of the proceedings public. There is, it seems to me a great difference between testimony, especially confidential testimony, and our final arguments. It was my understanding from the very beginning (June 11, 1973) that none of this former material was to be made public. However the fact that the final arguments could be presented in written form and copies made (at the option of each side) available to both parties indicates to me that this material is of a different character. Both the Department's representatives and the Chairman of the committee of Inquiry, it seems to me, agreed with this interpretation when we discussed the matter June 29, 1973. In light of all this, I find your present position highly questionable and clearly unjustified.

Sincerely,

Pauline Vaillancourt
Assistant Professor

PV/hs

cc.: Professors Johnston
              MacPherson
              Balthazar
              Malloch
              Wallerstein

Things grew even murkier by October. Dean Vogel informed Professor Vaillancourt that the tapes had not yet reached him, and were therefore still in the possession of Professor Johnston. One is inescapably reminded of the duel over the Presidential Tapes in the infamous case of Mr. Archibald Cox vs. Richard M. Nixon. The reader might well ask how it is the Dean alleged that Professor Johnston still had the tapes when he re-affirmed again that he had already sent them to Dean Vogel? (Johnston to Vaillancourt, October 19, 1973: "They are no longer in my possession. I have sent them to Dean Vogel at McGill.") And why pass the buck to Professor Johnston?

Tapes, tapes, where are the tapes . . .?
By October 29 McGill veterans got a strong whiff of something rotten in Montreal . . . Dean Vogel and Dr. Savage both signed the reply to Professor Vaillancourt, leading the cynical to scent an odour of collusion. It also appeared that Dean Vogel had the tapes all along, and was stalling when he first claimed that they "were being erased" and then claimed that Professor Johnston still had

them in his possession. The convoluted justifications in the Savage-Vogel letter had no basis, for Dr. Savage himself (Document #40) emphasized that authority over the disposition of the tapes rested with the Committee of Enquiry — destruction of the tapes (i.e., of Professor Wallerstein's final arguments) was in violation of Professor Johnston's permission to release a transcript of the summation. Dr. Savage and Dean Vogel were acting without authority. Why? And why the tone of veiled menace?

DOCUMENT 36

29 October 1973

Professor Pauline Vaillancourt
Department of Political Science
McGill University
P.O. Box 6070
Montreal 101, Québec

Dear Professor Vaillancourt,

This is in answer to your letter of 26 September. Since you address us jointly, and since the matters you raise relate to the joint agreement between the two of us, it is appropriate that we answer you in a joint letter. You raise two questions, (1) the disposition of the tape recordings that were made of the hearings before the Committee of Enquiry chaired by Professor D.L. Johnston, and (2) your wish to have a transcription made of part of one of the tapes.

It was not our intention that the tape recordings should constitute a permanent record of the proceedings before the committee. This is clear from the fact that our agreement contemplated the possibility that there would be no tape recordings at all. In our agreement the committee was given authority to require that all or part of the proceedings be recorded *for its own use*. The committee exercised that authority to require that all the hearings be recorded, but we do not see that the exercise of that authority alters the fact that the recordings were to be for the committee's use. Once the work of the committee was completed, and the committee itself ceased to exist, the purpose of the recordings was exhausted, and the mere fact that the recordings continue to be in existence for a period of time after the demise of the committee does not in our view mean that the recordings are to be treated henceforth as some sort of permanent record. The permanent record of the committee's review of your case is the long report it issued. We cannot imagine what relevance the tape recordings could have to future consideration of your appointment at McGill, unless it would be to reconsider the validity and correctness of the Johnston committee's decision. This is not a review that we wish to see undertaken, and we cannot think that you would either. In fact, the decision of the Johnston committee has been reviewed, and its recommendations confirmed by the Dean of Arts, the Vice Principal (Academic), and the Board of Governors at McGill.

We have discussed this matter together and are agreed that the proper disposition of the tapes is that they should be erased, and the tapes themselves returned for other use to the Instructional Communications Centre at McGill, which supplied them originally. Given the status of the tape recordings in our agreement, we consider this the only appropriate disposition of the tapes. We can see now that we should perhaps have made this whole matter clearer to the committee, to the Department of Political Science, and to you early in June, so that this issue could never arise. If we had fully clarified the matter, then Professor Johnston would undoubtedly have erased the tapes before returning them to McGill, and that would have been the best solution.

Our reason for coming to the agreement we did concerning the tapes was to avoid having the tapes (and matters relating to the tapes) become an extension of the dispute that was being adjudicated. We wanted the dispute concluded with the report of the committee. The very existence of this correspondence with you now indicates to us that our original agreement was wise.

(2) Given the status of the tape recordings in our agreement, we are not prepared to entertain the possibility of material being transcribed from the tapes for other than the committee's own purposes. We can understand that you might wish to have a memento of the summary argument of your academic advisor, and are sorry that we cannot accommodate your wish. But strictly speaking Professor Wallerstein's argument was directed to the deliberations of the committee; the committee has deliberated and made its decision, and given the nature of the decision, we must suppose that Professor Wallerstein's argument was not without effect.

Yours sincerely,

D. C. Savage, Executive Secretary
Canadian Association of University
 Teachers
66 Lisgar Street
Ottawa, Ontario

Dean R. Vogel, Faculty of Arts
McGill University
Montréal, Québec

Now is the hour of the mystery-story addict. Is the "our" a reference to McGill University and the CAUT? Is the "our" Dean Vogel and Professor Savage alone? If so, in what capacity, since neither has authority in either capacity to make the decisions contained in this letter. Then note "to avoid having the tapes (and matters relating to the tapes) become an *extension of the dispute.*" What on earth can the reference be to "an extension of the dispute"? We can think of two possible referents: (1) resumption of the proceedings in the Quebec Labour Court and (2) the question of "affirmative bias," *i.e.,* both testimony and Professor Wallerstein's case for "affirmative bias" presented in the final summation. If the tapes were to be subpoenaed there existed the excellent possibility that all the damaging testimony (to Political Science) would become part of the public record. Obviously, part of the deal that led to the Committee of Enquiry in the first place was to escape the dangers to McGill of the proceedings in the Quebec Labour Court. However:

We can understand that you might wish to have a memento of the summary argument of your academic advisor, and are sorry we cannot accommodate your wish. But strictly speaking Professor Wallerstein's argument was directed at the deliberations of the committee; the committee has deliberated and made its decision, and given the nature of the decision, we must suppose that Professor Wallerstein's argument was not without effect.

Note that this refusal is on the part of Professor Savage and Dean Vogel. Professor Johnston had written:

> I have written to Dean Vogel today to tell him that I would have no objection to the relevant portion of the tapes being turned over to you so that you may have a written copy of the relevant remarks.

The reader is reminded of item (h) in Document #32 (Savage to Vogel) that stipulates "that the parties would be requested to make a final summary, if they so wish, which would be presented simultaneously in writing at the close of all testimony." That final summary of Professor Wallerstein's must have been quite a final summary! "We must suppose that Professor Wallerstein's argument was not without effect" *indeed*! We shall return to the mystery of the purloined final summation. For the present, we shall only remind the reader of the truly outrageous action that was being taken (Vaillancourt to Vogel and Savage, Document #35):

> I was very surprised when I was informed recently that the chairman (Professor Johnston) had sent the tapes to Dean Vogel . . . It seems to me that the Dean is a very inappropriate choice as he has functioned as the Department's representative during the jointly initiated (CAUT and Dean Vogel) inquiry . . .
>
> I must also question the somewhat arbitrary decision made by yourselves in consultation with Professor Malloch that I not be allowed to make a typed copy of Professor Wallerstein's final arguments during the inquiry. I am most surprised about your decision since when I discussed this matter with Professor Johnston, in Professor Waller's office the evening of June 29, 1973, no objections were raised by Professors Waller and Mallory, and Professor Johnston agreed to send me a copy in the near future . . . I believe his decision (and the department's acquiesence) was based in part on his understanding that Professor Wallerstein and I were functioning under severe restraints of time and staff, since we had no special budget at our disposal for this . . .
>
> I must reject your suggestion that my having this text typed from the tapes would set a precedent for making other portions of the proceedings public. There is, it seems to me a great difference between testimony, especially confidential testimony, and our final arguments. It was my understanding from the very beginning (June 11, 1973) that none of this former material was to be made public.

Professor Vaillancourt was *not* requesting access to the confidential testimony on the tapes, only to her promised typescript of the final summation. We must therefore conclude that it is the final summation presented by Professor Wallerstein that Dean Vogel and Professor Savage are determined shall never greet the public eye. (Although at the time Professor Vaillancourt wanted the presentation for herself, and did not intend that it should be made public.) What could the final summation contain that it should be repressed?

Professor Vaillancourt was not to be intimidated, and her impatience and a perfectly justifiable suspicion that *something* (not in her interest) might be in the offing at old McGill is expressed in Document #37.

DOCUMENT 37

DEPARTMENT OF POLITICAL SCIENCE

McGILL UNIVERSITY

November 6, 1973

Dr. D. C. Savage
Executive Secretary
Canadian Association of University
Teachers
66 Lisgar Street
Ottawa, Ontario

Dean R. Vogel
Faculty of Arts
McGill University
Montreal, Quebec

Dear Sirs:

There is no question in my mind that the tapes were meant for the use of the Committee. However, when Professor Wallerstein asked Professor Johnston in the first session about the ultimate disposition of the tapes, he replied that they would remain either in his possession or that of the C.A.U.T. There was no suggestion then that they would be destroyed. Had there been, we would have asked for a formal discussion then and there.

I surely do not want to reopen the case, and regard it as totally closed. However, it was and is my contention that the Department of Political Science systematically introduced non-academic considerations in matters relating to me. I hope this is now a matter of the past. If it is, the tapes will gather dust.

Should it not be so, and the mere decision by others than the Department that I be reappointed is not sufficient to reassure me, then in any future situation the tapes would represent the best possible evidence of my contentions to any future body considering any future case.

They would, to be sure, not be my only resort. Both Professors Johnston and Wallerstein took detailed notes. But such notes, as Mr. [Archibald] Cox was reminding us all two weeks ago, are second-best testimony.

It seems to me that it is not merely the right, but the moral obligation of the C.A.U.T. to keep the tapes and that destruction of such testimony would constitute an abrogation of this duty.

Please remember it is the C.A.U.T. and not I that would still be in a position in the future to determine whether or not the tapes would in fact be relevant to any matter then at hand.

As to the matter of having a copy of Professor Wallerstein's final arguments, my case rests on Professor Johnston's word that he would provide me with a transcript of this material.

Sincerely,

PAULINE VAILLANCOURT
Assistant Professor

DOCUMENT 38

20 December, 1973

Professor Pauline Vaillancourt
Department of Political Science
Leacock Building
McGill University
P.O. Box 6070
Montréal H3C 3G1, Québec

Dear Professor Vaillancourt:

With regard to your letter of November 6th, 1973 concerning the disposition of the tape recordings that were made during the hearings before the Committee of Enquiry chaired by Professor D.L. Johnston, we do not feel that your letter raised points that had not been made in your earlier letter of September 26th, 1973 and answer in our letter of October 29th, 1973. We never considered it a function of the hearings to generate a body of potential evidence that might be drawn on in some hypothetical future hearing. The tapes have been erased, and the reels of tape have been returned to the Instructional Communications Centre at McGill.

Yours sincerely,

Donald C. Savage
Executive Secretary, CAUT/ACPU
66 Lisgar Street
Ottawa K2P 0C1, Ontario

R. Vogel
Dean, Faculty of Arts
McGill University
P.O. Box 6070, Station A
Montréal H3C 3G1, Québec

PV/hs

In Document #37 Professor Vaillancourt's suspicions have clearly been fully aroused:

> I surely do not want to reopen the case, and regard it as totally closed. However, it was and is my contention that the Department of Political Science systematically introduced non-academic considerations in matters relating to me. I hope this is now a matter of the past. If it is the tapes will gather dust.

Document #38:

> The tapes have been erased, and the reels of tape have been returned to the Instructional Communications Centre at McGill.

So much for trusting to the "honour of gentlemen". All that remains of the final summation is:

> Both Professors Johnston and Wallerstein took detailed notes. But such notes, as Mr. [Archibald] Cox was reminding us all two weeks ago, are second-best testimony. (Document #37)

In Document #37 Professor Vaillancourt indicates that she thinks a conflict of interest exists: that is, she is indirectly asserting that Dr. Savage and Dean Vogel are acting in the interests of McGill University — and insofar as Dr. Savage is not a professor at McGill but Executive Secretary of CAUT, why is he mindful of McGill's long-term interests? Who, after all, is the aggrieved party?

In Document #40 Dr. Savage argues very convincingly that he never had the right in the first place to agree with Dean Vogel to the erasure of the tapes — that neither had the right to destroy the record. Dr. Savage concludes by saying "The tapes were most emphatically *not* erased, as you wish to infer, because we objected to one of your subsequent arguments for their retention.". Indeed? Then why all the references to the possible "extension of the dispute", and why ignore Professor Johnston's promise, which he made in good faith?

Document #39, Vaillancourt to Savage and Vogel, brings us to the heart of the central issue in the "Battle for the Tapes." The tape-recorded transcripts (which contained not only all of the Political Science faculty's testimony but the devastating cross-examination by Professor Wallerstein) *could have been used in a second confidential hearing* involving CAUT, should one have ever occurred. The principle involved here is *not* to make the assumption that a purge once defeated, will not be attempted a second time; that the second time the offending department will not have covered its tracks much more cleverly; that Professors who have suffered an attempted purge deserve continued protection in the event of further unjust treatment. A precedent of great importance had been set, but the tapes might have been needed to implement it. Dr. Savage preferred to placate McGill University — at the expense of Professor Vaillancourt's future. In Document #39 this issue is raised and clarified, although it will remain in future to *win* the protections demanded by Professor Vaillancourt.

DOCUMENT 39

February 7, 1974

Dr. Donald C. Savage
Executive Secretary, CAUT/ACPU
66 Lisgar Street
Ottawa K2P 0C1, Ontario

Dean R. Vogel
Faculty of Arts
Dawson Hall
McGill University
P.O. Box 6070
Montreal H3C 3G1, Quebec

Dear Dean Vogel and Dr. Savage:

I am most dismayed at your having erased the tape recorded transcripts of the hearings of my case before the Committee of Enquiry. Your December 20, 1973 letter appears to indicate that you did not retain the tapes because you objected to my argument that the tapes could hypothetically be of value in future proceedings concerning my status at McGill.

Your erasure of the tapes is in clear violation of standard C.A.U.T. procedure since according to the C.A.U.T. Handbook (Sept. 1973; "Guidelines Concerning C.A.U.T. Investigational Procedures", page 68).

When an *ad hoc* committee is discharged, all documents relative to the case it has investigated shall be filed under confidential cover with the Executive Secretary of the C.A.U.T.

Your action in this matter is a blatant disregard of my rights as established under C.A.U.T. guidelines. In addition, your action may jeopardize any case I might wish to make should future investigations of my status at McGill be required.

Sincerely,

PAULINE VAILLANCOURT
Assistant Professor

PV/hs

cc: Professor Johnston
    Professor Wallerstein
    Professor Malloch

DOCUMENT 40

CANADIAN ASSOCIATION OF UNIVERSITY TEACHERS
ASSOCIATION CANADIENNE DES PROFESSEURS D'UNIVERSITÉ

March 18, 1974

Professor Pauline Vaillancourt
Department of Political Science
McGill University
P.O. Box 6070
Montreal
H3C 3G1

Dear Professor Vaillancourt:

I have a copy of your letter of 7 February addressed to Dean Vogel and myself jointly. I am not consulting him in my reply because I do not believe that as sponsors of the Committee of Enquiry we have anything further to say concerning the matter of the tapes. But since you speak in your letter of February 7 specifically to matters that concern CAUT, I want to reply in my capacity as Executive Secretary.

Your reference to the Guidelines concerning CAUT Investigational Procedures is not pertinent, since the committee in your case was not an ad hoc investigating committee of the sort governed by those guidelines; in fact it was not a CAUT committee at all. This is not a quibble over titles, but a matter of capital importance. The real authority of the Committee chaired by Professor Johnston lay in the fact that it was neither a committee of the University which had decided not to renew your appointment, nor a committee of the Association whose purpose is to champion the cause of the professoriat, but a committee authorized by both McGill and CAUT to conduct an independent hearing and to bring down a decision.

I do not accept that CAUT's actions in this matter have in any way disregarded your rights. Rather I would say that CAUT, in securing such a hearing for you, very clearly established your right to a proper consideration for the renewal of your appointment. As to the specific reasons for erasing the tapes, I consider that these were set out in the letter of 29 October from Dean Vogel and myself. The tapes were most emphatically *not* erased, as you wish to infer, because we objected to one of your subsequent arguments for their retention.

Yours sincerely,

Donald C. Savage
Executive Secretary

cc. A. Malloch
    R. Vogel

Mysterious Proceedings: Possible Solutions

What is the real difference between a faculty association and a faculty union? It is that for the faculty union no conflict of interest results from the necessity to serve two contradictory sets of interests. The faculty union explicitly recognizes a basic conflict of interest between professor and university: one is the employer and the other an employee. A syndicate exists to protect the interests of employees against the abuses of the employers. Not so with an "association", to which administrators may belong and in which the interests of faculty and university are implicitly assumed to be the same — hence the contradiction. We mentioned Dr. Savage, not to suggest that he behaved with malice, but to suggest our suspicion that he was caught in a contradiction: on the one hand, not to offend McGill or let any proceedings ensue from the Vaillancourt case that would deter other universities, in future, from abiding by CAUT policy and, on the other hand, Professor Vaillancourt's interests in having access to the explosive information contained in the tapes.

> The CAUT Policy Statement on Academic Appointments and Tenure makes provision for committees of enquiry agreed to jointly by the AF&T Committee and by the university concerned. On several previous occasions AF&T has proposed to universities that such a committee would be a fair and reasonable way to resolve a dispute, but until last spring no university had the audacity to agree. CAUT hopes that the example of McGill, in a case which appeared to have some of the ingredients of a *cause célèbre*, will persuade other universities to adopt this method of settling disputes over academic appointments.[1]

Of course, we know that "audacity" does not account for McGill's decision; desperation might be the more accurate designation. Neither McGill nor CAUT wanted proceedings continued in the Quebec Labour Court; McGill for obvious reasons (made even more acute by the findings of the Committee of Enquiry), Dr. Savage, on behalf of CAUT, reasoning quite probably that if such proceedings were to be continued, future recourse by other universities to the CAUT's arbitration scheme would be jeopardized — and indeed, it is a good scheme within the logic of a faculty association, infinitely preferable to the normal star chamber proceedings conducted through university channels.

What is offensive in the exchange of letters over the tapes is the implicit assumption which Dr. Savage seems to have made that Pauline Vaillancourt is not "one of the boys" and cannot be trusted to refrain from further attacks upon McGill. This assumption, if it indeed was operative, was most unwise to make, as the matter of the tapes was a last straw, a final proof that professional courtesy is not extended to radical women. If Pauline Vaillancourt had felt that prosecution of McGill was necessary, she would have continued with her legal proceedings. After long consideration, she chose the CAUT option. Her choice was dictated by her desire to clear her *professional* reputation.

---

1. "Committee of Enquiry Settles Dispute at McGill", *C.A.U.T./A.C.P.U. Newsletter*, November, 1973.

Was Dr. Savage reflecting or yielding to the McGill "old boy" prejudice when he treated her so shabbily in the affair of the tapes? He was constrained to protect McGill in order to protect CAUT, but he had no call to violate Professor Johnston's promise; to do so in obvious collusion with Dean Vogel; or to write letters that contain rather vague but unpleasant insinuations. In this instance, whose interests were being served? Everyone's interests *except* those of Professor Pauline Vaillancourt.

Dean Vogel, on the other hand, was quite obviously behaving just as a Dean of Arts and Science should behave. Dean Vogel was middle level management of McGill University and his first loyalty (particularly since the Committee of Enquiry found in Professor Vaillancourt's favour) must be to the University. While controlling Pauline Vaillancourt seemed to be what concerned Dr. Savage, Dean Vogel was looking out for McGill. *Question:* in the course of looking out for McGill, what do the tapes contain that he was so eager to see destroyed? We are sure that Dean Vogel would go to his grave before giving out such information, so we will rely upon content analysis and educated guessing.

In the first case Dean Vogel does not want the record of the Committee of Enquiry made public, *ever!* The publication in the *McGill Free Press* of the transcript of the meeting between Professor Vaillancourt and the Committee on Promotions, Rehiring and Tenure was sufficiently devastating — and in that case the Political Science professors had striven energetically to say as little as possible. What *confidential* testimony would look like very nearly overwhelms the imagination! Secondly, Dean Vogel did not want the testimony, so damaging to McGill, available in any legal proceedings that Professor Vaillancourt may deem necessary to continue. Well and good — these concerns were fully understood when the CAUT procedure was accepted; Professor Vaillancourt never requested a copy of the confidential testimony. She raised the issue of the value of the record in the event of further abuses at McGill, very likely, while trying to fathom: *why* the refusal to honour promises made to her and assented to by all parties? It is not unlikely, given McGill, that she began to suspect that something was up, and raising the legal question was the equivalent of a fishing expedition — that turned out to be a frustratingly successful fishing expedition.

Professor Vaillancourt was really protesting the refusal to provide a transcript of the final summation — to which she had a right and which she had been promised. She must have asked herself what we now ask: why was the final summation not made available to her? Could it be that the final summation, if made public, could be as damaging as the raw testimony? In this case one must consider both the general public and the McGill public: for what may be insignificant or abstract to the outsider may be pregnant with meaning to the insider, to those knowledgeable of the peculiar sociology of McGill University. Therefore we submit the following hypothesis: that the final summation presented by Professor Wallerstein was a powerful exercise in demonstrating and documenting "affirmative bias" on the part of the Political Science Department — that is, the practice of class prejudice, sexism and political hostility that culminated in a gross violation of Professor Vaillancourt's professional rights. Such disclosures would seriously undermine the "old boy" and extremely unprofessional hiring and promotion procedures at McGill and encourage who knows how many other junior professors to rebel!

Circumstantial evidence in favour of our hypothesis will be discerned in the Report of the Committee of Enquiry. Note Section VI. *Bias.* The Committee is troubled, and calls Dr. Savage as Executive Secretary of CAUT to testify as to the meaning of bias and inconsistency. The Committee comments: "While the statement was extremely helpful it still leaves the meaning of bias in some doubt." Then, in Item #32 the Committee, in Byzantine language, states:

> We are clear that bias it not the opposite of integrity or good faith, and that recognition of integrity and good faith does not establish lack of bias. We are fully persuaded of the integrity and good faith of the DC [Departmental Committee], but find this irrelevant to the question of bias.

In short the Committee never does solve the question of just what bias is. What is at issue, obviously, are the arguments put forward in Professor Wallerstein's final summation but which seem to appear in condensed form in Item 33 of Document #34:

> We considered an affirmative theory of bias put forward by Professor Vaillancourt. She alleged that shortly after she was initially invited to consider joining the Mc-Gill Department, reports from Berkeley suggested that she was a political activist and a non-conformist; that a climate of opinion developed over her time at Mc-Gill with her association with dissenting causes in several discernible stages; that it culminated in a desire on the part of more traditional oriented members of the Department to eliminate from the Department someone who was not congenial, who challenged many of the customs that had developed in the Department over the years and whose own political views were associated with minority causes; that the desire to sever crystallized in the quiet and polite decision to let Professor Vaillancourt go at the first convenient opportunity.

The Committee concludes:

> We found no sufficient evidence to support this affirmative theory of bias.

The reader will recall that Professor Johnston is a member of the Faculty of Law, University of Toronto. Note that Item 33 does not say that *no* evidence was found, but that "no *sufficient* evidence" was found. Given the Committee's admission that "The allegations of bias were the most difficult for us to assess, since the definition of bias is quite unclear" the Committee cannot be faulted for caution. [2]
Furthermore, to have found *sufficient* evidence to support an affirmative theory of bias would immediately have moved the report from the realm of professionalism to the realm of politics in a case that contained explosive elements in the Quebec situation. We again stress that we do not fault the Committee for displaying caution: we suggest that the latitude of admissible evidence may vary under varying conditions.
Indeed, the Committee retreats from "affirmative bias" but *not* from the key issue, to their deliberations, of professional rights:

> 34. We note however that the Chairman in his submission of the Department's case put the question whether it was not proper for a department to use a probationary period to decide not to renew a member "who seems to create so many problems and difficulties" in the department?

---

2. Bias: the intrusion of sex, class, ethnic, racial and political prejudice in the evaluation of a scholar's work, or upon consideration for renewal of probationary appointments or promotion and tenure; evaluation on professionally inappropriate considerations. Might one suggest that the Ethics Sub-Committee of the C.S.A.A. might undertake to discuss and issue a policy statement on the question of bias — for is not academic freedom and its protection *in spirit* an ethical question in the last analysis?

This depends on the kind of problems and difficulties. Scholarship often makes problems. A new style of scholarship introduced into a department where a different style has prevailed is very likely to disturb the smooth congeniality of the department. But the claims of congeniality must not be allowed to outweigh the claims of scholarship, and a problem of this kind is an entirely improper reason for non-renewal.

Hooray for the Committee of Enquiry! Item 34 should be inscribed in gold over the Roddick Gates. The author is reminded of Professor Solomon (who is Jewish) telling her he could not understand why she was shocked when he told her that he disliked Jewish career women, and most especially Jewish women like Pauline Bart, and that was good and sufficient reason not to hire her, SSU or no SSU! Alas, we have no reason to believe that this inscription will ever adorn a bronze plaque at McGill to guarantee a magna carta of academic freedom in the jungles and swamps and "old boy" networks.

The Committee of Enquiry had done its duty, fulfilled its mandate, vindicated Professors Vaillancourt and Wallerstein, set precedents which if followed might bring relief to dissenting junior faculty at McGill. The Committee can only be judged "good men and able scholars". It is not for the Committee to reform McGill: cleaning up McGill must be done by the McGill community.

It is in the "Battle for the Tapes" that the inferential evidence for "affirmative bias" (and its instant recognition by knowledgable McGill faculty) is found — and that it was *exactly* the persuasive and documented argument for affirmative bias that McGill wanted covered-up, and to that end refused to release Professor Wallerstein's concluding statement.

PART 6: The Purge

*But in the West, the intellectual and
moral rule of the bourgeoisie had won the
consent of the great masses of citizens
to a liberal State form, so that here
'the State is merely a frontal trench, an
advanced line of defence, and behind it
there is a powerful fortress of concrete
pillboxes.' This 'fortress' consists in
the ways of living and thinking, the
ambitions, morality and habits which
most people have absorbed as they adapt
themselves to the prevalent* Weltanschauung *diffused by the bourgeois ruling
class; and this is what makes civil
society' resistant to catastrophic eruptions
arising out of immediate economic
causes . . .' Hence, in western liberal-
bourgeois States, open warfare must give
way to a war of positions . . .*
*The task of the intellectuals
organically associated with the working
class is to win over the traditional intellectuals to socialism; then they must together transform the new conception of
the world into 'common sense . . .'*

Giuseppe Fiori, Antonio
Gramsci, Life of a
Revolutionary[1]

Introduction

By 1974 the call for socialism in Quebec *and* the call for independence
were no longer "extremist". These feelings entered the general consciousness
of the working class — and *this* is the ideological essence of the task of the
intellectuals organically associated with the working class in politics. For it

---

1. Guiseppe Fiori, *Antonio Gramsci, Life of a Revolutionary*, NLB (London) 1970 pp. 242, 245.

represents the defeat of the "prevalent *Weltanschauung* diffused by the bourgeois ruling class" that makes civil society resistent to catastrophic eruptions arising out of immediate economic causes. If we trace the evolution of this remarkable victory in the realm of politics we cannot avoid seeing the role of Francophone intellectuals — in the trade unions, in the schools, in the student movement — who have in less than ten years organically associated themselves with the working class and won so many of the traditional intellectuals to socialism. Quebec is a living, contemporary model of Gramsci's theory of the role of intellectuals in the conditions presented by mature capitalism and bourgeois democracy.

In this perspective we may understand that McGill plays a very special and unique role. It is perhaps unique in Canada (or in North America for that matter) because it has been from the day it was founded a fortress in defense of colonialism in Quebec (first for the British Empire and then for English Canada and the United States); McGill is at the very heart of the moral and intellectual colonization of French Quebec so necessary to the colonizers and their agents, the privileged Anglo managerial class. Consequently, McGill's very nature places it in a hostile and antagonistic relationship to the vast majority of the Quebec people.

Therefore, much that is mystifying about McGill is illuminated when we realize that McGill in Quebec is, in essence, a fortress under siege. The external threat to McGill, which has continued unabated since *Opération McGill* (although the forms and actors may change), is reflected in the *internal* "fortress mentality" of the whole institution. McGill cannot afford real liberalism; it has insufficient political manoeuvring space to practice co-optation; but above all, McGill cannot afford to have a fifth column within it — for what is more dangerous to a fortress under siege than to fall because of betrayals from within? Top administrators had drawn their lessons from Stan Gray — a Stan Gray was not to be permitted to flourish a second time. McGill is the principle "fortress of concrete pillboxes" that stands behind the "liberal state form" in order to secure for the Anglo minority "rule by intellectual and moral hegemony"

> Lenin himself, Gramsci points out, stressed the importance of the cultural struggle, in opposition to the various 'economist' trends. He developed the theory of "hegemony' (domination plus intellectual and moral direction) as the complement to his theory of the State as force... Its significance was clear: domination (coercion) is one form of power, and historically necessary at a given moment; rule by intellectual and moral hegemony is the form of power which guarantees stability, and founds power upon wide-ranging consent and acquiescence. [2]

What had happened in the 1960's in Quebec was a successful assault upon the "hegemony' of the Anglo managerial class; the widespread undermining of the "rule by intellectual and moral hegemony" which was McGill's crucial role in colonized Quebec:

> [Gramsci's originality lies] in his argument that the system's real strength does not lie in the violence of the ruling class or the coercive power of its state apparatus, *but in the acceptance by the ruled* of a 'conception of the world' which belongs to the rulers. The philosophy of the ruling class passes through a whole tissue of complex vulgarizations to emerge as 'common sense': that is, the philosophy of the masses, who accept the morality, the customs, the institutionalized rules of behavior of the society they live in. The problem for Gramsci then is to understand *how* the

2. Fiori, *op. cit.*, p. 243

ruling class has managed to win the consent of the subordinate classes in this way; and then, to see how the latter will manage to over-throw the old order and bring about a new one of universal freedom.[3]

Gramsci answered the question of *how* consent is obtained by arguing that it first derives from the prestive and power which the dominant group enjoys "because of its position and function in the world of production." However ideological conquest is mediated:

by the whole fabric of society and by the complex of superstructures, of which the intellectuals are, precisely, the 'functionaries.' . . . What we can do, for the moment, is to fix the two major superstructural 'levels': the one that can be called 'civil society', that is, the ensemble of organisms commonly called 'private', and that of 'political society' or the 'State.' These two levels correspond on the one hand to the function of 'hegemony' which the dominant group exercises throughout society and on the other hand to that of 'direct domination' or command exercised through the State and 'juridical' government. The functions in question are precisely organizational and connective. *The intellectuals are the dominant group's 'deputies' exercising the subaltern functions of social hegemony and political government.*[4]

The intellectuals of McGill University had, since its founding, produced the ideologies (and the government intellectuals) by which Anglo moral and intellectual hegemony had been secured. McGill University, as an institution within the superstructure, served as the "deputy" of whatever economically dominant group held power, "exercising the subaltern functions of social hegemony". As we have seen, McGill was forced to the adoption of a thin veneer of "liberalism" by the late and rapid modernization of Quebec, but the period of "liberalism" was short lived, for the Quebec people, especially by the late 1960's, were rejecting the "conception of the world which belongs to the rulers" in favour of new conceptions, of their own making, increasingly formulating the interests of the "subordinate classes" in opposition to the rulers. It was for this reason that McGill was assaulted in *Opération McGill,* that it finds itself at war with the Francophone civil service, that *it cannot tolerate within itself* any opposition of an ideological or political nature and above all, cannot tolerate the existence of any allies of the "subordinate classes".

The internal nature and functioning of McGill cannot be understood in isolation from its external social and political relationship to Quebec. Within McGill itself we may discern reflections of the superstructural forms of civil and political society. The top university administration and the Board of Governors are the equivalent to the State, while the Senate, Deans and Department Heads correspond to the "deputies" charged with maintaining "moral and intellectual" hegemony of the dominant group. In this light we may understand why, by the spring of 1975, the three oppositional figures in the final scenes of our drama — Marlene Dixon, Pauline Vaillancourt and Immanuel Wallerstein — were all leaving McGill. From 1971 to 1973 all three had been engaged in a defensive war that had developed from the defeat of the confrontations of 1968-1970. The advanced line of attack — out and out firing of Dixon and Vaillancourt — had failed, Vaillancourt and Dixon winning re-appointment. Yet behind the "first line of attack" lay the Departments themselves, the fortresses *within* the fortress for the defense of ambition and habit by which the faculties had adapted

3. *Ibid.*, p. 238. Emphasis added.

4. Antonio Gramsci, *Selections from the Prison Notebooks,* edited and translated by Quintin Hoare and Geoffrey Nowell Smith, International Publishers, 1971, "The Intellectuals", p. 12. (emphasis added).

themselves to the "prevalent Weltanschauung diffused by the bourgeois ruling class". It would be this departmental "concrete pillbox" of prejudice, hostility and slander that would carry through the purge, the departments and the Administration having failed by "legal" and "liberal" means to rid themselves of these stubborn combatants.

The lessons ought to be very clear: there is more than one way to conduct a purge! When the majority of faculty are immoveably opposed to any genuine intellectual pluralism, when they are convinced that they are menaced by "socialism", when they feel threatened personally and professionally, their monopoly of power and influence gives them the greater balance of power in what is, in the nature of things, an unequal combat.

By 1975 the opposition had been driven out of the sacred groves of McGill. Repression and purge had indeed come to pass, but under the *appearance* of the "voluntary" withdrawal of the "foreign bodies" that had infected the body politic at Old McGill. This section sets out to show how a workplace can be turned into a "prison of the mind and spirit", how a purge can be conducted after legal attempts by "procedural means" have failed to discredit the target and justify the expulsion. It is an ugly and brutalizing process, that leaves its scars on all participants.

The Political Purge and Character Assassination

Both have stepped on lots of toes and have violated a basic if unmentioned rule in academic life that first be a member of the team, then say and do what you like . . . Many of the professional sociologists are rather defensive about their work, often because they are not sure of its validity or relevance. This has lead to expectation of conformity and a disinclination to take risks. Add to this the political and budgetary pressures a university faces, one can easily understand this predilection for conformity. But sociologists continue to insist they really would welcome true intellectual excellence. But they must recognize that such excellence comes from the turbulence of involvement, and an involvement refined by thought.

Professor Franz Schurmann to Professors Wallerstein and Ehrensaft, November 10, 1971

I am referring to the appointment offered to Mrs. Pauline Vaillancourt. I think you should know that Mrs. Vaillancourt has impressed several of us as a person much more interested in political agitation than in scholarship. She combines a rather unpleasant personality with a tendency to read political motives into every relationship between herself and the faculty, a tendency which of course contains its own self-fulfilling prophecy.

Professor Ernst B. Hass to Professor J.R. Mallory, June 6, 1969

In the greater number of cases of individuals purged in recent years the virulent personal and professional attacks against the integrity, decency, good sense and plain humanity of the individuals purged is almost never questioned. Every disgusting bit of second hand gossip, plain invention, and malicious slander is sucked up as if it were revealed truth, unquestioningly accepted as the "real" reason these "impossible" people were purged — and often destroyed, at least professionally. One speculates that this personal brutality and repulsive slandering is one of the roots of the growing hatred between liberals and radicals or Marxists. A famous victim of a purge wrote recently, in personal correspondence:

Other interviews, such as at_____, which turned me down, included political grillings. There, the president asked me about my "brand" of Marxism. When I wouldn't reply in a straightforward manner, he insisted that he had a right to ask questions of this sort. Presumably he needed the information to find out whether I would conduct myself as a "good Marxist" (or what was frequently called an "academic Marxist" on our job-seeking tour) rather than a downright "bad Marxist" (-Leninist!). In addition to questions of this kind, I was asked in a number of places by liberal faculty members about whether I would support *their* right to teach, presumably because Marxists are notoriously opposed to liberalism and liberal teachers. One would think that liberals were being purged and black-listed from campuses and not Marxists. [5]

As *Academic Roles and Functions* makes quite clear, one cannot be in political opposition and be a member of the team.

Where there exists conflict over basic goals and means of work the 'boat is rocked' and the 'team spirit' impaired. In periods of conflict, the basic power structure of the group rises clearly to the surface, cliques and coalitions are formed, polarization occurs along lines of disagreement, and the more powerful seek to contain or to expel the contending faction.

---

5. From a friend to the author.

The faculties in both political science and sociology are incapable of intellectual pluralism: they are far too defensive about their work, "because they are
not sure of its validity or relevance;" in the repressive milieu of McGill, they are
completely unprepared to take risks; in the frantic career-hustling that marks the
academic climber with little to recommend him but departmental power, the
obsessive mania for up-grading leads to an equal obsession with conformity as if,
by some alchemy, being socially "compleat" petty bourgeois professionals will
promote their achievement, or win them an envied place in the "old-boy" network.
The hunger for social acceptance, particularly within McGill, belongs in a novel
by Emile Zola — we cannot pretend to do it credit. Its result at McGill is a
milieu of such rigid and artificial social rectitude as to approach the heights of
parody, a veritable three-ring circus of parvenus from the lower petty bourgeosie
or upper working class striving with might and main, pipes and turtle-neck
sweaters, grey suits and swagger sticks to forget their origins, having "descended
on the known world from hunger, from vague and unwarranted ethnic origins."
It is an irony of our culture that the very rich and the very poor (or the once
poor who refuse to be ashamed of it) are free to be unconventional: they have
little to lose, and so enjoy their freedoms (albeit in different ways and at different costs). It is the petty-bourgeois, the parvenu, who must be, "like Ceasar's
wife, above reproach." And so we have a gallery of academic types: the Ersatz
Old Boys, the Intellectual Snobs, and the Social Snakes, the Social Politician,
the Coquettish Dragon Lady, and last but not least, the Culture-vulture, newly-
arrived, Bourgeois Manqué. Like all people nursing precarious pretensions, the
virulence of their insecurity (their subterranean fears of descending back into
vague and unwarranted origins) leads them to a level of personal viciousness and
malevolence whose brutality and cruelty is tyrannical.

It is a culture of insecurity, competition, individualism, pretension and
petty ambition:

> The petit-bourgeois: of all the products of capitalism, none is more unlovely than
> this class. Whoever does not escape from it is damned. It is necessarily a class
> whose whole existence is based on a lie. Functionally, it is exploited, but
> because it is allowed to share in some of the crumbs of exploitation that fall from
> the rich bourgeois table, it identifies itself with the bourgeois system on which,
> whether as a bank manager, small shopkeeper or upper household servant, it seems
> to depend. It has only one value in life, that of bettering itself, of getting a step
> nearer the good bourgeois things so far above it. It has only one horror, that of
> falling from respectability into the proletariat abyss which, because it is so near,
> seems so much more dangerous. It is rootless, individualistic, lonely, and per-
> petually facing, with its hackles up, an antagonistic world.
> (Christopher Caldwell, *Studies and Further Studies in a Dying Culture*)

Their fear and hatred of the working class, particularly of those most recently
risen from the depths, results in such mindless prejudice against working class
mannerisms, styles, even language, as to be very nearly indistinguishable from
their racism or their jingoistic liberalism. Racism, being not "nice" to parade in
public, is ritualistically denied even while enthusiastically practiced behind the
scenes (for example, Wallerstein was accused of attacking standards because he
would "lower standards to admit more leftists or Third World students"). Hatred,
loathing, and blind prejudice against anything working class is a fundamental
tenet of modern corporate liberalism. Middle-class liberalism is held as enlight-
enment against the beer-drinking fascist ignorant vulgar and violent working
class. The mythology of corporate liberalism in the university gives complete

license for this class hatred — and all the more, that so many professors have been creamed from the milk of the working class, turned into class collaborationist "professionals", stripped of their class roots (and their ethnic identities) the ex-working class professors are reduced to being viciously competitive parvenus. The social crimes of both Dixon and Vaillancourt were not only rooted in the fact that they were "uppity women" but that they were strong, outspoken and principled *working class uppity women* who refused to play the games of social pretension.

One characteristic that is generalized in the "most unlovely class" is the nasty trait of subservience to their "betters" (be it full professors or "old boys") and arrogant and petty "lording" it over their inferiors: students, faculty of lesser rank, lower class people, ethnic minorities, and above all, women. The full virulence of their insecurity and competitive mania may be freely vented upon women, without regard to the intemperance and general ugliness of the verbal degradation and violence that threats women as both punching bag and garbage dump for the petty frustrations, fears, and hatreds of these almost universally sexist men. Uppity women are intolerable principally because they refuse to act as if they are social or academic inferiors.

Of course, such punishment is not meted out equally to all academic women: there are "good niggers" and "bad niggers". What are the characteristics of the "good females"? First, that they never remind any male "colleague" that they *are* women, unwanted and unwelcome invaders and disruptors of the secure male preserve of the university department. Such women are expected to act as the men do (keeping children, menstrual cramps, household duties, the wife-role always out of sight) even though they will never be accepted into the "real" male world of "The Boys". These women are forever claiming that there is no discrimination against women; that women need only subserviently ape the pretentious manners, attitudes, and prejudices of the men in order to "make it" upward and onward in the professional world.

One such "good female" wrote a negative letter to the Committee of Enquiry attacking Professor Vaillancourt:

> I believe [Vaillancourt's] attitude towards students reflected her rigid ideological views of society which condemn students on the basis of status, income, language, etc. and not on the basis of academic merit. Because I am a female, I was fortunate enough to escape some of her more barbed comments.

In translation, this passage reads: "her rigid ideological views", i.e., that Professor Vaillancourt was a "radical" which by definition is to not be "one of The Boys". Professor Vaillancourt's "intolerable" actions in this line included such things as taking McGill Faculty Union petitions to faculty meetings to obtain faculty signatures; circulating petitions demanding that Gabriel Kolko be admitted to Canada; raising embarrassing political issues such as the fact that Political Science Department was a member of the Inter-University Consortium of Political Research at Ann Arbor, Michigan which was being offered money by the U.S. Navy. Professor Vaillancourt, in this instance, was able to force the Department to threaten to resign if such funding was not refused and also moved that a copy of the letter of resignation be sent to the other 200 members of the Consortium, many in foreign countries, drawing attention to the Navy funding and McGill's intention to withdraw. It is significant that a few months after this incident, Professor Richard Hamilton was named to replace Professor Vaillancourt as the representative to the Consortium from McGill.

203

The translation continues: "her rigid ideological views of society which condemn students on the basis of status, income, language, etc . . ." reads: Professor Vaillancourt's courses had reading lists with too many people like Jerry Rubin, Pierre Vallières, Charles Gagnon, Germaine Greer; the course lectures contained too many references to workers, the working class, students, women, Blacks, anti-colonialism and the Quebec situation. Professor Vaillancourt did not let her students "forget" that they were a privileged class in Quebec society, requiring them to reflect upon this. Furthermore, her courses were lively and unorthodox, so that leftist students directly took on the conservative students in classroom debates. This raised questions in the minds of uncommitted students, questions that would be taken into conservative classrooms, where the replies, more often than not, would be found wanting by students. Nor did Professor Vaillancourt let the Department forget that it existed in Quebec. Many members of the Political Science Department are fanatically hostile to the Quebec prople, above all to the notion of Quebec independence. The fact that Professor Vaillancourt was married to Jean-Guy Vaillancourt, a Quebec militant who had involved himself in the sacred groves of McGill (in the Dixon case), made her a living symbol of the "enemy within", a veritable agent of the feared Francophone horde whom they imagined to be perpetually massed at the Roddick Gates.

The concluding phrase, "Because I am a female, I was fortunate enough to escape some of her more barbed comments", translates as Vaillancourt is a "female chauvinist" who broke the basic rule that we "good niggers" among the women academics *never* violate: to avoid at all costs reminders that we are women. It must be admitted that Professor Vaillancourt *is* guilty of this transgression. Vaillancourt took seriously her duty to represent the interests of women (including students) in the Department. She condemned, for example, the Department's continued administration of scholarships that restricted awards by sex, race and religion. She raised issues and questions such as why more women were not admitted to the Department, why more women did not receive fellowships, and so forth. She included reading material and lecture content on the secondary status of women, the discrimination against them, and women's struggle to overcome the injustice of their "place". The other women in the Political Science Department, Professors Haskell, J. Stein, and Steinberg did not raise these questions, and feared and resented Professor Vaillancourt's raising them. The Department, and its female "good niggers", made it clear, repeatedly, that Vaillancourt was *not* the "sort of woman the Department needs or wants". This issue, of course, begins as early as the original Vaillancourt appointment. The reader will recall that Vaillancourt, while a graduate student, had been active in the Berkeley Political Science Woman's Caucus, which was part of the reason why Professor Haas so detested her. Professor Haas, it will be recalled, alleged that Pauline Vaillancourt "combines a rather unpleasant personality with a tendency to read political motives into every relationship . . ." while "I have just heard from Miss Barbara Haskell that she will be joining your department in September. I am familiar with Miss Haskell's work and have known her for some time, and I feel that you made an excellent choice. She provides a good example of all the personal and professional qualities which Mrs. Vaillancourt lacks.". "Bad nigger" and "good nigger". Sources at Berkeley report that Professor Haas felt that women were more dangerous than Blacks — presumably because there are more of them in direct service to white male supremacists. The fact that Professor Haskell is nowhere as professionally recognized as is Professor Vaillancourt and receives the *worst* teacher ratings in the Department never becomes an issue, nor is there any spurious question of an "unpleasant personality". The admirable Miss Haskell is *not* an "uppity nigger".

There are two documents (Document #16 and Document #23) that reveal the combined operation of class prejudice, sexism and political hostility. Taken together, they reveal another subterrannean process: the collective definition of the professional pariah. The reactionaries in both Political Science and Sociology, acting in effect as one social group, created among themselves a collective definition of both Professors Vaillancourt and Dixon as two women without any redeeming virtues: bogey-women who trampled on all that was near and dear, who create "tension" and anguish and who will not cease protesting against faculty "old boy" prerogatives to arbitrary and prejudiced judgement, so long defended at McGill. The tone and style of the collective definition is based on slander by innuendo. No proof is ever given, because none is needed: reference is made to "collective understandings" that have been reached through countless informal sessions in which these women have been the butt of gossip and vilification. The art of unsubstantiated vilification is highly developed by Professor Von Eschen.

> [In reference to unsubstantiated and alleged unfavorable student comments on Professor Vaillancourt's teaching] : Here again, Mr. Spiegel had told me in private conservation that the course he had taken from Professor Dixon was bad. I have reason to believe in the case of Professor Dixon at least, that Mr. Spiegel was not alone in saying on thing in conversation and another in a letter. (Document #16)

Of course, Professor Von Eschen does *not* mention that when course evaluations were determined by a Sociology Department survey supervised by Professor Larry Felt, Professor Dixon scored higher on all categories of evaluation than *any* other member of the Department! Nor does he refer to the high course evaluations for many of Professor Vaillancourt's classes. All that he means to do is use some nasty gossip he claims to have heard from a student to discredit all student evaluations, and by innuendo assert that both Professors Dixon and Vaillancourt are bad teachers, no matter what the evaluations show! However, he means to do more than that:

> If student views are going to be used, and they should be, the opinions of a *cross section* of students should be solicited and this should be done *prior* to renewal consideration time when students become pressured by those soliciting letters to change their views. (Document #16)

Professor Von Eschen, without proof, is accusing both Professor Dixon and Professor Vaillancourt of "pressuring" students to change their views. He has absolutely no evidence to back this up (because neither woman ever pressured any student into writing such letters). There is, however, a great deal of evidence, including Von Eschen's own letter, that students *were* pressured by reactionary faculty to "change their views."

> It is as important that political consideration not be used to force retention of an incompetent person as it is important that they not be involved in firing a competent one. Justice should be even-handed. (Document #16)

One cannot help but observe that for Professor Von Eschen to invoke "justice" is equivalent to his assertion that he is a "political radical." In the passage quoted above a pious liberal invocation is actually an accusation that "political consideration" was used to "force" the retention of "an incompetent person" (who could this be but Professor Dixon?) and that the same "force" was about to be used to retain the incompetent Professor Vaillancourt. The reader should keep in mind that Professor Von Eschen does not have professional accomplishments even approaching those of either woman he is asserting to be "incompetent."

If we now turn to Document #23 from Professor Bruneau we find the theme of teaching treated in an almost identical way to Professor Von Eschen's. First, accusations of "pressuring" students and exploiting radical students:

> I remember distinctly how a group of her students were mobilized, claimed to speak for all the students, and thereby exerted pressure on the Department for her renewal.

Professor Bruneau, of course, does not mention that this "group of her students" was nothing of the sort; it was the Political Science Students Association (PSA) once again protesting against the firing of a radical, just as they had in Stan Gray's case, and for the same reasons: the need for a critical political scientist to teach in the department. The attempt to discredit the students by suggesting that they are "mobilized" merely to defend Pauline Vaillancourt apes Professor Von Eschen's innuendoes — as if the PSA had not been fighting these issues since 1967!

> After the decision was made, a number of the 'silent majority' came to me and asked why Professor Vaillancourt had been retained as in their view she was an incompetent and unpleasant teacher.

Professor Von Eschen's "Mr. Spiegal" has now blossomed into a "silent majority." It would seem that Professor Bruneau finds the "silent majority" tactic as useful as did the ex-President of the United States, Richard M. Nixon. Yet all that demonstrates the existence of a "silent majority" is Professor Bruneau; and all the evidence he puts forward is his alleged collection of student complaint and gossip — as if every student with a grudge would not select a person like Professor Bruneau, ever-eager for the latest bad word. McGill students are vociferous complainers, particularly the conservative students, as great numbers of such letters regarding Professor Dixon may be found in the Departmental files, in the Dean's files and in the Principal's files. Yet, when a real "cross-section" of students is taken, as it was in Sociology, Professor Dixon received the highest ratings. In short, the pressuring of students and manipulation of complaints is a practice of the reactionary faculty, not the progressive faculty.

DOCUMENT 23

McGILL UNIVERSITY

16th November 1972

Professor Robert Vogel
Dean of the Faculty of Arts
McGill University

Dear Dean Vogel:

I am writing regarding the recommendation of our Committee on Tenure and Promotions in the case of Professor Vaillancourt and I would strongly encourage you to accept their decision. This Committee is composed of extremely good men and able scholars who are solely interested in improving the quality of our Department; I intend to remain at McGill for some time and thus have a vested interest in university affairs as well. I have seen how Professor Vaillancourt was able to extend her one year appointment to four years and am of course familiar with the case of Professor Dixon last year. I have known Professor Vaillancourt since 1964 when we were graduate students at Berkeley, and I assure you that I am writing not out of a feeling of malice but rather from a sincere desire to up-grade our Department.

Almost three years ago Professor Vaillancourt's contract was up for renewal and the Department was apparently intending to let her go. I remember distinctly how a group of her students were mobilized, claimed to speak for all the students, and thereby exerted pressure on the Department for her renewal. After the decision was made, a number of the 'silent majority' came to me and asked why Professor Vaillancourt had been retained as in their view she was an incompetent and unpleasant teacher. In short, the spokesmen for the group did not represent all the students although it is not possible now to ascertain what percentage they did speak for. In following years a great number of students have come to me (completely unsolicited, I might add) to complain about her performance in teaching and evaluation. I might mention that one of these students was one whom you coached in that television competition program. This year I am Honours advisor and during the first three weeks of school three students came and transferred out of Professor Vaillancourt's course as they felt it would be a waste of time. In short, regardless of how many letters you receive from students testifying to the excellence of her teaching I would suggest that you accept these with great reservations.

When we were graduate students at Berkeley I was quite close to Professor Vaillancourt and her husband. Since coming to Montreal, however, our relationship has deteriorated and I am somewhat at a loss to explain this as I have not been active politically either within the province or the university. However, it is undeniable that she has never sought to establish rapport with many members of our Department. As a colleague I find her intolerable as great tension arises in our meetings over relatively unimportant matters. I would like to see more of an academic community emerge at McGill, particularly within our Department, and I feel that this atmosphere would be impossible to achieve with her presence. I cannot remember when she last contributed anything constructive to the Department and her bringing a crying baby into meetings is an insult to our efforts. Her grading system has made a joke out of our desires to improve the image of the Department and the comments she has made in public to students about how she perceives McGill vis a vis other Montreal universities suggests she might be intending to sabotage our university. Professor Vaillancourt is at best negative for the Department, and it is extremely frustrating to consider the many qualified people that might be selected to replace her.

I therefore encourage you to accept the recommendation of our full professors. I would be happy to discuss these matters at your convenience.

Sincerely yours,

Thomas C. Bruneau
Assistant Professor
Dept. of Political Science

TCB:lb

The very fact that teaching, the least important professional criterion in judging scholarly competence, appears so often surely suggests that besides the collection or invention of "bad teaching stories" the men of Political Science and Sociology have very little to back up their constant accusations of "incompetence". As the Committee of Enquiry confirmed, it *was* all they really had, and it was suspect and not crucial in any case.

The heart of the Bruneau letter comes at the end, and merits an exercise in content analysis:

> When we were graduate students at Berkeley I was quite close to Professor Vaillancourt and her husband. Since coming to Montreal, however, our relationship has deteriorated and I am somewhat at a loss to explain this as I have not been active politically either within the province or the university.

One wonders how it is that Professor Vaillancourt, who seems to be an ordinarily pleasant human being to whom one could be "close", might suddenly turn into a monster at McGill?

The secret of the "deteriorating" relationship is quickly revealed:

> However, it is undeniable that she has never sought to establish rapport with many members of our Department.

Read "conformity with" for "rapport" in "our" Department — the "our" not inclusive of Professor Vaillancourt.

Professor Bruneau's most devastating condemnation, however, is the final crushing observation that:

> I cannot remember when she last contributed anything constructive to the Department and her bringing a crying baby into meetings is an insult to our efforts.

The controversial matter of Pauline and Veronique Vaillancourt was not viewed by all with Professor Bruneau's outrage. An example of how the majority of students, secretaries and non-sexist individuals in general viewed Veronique was written up in the *Montreal Star,* (November 15, 1972). The article described the both practical and loving way in which Professor Vaillancourt combined her professorial job with caring for her child in her McGill office.

> Students often pop into the office to see and play with the [baby] and fellow professors are friendly. 'There has been some opposition (says Vaillancourt) to the idea of bringing a baby to work regularly, but mostly it comes from men with stay at home wives. They don't know how to react . . .'. She insists that the idea of taking a baby to work 'is no longer revolutionary' and hopes that more mothers will follow her example.

We shall end our analysis of the processes of prejudice with a last passage noting the common themes present in the Von Eschen and Bruneau letters;

> I have seen how Professor Vaillancourt was able to extend her one year appointment to four years and am of course familiar with the case of Professor Dixon last year . . . I assure you that I am writing not out of a feeling of malice but rather from a sincere desire to upgrade our Department.

This book has amply documented that the allegations of incompetence made by the Sociology and Political Science faculties against both women were groundless. Both were not only competant, they were *more* competant than the individuals making the virulent character assassinations documented here. These individuals, quite obviously, were writing out of deliberate and habitual malice.

The object of this section on the hidden subterranean processes of the political purge is to make the reader aware of the social underpinnings that explain the otherwise bizarre and intemperate behavior of the entrenched faculty in these cases — and to show how the liberal recourse to "procedures" cannot be made to function unless there is a sincere commitment *to* those procedures and the norms and values of academic freedom and unbiased professional judgement upon which they are based. Actions *do* speak louder than words. The spokesmen of Political Science and Sociology were almost hysterical at the end, asserting their "integrity" and "honesty" and "sincere desire to up-grade *our* department" and "protect standards". Yet, the gentlemen "do protest too much".[6]

---

6. A footnote on the practice of sexism: Both Departments, Sociology and Political Science, have progressive men — none of whom have been subjected to the systematic abuse and character assassination that the two women have received. It must be pointed out that one man is a protégé of Charles Taylor and a "philosophical anarchist", who refused to support Pauline Vaillancourt because he "disliked her personally". A second man is a genuine progressive, but is tolerated in the Department because he keeps his politics largely off the campus (until recently, when he began to expose Canadian complicity in American militarism). His position is far from secure. In Sociology, Professor Spector was "one of the boys" until he defended Professor Dixon — which he did because he thought it absolutely unfair not to renew her contract after the Department had renewed his! Professor Spector is not "political" but he is honest and he does believe in fair-play. Since the 1971 re-appointment battle his life has been made virtually intolerable and he was very nearly denied a second renewal of his contract — in fact, renewal had actually been denied, only to be reversed the following morning in a move catching all by surprise. The Spector case led a certain Dean to remark that he (the Dean) knew very well that two standards were used in the Sociology Department. Sociology's last moment reversal may have been the result of the certain Dean's growing impatience with the botched record of purges in Political Science and Sociology. It is interesting to note htat after this instance (and one or two others that must remain unspecified) Professors Hamilton, Harold Waller and Von Eschen tried to "get" the Dean!! Professor Felt gave some support to Professor Dixon and then resigned from the Department. Professor Philip Ehrensaft, at first welcomed, was consequently expelled from the club. His life was one of constant frustration and increasing alienation. Professor Wallerstein was systematically and outrageously mistreated. The Sociology Department's mindless vendetta, in the long run, turned into a form of professional suicide — by 1976 the total number of departures and resignations may excede six!
Had these men defended a man, it is highly improbable that they would have become the object of such blind animosity. One speculates that they are not only viewed as "traitors" to *the* (our) Department but far worse, are viewed as betrayers of the prerogatives of male supremacy in the academic community. In this light (of men who were willing to defend a female colleague on principle) it is crucial for young academic women to know that Professor Gertrude Robinson, a protégé of Professor Richar Hamilton, has not been a noticeable friend to either Professor Dixon or Professor Vaillancourt. Professor Prudence Rains has been a genuinely warm and decent friend (although she is not active in the women's movement). Professor Rains has been made to suffer, as her memorandum will testify. We have already noted that the three women in Political Science, Professors Haskell, J. Stein and Steinberg, were hostile and active enemies of Professor Vaillancourt.

Chronology:

Department of Sociology, ANNUAL REPORT, 1971-1972:

> *Departmental policy should be formulated against the background of the recent history and immediate prospects of the discipline concerned, as well as the recent history and prospects of the particular department . . . society and perhaps university campuses in particular have been in turmoil, and sociology and other social science departments have frequently been at the centre of conflict and confrontation. Within this context, sociologists have been examining and re-examining their own present roles and future directions. At the one extreme, are those who hold to what perhaps might be regarded as a traditional view: that the main job of sociology is to know what is going on in society and to develop theories for explaining and understanding social systems, or aspects of them, while at the same time hoping to influence society for the better by being available for consultation, by studying things which are problematic to the society, and by teaching students. At the other extreme are sociologists of the new left, who often hold these traditional views in contempt, and argue that the business of sociology is to change the world, not just help it to change, sometimes with revolutionary fervour. In the middle, and probably less numerous than those at either extreme, are some sociologists who feel that more could be done which is of an applied or practical nature, without either abandoning the traditional view or espousing more activist philosophies. These conflicts within sociology are to some degree reflections of conflicts and strains which are in the society, but in any case are bound to be reflected in the life of any intellectually lively department . . .*
>
> David Solomon, Chairman
> Department of Sociology
> to Principal R.E. Bell,
> July 10, 1972.

November, 1971   The Dixon Re-appointment Battle.
Immanuel Wallerstein defends Dixon through some 72 hours of argumentation, supported by Spector and Ehrensaft. Last moment swing votes by Westley and Solomon decides for re-appointment as the battle threatens to become public beyond McGill. Von Eschen, Pinard and Hamilton polarize the Department, vowing never to forgive or forget.

September, 1972   Wallerstein becomes President of MFU.

October, 1972   Pauline Vaillancourt is informed that Political Science refuses to renew her contract on grounds on incompetence.

210

November 23, 1972 Von Eschen writes letter attacking Vaillancourt and Dixon to Harold Wallen, Chairman of Political Science.

November 29, 1972 Chairman Solomon writes to Chairman Waller attacking Vaillancourt, "I hope these comments will be helpful to you.".

January 16, 1973   Wallerstein and MFU take on appeal of the Vaillancourt case.

January 29, 1973   Maurice Pinard writes letter attacking Vaillancourt to Harold Waller.

January 30, 1973   Richard Hamilton writes letter to *Gazette* attacking Vaillancourt.

The Interregnum, 1971-1972:

> Where there exists conflict over basic goals and means of work the "boat is rocked" and the "team spirit" is impaired. In periods of conflict, the basic power structure of the group rises clearly to the surface, cliques and coalitions are formed, polarization occurs along lines of disagreement, and the more powerful seek to contain or expel the contending faction . . . The most common answer to the activist professor who sought freedom to pursue his own style of work and teaching was: get out of *our* university if you cannot submit or our departmental organization. The activist was rejected as a colleague and treated as an outsider, often as an enemy — a practice which almost guarantees creating an enemy where none might have existed before.
>
> Marlene Dixon, "Collegiality," *Academic Roles and Functions*

The Dixon reappointment split the department right down the line. As we shall see, there were those who were implacable in their opposition to Professor Wallerstein after his defense of Professor Dixon. Others attempted to bring him back into the fold in order to capitalize upon his professional standing in the great calling of "upgrading our department." The Right, like the Left, demands *proof* of reliability and loyalty. The proof demanded of Professor Wallerstein by the Right was that he repudiate Dixon. This he would not do.

The Right in the Sociology Department seemed incapable of comprehending that Professor Wallerstein was taking a principled stand. The plots that so haunted the Sociology faculty were figments of their own witch-hunting mentalities; positing a non-existent alliance based upon an equally non-existent joint membership in an "international socialist network" was the only way they could make sense of Wallerstein's refusal to take the easy, opportunist road of joining the general denunciation.

What would happen between 1971 and the spring of 1973 was that Dixon and Wallerstein would keep landing on the same side of controversies because of their fundamentally common commitments to academic freedom, intellectual pluralism and social theory.

The greater part of 1972 passed in what appears to be "recovery, reorganization and attempts to regain stability," in Solomon's words from the Annual Report. The quiet surface is deceptive. While Wallerstein still held hopes of being free to engage in actions in the light of his ideals, and even Dixon did what she could to mend fences, the Department was unprepared to easily forgive what they considered out-and-out betrayal, for their hatred of Dixon was greater than before. The *Insurgent Sociologist* had reprinted *Academic Roles and Functions* with a short covering statement gleaned from *McGill Daily* stories. Consequently, the *Insurgent* presented the Dixon re-appointment as a political victory against an attempted purge. The *Insurgent* had doubtless taken materials from the *Daily* as the quickest expedient in introducing the document, but the Sociology Department interpreted the *Insurgent's* introduction as the vilest perfidy on Dixon's part. In private, Solomon had told her he considered it proof of her "dishonesty." Of course, what had enraged the Sociology faculty was to have been exposed for an attempted political purge when they had made their midnight reversal *in order to circumvent exposure of just that fact!* Their attitude was doubtless so bitter because given the *Insurgent's* introduction, they might as well have fired her! Now they would have to live with her for three more years on top of the *Insurgent's* bad publicity. The truth was that the North American radical academic community took it for granted that Dixon would be purged, that any firing of Dixon would, on the face of it, *be* a purge, and was as astounded as Dixon had been at the outcome. Also, it was important at that time to score a victory, it had improved the morale and spirit of many people fighting purge actions at the same time. Furthermore, after the vile things that had been said and done for two years, and during the hearing itself, why did these men think that Dixon would collaborate in their cover-up? The least attack on themselves lead to frenzied vindictive behavior — but somehow they actually expected that Dixon would be "grateful," despite the virulent attacks on her work, her personality, her politics, even her qualifications to be counted as a female.

Furthermore, desires to pacify Wallerstein must also have entered into the swing-votes for Dixon's renewal. Wallerstein had "done his thing", and it was now time for him to shape up and begin "up-grading" the Sociology Department — for after all, that was why he had been hired. But Wallerstein did not "shape up", at least not in ways acceptable to many members of the Sociology Department. In the Spring of 1972 Wallerstein had agreed with David Solomon that an academic conference sponsored by the Sociology Department would be a useful thing to do — but whom did he agree to work with on such a conference? Professors Dixon and Ehrensaft! Did this perhaps portend things to come? Dixon as an isolated "extremist" was one thing: but Dixon and Wallerstein, and Spector and Ehrensaft — that was without question the makings of a deadly fifth column to undermind standards, seize "their" Department and threaten to destroy McGill and thereby society. The initial set of volunteers to work on Sociology's conference (Wallerstein, Dixon, Ehrensaft, Von Eschen and Robinson) was sabotaged by Von Eschen, who manoeuvered to block all the proposals suggested by Dixon, Wallerstein and Ehrensaft. The final blow took the form of a "Chairman's ukase" from Solomon, proposing to reconstitute the "conference committee" making Pinard a co-chairman with Wallerstein — in order to "control" him while securing Von Eschen's position. That, of course, put an end to the Conference. A petty little machination? Indeed, but one of an endless series of such shabby plots, effectively cutting away Wallerstein's freedom of movement. The whole parade of plots was designed to punish Wallerstein for refusing to ostracize or to repudiate Dixon — which is to say the heart of the junior faculty opposition.

To make matters more difficult, there were the graduate students. Early in 1971 (the renewal was not until November) Dixon had given up on working with graduate students. Any student with the temerity to work with Dixon was punished. It was said that grades from her courses were worth nothing, because they were too "political" and too "high", and therefore did not count (or counted negatively) when the student was evaluated for scholarships or assistantships or in the reading of area examinations. The students were often suspected of being part and parcel of the "Bolshevik menace"; they could be punished with low marks in other graduate seminars if they were known sympathizers of Dixon. [7] Dixon had responded by shifting towards undergraduate teaching: a professor was hardly a help to graduate students if effective barriers to their certification were erected because they wished to study with the resident Bolshevik. Such reprisals against students had begun in the SSU period, and continue to this day. The result of such abuse of students was that many flocked to Wallerstein, overloading his time, while Dixon and others tended to shift students over to him, or to appeal to him on behalf of a student — since only he had sufficient clout to protect them. This also cut into Wallerstein's space, for one does not write major books on the development of the capitalist world system if one spends the greater part of one's departmental time fending off repressions.

Then there was the matter of the reading of graduate student examinations. The Department invented a new procedure: there were to be three readers on area examinations — two readers expert in the area and a third from outside the area — in order "to protect standards". What this plot was designed to do was place one member of the reactionary faculty bloc in each student's committee, and thus control and monitor every academic function performed by a member of the opposition bloc.

Then there were the departmental "theory" seminars, presided over by Hamilton. It was at one of these seminars that Dixon was expected to come and "perform" for Hamilton and a small group of students who understood nothing about dialectical materialism. In this absurd situation Dixon decided to play "It's just little ole' me, boss (shuffle, shuffle)" to Hamilton's set-up. The reactionaries never did get on to Dixon's refusal to perform for them under any conditions, at any time. Others of the junior staff did perform, with much cursing under the breath and outrage in their hearts.

It was also at this time that the attacks against Professor Wallerstein for disrespecting standards, for being "soft" on standards where radicals were concerned began. As we shall see, these accusations are part and parcel of the assault on Wallerstein's professional reputation that the Department undertook in response to his defense of Professors Vaillancourt and Dixon and for his general political position within the University in defense of both academic freedom and

---

7. After Dixon's purge from Chicago, it is interesting to note, one student she had trained and supervised was refused certification until he agreed to remove her name from his doctoral dissertation.

(by necessity) of the right for radical thought to exist within McGill.[8] The mediocrities in the McGill Sociology Department did not dare to attack Wallerstein's own work but instead attempted to impugn his motives by attacking Dixon and Vaillancourt, saying if these no good women are defended by Wallerstein, then he must be soft on standards. Yet in "Radical Intellectuals in a Liberal Society" he is also quite clear about his position on the necessary quality of radical throught:

> This revolt by young people has also been, in many ways, intellectually liberating for the entire American left. It liberated the left from the cramping fears instilled in them by the anti-Stalinism of the cold war period. Analyses bearing the terminology and methodology of leftist thought have become intellectually respectable once again, at least in the academy . . .

> The first need for the American left is intellectual clarification of the ways in which American and world society can and will transform itself into a socialist society. The left, no doubt, has a sociological perspective that is different from that of the liberal center. It also has the outlines of a theory of historical change that is distinct from that of liberalism, which explains why, even when their ultimate objectives seem to converge, radicals seldom agree with liberals on the efficacy of their methods for promoting change. The left is far from having a clearly developed social theory that can account for the continued resiliency of the existing world social system, and clearly indicate the modalities of transforming it.

> There is much hard intellectual work to be done by the left. This intellectual work will never be done well if it is isolated from praxis, from involvement in a political movement and political action. But neither will it be done well if it is isolated from the pressure of competing intellectual ideas in the mainstream of intellectual debate.[9]

What divides Hamilton (the chief defender of "standards" in the Sociology Department) from Wallerstein is not respect or disrespect for standards, but Wallerstein's respect for radical and Marxist thought and Hamilton's hatred of *radicals;* Wallerstein's conception of the essential role of pluralism — competing ideas — and Hamilton's fanatical defense of his own brand of main-stream "empirical" sociology as the only legitimate sociology, that is, his hostility to pluralism, to any sociology other than his own.

It is equally absurd to accuse Professor Wallerstein of being "soft on radicals". *University in Turmoil*[19] contains a long political and tactical critique of the student movement: "Radical Intellectuals in a Liberal Society" is, in one sense, an extended critique of the left, specifically for tendencies towards "witch-hunting, adventurism and the cop-out". Nor can Wallerstein be accused of being "loved by the left". The Columbia S.D.S. was almost virulently critical of the role Wallerstein played during the Columbia strike and other segments of the left had attacked him in various ways. These attacks had not turned Wallerstein into a vengeful renegade; but they had made him critical of the left and careful in

---

8. At this point it is important to know that in his role as President of MFU, Wallerstein undertook the defense of any individual whose professional rights were being threatened, irrespective of intellectual orientation or political commitment. This was clear from the two cases subsequent to the Vaillancourt case in which he acted as academic counsel to an assistant professor in English and to an assistant professor in French. Neither were leftists or activists. Both had been shabbily treated because of the internal needs of the departmental mandarins. In both cases the academic freedom of the assistant professors had been grievously assaulted. Both cases eventually were won on appeal, but after long and arduous battle.

9. *Ibid.*, p. 471, 475-6.

10. Immanuel Wallerstein, *University in Turmoil.*

his relations with it. The left had not been "soft" on Wallerstein, and Wallerstein had not been "soft" on the left.

As for Dixon, she played a supporting role backing up Wallerstein's attempts to operate rationally in an irrational situation. If she had expressed any personal preferences for anything, its chances would have dropped to zero immediately. She was therefore in a position of detached cynicism salted with ironical amusement: she might not yet have made up her mind just what Wallerstein's "politics in the world" might be, but she knew what his "politics in the university" were (and she agreed with them, including the necessity for opposition and contradiction). The cant about "standards" made was absurd, a child could not help but observe the real fear of any genuine competition on the part of a person like Von Eschen or the defensive rejection of competing styles of sociology by Hamilton. Within his own field, Hamilton at least could legitimately claim to judge standards, but not the likes of Von Eschen. Von Eschen had been promoted to Associate on the promise of finishing a book within the year. Four years later there was no book. Solomon had barely published anything, and Westley's "classic" contribution was 20 years in the past. One could go on and on, but why? Why fall into the same nasty carping about non-existent intellectual concerns. The reactionaries were obsessed with political concerns, principally their retention of power in the Department, and neither cared about nor understood the intellectual debates that were raging in the great world outside.

Plots and Conspracies: 1971-1972

> For the majority of faculty the course of action has been liberal or radical rhetoric and reactionary action. For example, in the mid and late 1960's when students began to combine action and thought, when the forces of America's imperial expansion began to steadily sharpen the contradictions at home and in the Third World... academic liberals and many so-called "socialists" and "radicals" in the interests of their privilege, their economic security and their intellectual pretensions, became reactionaries: they became the enemies of university reform, apologists for repression, and sometimes the new ideologues of anticommunism...
>
> Marlene Dixon, "The Failure of the Sociology Liberation Movement, Revised," *The Human Factor,* Columbia, Spring, 1971

An alternative title for the controversial "Failure of the Sociology Liberation Movement" might well have been: *Portrait of McGill.* In the concrete pill-box of the McGill Sociology Department, events were occurring beginning in 1969 that would not come to full bloom until three years later in the United States. The essay at the time ruffled the feathers of untold numbers of "radical" academics who may be discovered today grilling Marxists on their attitudes towards "permitting" liberals to teach — as if it were liberals and not Marxists being purged and black-listed. A gift for Cassandra's prophecy carries no pleasure. Indeed, the gift has no mystical origins; its roots are in the peculiar nature of the McGill Department.

The mystery that we set out to solve is how and why do the progressives of 1968 transform into the opportunists and reactionaries of 1969-1970? The answer, of course, lies in the observation that opportunists always adopt protective covering. When it is convenient to be progressive, they toot for reform; when impolitic to toot for reform, they join the chorus of reaction. It is the course of such opportunists that we shall presently attempt to discern.

More is at stake than sheer politics, however, as the virulence of the character assassinations make clear. A second factor was that the events of 1969-1971 exposed the pretensions of individuals whose life breath is pretension and whose whole milieu — the academy — is governed by the shameless practice of hypocrisy and self-righteousness. Both of these academic characteristics, one cannot help noting, are typical of academics in power, amply demonstrated by the murderous or absurd posturings of a Kissinger or Moynihan.

As an aid to the reader in following the tortuous path of Sociology's plots and conspiracies, the following set of maps are provided. The key individual plotters will be Von Eschen, Hamilton and Pinard. The Rightist kingpins are Solomon and Westley. Key Leftists are Dixon and Wallerstein. Note how political definition and role shifts with the successive polarizations in the Department. The overall shift to the right was caused by the sharp swing to reactionary measures by the McGill Administration.

If we were to draw an approximate set of maps for 1968 they would look like this:

Progressive	Centre	Right
Von Eschen	Rosebourgh	Solomon (on Leave)
Pinard	(deceased)	
Felt (resigned)	Westley	
L. Goldberg (resigned)	Krohn (waiting for	
Spector	renewal and pro-	
(SSU)	motion)	

1969 Alignment

Progressive-Left	Centre	Right
Dixon	Von Eschen	Solomon
Felt (vacillating-resigned)	Pinard	Westley
Goldberg (vacillating-resigned)	Spector	Krohn
(SSU) (expelled and repressed)		

If we were to draw political maps of the Department for 1970 and 1971 they would look like this:

Pre-Dixon re-appointment Political Alignment (1969-1971)

Left	Centre	Right
Dixon	Wallerstein	Solomon
	(newly arrived)	Westley
	Ehrensaft	Hamilton
	(newly arrived)	Pinard
	Spector	Von Eschen
	Rains	Robinson (new)
		Carroll (new)
		Krohn

Political Polarization Post Dixon re-appointment (1972)

Left (Votes 5) (Left-Liberal Coalition	Right (Votes 8) (Right-Opportunist Coalition)
Pragmatic Leftists:	**Pragmatic Rightists:**
Wallerstein	Solomon
Ehrensaft	Westley
Honest Liberals:	**Dogmatic Rightists:**
Spector	Hamilton
Rains	Pinard
Marxist Leftist:	**Opportunists:**
Dixon	Von Eschen
	Krohn
	Robinson
	Carroll

Thus (after the expulsion of SSU and isolation of Dixon) the Department split along lines of support or non-support for Dixon's renewal. The resolution of the split would be the departure of the Left, the triumph of the Right, and the consolidation of the Second Von Eschen Plan.

To begin our drama: in 1968 both previously joint departments — Economics-Political Science and Anthropology-Sociology — were split into four separate entities. The "progressives" in Econ-PoliSci were in the Economics Department while Political Science, dominated by conservatives, began their vendetta against Vaillancourt. In Anthro-Socio a overwhelmingly *junior* faculty in sociology had been dominated by the Anthropology senior faculty — a split in Anthro-Socio put the departmental majority into the hands of junior faculty — led at the time by Von Eschen and Pinard. The Von Eschen-Pinard axis included a friend they had hired from their alma mater Johns Hopkins, Luis Goldberg, and two other newly hired junior professors, Larry Felt and Malcom Spector from Northwestern. They formed a bloc against the now out-numbered senior faculty. The junior faculty were all Americans (except for American-trained Francophone Pinard), friends, all inexperienced and virtually unpublished and *all* dreaming that the Department would now be "theirs" given their majority vote and the removal of the control previously exercised by Anthropology senior faculty. Into this dream intruded the SSU. Faculty who were not even competent to train graduate students (never having had any to train) were now faced with the student movement. Given the honeymoon with radicalism and to co-optative policies of the out-numbered senior Westley, capitulation to SSU was swift. However, the basis of the junior faculty's capitulation, disguised though it was in radical rhetoric, actually rested upon its political inexperience and fear of a strike. No sooner did they have the Department in their grasp than the students threatened it! Opportunism presented itself as the most expedient tactic. The price of that opportunism was Professor Dixon.

Dixon was actually senior to most of the junior faculty, with experience in training graduate students, and having written "The Rise of Women's Liberation" in her first term at McGill. Thus Dixon was, at the beginning, a professional threat. That, however, was not to be her principal threat; it was her refusal to repudiate the SSU, and to ally with the junior faculty, resulting in their failure to consolidate their control of the Department. *Control of the Department had always been the real objective.* The Dixon-SSU alliance *and* the return of David Solomon from leave was to wreck (at least temporarily) what may be termed the Von Eschen Plan: to turn the McGill Sociology Department into a sinecure for the junior faculty. This plan was outlined to Dixon privately when she was interviewed in the form of assurances that junior faculty would never be fired from McGill. At that time, Dixon thought it very odd, but Von Eschen had continued his assurances that vast powers were enjoyed by junior faculty. Dixon assumed, given her experience with the extremely conservative and traditional University of Chicago, that Von Eschen was basing his "Plan" upon the SSU alliance. Such was not the case. Von Eschen's plan was to consolidate control by expelling the SSU at the earliest opportunity. Dixon's refusal to join the plot and her open alliance with the SSU created the stalemate (and nascent splits within the junior faculty bloc) that made the Solomon-Westley *coup d'etat* possible. Reassertion of senior faculty control in Sociology required that the Von Eschen-Pinard axis shift into the senior faculty camp if they were to remain insiders. At this point the splits that had been brewing in the junior faculty's ranks burst into the open: Felt and Goldberg both left McGill soon thereafter and Spector defected.

The Von Eschen Plan having failed, the Second Von Eschen Plan began to work itself out: rapid promotion. This was secured for Von Eschen and Pinard (and more recently for Robinson and Carroll) in which their subservience to the Hamilton-Westley-Solomon senior bloc received its final reward. Von Eschen's success in getting Professor Carroll (so marginal that both he and everyone else thought he would not be renewed!) *promoted*, assured in 1975, Von Eschen's second plan[11] — especially given the eventual departure of the one man whom he could not manipulate, Professor Wallerstein. Von Eschen's first success rested upon his ability to swing the junior faculty over to Solomon-Westley in the repression of the SSU; his continued success rested on his early promotion (based on the promise of a still non-existent book, that is, an obvious pay-off for services rendered) and his role as chief plotter and ideologue of departmental politics under senior rank. Pinard's conservatism and Hamilton's hatred of radicals lined them up in the Von Eschen camp. The basis of the hysterical hatred of Dixon may now be understood: she was a constant threat to the powerful alignment of a professional hustler (Von Eschen) and his opportunist rank and file and professional or departmental conservatives.

In 1971 Dixon was due to be summarily expelled. The newly arrived Wallerstein and Ehrensaft were quietly but fervently hoping that they would not be drawn into the renewal issue. Indeed, it is ironical that it was an Honest Liberal (taking decency, fair play and professional criteria seriously), who did not even like Dixon personnaly at the time, Professor Spector, who would actually push Dixon into fighting the purge. Prior to Spector's unexpected visit Dixon had resigned herself to what seemed inevitable but she also knew that she was black-listed; being fired from McGill would be the end of teaching, writing, all the things that one could hope might be possible in a university. Why let them take it away *and* "pull it off" as they had boasted of doing with the repression of the SSU? The die was cast; once the game began there was no turning back for any of the players.

Wallerstein was Left politically and professionally, but all his instincts in departmental and university politics were to operate in the Centre: to compromise where necessary, to advocate no extreme positions, to press for professional and intellectual goals within the limits and boundaries of the system. Wallerstein had been led to believe that McGill offered a sort of "radical repose" and Ehrensaft that the university was a place where radical junior faculty pursued intellectual excellence. The political basis of the attempted purge would not be clear to either until they had spent many hours listening to the arguments from the Right. Wallerstein's agreement to represent Dixon was based upon her publications file, that is, her professional work. The stories that each or these men had heard about "the woman" were so horrid as to scare off almost anyone, therefore, their decision was hardly influenced by favourable personal knowledge of Dixon *or* by politics. Furthermore, they had been repeatedly told that politics had nothing to do with the firing of Dixon — she was to be fired because she was an intolerable human monster that "disrupted" the Department.

The first and unalterable split was into Pro and Anti Dixon: this was the defining line of political demarcation. Wallerstein, Ehrensaft and Spector had sincerely believed that when the renewal battle was over, bygones would be

---

11. The result of the politically motivated promotions in Sociology is faculty at the associate rank who were marginal at the junior rank, with one exception.

bygones and normal life would resume in the Department: *they actually hoped that there would be no reprisals:* Yet there were reprisals, three long years of reprisals from a solid bloc with a three vote majority (not that votes were ever taken in Sociology!)[12]

The motives and politics of various allied cliques in the Right wing bloc differed. The *Pragmatic Rightists* [Westley (tactics) Solomon (operations) in which Solomon fronted and took the rap for Westley — who dearly and fervently pursues a deanship] are right-wing politically and professionally but are also essentially *locals* (concerned with the Department and McGill University) because they cannot really move out of McGill. Consequently, they are tactically more flexible and less reckless than the *Dogmatic Rightists.* The Dogmatic Rightists (Hamilton and Pinard) are *cosmopolitans,* not really attached to McGill because they can move on to other jobs; their "cause" is defense of the *professional* right-wing against the threats, challenges, disruptions and heresies of the radical and Marxist tendencies within Sociology (perceived to attack their work and professional hegemony as Super Scientists, i.e., use of survey techniques and statistical methodology). *The Opportunists* were motivated purely by the "politics of self-promotion". They are *locals* because they are without exception so marginal professionally that their ability to move beyond McGill (especially in a "tight market") is severly restricted and would have to be to institutions of considerably less prestige. Had the Left controlled the Department, they would have all become "radicals". With Solomon-Westley in *de facto* control, and opposed to Wallerstein — or at least fearful of him — as a consequence of the Dixon renewal, their alignment with the Right was assured. *The Opportunists are the real victors, of course, parlaying their swing-vote into promotion and tenure!* The leader and tactician of the Opportunist bloc was, of course, Donald Von Eschen. His task was to keep the other opportunists in line and to carry out the busy work of purges, repressions, slanders, social relations. Von Eschen was the pivot between the right-wing blocs: through Pinard to Hamilton; from Solomon-Westley to Hamilton; keeping Krohn in line while attempting to cultivate Ehrensaft as a source of left-wing intelligence. Krohn, Robinson and Carroll bent with the wind: Robinson's wind was Hamilton. Carroll had initially sought Hamilton's protection, but for some reason lost it — indeed, the cause for much cynical merriment in 1975 was Carroll's sudden "shift to the Left" in joining the MFU when the thought he would not be renewed.

The *Pragmatic Leftists* (Wallerstein and Ehrensaft) were left-wing politically and professionally but (unlike Solomon-Westley) were *cosmopolitans* whose first loyalty was to their intellectual work and not to McGill University, since both could move to favourable alternative jobs with minimum difficulty. Wallerstein consistently attempted to regain the Center since, being an astute university politician, he could not fail to see that the post-Dixon polarization gave hegemony to the Right. One imagines that he hoped to be able to manage an accomodation with Solomon-Westley, at least sufficient accommodation that he could pursue his work, intellectually and departmentally, with some measure of freedom.

---

12. Votes were never taken because voting records would have shown the discrimination against minority bloc faculty. This could have resulted in intervention by the Dean. Refusing to vote, in favour of "consensus", left Von Eschen free to use his manipulative tactics; it also left Westley-Solomon free to claim that "no decisions could be made" in order to justifiy their administration of the Department by fiat.

Solomon-Westley were open to a limited accommodation, having enough sense to see that no good would come to them from abusing so great a power; but they fundamentally distrusted Wallerstein's leftism, and were limited and constrained by the demands of the Dogmatic Rightists (fanatical in their opposition to Wallerstein, the heretic) and the Opportunists (who greatly feared both Wallerstein's professional reputation and his defense of improved standards and procedures for professional judgement in the Department).

The *Marxist-Left* (except for 1973-1974 when she was on sabbatical leave) took notes for this book. Dixon tactically understood Wallerstein's attempt to re-establish the Center although she felt it doomed to failure, and simply tried to stay out of his way in order not to compromise him further. This could reach hilarious heights at faculty meetings Dixon would sometimes force herself to attend: she would sit as far away from Wallerstein as possible in order to emphasize physically the lack of collusion!

The *Honest Liberals,* [Spector and Rains] attempted to operate according to principle. Professor Rains tried with tact and diplomacy to stay out of the line of fire as much as possible. Professor Spector had a tendency to outraged indignation, which often put him in the line of fire. Neither of the Honest Liberals "voted" (*supported* would be the more accurate term in the absence of voting procedures) as a bloc with the Left — they supported issues according to their own lights (sometimes Left, sometimes Right) causing considerable tooth-gnashing on the Left for their failure to see that by *not* bloc-supporting they were making their own persecution and mistreatment easier to conduct. Professor Rains would often, as a result, be a compromise "peace-maker" and token bow to the Left on certain committees (including the crucial Chairmanship Search Committee). Spector and Rains do not fit the cosmopolitan-local distinction, being young professors principally concerned with carrying out their teaching and intellectual obligations as juniors on probationary appointments, although this began to change as Spector's professional career began to be threatened by the aborted purge and hounding attacks on his work.

If the internal politics of the Left-Coalition in the Sociology Department *had in fact been a socialist plot* there is good reason to believe that the Right would not have been victorious; or at least would not have successfully expelled the Left-Coalition. The Honest Liberals, given patient political education, might have been brought to see the foolishness of "principle" in the face of conspiracy. Assurances to the rank and file opportunists might have won at least two over to the Left. But Wallerstein did not share Dixon's cynicism and did not have her knowledge of what the Department really was like, and he did initially understand the motives of Von Eschen or Hamilton.

The Cold War in the Sociology Department

Hamilton's political use of standards is clearly illustrated in the Secret Sociology Document and in his role in the Vaillancourt case among others. What is meant by Hamilton's commitment to "standards" and "objectivity"... It is simply the false identification of status quo, uncritical, positivistic social science research with "quality" research. In other words, Hamilton conveniently equates his own status-quo-don't-rock-the-boat orientation to sociology with "quality mainstream" and thus defines any other type of sociology (most particularly radical sociology) as illegitimate and substandard... It is clear that "standards" are applied only when it is politically convenient. For example, why weren't standards applied last year in the political science department renewal of Barbara Haskel (whose teaching was called into question to such a degree that a departmental meeting was called to settle the matter). "About 75% of Professor Haskel's students cut down her 251 course as vague, redundant, boring" according to a Political Science Students Association Survey... Why doesn't Professor Waller or Professor Hamilton talk about standards in connection with the Vaillancourt case? To have invoked standards would require that Vaillancourt be renewed and Haskel fired...

"The Political Use of Standards," *McGill Free Press: The Vaillancourt Papers,* April 10, 1973

After the expulsion of the SSU the Department of Sociology had become almost completely politicized: the struggle for voting procedures and a voice in hiring followed by the guerilla tactics employed by the SSU in retaliation for their expulsion united the faculty in opposition to Dixon-SSU. This meant that every event, personality and issue was political. It was the fact of the overwhelming politicization of the Department that Wallerstein was so slow to comprehend. Wallerstein, the *de facto* leader of the Left-Liberal Coalition, never thought of himself as such: it was clear that he continued to act on a presumption of "departmental politics" in the usual *professional* sense of the word, rather than in the conflict-bred true sense of a *politicized* conflict. This put Wallerstein at a disadvantage, politically, because it meant that at a higher level of sophistication he was making the Honest Liberal's mistake: he acted on "principle" (making a presumption of principle on behalf of his adversaries) in the face of conspiracy. The conspiracy began on the day after the Dixon renewal, a conspiracy to keep Wallerstein from exercising the power normally due him by rank and reputation; a conspiracy to foil any plans or goals he might entertain for the department; a conspiracy on the part of Von Eschen-Pinard-Hamilton to drive him out of the Sociology Department. Von Eschen's motives were both fear and envy. Von Eschen's fear and hostility towards talented people, students or faculty, is legendary in the Sociology department — as many students have learned to their sorrow. Pinard is a pure case of *ressentiment*; a smouldering, resentful envy for the glamourous super-star, who needed to be cut down a notch or two. Hamilton detested Wallerstein after the Dixon re-appointment for being a heretic, a renegade, a destroyer of the hegemony of mainstream sociology — and thereby, the hegemony and honour, power, grace of Hamilton. Solomon-Westley did not desire his expulsion (still dreaming of up-grading) but they opposed the changes they feared he might bring, changes in staffing procedures, application of professional judgements, the political tone of the department: changes that would break their almost unchallenged power in the department, founded on mediocrity and guarded by the old-boy norms prevalent at McGill. Tactically they moved to "control" Wallerstein, to set limits and watch-dogs on every move he tried to make.

The key area in which the cold war in Sociology was waged, prior to the show-down over the chairmanship, was hiring. Hiring is always the pivot: hiring in the long run determines the nature of any department; in politicized departments factions, cliques and coalitions move to strengthen their position by recruiting allies and blocking the potential allies of the adversary. If hiring is effectively blocked, assuring the isolation of a key faction in a faculty, that faction has lost the cold war — the opposition is then free to gobble up "territory" (appointments) and thereby assure its permanent hegemony.

The lines of conflict over hiring were drawn ideologically, since political struggle within the academic professional social studies takes place in the framework of the larger struggles being waged within the profession itself for styles and conceptions of research and theory development. In the Sociology Department, given the stakes riding on the outcome of new appointments, the critical area of hiring was removed from the jurisdiction of departmental meetings and placed in a special, "balanced" committee, that is, having representatives of the contending factions. The result was that it was impossible to seriously consider a candidate in terms of intellectual work alone, since by now all intellectual work had a political colour. A candidate working in economic sociology, historical sociology, or carrying any taint of possible "Marxism" was viewed principally in terms of "estimated political allegiance". The so-called "opposition bloc" contained two Marxists (Ehrensaft and Dixon) and two symbolic interactionists (Rains and Spector). Thus any additions in those areas was out of the question. To hide the political tone of the purge, the Committee was instructed to not look for "political sociologists" since it was thought most Marxists would so define themselves. In the space remaining, Wallerstein manoeuvred to get candidates with the best possible intellectual credentials. Of course, the reactionary bloc (Westley, Solomon, Hamilton, Pinard and Von Eschen, tailed by Robinson and Carroll) opposed any candidate acceptable to Wallerstein. In this deadlock Von Eschen invented the "desperate need for a methodologist". The desperate need was a tactic to close off new faculty slots to any potential allies of Wallerstein. The only speciality that seemed "safe" was, of course, methods. (See Documents #50 & 51)

The reader is reminded of Part I which makes clear that statistical and survey methods are hardly "apolitical". Socalled "empirical sociology" arose in North America as the positivistic and pragmatic alternative to Marxian and Socialist sociology.

The end result of "value free" empirical sociology (as C. Wright Mills pointed out in a 1954 essay) was the production of increasingly trivial masses of work of extremely dubious merit:

> Sociology, judging by the books of its practitioners, is a strange field of learning.
> In the libraries of its professors you will find books containing announcements

like this: p^1 $(=p^2ij)$. As well as books, also called sociology, full of mumblings like this: Sociological theory, then, is for us that aspect of the theory of social systems which is concerned with the phenomena of the institutionalization of patterns of value-orientation in the social system, with the conditions of that institutionalization, and of changes in the patterns, with conditions of conformity with and deviance from a set of such patterns and with motivational processes in so far as they are involved in all of these.'[13]

In this essay, as in others, Mills argues that there are types of sociologies:

> The first camp is that of The Scientists, who are very much concerned to be known as such. Among them, I am sure, are those who would love to wear white coats with an I.B.M. symbol of some sort on the breast pocket. They are out to do with society and history what they believe the physicists have done with nature. Such a view often seems to rest upon the hope that if only someone could invent for 'the social sciences' some gadget like the atom bomb, all our human problems would suddenly come to an end. This rational and empty optimism reveals, it seems to me, a profound ignorance of (1) the role of ideas in human history, of (2) the nature of power and its relations to knowledge, and of (3) the meaning of moral action and the place of knowledge within it.
>
> Among The Scientist, the most frequent type is The Higher Statistician, who breaks down truth and falsity into such fine particles that we cannot tell the difference between them. By the costly rigor of their methods, they succeed in trivializing men and society, and in the process, their own minds as well.[14]

Mills' real fight with The Higher Statisticians and with The Scientists is precisely that they trivialize man and history, for want of any genuine intellectual enterprise:

> In fact, several men in the social studies now enjoy enormous reputations, but have not produced any enormous books, intellectually speaking, or in fact any contributions of note to the substantive knowledge of our time. Their academic reputations rest, quite largely, upon their academic power: they are members of the committee; they are on the directing board; they can get you the job, the trip, the research grant. They are a strange new kind bureaucrat... They could set up a research project or even a school, but I would be surprised if, now after twenty years of research and teaching and observing and thinking, they could produce a book that told you what they thought was going on in the world, what they thought were the major problems for men of this historical epoch; and I feel sure that they would be embarrassed if you earnestley asked them to suggest what ought to be done about it and by whom.[15]

Mills' description of the profession at large is also quite accurate for McGill sociology department, for all of the senior reactionaries are Scientists of the type Mills describes, whose power rests upon the same bureaucratic foundation. Of course, what is a Scientist without a Higher Statistician? Still, it is odd that such a desperate need for a Higher Statistician did not arise until Wallerstein came to McGill.

In opposition to The Scientists, the Higher Statisticians and The Grand Theorists Mills argues that:

---

13. C. Wright Mills, "IBM Plus Reality Plus Humanism = Sociology," 1954 in C. Wright Mills, *Power, Politics and People,* Irving Louis Horowitz, editor, Ballantine, p. 568-576.

14. *Ibid.* p. 569.

15. *Ibid.* p. 570.

Serious differences among sociologists are not between those who would observe without thinking and those who would think without observing. The differences have rather to do with what kind of thinking, what kind of observing, and what kind of link, if any, there is between the two.[16]

Mills then describes the "third camp" and his own:

> The third camp is composed of sociologists who are trying to perform three major tasks, which may be stated in this way: Whatever else sociology may be, it is a result of consistently asking: (1) What is the meaning of this — whatever we are examining — for our society as a whole, and what is this social world like? (2) What is the meaning of this for the types of men and women that prevail in this society? and (3) How does this fit into the historical trend of our times, and in what direction does this main drift seem to be carrying us? No matter how small-scale what he is examining, the sociologist must ask such questions about it, or he has abdicated the classic sociological endeavor.[17]

Wallerstein pre-eminently fits into C. Wright Mills' "third camp". The third camp describes his work better than "Marxist" or "economic sociology" or any other appellation we can think of. His own work on the capitalist world system and his concern with the major trends and outcomes of the world distribution of wealth are outstanding examples of what Mills would term the "classic sociological endeavor". The author was later to learn that Wallerstein's designations in terms of Mills' "third camp" was not fortuitous: he had known C. Wright Mills first as a student and then as a colleague at Columbia — in fact, Mills accounted for Wallerstein's choice of study in sociology. This relationship was also manifested in the fact that Wallerstein wrote the essay on Mills for the *International Encyclopedia of the Social Sciences*. Nor is it in any way insignificant that *The University Crisis Reader* is dedicated to the memory of C. Wright Mills.

Therefore, in the question of hiring (as in so many other departmental issues) Wallerstein was not engaged in departmental "power politics"; he was looking for neither Marxists nor allies, and was looking for candidates whose work would be concerned with Mills' three questions and so measure up to his "standards", which were the quality of work within the boundaries of the classic sociological endeavor.

The Sociology faculty with their fears of political plots and conspiracies, with their poorly disguised envy, and their anxiety to protect their control over the committee; the directing board; the job; the trip; the research grant, had no grounds upon which to impugn Wallerstein's motives or to claim that "you never know what he's thinking". Anyone who wanted to know what he was thinking only had to be familiar with his published work:

> For me, the primary function of a university is neither professional training nor general education nor intellectual research. These are all tasks assigned to it. But its primary function is in fact perpetually to question the truths of the time — whether they are the truths of the universe or of the social consensus. It is the Socratic task 'to corrupt the youth'. To be sure, I would counsel diffidence because the risk of hubris is monumental. But silence is the worst of all solutions, because the most cowardly.
>
> . . . A critical university cannot enshrine orthodoxy, since it is critical — that is, it exists to question accepted truths — which means that it is engaged in a perpetual debate, open, intellectual, and rational, with others who are, in social terms, more powerful.

---

16. *Ibid.*, p. 571.

17. *Ibid.*, p. 571-572.

The critical university will not, or should not, foster contempt for opposition and contradiction, since the existence of such alternative views are its raison d'etre, and since the quality of its criticism is a function of the quality of the intellectual defense of the accepted truths.

Far from being anti-intellectual, the critical university — and it alone — will demonstrate that intellect and reason are the essential weapons of social analysis and change . . .[18]

As for "standards", the intellectual demands of the "third camp" transcend any requirements, as Mills has written, for the "costly rigor of their methods, [which] succeed in trivializing men and society, and in the process, their own minds as well".[19]

We may now comprehend the real lines of ideological and "territorial" struggle in Documents #41 through 43. In 1972-73 the Sociology Department created an Appointments Committee to search for one assistant professor. Previously, appointments had been discussed and decided by the whole Department; the Appointments Committee was an artifact of the post-Dixon polarization, part of the control mechanism to contain Wallerstein. The Appointments Committee was "balanced;" that is, it comprised one representative from the Dogmatic Right (Pinard), one from the Pragmatic Right (Solomon), one, (Wallerstein), to represent the "others" (the euphemism used by the Right to characterize the Left) and one weak member who presented himself as independent of factions, Krohn — this, of course, was not true: Krohn followed the main chance, tailing the Opportunists, even though he was considerably senior to them. Krohn is one of those weak characters who likes to make virtuous noises before collapsing.

The Appointments Committee spent three months of intense meetings and consideration of dossiers (looking for *one* assistant professor!). The Committee, predictably, was constantly deadlocked: Pinard, sometimes Pinard and Solomon, would veto any candidate supported by Wallerstein. Even Krohn's candidates would be vetoed (for Krohn was only a partially reliable low rooster in the pecking order). As the deadlock dragged on, Wallerstein's patience became frayed to the breaking point, as expressed in Document #41. The exchange of memoranda might take its title from Wallerstein's opening cry of anguish: "The operations of our committee continue to astonish me, and quite frequently appall me." The sentence is, indeed, applicable to the operations of the entire Department.

Document #41 contains two themes that may tell us much about Wallerstein's comprehension of the nature of the Sociology Department. He begins with a plea to consider what hiring ought to be about. The only problem with this expression of frustration is that it rubbed salt into the wound of Pinard's insecurity and *ressentiment* ; it was guaranteed to terrorize Solomon, for whom the very thought of hiring on the basis of "talent, no matter how offbeat," and being willing to give it its head," had to conjure up visions of Stan Gray and Dixon or, at the very least, disrespecters of "old boys" and the hallowed traditions of McGill that assured repose to mediocrity.

The second paragraph must have served to reinforce fears inspired by the first. Candidates from Harvard! from Berkeley (remember Vaillancourt!) and Columbia! Wreckers, every last one of them, without a doubt!

---

18. Wallerstein, "Academic Freedom and Collective Expressions of Opinion", *loc. cit.*, p. 719.
19. Mills, *op. cit.*, p. 569.

The last two paragraphs are the clearest indication of patience tried past endurance. Wallerstein indicates that while willing to resort to reason within the framework of professional norms (first two paragraphs) he is at the point where he is on to the game and heartily sick of playing it (last two paragraphs). Wallerstein is a man of extraordinary self-control and patience: the reader will have to try to imagine what the three month existence of the Appointments Committee must have been like to provoke the concluding sentence, which simply blows the whole charade apart: "In any case, our collective actions amount to a confession of mediocrity and fear."

DOCUMENT 41

McGILL UNIVERSITY   INTER-DEPARTMENTAL MEMORANDUM

8 May 1973

To: Committee on Appointments: Roger Krohn
                                   Maurice Pinard
                                   David Solomon

From: Immanuel Wallerstein

The operations of our committee continue to astonish me, and quite frequently appall me. I come to the committee with some experience in looking for assistant professors. For some 6-8 years I was a member of the Columbia Department's Search Committee composed of Si Goode, me, and for most of the time Lazarsfeld. Each year we got from the 8-10 leading departments in the U.S. their choice names and took it from there. We looked for talent, no matter how offbeat, and were willing to give it its head. Because of the rather oligarchic structure at Columbia at the time, our decision was more or less fiat. Over the years we no doubt made mistakes. But using such a system we managed to amass a group of assistant professors who could hold their own in a department of senior giants, and we were able thereby to maintain a level of intellectual activity and excitement which, at least at the assistant professor level, never waned.

Of the batch of names that have poured into McGill this year, there are only three the Committee at Columbia would have hired: [names omitted].* If we were truly interested in raising "standards" in this department, then we would have been scrambling to get these three instead of thinking up laborious explanations of their intellectual limitations or our supposed organizational needs. We should have had all three up here long ago and have been spending our time debating which is the strongest.

---

* One was from Harvard, one from Berkeley, one from Columbia.

227

Instead, because of the persistent efforts of some to keep the place vacant for a candidate not wanted by the majority of the department, we have refused even to consider them seriously. By now it may be too late to get them (with the possible exception of . . .) since first-rate products of Harvard, Berkeley and Columbia are not being sneered at elsewhere, even in these days of tight budgets.

Perhaps these candidates are not being rejected for political reasons. Perhaps it is that we are afraid of high-powered junior colleagues. In any case, our collective actions amount to a confession of mediocrity and fear.

Document #42 shows how reckless the Dogmatic Right could be, for it reveals that it is precisely "political reasons" and fear of "high powered junior colleagues" that have been at work in the Appointments Committee. Yet Pinard's reply reveals more than that. The *ressentiment* is transparent in the astounding first paragraph! The reader ought not to be taken in by the characterization of Wallerstein as the "colonizer;" Pinard is American trained, American identified, opposed to Quebec independence, a Liberal party stalwart, a supporter of Trudeau, a defender (with Hamilton) of the most "colonizer" social science to be imposed upon Canadian social studies. The first paragraph indicates to what lengths Pinard was willing to go to bring Wallerstein "down a notch or two" beyond blocking every candidate he proposed. The reader will also discern the Von Eschen "desperate need for a methodologist" smokescreen. (To which we shall return).

DOCUMENT 42

McGILL UNIVERSITY   INTER-DEPARTMENTAL MEMORANDUM

June 27/73
TO: Immanuel Wallerstein
FROM: Maurice Pinard
SUBJECT: Committee on Appointments

I very much appreciate your recent memorandum. Out here in our little branch plant it is sometimes difficult to appreciate and understand the superiority of your procedures in the New York office. For your kind and generous aid in explaining to us the error in our ways, I would like to offer my sincere thanks.

There is, nevertheless, a detail that I fail to understand. You say the front office just hires the best people. But then, when we have someone recommended as a future

Blalock ("If I were to compare him with better known figures in the field, I would say that ten years from now he will be another Blalock . . . His preparation to do advanced work in this area (methodology) . . . surpasses that of any student who has graduated here during the past five years" — Donald J. Bogue, Sociology, Chicago) and yet you have given him a "2" rating meaning "very marginal". To me, a poorly educated product of the colony's schools, this seems an inconsistency.

I am sure it is not an inconsistency, but I would like you to indicate how your recommended practice is to be reconciled with your recommended principle. I am sure that you have not rejected him for political reasons or because you fear a high-powered junior colleague or because you wish to confess mediocrity and fear. But I must say there does seem to be some problem here.

c.c.: David Solomon
      Roger Krohn

Documents #42 and 43 amount to a declaration of war. Yet Pinard is too insecure and too McGill-parochial to realize that what he conceives as "winning," that is, the political defeat of Wallerstein in the department, is professionally, *losing:* for Wallerstein was not to put up indefinitely with bites from gnats like Pinard. That McGill could not keep a man like Wallerstein is a negative reflection upon McGill and the McGill Sociology Department.

Wallerstein's reply (Document #43) is an interesting study in the man: #1 is a devastating (but indirect) analysis of the actual nature of the McGill Department. It also carries a very clear warning: "I do not work in branch plants." Wallerstein also de-mystifies the cant about standards at McGill, "The faculty, mostly third-raters who couldn't get decent jobs in England, were obsessed with standards."

DOCUMENT 43

McGILL UNIVERSITY   INTER-DEPARTMENTAL MEMORANDUM

29 June 1973

TO: Maurice Pinard
FROM: Immanuel Wallerstein
SUBJECT: Committee on Appointments

1. My comparison of the Columbia and McGill modes of operation was between peer Departments. I do not work in branch plants. For those of branch plant mentality, however, it is easy to see how they might arrive at some of the absurdities to which we have been occasionally reduced.

In 1956-57 I was doing research in Ghana and lived at the University College of the Gold Coast. At the time, the University College was affiliated to the University of London and furthermore had a Principal who thought it pedagogical wisdom to replicate the structure of Cambridge. The faculty, mostly third-raters who couldn't get decent jobs in England, were obsessed with standards. They talked of the matter ceaselessly, especially if any African mentioned the possibility of adjusting academic structures to local needs. The result was predictable and ironic. It regularly happened that students who were refused admission to the University College of the Gold Coast were admitted to the University of London (The parent institution) as well as to Oxford or Cambridge. Did this mean that Oxford, Cambridge and London had lower standards than the University College of the Gold Coast? No, it meant that the rigidities of the faculty at the University College of the Gold Coast found expression in an abhorrence of deviance from a narrow path and resulted in objectively lower standards for both faculty and students.

I recommend we abolish the mentality that has such consequences.

2. On the matter of Mr. X to whom I gave a "2" I cannot say why, without looking again at the dossier. There are two possible reasons which come to mind. One is that there were things in the dossier that made me conclude thus. The fact that someone is the best methodologist Chicago produces in five years is not in itself a telling compliment. Or it may be that I read the dossier too hastily and was wrong. We read the folders the first time around very fast to make our initial assessments, and no doubt we made many errors.

The difference between Mr. X and the three persons of whom I was speaking in the previous memorandum was that the latter three were the subject of close attention by the Committee and hence each member was able to give a considered judgement on the individual merits.

cc: David Solomon
    Roger Krohn

The result of the tactics of the Right was that in 1972-73, after three months of frustrating and time consuming meetings, the Appointments Committee *recommended no one* — and that in a year when candidates were plentiful, jobs few — a year when candidates from Harvard, Berkeley and Columbia would apply to McGill in the first place. In the end, the McGill Sociology Department hired on one.

Chronology:

Department of Sociology, ANNUAL REPORT, *1972-1973:*

> *During the past five or six years, of which I have been chairman for only four, there have been four outstanding features of the situation of the Department. First, there was a very great expansion in the number of students registering in the Department's courses. Second, and concomitantly, in universities generally, there was a period of considerable turmoil which frequently centered in social sciences departments. While McGill was perhaps less disturbed than many others, 1967-68 and 1968-69, were years of tension and turmoil in the Department. Third, 1970-71 and 1971-72 were years of recovery, reorganization, and attempts to regain stability. Finally, a number of new appointments were made during this period so that the Department became larger than it had been before the period of greatest tension.*
>
> *During the early part of 1972-73 the preceding years' efforts to stabilize life in the Department began to bear fruit in the form of improved departmental administration as well as review of graduate and undergraduate curricula in terms of both content and standards of student achievement. There have been substantial achievements in all these aspects of the operation of the Department. The last two or three months of 1972-73, however, have been a period of some tension, centering mainly around the selection of a new chairman, a problem which is yet to be resolved...*
>
> David Solomon, Chairman
> Department of Sociology

January 16, 1973	The Grievance Committee of the McGill Faculty Union sends a memorandum to Dean Vogel supporting Vaillancourt.
January 29-30, 1973	Hamilton and Pinard attack Vaillancourt and MFU (i. e., Wallerstein).
March 30, 1973	CAUT agrees to arbitrate the Vaillancourt case.
April 10, 1973	The Report of the Chairman's Search Committee (to select a Chairman for Sociology since the Department was incapable of doing so) published in the *Free Press.*

June 26, 1973	Solomon and Westley assume power as Co-Chairmen to "save" Department from receivership when Wallerstein refuses post. The Co-Chairmen have the sole power to make any decision that cannot be resolved by consensus (i. e., *all* important decisions). Democracy ends for faculty in Sociology.
August 20, 1973	Committee of Enquiry decides in favour of Vaillancourt.
September 26, 1974	Sociology Graduate Students demand a reply on the question of student participation and representation on departmental committees.
October 3, 1974	William Westley informs the students that they will not be allowed to participate.
October 8, 1974	Marlene Dixon resigns from the Department of Sociology.
November 20, 1974	Graduate students again appeal for representation. The Department of Sociology decides not to decide upon their appeal. Democracy ends for the students in Sociology.
April, 1975	Immanuel Wallerstein informs the Department that he is seriously considering specific offers from three major universities.
1976	Wallerstein resigns, accepts offer at State University of New York at Binghamton.
	Ehrensaft resigns, joins Vaillancourt at Université du Québec à Montréal.

The Second Colonels' Coup: Pyrrhic Victory

> In the world I live in it is possible to disagree with someone and it is possible to correct someone without wanting to destroy them. You treated me as if I stood for the decline of all that is right, honourable and intellectually dignified. In fact, all I have done is to have an opinion about student representation in the Sociology faculty . . . and to express a possibly mistaken opinion about our hiring priority. These are not in fact issues for which I am about to die; they are not even issues for which I am prepared to undergo another experience like yesterday's. You once quoted Bertold Brecht to me to the effect that the man who was smiling hasn't heard the bad news. Impending doom is not my own view of life. I don't want to experience your presence as impending doom, nor do I wish to represent impending doom to you. More simply, I do not dislike you. I have never treated you meanly and it is unlikely that I ever will. You did treat me meanly and inappropriately and I think you owe me an apology, although I do not really expect to receive one . . .
>
> Professor Prudence Rains to Professor Richard Hamilton, Inter-Departmental Memorandum, inserted into the Minutes of the Sociology Departmental Meetings, dated May 10, 1974

The showdown between the Left and the Right came in the Spring of 1973. The showdown would result in the second Solomon-Westley Colonel's Coup, the "joint-chairmanship" resolution rammed through the Department in June, 1973. Neither the showdown nor the second *coup d'état* in Sociology would resolve any of the conflicts in the Department. *Detente* was beyond the diplomatic capacities of the Right-Opportunist Coalition. Dixon's absence in 1973-74 on sabbatical leave would change nothing, except to remove a scapegoat upon whom blame for the antics of the Right-Opportunists could always be deflected. Indeed, Dixon continued *in absentia* to perform the role of scapegoat: opposition to Professor Wallerstein now was excused by the menace of his future support for Dixon's *promotion*. The Sociology Department was haunted by legendary Wallerstein victories and the nightmare of *permanent* life with "The Woman." Of course, Dixon was no more than a symbol of the deep divisions that existed quite independently of herself; divisions within sociology at McGill and in the whole profession in North America.

The subsequent history of the sociology department after 1971 must appear very odd to ordinary, sensible people. The fears and machinations of the majority faculty take on a bizarre quality when one considers that the centre of their agitation was their fear of two women, effectively powerless in the university, of junior rank and largely isolated, thanks to the busy and malicious tongues of their "colleagues." All would have proceeded ordinarily at McGill, which is to say that both Vaillancourt's and Dixon's contracts would have been terminated, their professional reputations in shreds, and North American Universities preserved from their subversive and revolutionary activities. Such professional destruction and effective purging has been carried out countless times in the last five years all over the continent. What changed the situation at McGill was a man who refused to join the conspiracy, thus wrecking the best laid plans of the defenders of "academic standards" and witch-hunters against the "bolshevik menace" whose evil tide threatened to "destroy McGill and thereby society."

Both Professors Hamilton and Wallerstein had been eagerly sought by the Sociology Department as part of its program to "upgrade". McGill's traditional orientation towards science and engineering and the late development of the social science departments led the Sociology faculty to feel like "outsiders" under threat from an everhostile old guard in the science faculties. With the acquisition of such marketable commodities as Hamilton and Wallerstein the department heaved a collective sigh of relief: even with the embarrassment of Dixon and Vaillancourt (who had a half-time appointment in Sociology) these latest acquisitions promised to be the salvation of the Department — particularly since the Department would soon be relieved of the detested women.

Following the re-appointment of Dixon, Hamilton and his supporters pursued further political polarization of the Department . The subsequent academic degeneration of the Sociology Department finally came to a head in the Chairmanship battle that ended in a second Solomon-Westley *coup d'état* in April, 1973. The *coup d'état,* as we shall see, was made possible by the effective stalemate between Hamilton and Wallerstein.

Hamilton and Wallerstein both came as full professors: professionally, they were the Department's "stars". In the normal course of things, one, then the other, would have occupied the chairmanship of the Department (especially since senior resident faculty had served previously as Chairmen). However, the McGill Department did not represent the normal course of things. While power struggles between tenured senior men are the bread and butter of academic cocktail gossip, these struggles are normally "apolitical", limited in scope to intra-university and intra-professional competition and empire building. In 1971 neither the university *nor* the profession were "apolitical". As we have seen, McGill University was pursuing a repressive course in response to Opération McGill; the McGill Sociology Department was following suit against its one, and effectively "contained", Marxist; the profession of Sociology in North America was itself deeply torn by a bitter and prolonged struggle between the mainstream and emergent Marxist tendencies — a struggle which had ceased to be any kind of pretense to intellectual debate with the purging of Marxist activists which began in 1969 but was hugely accelerated by 1970-71. When the power struggle came in Spring of 1973, there was none of the jocular manoeuvering for position which occurs in "the normal course of things". Lives and careers and the fate of the Department rested with the resolution of the Chairmanship "problem" that Spring of 1973.

In the fortress mentality which dominated both the Sociology and Political Science faculties, it must have been beyond comprehension that any one of "the boys", that is to say, successful "stars" and "big reputations" of senior rank, would betray the Department and its long-term interests and immediate concerns with survival. While Hamilton turned out to be wonderfully satisfactory, hating the student movement and its junior faculty allies even more virulently than the resident faculty, the "enemy within" turned out to be the very "star" upon whom the Department had pinned its highest hopes: none other than Professor Wallerstein.

The entire scenario is a study in irony. Both Hamilton and Wallerstein were seekers after peace. Hamilton (it must be presumed) wanted to leave Wisconsin because the University was too "soft" on the student movement, while Wallerstein wanted to leave Columbia because of the general stupidity with which the student movement had been repressed — particularly the Black student movement, given the fact that Columbia's "community" was Harlem. Wallerstein's thought at the time was available to anyone who wanted to take the trouble to read *University in Turmoil* (which preceded *The University Crisis Reader*) in which Wallerstein attempted to make sense out of what the university rebellions of the late 1960's had been about, and indeed, what the university was or ought to be. In fact, Wallerstein's behaviour is completely consistent with the positions he had taken in *University in Turmoil* — and, as we shall see, consistency is one of Wallerstein's defining characteristics intellectually and morally in the context of the Department.

Rarely is the contemporary historian granted a glimpse of the subterranean processes at work in closed social groupings like university departments, yet we have such a treasure in the "Secret Proceedings of the Department of Sociology", Document #45. The somewhat dramatically headlined "Secret Proceedings" were, in fact, no more than a confidential report prepared by Professor Frances Henry, Chairwoman of the Chairmanship Search Committee, summarizing faculty sentiments towards the two candidates, Professor Hamilton and Professor Wallerstein. Professor Henry prepared the report because the situation in the Sociology Department was so "hot" that the Committee felt faculty would speak honestly only to an outsider. It would appear that the Committee was correct.

Free Press, April 10, 1973

The Secret Proceedings from the Department of Sociology

The following document was found slipped under the *Free Press* door on March 26, 1973. It appears that this document relates to the question of the chairmanship of the Department of Sociology and that it was not intended for public consumption. Upon our review of the document, we consider that it bears directly upon the Vaillancourt case, on union repression at McGill, and that it therefore is of great interest to the general McGill public. We also feel that the habits of "secrecy and confidentiality" and the decisions made behind closed doors utilized by the ruling class should be exposed wherever possible. Therefore, it is in the interest of justice that we publish this document. We think that it is important to point out to our readers the special references made to Professor Wallerstein concerning his politics, his union activities, and his relationship to both the Dixon and Vaillancourt cases.

TO: Members of Chairman's Search Committees
FROM: F. Henry

Report of discussions held with all members of the Department with respect to the chairmanship of Wallerstein or Hamilton. Discussions were unstructured and the report contains paraphrases and quotes from what people said. No organization has been attempted. In some instances, detailed interviews were edited because they referred to incidents or named people. Editing has been done only when the informant would become identifiable.

HAMILTON

His personal relationships are unfortunate. He is somewhat arrogant. Might have trouble holding Department together. Looks as if he has little respect for how other people do things. He is needlessly abrasive to certain members of the Department. Does not instill confidence in people. Very concerned with standards which may frighten some people who do not do his "hard nosed" kind of sociology.

Will polarize Department along dimensions of hard and soft sociology. The rightist professional faction will become dominant. Might make a few compromises to the left but only gestures. People who don't align with either faction will be forced to align themselves politically. Marginal interests in sociology will not be represented because both factions reflect these interests (these interests were spelled out but to disclose them would probably identify the informant).

Has lack of diplomacy. Doesn't even speak to some members of the Department. He is not principled — will undermine faculty rights in order to get his way. Does not involve other people in decision making — does not even meet his own committee because he doesn't speak to some of its members. Will handle things on his own despite the theoretical decentralization of the Department. Has had unpleasant experiences with H. when he has tried to use morality as a weapon. Would not personally fear his chairmanship but thinks that other people would.

H. Will create issues where there are none. A member of the staff might have a complaint. H. would not treat the complaint seriously and other staff members would then have to take their time to deal with the complaint. This would create an issue that the whole Department might have to handle. If a good student came up with a request, H's rigidity would go against the student who would then take it to the Department and another issue would be created. H. would not be fair to staff either. His general insensitivity to other people's problems would lead to the creation of new issues constantly. Will use his post to be vindictive because he is narrow minded and rigid. Would be unpleasant to deal with on day to day business:

Would make my life miserable. This Department is polarized because of the two approaches to sociology — the new Marxism versus traditional sociology. H. and his group want to define sociology in a traditional sense and will not accept alternatives to what they define as acceptable sociology. This Department has been fighting for pluralism and it would not be pluralistic at all were it not for Wallerstein and his group. Wants a pluralistic Department and the liberty and right to have dissenting position. Wants criticism but also wants to criticize the more traditional group. The issues surrounding polarization, pluralism, are important when they relate to curriculum, recruitment, etc. These should be intellectual decisions and not become personalized issues. Currently, what should be intellectual debate has become political debate and the Department is now incapable of making intellectual decisions. H. is antipluralistic. Wants centralization because of standards. Training of students would not be free. Would not give fair treatment to certain members of the Department. H. would want to carry out a purge.

H. is arrogant. His authoritarian actions could lead to conflict with members of staff. This might lead to his leaving the Department. He is in favour of a kind of intellectual elitism.

H. would retaliate politically in any way he could to those against him. He has had conflicts elsewhere — sees world in black and white terms. Once he has had a clash, he never forgets. Since Dixon's case, he has pursued the same battle. Is not open to concilliation. Anyone who has supported Dixon is considered dishonest. He is disliked by students — cannot get discussions going with him in class. Even his T.A.'s have difficulty with him. He would try to get me fired: would make life in this Department miserable.

H. never speaks to me and one does have to speak to one's chairman. H. will try to get me. I'm offensive to him because I supported Dixon. I fear his vindictiveness. He is a bad member of the Department. Students hate him. He has a condescending relationship with students and staff. As chairman he would poison the atmosphere of the Department. Nothing is good enough for him. All he talks about is his high standards.

His personality is too rigid. Too black and white. His own values too accentuated. Can't change this, its his personality. Therefore he is not suitable to be chairman.

H. is fairminded within his own lights. Has very high standards but his point of view is not only dimension of the field. Has very particular view of sociology but does not accept other areas as being valid. Applies overly puritanical and methodological standard to work. Is very uptight when attacked. May react irrationally, even in vindictive ways. Has intellectual arrogance when attacked.

WALLERSTEIN

Might want to change Department to Department of radicals. Pick appointments: get rid of people. Might need only one or two more radicals to change existing Department. Could influence these appointments because chairman can influence appointment process. The group of Wallerstein's group of supporters gives impression that they have no standards; accept people on political affinities. Wants to give access to various discriminated groups at cost of lowering of standards. May also encourage students to take sides and create more polarization of Department. Defense of Vaillancourt and general union activities suggest creation of a radical faction in order to increase potential power of the left in the Department.

Lower standards to admit more leftist people or third world students. Sets precedent for lowering of standards generally. These students would later have to be weeded out —

make process more difficult for all. On appointments, there is intolerance for research that is not directly problem-oriented. Only research accepted is that oriented to social change. Only people with these kinds of research interests would be accepted no matter what the quality of the person. Anyone who attacks this position is automatically right wing or conservative. There is already conflict on appointment now in progress — right wing "hard nosed" methods type versus radical type.

The Department is a staging area for his outside political interests. Department decisions will revolve around his role outside the university. This started with Dixon's case — can't see this as a reasonable appointment, yet W. still maintains that it is. More new evidence that Dixon is not good, yet W. continues to support her. Evidence that he is more concerned with his outside activities than with Department needs. He is not an open person. Other people don't know where they stand with him. Don't know where he himself stands since he will not reveal his position. Arguments go on in the Department and with him making decisions, would never know his reasons for the directions he takes. W. attempts to lower standards: supports the wishes of some other colleagues who also want to lower standards.

His policies are not consistent with Department needs: tendency to reduce standards. W. is never open about his policies and where he stands. Would not trust him as a chairman.

W. can't be trusted. He has political motives and we don't know where he draws the line. Never know his cards. Is always secretive. At committees, he remains silent until everybody else has spoken. He is always playing a game. On reappointments, W. will defend any radical. Standards will go down. If non-radical, W. acts like a pure academic like everyone else. Has double standards based on a person's political affiliations. He has created wide-spread suspicions in the Department. Did this at Columbia as well. He must make clear his position on hiring etc. and other decisions. He has to show his cards. He is trying to look moderate while being a radical.

There is conflict of interest with his union activities. As president of union, he will defend anybody including members of his own Department on whose review committee he sits. There is clear conflict of interest here.

Does he accept a pluralistic view of Department? I think that if he had his way, he would build Department in his own image. No room then for half the people here. Will he accept those of other views in new appointments? He already has views on building a social science faculty — would probably be a leftist radical faculty with no room for others.

Can't trust him. Don't know what he would do with Department. He has set of ends outside of the university. Will have trouble balancing this with making the Department work. Does not have enough commitment to the Department to create this balance between his outside role and the running of the Department. Department would become an instrument to these outside ends.

W. has used double standards in his reappointments review. Supported one who was radical. Did not support other who was not radical. W. could support anybody who is in the international socialist network even if person is incompetent.

W. is not straight. Would put political considerations in front of Departmental affairs. Plays a diplomatic game — does not say where he stands. Would want to create a politicized Department.

Standards will slip. Make ad hoc exceptions in hiring or getting in graduate students for non-academic reasons. Tends to oppose any attempt to add requirements to graduate programme whose purpose is to raise the standard of graduate education. Department has just begun a good graduate programme. W. is against stringent standards and requirements for graduate students.

IDEAS ABOUT SAFEGUARDS, STRUCTURAL ARRANGEMENTS, ETC.

Checks and balances are already there. Would be hard for anyone to scuttle the Department, but it might be possible. Appointments and reappointments are key issues. Must have agreement from both candidates that they would conform to the decisions reached by the review committees. Neither candidate should sit on anyone's review committee or some other arrangement whereby they upheld the committee's decisions. Perhaps we should not consider politicized people for appointments in the future or make sure that political activities are not considered in an appointment.

Recruiting only non-political people closes out too many creative people. Does not like idea of vice-chairmanship since this will immobilize the Department and may turn into veto power for the vice-chairman. Doesn't want an outside chairman since it would take either a dictator or a mere caretaker to handle the splits in the Department.

No structure will control how the chairman talks to the Dean. If an ombudsman were to work, he might just as well be chairman. No way of legislating malevolence out of a person's personality.

No arrangement or safeguard can guarantee trust. Things of common concern to the Department should be thoroughly aired and discussed before a new chairman takes over.

Have a third person in charge of review committee if candidate fears the chairman. All hiring should be done with the view of the needs of the Department in mind. Select areas of field which should hire or be covered; not political grounds.

Third person in charge of each review committee and in charge of negotiations with the Dean. Ombudsman is a good idea but does not control the problem of lack of trust.

Ombudsman would decrease the power of the junior staff. Ombudsmen are likely to be senior people. Therefore more power in hands of senior staff.

No safeguards can work. Chairmen would not abide by review committee. Chairman can still influence the Dean even if the review committees are headed by third parties. Only safeguard which can work is to have a chairman with a genuine commitment to pluralism

No prior arrangements can work. Rebellion is only check against a chairman. Two year term might work to alleviate fears of some people.

Chairmen's discretionary power cannot be checked. Guarantees of candidates would not be good enough. Can't trust them.

Third party in charge of review committees is not acceptable, would not work. Chairman will still have his influence.

Can't imagine any safeguards which would work. Both candidates have to make peace with people in Department. Means coming to their opponents and talking seriously to them. Chairman can still subvert the review committees' work by a word here and there.

The Department now is run in a straightforward manner. It should continue to be run in this manner. New chairman must adopt Solomon's style in order to keep Department efficient and running.

No arrangements or safeguards can work. Chairman is at nexus of communication network. A lot of day to day decisions would be made against which there can be no safeguards.

GENERAL COMMENTS

Neither are as evil as they are taken to be. Both good workers, good administrators and good scholars.

Latent polarization will become overt if either one is selected. Factionalism will increase. People will be forced to join one side or the other. Atmosphere in Department will become too politicized.

I could live with either one of them as chairman as long as other people are equally flexible.

Neither is a good choice. Both are distrusted, cannot legislate away distrust.

Am not threatened by either one of them. I have preference for one but would also accept the other.

I have no evidence against either one of them. Have heard only the evidence of others.

People who are really strongly for or against these candidates are paranoid.

copies to:

F. Henry
P. Boulle
D. Woodsworth
D.N. Solomon
I. Wallerstein
P. Rains
G. Robinson
M. Pinard
R. Krohn
W. Westley
R. Hamilton

The first interesting revelation contained in Document #45 is the obvious split in the Right. The Right-Opportunist Coalition is united in its opposition to Wallerstein, but it is split on the question of Hamilton. It is obvious that while it was politically expedient to use Hamilton's defensive mania for "standards" (i.e., a code-word for defense of mainstream sociology) as a weapon against Wallerstein, the Opportunists are just as frightened of Hamilton as they are of Wallerstein, and for precisely the same reason: what will become of *them* if either man succeeds in establishing a' uniform and demanding set of professional standards? The hostility to Hamilton is clear proof that a concern for "standards" was never more than a propaganda attack against Wallerstein. (Of the 10 comments listed against Hamilton, only 4 come from the Left, as near as the author can determine, knowing people's stances as well as she does; by the politicals, no reference is made to Hamilton's personal style, but to his intolerance for radical or Marxist sociology while fear is expressed that he is irrationally vindictive, which is, of course, based on his active participation in both of McGill's two most famous attempted purges. The Left was never fooled by the red-herring of "standards". The remaining comments belong to members of Hamilton's own faction.)

Hamilton's blind hatred of radicals has been his consistent error. Someone says of Hamilton that "he is fair minded within his own lights" and the author believes this to have been true in non-political circumstances, but when it comes to radicals Professor Hamilton has applied his famous "standards" unfairly and inappropriately, as the Vaillancourt case emphatically demonstrated. Hamilton's irrational hatred for Dixon seemed to have blinded him to the obvious incompetence (in Hamilton's own terms) of the mediocre "old boys" and genuinely incompetent Opportunists in Sociology. Richard Hamilton had simply been used by types like Harold Waller, Maurice Pinard and Donald Von Eschen. All they had to do was push the button marked "radical" to set Professor Hamilton off. Yet Professor Hamilton, as a consequence, was left wide open, for the people he defended were indefensible while the people he attacked were eminently defensible, as we have twice documented. In the end, Hamilton was betrayed by his "honest" friends, who were willing to use him against Wallerstein but were unwilling to support him for Chairman; the Right, not the Left, blocked Richard Hamilton.

The split in the Right created a situation in which Professor Wallerstein could have "seized" the Chairmanship: Wallerstein had the support of a majority in the Chairmanship Search Committee; he would have had the backing of the Dean; he had the unified support of the Left-Liberal Coalition. With such a constellation it is almost certain that Solomon-Westley would have swung at the last moment, withdrawing their opposition. Yet Professor Wallerstein did not "seize" the Department chairmanship. How can we solve this mystery? For if the fears expressed in Document #45 had any substance at all, then Wallerstein ought to have pressed his advantage to victory.

Professor Wallerstein's failure to "seize the time" is proof in itself of the foolishness of the mythology that had been constructed around him by the Right-Opportunists. It seems quite clear that in practice Professor Wallerstein *never* wanted to "seize the Department" and had never schemed to "take power;" indeed, he did not *want* "power." What Professor Wallerstein had consistently sought was "peace with honour," in order to carry on with his intellectual and academic work. Professor Wallerstein's "crime" in the little world of McGill was that he refused to sell honour to buy peace.

We do not know what transpired between Professor Wallerstein and the members of the Chairmanship Search Committee. Yet, based on our general knowledge, we may certainly hazard an educated guess: the *last* thing Professor Wallerstein could have wanted was to preside over a divided department, wholly without collective commitment to a consistent set of academic standards and values, and containing a majority faction whose sabotage and harassment would continue (just as it had in the past) whether he was Chairman or not. It is also possible that Professor Wallerstein was not much interested in remaining in the Department where mediocrity had the power to prevail *uber alles*. Under the circumstances the author thinks it likely that Professor Wallerstein *refused* the Chairmanship. This must surely have been beyond the comprehension of the Right-Opportunists, for not *one* of them would have been deterred by Wallerstein's scruples.

We wish to make only one more observation concerning Document #45. The reader will recall that we sketched the processes of the "collective social definitions" that operated against Professors Vaillancourt and Dixon. We see the same process at work here against Professor Wallerstein. The Right-Opportunists alleged that he had "outside political interests", that he entertained untrustworthy "political motives", that he was "secretive", that he had "ends outside of the University", and finally, ultimately, there was the alleged, menacing membership in "the international socialist network". One respondent charges that:

> He has created widespread suspicions in the Department. Did this at Columbia as well. He must make clear his position on hiring, etc. and other decisions. He has to show his cards. He is trying to look moderate while being a radical.

As Documents #41-43 show, Professor Wallerstein made his position on hiring crystal clear, much to the displeasure of the Right-Opportunists. As for "showing his cards" he certainly did so, and consistently, in print, in the MFU, in the Dixon and Vaillancourt cases. As for creating suspicions, *what* suspicions? That he is a radical? Indeed, he *is* a radical and has said so frequently. That is the root of the attack against Wallerstein, for according to dogma at McGill, being a radical is synonomous with "lack of respect for standards".

McGill covered itself for its purges and its mediocrity by insisting that excellence and radicalism are mutually exclusive. The same tactic has been consistently used all over North America to disguise political purges. Wallerstein's insistence on the basic compatibility of both, threatened the whole mythology that had arisen in response to the challenge that began in 1968. Just as Stan Gray and his "critical university" ideas had to be driven out, so did Immanuel Wallerstein and his equally subversive notions of the "critical university" and the necessity of both praxis and pluralism.

The result was that throughout March, April and May the Sociology Department was deadlocked. The two men who would normally succeed to the Chairmanship, on the basis of rank, would have been Hamilton and Wallerstein. The deadlock produced a power vacuum, which Solomon-Westley exploited in June to effect another *coup d'etat*. (Document #46, June 26, 1973) The only alternative, given Professor Wallerstein's refusal to accept the Chairmanship, would have been to put the Department into trusteeship (that is, turn over its governance to an outsider appointed by the Dean as had been done in the French Department). The Left-Liberal Coalition rank and file favoured trusteeship, but Wallerstein opposed such a move. It is the author's belief that the whole affair of the Chairmanship had, in fact, crystallized Professor Wallerstein's doubts and frustrations about the Department; that is, Professor Wallerstein had probably decided, *at that point,* to leave McGill. Given a decision that it was impossible to salvage the Department, Wallerstein must have reasoned that for the remaining period of his residence he still had the capacity to fend off the worst of the repressions against the Left-Liberal Coalition, while a trustee appointed by the University was an unknown, and might make the situation even more intolerable than it already was. The author knew that the game was over when the Chairmanship deadlock was "resolved" with the second Solomon-Westley *coup d'etat*.

Document #46, "Excepts from the Minutes of the Sociology Department Meetings", is an edited version of the departmental minutes. All that has been edited from the Minutes are matters of little concern to the outsider or to the topic. It should be remarked that the McGill Sociology Department has an explicit policy not to take *verbatim* minutes, for what should be obvious reasons.

EXCERPTS FROM THE MINUTES OF THE
SOCIOLOGY DEPARTMENTAL MEETINGS
MCGILL UNIVERSITY

APRIL 24, 1973

Security Risks

During the last 13 months the keys of the general sociology offices have had to be changed three times. Various other offices have had new locks and it is felt that all other offices which have not been changed may be compromised and will therefore be changed as soon as possible . . . Keys for L710 will not be available to minimize the risk of the great number of keys in circulation up to now.

JUNE 26, 1973

Present: Professors Solomon, Westley, Pinard, Carroll, Hamilton, Wallerstein, Rains and Von Eschen

1. *Chairmanship Selection*

All faculty members of the Department were present at the Department Meeting, June 15, 1973 when Professors Solomon and Westley consented to act as co-chairmen for the academic year 1973-74.

It was agreed that a) the Minutes should contain written comments from faculty members, and
b) a copy be sent to Dean Vogel

RESOLUTION ON CHAIRMAN OF DEPARTMENT*

1) The Department appoints David Solomon and William Westley as co-chairmen for the academic year 1973-74.

2) Their duties shall consist of all matters relating to budget and personnel and those other matters not specifically turned over to chairmen of standing committees.

3) All business decided unanimously by standing committees within their purview sha.. take effect.

4) Standing committees shall, however, distribute agendas of their business to all members of the Department sufficiently in advance of their meetings so as to permit members not serving on the committee to express their views. ·

5) Standing committees shall distribute minutes of their decisions to all members of the Department. If other members of the Department feel that decisions were unwise or incorrect, they may raise the issue at the next Department meeting, not in order to reverse the previous decision but to instruct the committee how to handle future decisions.

6) If a Standing Committee cannot resolve a matter unanimously, any member may request the Department collectively to take action.

---

* proposed by Solomon-Westley as "solution for deadlock".

7) If the Department collectively arrives at a consensus on such referred issues, their decision shall take effect. If not, it should be referred to the co-chairmen.

8) The co-chairmen may decide upon such a referred issue, in which their decision shall take effect.

9) The selection of committees for 1973-74 shall be balanced. The mode of selection shall be the subject of a further resolution.

All except Professors Spector, Dixon and Carroll supported the motion on the election of co-chairmen.

Professors Wallerstein, Spector and Dixon have asked to have their views included in these Minutes:

Reservation of Immanuel Wallerstein:

I support this motion on the election of co-chairmen on the following assumptions and reservations:

a) This is an interim measure to resolve a deadlock and enable the Department to move foreward.

b) I hope and expect that Professors Solomon and Westley will attempt to use the year to check corrosive differences in the Department and to find new and more permanent solutions.

c) I think in general the only desirable form of departmental government is one in which all faculty members are peers and have equal influence in deciding the affairs of the Department. The structure now voted is not such a form of government, in that it allows under specified circumstances the will of two members to prevail.

d) While justifiable as a *pis aller* (a last resort-Ed.), it would in my opinion be a sign of grievous ill-health if we used such a structure for more than a year. I would be opposed to any such suggestion, and wish to return at the end of the year to a mode of decision-making that grants all faculty an equal voice and vote.

Reservation of Malcolm Spector:

I favor putting the Department into trusteeship because the alternative plan will not solve, but only increase the lack of trust and unfairness as well as the extent of the dishonesty in the Department this year.

The department has disgraced itself in several activities and we are in need of a good cleansing, not a cover-up.

Reservation of Marlene Dixon:

I cannot in this memo reconstruct all of the argumentation presented at to-day's meeting, but I will try to summarize the major points accounting for my dissent from the majority position. I will also place my decision in context.

Context: In the four years I have been employed by this Department I have witnessed the steady erosion of democratic procedures. The Department was, in 1969, a model of progressive procedures and of democratic governance. By one means or another, year after year, democratic procedures have been replaced by (1) bureaucratic methods in which decisions are made by few people, or (2) coalitions of people manipulating situations outside of the jurisdiction of the departmental meetings. The result, in my opinion, of the erosion of democratic procedures has been the rise of distrust, of behind the scenes manipulation, and the extensive use of *ad hominem* criteria. In this situation the professional rights of numerous people have been subjected to threat. To date, most people have weathered these crises, but the situation is such that no one can feel really secure. There is an atmosphere which is hostile to work, which is hostile to the minimum tranquility which is required for intellectual work. In short, this Department has become oppressive and depressing, not the least factor being that no one can feel secure when justice has to be won at such price and effort time and time again.

The cure for this deteriorating situation does not seem, to me, yet another loss of democratic liberties. Now it is proposed that a two-men committee — or a "joint chairmanship" — is to be given the right to decide issues which the Department as a body is unwilling to debate to conclusion. Rather than addressing the fundamental issues of personal and professional liberty which are before us, this Department is choosing to give up the right to make decisions — thus people are abrogating not only their own rights, but the rights of others. Such a system, with the danger of the exercise of arbitrary power, can hardly solve the underlying issues. Justice now may be even more precarious than it has been.

Indeed, the proposal not only requires that we give up our right to make decisions, and to insist that issues be struggled through to conclusion, the proposal also effectively curtails or even removes the possibility of dissent and conflict — at a time when the larger profession is characterized by the dissent and conflict which attends reformulations of intellectual positions.

For these and other reasons, I cannot be reconciled in principle with to-day's decision, and I wish to make my dissenting position very clear.

Postcript: I should like to add that this memo should not be construed as an attack on either of the volunteers for the joint-Chairmanship, but refers to the dangers inherent in a system which is fundamentally undemocratic.

(Reply of) Professors Solomon and Westley:

While we agree that all members of the Department have the right to register their objections to departmental decisions in the minutes or otherwise, we regard the statements of Professors Dixon and Spector as irresponsible and untrue since none of their comments are supported in any way. We feel, therefore, that these two statements are a discredit to their authors.

(The following statement by Professor Michael Carroll was appended to the minutes of the meeting of June 26 but he requested that it not be forwarded to Dean Vogel)

Reservation of Michael Carroll:

I am strongly opposed to the re-organization of the Department according to the plan suggested by Professors Solomon and Westley for the following reasons:

1. It is clearly undemocratic, in the sense that the decision-making power in the Department would be far less diffused than is presently the case. The constriction of decision-making power occurs in two ways. First, it is now possible for one of the major committees — undergraduate or graduate — to make departmental *policy*, rather than simply policy *recommendations*. While this may indeed lead to increased efficiency, it does so by disenfranchising whole segments of the Department. (Thus, for instance, a member of the undergraduate committee might not have any real authority with regard to graduate regulations.) But, the clearest erosion of democratic procedures results from the arbitrary authority given to the co-chairmen. I certainly agree that there will probably be few occasions in which consensus is not reached by the Department (thus throwing the matter to the co-chairmen), *but,* if the past year is to be any guide, the problems least likely to result in consensus are those *most* likely to revolve around the issues most important to the future course of the Department. To have these really important issues arbitrarily decided by two members of the Department is intolerable.

2. I disagree that the Department has been paralysed under the present system. There have been only two issues that this Department has not been able to resolve — the selection of a new chairman and the appointment of a new staff member. *The issue of the chairmanship has only once come to the level of the Department,* previously it had been discussed only in the chairmanship selection committee. However, much effort was put into the discussion by this committee, its membership was only a subjet of the Department as a whole. Further, the experience of a given committee does not always replicate itself in the full department. For instance, in the case of appointments, only *one* substantive case was ever brought before the Department as a whole (all other discussion went on in the Appointments Committee). In this case (the appointment of Mr. Eaton $^1/_4$ time), a decision *was* made by the Department despite the fact that the Appointments Committee itself could not devolve upon a clear recommendation. I present the fact that the present re-organization plan was presented in the middle or a very long meeting, with no advance notice and with the implication that a rapid decision was necessary, even though, as mentioned above, this was the first department meeting at which the chairmanship issue was discussed.

3. Although the present plan is billed as an interim measure, my own experience has been that once organizational structures are institutionalized, they prove more resistant to change than had been expected. For instance, it is now argued that the present plan is necessary because there is no alternative. But it is difficult to know how the situation will be any different a year from now. Since the current divisions within the Department are not borne of momentary anger, but of deep philosophic differences, it is not likely that a "cooling off" period will do any good. Thus, if at the end of the present year we decide that an outside chairman is after all necessary, we will simply have wasted a year that could have been spent searching for one.

4. Once the current plan was presented, the speed with which it was rushed through prevented any attempt to compare it with previous plans and to see if various members of the Department might want to revise their opinions concerning these previous plans.

The following memo was inserted into the Departmental minutes:

TO: All Faculty
FROM: Michael P. Carroll
DATE: October 11, 1973

As it now stands, the only persons who can refer an issue to the department level are persons who happen to be members of the department committee at which the issue is first discussed. It is nevertheless true, however, that many of the issues discussed at the committee level involve policy decisions that will have consequences for *all* members of the department. It does not seem unreasonable to ask that if a decision is going to affect all members, then all members should, at the very last, have the *potential* for influencing that decision. I would therefore like to propose the following revision of our current procedure:

If any faculty member feels that an issue on the agenda of any department committee is an issue that might entail a substantial change in current department policy then that faculty member, if he or she wishes, may require that any *final* decision on that issue be made at the departmental level.*

---

* This memorandum from Professor Carroll was a result of the fact that he was not a member of the Graduate Committee and felt that the Committee's decisions, even if unanimous, were too "lax" or too "pro-student."

5) Standing committees shall distribute Minutes of their decisions to all members of the Department. If other members of the Department feel that decisions were unwise or incorrect, they may raise the issue at the next Department Meeting, not in order to reverse the previous decision but to instruct the committee how to handle future decisions.

Any member of the Department may call for the final decision on an Agenda item affecting policy to be reserved for the Department.

January 18, 1974

1. Questions re: letter of Curriculum Committee, dated Jan. 2/74

DECISION: Prof. Wallerstein will reply to the general questions as Prof. Dixon's proposed courses cannot be discussed during her absence. More detailed information is needed from Prof. Dixon.

Undergraduate Committee Report

DECISION: Prof. Krohn's new course proposal 552B Current Sociological Theory is returned to the Undergraduate Comm.

(Editor's note: Since the Minutes are *not verbatim* the reader has no way of knowing the machinations that were being conducted behind the scenes in Sociology as well as other departments. What the decision on Prof. Krohn's course meant was that Prof. Carroll had opposed Prof. Krohn's course, *then* himself circulated a new course proposal, almost duplicating Krohn's.

FACULTY OF ARTS

COURSE PROPOSAL

Distributed between
22-25 Jan. 74
Revised

Department: Sociology

Title of Course: Theoretical Paradigms in Sociology

Proposed Number: 166-5

Responsible Instructor(s): M.P. Carroll

Description of course:
The course will deal with some of the major paradigms used in sociology, including the evolutionary perspectives of the last century (Spencer, Morgan, Engels) and its modern variants, functionalism (both the Durkheim-Radcliffe-Brown-Merton and the Durkheim-Mauss-Levi-Strauss traditions) and Freudianism, and then upon more limited paradigm traditions, including Durkheim on suicide and on religion, and Weber on bureaucracy and the rise of capitalism. Permission of the instructor required.

Reason for Proposal:

I have talked with Professor Krohn, and it is clear (to me) that there will be little overlap between the two courses. First, he covers several theorists that I don't cover and vice-versa. Second, with regard to those theorists in common to both courses, it is clear that we emphasize — in all the cases we discussed — different aspects of the person's work. But perhaps the most important difference concerns the perspective. Prof. Krohn teaches all this theory course from a sociology of knowledge perspective, which emphasizes, among other things, the social traditions and background variables that led a theorist to construct his particular theory. I am interested not in the sociology of knowledge but rather in the *empirical validity* of these classical theories, that is, in questions like what does the theory assert, which predictions and explanations does it generate, and are these supported by the data, both the data presented by the theorist in question and that accumulated since.

> (Editor, continued: This was too much for Prof. Wallerstein coming as it did on the tail of a tri-departmental attack on Prof. Dixon's new course proposals. Prof. Wallerstein responded as follows:)

To: William Westley

From: Immanuel Wallerstein

Re: Course proposal, "Theoretical Paradigms in Sociology"

Unfortunately, I am unable to attend the Department meeting on Feb. 1. It conflicts with the semi-annual meeting of the Research commission of the Centre Quebecois des Relations Internationales, of which I am the Vice-Chairman.

I am very strongly opposed to granting departmental approval for this course on both substantive and procedural grounds. Prof. Carroll says he wishes to test the empirical validity of the classical theories, using not only the data presented by the theorists in question but also the data accumulated since. I suggest this is nothing less than the totality of sociology. In any case, it is to say the least a doubtful proposition that one could decide between the so-called evolutionary paradigm and the unnamed Weberian paradigm on the basic of some crucial data that could be presented within the framework of a short course.

The course points to a more fundamental intellectual fraud involved in "theory" as a field of pedagogy. It is no accident that none of the natural sciences have courses called "theory". Nor does psychology or economics. In political science, "theory" simply means "philosophy". And anthropology courses in "theory" are courses in the history of ideas. Only in sociology departments do some people pretend to teach a non-existent subject, disembodied "theory".

Every course in sociology involves the presentation of theories and the testing of their empirical validity. I have no objection to discussing the difference between an "evolutionary" perspective and a "Weberian" one in the analysis of stratification, or religious institutions, or large-scale social change. But then this should be done in courses on stratification or religion or social change.

It is fundamentally misleading to students to abstract the formal frameworks and suggest they should evaluate them. Of course, it may be of interest to the student or useful to him to know the history of ideas in the field and especially their social roots, but presumably this is what Prof. Krohn's course does and which Prof. Carroll states quite clearly he will not do.

248

In short, I think a course in the "theoretical paradigms of sociology" is akin to astrology or alchemy and should be rejected as such.

In addition, quite apart from the substantive objection, I think it highly inappropriate procedurally to consider this course other than in conjunction with Prof. Krohn's proposed new course. We can only make rational allocations of our limited collective resources if we consider simultaneously potentially conflicting courses. I therefore propose putting off consideration of this course until the March meeting, at which time prosumably Prof. Krohn will have responded to the queries put to him at the last meeting.

ADDENDUM TO MINUTES OF THE DEPARTMENT MEETING, FEBRUARY 1, 1974

I wish to protest in the strongest possible terms some of the statements contained in Professor Wallerstein's memorandum concerning my new course proposal. Specifically, I object to my proposal being labeled an intellectual fraud, and to the implication that my work is of the same intellectual worth as alchemy and astrology. Such comments would be out of place in any discussion involving educated persons; they are especially out of place in a discussion among colleagues within the same department.

M. Carroll
Department of Sociology

THE FOLLOWING PETITION WAS INSERTED INTO THE DEPARTMENT MINUTES: GRADUATE STUDENTS MEETING, DEPARTMENT OF SOCIOLOGY, APRIL 4, 1974

Central to the experience of all graduate students in the Department of Sociology is the lack of information on departmental decisions. This reflects the paucity of formal representation on departmental committees and an apparent general unconcern with student needs and interests. Furthermore, we are distressed at the uncoordinated and directionless manner in which departmental affairs are conducted; individual issues are resolved through uneasy compromise, and the implications of these piece-meal solutions are not clarified. Continuous uncertainty and a lack of trust at all levels of the department has led to our present state of despair.

Two recent events exemplify the gravity of these problems: First,

The issue of faculty appointments

At an *ad hoc* general meeting of faculty and graduate students, held at student request in March, a number of issues were raised about student/faculty relations, among them the questions of faculty policy on hiring. The basic question asked by students was whether the faculty intended to build on certain "strengths" already existent within the department — those formalized in the recent establishment of Collegia focused on five areas in sociology. Anxiety was expressed (and apparently appreciated by some members of the faculty) about the fate of one of these strengths — Deviance — which is now represented at the faculty level by only two staff members, one of whom will be on sabbatical leave next year. This is also an area which is popular with both graduate and undergraduate students.

The outcome of our discussion was that no overall departmental policy existed on hiring and the future composition of the department. This, in itself, did little to alleviate the anxieties of graduate students committed to degree programs in the department and already following defined interests which, at the time of application, were said to be well represented at McGill.

Of more pressing concern, however, is the fact that the information then relayed to graduate students on the number of appointments available and the criteria being used to differentiate between potential candidates bears little ressemblance to the actions subsequently taken.

At the meeting the immediate situation was presented to us as follows:

1) One position was available for the coming year;
2) The principal criterion being used to select a new appointee was ability to teach demand undergraduate courses not now offered within the department;

3) If at all possible, a visiting professor specializing in deviance would be sought for 1974-75.

It was stressed by the faculty that difficulties would be encountered in doing this, it being already extremely late, in the year to resolve this problem. However, the grave imbalance between student interest and faculty support in the area of deviance was acknowledged.

We now understand that as a result of negotiations with the Dean, not one, but two paid positions are available for next year. While the possibility of hiring a second new faculty member may have been unknown to some members of the department at the time of the meeting, we feel that it must have been apparent to some others — either then or very soom afterwards — in order for the negotiations to have been undertaken. In view of the concern expressed by students at this time, we feel that we should certainly have been informed as soon as this second position became available. We would also like to point out that the candidate to whom the appointment has been offered will not be teaching demand undergraduate courses which are not currently offered, and in no way provides support to the area of Deviance. Moreover, a third position, that of visiting professor, has been offered to someone in complex organizations — a candidate 1) whose presentation was scheduled on such short notice that no student heard about it, 2) who is in an area that is already well represented in the department, and 3) who is not in one of those areas indicated to us at the staff-student meeting as being of high priority.

A second example involves:

The history of student representation on one committee

A further very disturbing issue is the question of student representation on the committee selecting new graduate students. Last year we had representation on the graduate committee and through this, also on the sub-committee set up to process student applications. Our representative, Joan Hoffmann, put in many hours reviewing files — more, indeed, than several of the staff members of the committee — only to be informed in the final days that she did not have a vote on this committee. At that time she made a formal objection to this position, especially in the light of the time that had already gone into evaluations and in the light of the fact that we has assumed that our representative had all the rights of other committee members. Furthermore, she submitted a formal request that this issue be taken to the departmental faculty and resolved. It now appears that this request never got transmitted to the department, that the request has been lost, and that even the minutes of the meeting have disappeared. The issue was so completely ignored that this year there appears to be confusion among the sociology faculty as to whether in fact students are even to be included in student admissions, the claim being made that last year's representation was some how *ad hoc*, i.e., a whim of that particular year's committee. Such complete disdain for our participation has upset us enormously.

The two episodes described above demonstrate a distressing unwillingness on the part of faculty in the sociology department to confront either immediate organizational difficulties or the necessity for long-term policy. They also demonstrate a blatant lack of commitment to student interests; they are in no way isolated incidents. Repeated meetings with individual staff members have made it clear to us that the faculty as a whole will not resolve these issues unless some formal mechanisms are instituted whereby problems can no longer be evaded.

We therefore demand:

1) Two elected representatives, with vote, on the graduate committee, who will also act on sub-committees.

2) An elected representative, with vote, to act on the hiring committee of the department.

3) Two elected representatives, with full rights, at departmental meetings, who will be a part of curricular and other decisions which directly affect graduate students

4) An immediate response from the sociology faculty with regard to these requests.

MAY 9, 1974

Present: Professors Westley, Hamilton, Pinard, Carroll, Robinson, Krohn, Von Eschen and Rains

1. Graduate Students

Discussion of the memorandum issued by the graduate students on April 4, 1974

DECISION:

Two graduate student representatives shall serve on the Graduate Committee. They will be elected annually, in the Spring, by secret ballot. They will then be recognized as fully fledged members of the Graduate Committee with the proviso that they will have only a consultative role on the selection of new students.

Paragraphs 2 & 3 deferred for later discussion.

THE FOLLOWING MEMORANDUM WAS INSERTED INTO THE MINUTES:

TO: R. Hamilton

FROM: P. Rains

DATE: May 10, 1974.

I think you ought to be ashamed of the way you treated me at the faculty meeting yesterday. The degree of your anger was entirely out of proportion to anything I might have said or done, and in fact I cannot imagine myself ever saying or doing anything which could possibly justify such an act of interpersonal violence.

Your verbal onslaught on me was so sudden and so fraught with unspoken innuendoes as to my motives and character, and was so underlaid with violence that neither I nor anyone else who was present could gather sufficient presence of mind to do anything but sit there and watch.

In the world I live in it is possible to disagree with someone and it is possible to correct someone without wanting to destroy them. You treated me as if I stood for the decline of all that is right, honourable and intellectually dignified. In fact, all I have done is to have an opinion about student representation in the Sociology faculty meeting at McGill University in 1974, and to express a possibly mistaken opinion about our hiring priority. These are not in fact issues for which I am about to die; they are not even issues for which I am prepared to undergo another experience like yesterday's.

You once quoted Bertold Brecht to me to the effect that the man who was smiling hasn't yet heard the bad news. Impending doom is not my own view of life. I don't want to experience your presence as impending doom, nor do I wish to represent impending doom to you. More simply, I do not dislike you, I have never treated you meanly and it is unlikely that I ever will. You did treat me meanly and inappropriately and I think you owe me an apology, although I do not really expect to receive one.

More generally, I find it distressing that as a department we have become so hardened to conflict and so adapted to subtle forms of violence that we simply sit and hope that it will pass quickly and that we can forget about it as soon as possible.

251

MAY 21, 1974

Present: Professors Solomon, Krohn, Rains, Wallerstein, Pinard, Von Eschen, Robinson, Hamilton and Carroll

1. *Graduate students* continued from the last meeting —
Discussion of the memorandum issued by the graduates students on April 4, 1974.

Page 3, para 2 (An elected representative, with vote, to act on the hiring committee of the department) DECISION:

It is assumed that the Appointments Committee acts as a Search Committee fulfilling the same functions as last year. Under these circumstances there will be one graduate representative with full rights, to be elected by secret ballot, annually, in the Spring.

Discussion page 3 para 3 (Two elected representatives, with full rights, at departmental meetings, who will be a part of curricular and other decisions which directly affect graduate students)

ACTION

Due to lack of consensus no decision has been reached. The decision will be made by the co-chairmen.

The last meeting for 73/74 will be held on Thursday, May 30, 1974 at 4 p.m. in L738

ON MAY 30, 1974 THE LAST *LEGAL* MEETING OF THE SO-CALLED "CO-CHAIRMEN INTERIM SOLUTION" WAS HELD. THE SYSTEM, NEEDLESS TO SAY CONTINUES, *WITHOUT* THE FORMALITY OF AN EXTENSION VOTED BY THE DEPARTMENT. THE OPERATIVE DECISION-MAKING UNDER THIS SYSTEM IS CONTROLLED BY THE FOLLOWING EXTREME RIGHT COALITION: PROFS. WESTLEY, SOLOMON, HAMILTON, VON ESCHEN, AND PINARD.

Document #46 should give a flavor of what daily life was like in the Sociology Department at a formal level. What it cannot communicate is what existence was like for the "out-group" in which every word was twisted to be used against the "professional pariahs"; in which every mistake, no matter how slight was capitalized upon; in which students were harassed, every suggestion blocked, every effort to accomplish even the tiniest change sabotaged. What had previously been visited upon Professor Dixon alone now became the daily bread of Professors Spector, Ehrensaft, and Wallerstein. It was an intolerable existence. Harassment is the way to effect a purge when legal means (out and out firing), fail. It was a conspiracy and a campaign to drive out the pariahs.

The Graduate Student's Petition, inserted into the minutes, April 4, 1974 begins a series of documents which show that the lives of graduate students were also miserable, their conditions having steadily deteriorated since the defeat of the SSU. Furthermore, Professor Von Eschen (and doubtless others) filled the heads of the graduate students with anti-Dixon, anti-Ehrensaft *and* anti-Wallerstein propaganda to the point where the frightened and gullible students were scared away from the very professors who would fight for them. Von Eschen's tactics were also designed to increase his graduate student load, the better to secure his position and grant him a captive audience. In 1971 Dixon had begun to warn good students away from the Department and had stopped trying to work with graduate students the same year, especially after reprisals had been inflicted upon the graduate students who had supported her during the renewal battle.

Document #47 is a protest from the graduate students against the faculty's refusal to respond to their petition, submitted April 4, 1974. Note, Document #46, May 21, 1974 the resolution to the discussion of the memorandum issued by the graduate students: "Due to lack of consensus no decision has been reached. The decision will be made by the co-chairmen." From May to September: decision, decision, where was the decision?

DOCUMENT 47

September 26, 1974.

To:
All Members of the Faculty,
Department of Sociology,
McGill University.

As the graduate student representatives elected last year to discuss student representation on departmental committees and in departmental meetings, we would like to draw your attention to the fact that, despite assurances made last spring that this matter would be quickly resolved, no action has been taken on this issue. Our understanding is that, after the department failed to reach consensus, responsibility for the final decision rested with the Chairmen. However, although each of us has been in town for all or part of the summer, no word has been received from them.

We feel that, since our requests were circulated on April 4th, a reply is long overdue.

Sincerely,

(Names deleted)

Document #48, Co-Chairman Westley's reply to the graduate students, merits extended translation. It will be recalled that the graduate students charged, and quite rightly, that:

> The two episodes described above demonstrate a distressing unwillingness on the part of faculty in the sociology department to confront either immediate organizational difficulties or the necessity for long-term policy. They also demonstrate a blatant lack of commitment to student interests; they are in no way isolated incidents.

The graduate students then went on the set forth four very tame demands: two elected representatives to the graduate committee and two representatives to the departmental meetings.

To these modest demands Westley replies: No! It is the rationale for the refusal that holds so much fascinating information and telling revelations. Westley begins with the same old refrain that Political Science and Sociology faculty had used against the PSA and SSU:

Obviously if we are to reach these objectives a number of different conditions must prevail within the department but two are of paramount importance: The highest possible standards of professional competence reputation [sic] among the faculty, for it is the national and international reputation of the faculty for excellence in their field that provides the graduate students with appropriate role models and with effective job sponsors . . . we would argue that it is only people with these qualifications who are competent to train graduate students.

Of course, one of the few men to meet those qualifications for "national and international reputation" was Professor Wallerstein, who supported the student demands! The old refrain: only faculty are competent, the six-year stanby. One wonders why faculty are so afraid of their students?

However, Westley very quickly moves to the real reason for his refusal:

Secondly, the department must make strenuous efforts to develop sufficient harmony and a working consensus which will enable us to cooperate in educating and placing our graduate students . . . More simply stated we were more concerned with the effect of your participation on the capacity of the department to meet these objectives than we were with how you feel about our decisions . . . I want to make it clear, however, that the problem does not arise so much from the actions of the students on departmental meetings, for they seemed to be both useful and detrimental, but from the effect which the presence of students had on the decision making processes of faculty. The presence of students seemed to transform departmental meetings into public forums, leading members of faculty to take public and political postures, and thus to deepen existing cleavages and antagonisms within these departments.

It should be noted that the only two departments, even at McGill, that bar student representation and participation are Classics and Sociology. Other departments at McGill seem to have weathered the terrible stresses and strains of "public forums and political postures." Why not Sociology? First, because Sociology was engaged in a triple purge, and did not want the students involved. Secondly because the Right-Opportunitists did not want student observers getting a first hand look at the cause of their grievances. And finally, because the Right-wing has been consistently anti-student, because they feared the students.

It will also be noted that Westley did not mince words when he tells students what he thinks of their opinions: "More simply stated we were more concerned with the effect of your participation on the capacity of the department to meet these objectives than we were with how you would feel about our decisions." Westley is a great advocate of "worker's participation" in industry: let the workers beware!

To be sure, Westley is willing to (1) tell students how to organize themselves (stipulating secret ballots, etc.) and (2) to grant two perfectly useless token observers to the appointments and graduate committee. One incident should serve to show the utter uselessness of such representation:

Our representative, Joan Hoffmann, put in many hours reviewing files — more, indeed, than several of the staff members of the committee — only to be informed in the final days that she did not have a vote of this committee. (Document #46).

The students are too cautious to tell the whole story. At the time, Professors Ehrensaft, Dixon and Westley served on the graduate committee along with Joan Hoffmann, who was every bit as conscientious and responsible as the students indicate in their petition. Her right to vote was taken away by Westley in a successful move to bar Nesar Ahmad (who had been editor of the McGill Daily, a known progressive student) from admission to the graduate program. Indeed, the incident of Nesar Ahmad was the last straw for Professor Dixon, who refused to attend one more meeting. Westley, prior to the consideration of Ahmad's dossier, was overheard by a departmental secretary (no longer employed by the department) to say that "Nesar Ahmad would be admitted over my [Westley's] dead body." The secretary repeated this information to a graduate student, and the tale quickly spread. When Professors Ehrensaft and Dixon challenged Westley's obvious prejudice against Ahmad, Westley retaliated by accusing *them* of "breach of confidentiality", when in fact it had been Westley's *own* lack of discretion that had made the reasons for his opposition transparent. So much for the stories of "dishonesty" on the part of Dixon and Ehrensaft. Ms. Hoffmann lost her vote so she could not cast it for Ahmad and very possibly for several other progressive graduate students that Westley was determined were not to be admitted. Later, Ms. Hoffman was to pay for her part in the "Memorandum from the Graduate Students", which was to cause her great anguish and anxiety: Westley is very quick to discipline "inferiors" who step out of line. Indeed, Westley says as much in his reply:

> These are all effects which are seriously detrimental to a healthy graduate department, and to the fate of graduate students *within* the department. (emphasis added)

One last point remains to be made from Document #48. It will be recalled that Co-Chairmen Solomon and Westley had replied to the protests (Document #46) of Professors Dixon and Spector against the Solomon-Westley *coup d'etat* as follows:

> While we agree that all members of the Department have the right to register their objections to departmental decisions in the minutes or otherwise, *we regard the statements of Professors Dixon and Spector as irresponsible and untrue since none of their comments are supported in any way*. We feel, therefore, that these two statements are a discredit to their authors. (Document #46, June 26, 1973, emphasis added)

In Document #48, dated October 3, 1974, Westley tells the graduate students:

> This both seriously interfered with the business of the department, and with the capacity of the departments to negotiate normative orders necessary to making decisions and getting the work of the department done. *This being the case it tended to drive business underground and into factions and cliques* . . . It was with knowledge of this kind of experience that we made the decision to reject graduate student membership in departmental meetings. (emphasis added)

The author rests her case.

DOCUMENT 48

Department of Sociology
October 3, 1974

To Graduate Students:

In response to your letter of September 26th, 1974 I must apologize for this delay in replying. However, on one of the questions you raised — that is student membership in the department meetings — the Department was unable to reach a decision and left it up to the Chairmen. We needed time to find out how colleagues in other departments and universities having students in the department meetings felt about it.

As you must know members of the faculty share with the graduate students an interest in and deep commitment to provide within the department an environment where the student can receive the best possible training and opportunities for personal growth. With this concern in mind we appreciate your efforts to seek out way in which the graduate program can be improved and in which the graduate students can make a maximum input. We also share with you another concern which is to provide you with the kinds of training and levels of competence which will maximize the probability that each of you will upon receiving your degrees, be placed in positions which fully challenge your competencies and provide opportunities for your advancement and development, and have given much thought to this, for the job market has already shrunk and will become more difficult in the future. Obviously if we are to reach these objectives a number of different conditions must prevail within the department but two are of paramount importance: The highest possible standards of professional competence reputation among the faculty, for it is the national and international reputation of the faculty for excellence in their field that provides the graduate students with appropriate role models and with effective job sponsors. At the same time, we would argue that it is only people with these qualifications who are competent to train graduate students. Secondly, the department must make strenuous efforts to develop [sic] sufficient harmony and a working consensus which will enable us to cooperate in educating and placing our graduate students. I would emphasize at this point that our self-esteem and success as serious members of faculty is closely related to our success in providing excellent graduate training and in placing our graduates in good jobs. (I am happy to report in this connection that a recent survey of sociology departments in Canada indicate that the McGill department was fare [sic] ahead of any other department in Canada in terms of the reputation and productivity of its faculty).

It was with these considerations in mind that members of the faculty addressed the suggestions which the graduate students made concerning their participation on various departmental bodies. More simply stated we were more concerned with the effect of your participation on the capacity of the department to meet these objectives than we were with how you would feel about our decisions. I am happy to be able to say that with respect to two bodies (the graduate and appointments committees) we definitely felt that the students participation would have this effect, but must regretfully report that with respect to participation in the departmental meetings this would not be the case. Thus the department decided:

1. There will be one graduate representative on the Appointments Committee with full rights, to be elected by secret ballot, annually, in the Spring. The business of this Committee is to search and screen candidates for position on the Faculty.

2. Two graduate student representatives shall serve on the Graduate Committee. They will be elected annually, [sic] in the Spring, by secret ballot. They will then be recognized as fully fluedged [sic] members of the Graduate Committee with the proviso that they will have only a consultative role on the selection of new students and shall not participate in decisions involving a clear conflict of interest such as the evaluation of other graduate students.

The Department was unable to reach a consensus — and left the decision about student membership in Department Meetings to the Chairmen. After consulting colleagues in other departments at McGill and elsewhere where the students did participate in departmental meetings, and finding that many colleagues were critical and none were enthusiastic and after a personal review in which we were unable to see gains from student participation and could see some possible serious disfunctions, we felt that we could not break the deadlock. This has the effect of rejecting the student request of membership in Department Meetings.

I want to make it clear, however, that the problem does not arise so much from the actions of the students on departmental meetings, for they seemed to be both useful and detrimental, but from the effect which the presence of students had on the decision making processes of faculty. The presence of students seemed to transform departmental meetings into public forums, leading members of the faculty to take public and political postures, and thus to deepen existing cleavages and antagonisms within these departments. This both seriously interfered with the business of the department, and with the capacity of the departments to negotiate normative orders necessary to making decisions and getting the work of the department done. This being the case it tended to drive business underground and into factions and cliques. These are all effects which are seriously detrimental to a healthy graduate department, and to the fates of graduate students within the department. It was with knowledge of this kind of experience that we made the decision to reject graduate student membership in department meetings.

Yet, we have made this decision with regret, for we feel fortunate to have a group of graduate students who are both interested in and willing to help in the work of the department. We were mindful of your need for fuller communication from the department and feel that to meet this need that — we should explore alternative means. One such suggestion has been to have regular meetings of the faculty and graduate students in which we keep each other informed of developments, ideas, needs and problems, through we hope that most of this business can be transacted within a graduate committee. However, we would welcome alternative suggestions.

I would be pleased to meet with any or all of you to discuss these matters at an early and mutually convenient date. Should such a meeting result in what we would both see as viable alternatives I am certain that the department would be interested in meeting to consider them.

Yours sincerely

William A. Westley
Co-Chairman

WAW/cc

Document #49 is the reply from the graduate students. This reply led to an "informal" meeting between faculty and graduate students, at which the author (having just returned from her sabbatical leave) was a distant and amused participant. Professor Wallerstein, having the misfortune to have spent the last year in the company of the Sociology faculty, was *not* amused: indeed, the author had rarely seen Professor Wallerstein display (by attitude, not words) such overt disgust with Sociology's performance. The good faith, but growing impatience, of the students was painfully obvious. Student spokespeople persuasively, patiently, convincingly asked for almost *nothing* in the way of representation. The news that only Classics and Sociology were without student representation was a bombshell, to which the faculty had no reply at all.

THE CASE FOR GRADUATE STUDENT REPRESENTATION
Presented to the Faculty:
November 20, 1974

As we have stressed in earlier discussions on representation, students are concerned with three issues: disregard by faculty for our interests, lack of information, and our apparent irrelevance to the functioning of the department. We wish to move towards a stable structural solution to these problems. Representation provides a voice for our interests in the department, and is thus a first step toward realizing more general aims.

Representation for graduate students on department meetings could inject a portion of democracy into the decision making of the department. More realistically, representation might at least provide protection for students within the present uneasy climate. Certainly, representation will insure that graduate students have access to information about the department.

The Inadequacies of the Present System

In the existing organization, graduate students have representation on the Graduate Committee and the TA Grievance Committee; a recent proposal involves representation on the Appointments Committee. The decisions of these committees may be overturned in department meetings. Even if the individual committee concerned reaches consensus, a tiny minority of the faculty can reserve this consensus. The current committee structure then creates only *apparent* student participation in decision-making. Final decisions are in fact taken at a level that is removed from student input. Quite apart from the inequities of this system, it would seem to be of practical importance to include students with their own specific arguments — in the final decision-making process. Our experience is that student interests are treated at the department level in a cavalier fashion.

We need guarantees that student arguments are aired and seriously considered; that decisions, when taken, are conveyed.

The Question of "Special Interests"

Student interests are different from faculty interests, yet both are central to department business. Recognition and representation of our interests are crucial to the successful functioning of the department. Briefly, our academic progress in the department is directly affected by the variety of courses offered, degree requirements, and the structure of the graduate program. Proposals and suggestions for academic changes are the legitimate and pressing concerns of graduate students. Our academic lives are similarly affected by the money available for support and by the way it is distributed. This in turn affects the arrangements made for research facilities, office space, and so on.

Students have in the past been refused participation in department meetings on the basis of these "special interests". We have been presumed unable to contribute to the rational planning of the department because of our limited and specific commitments as students. It is true that we have some interests to protect — and that our participation will reflect these concerns. It does not follow, however, that we are unable to understand the importance of long as opposed to short-term planning.

In fact, *without* student representation adequate planning has proved impossible over any time span. In the history of the department, disregard for student interests has been mystified by this supposed distinction between long and short-term interests. The evidence indicates that, without student input, short-term planning (reflected in the hiring policy of the department, the provision of courses appropriate to current students, and the maintenance of the appropriate balance between faculty and student interests) has been sadly lacking. We have experienced the detrimental effects of this haphazard short-term planning. Students fail to see evidence of a coherent long-term policy.

The development of an overall plan is central to the creation of a vital department. Current research, the reputation of the department, and graduation of students all depend on the ability of faculty and students to perceive the direction of the graduate program and the means to move toward chosen research paths. It may be more peaceful to avoid the question "What is the department really about?" — it is also unfortunately unrealistic in the contemporary sociological context.

"Polarization"

Student participation in department meetings has been rejected in the past on the grounds that it will polarize the faculty. Professor Westley's letter to graduate students on October 3rd clearly indicates this:

> I want to make it clear, however, that the problem does not arise so much from the actions of the students on departmental meetings, for they seemed to be both useful and detrimental, but from the effect which the presence of students had on the decision making process of faculty. The presence of students seemed to transform departmental meeting into public and political postures, and thus to deepen exisiting cleavages and antagonisms within these departments. This both seriously interfered with the business of the department, and with the capacity of the departments to negotiate normative orders necessary to making decisions and getting the work of the department done. This being the case it tended to drive business underground and into factions and cliques.

This statement is disquieting for a number of reasons. First, it is difficult to see how the present balance of power within the faculty would be substantially altered by student participation. Second, it leaves to the imagination the particular sensitive issues within the department which require privatized negotiation. Third, it seems that graduate students are expected to pay the price of faculty polarization. In effect, we are asked to leave decision-making to a group that cannot resolve its own problems. but sees fit to resolve ours.

Representation in Practice

Students are working towards a department which is responsive to our interests. It should be clear that the form of representation we aim for will be one which can ensure accountability to the graduate students as a whole. We see the active participation of our representatives, their commitment of time and energy, as essential to this goal. Representatives would normally be chosen in the spring, at a time when graduate students can assess each other's relative capability and commitment. We feel that the continuing efforts we have directed towards attaining representation demonstrate the active concerns of students as a group, and of our representatives.

We do not view participation as a panacea, nor do we expect the representative's role to be problem free. Some business may go more slowly. This is to be expected when additional groups are operative in decision making. However, this problem can be minimized both through access to clearly stated agendas of business and with a more open forum, informal and formal, for decision making.

We see the need to create flexible representation. The consensus system involves a shifting resolution of issues. The system is, however, non-participatory in the wider sense. In view of this, it seems overly optimistic to anticipate that student representatives would not, on occasion, need to consult their wider constituency. This is, after all, our only guarantee that the collective voice of students will be heard on critical issues.

The case for representation made here rests chiefly on the inclusion of student interest in decisions. This solution is addressed to larger problems, common to both students and faculty. It is our hope that life in this department can be more than a matter of survival.

Document #50 (Hamilton to "Whom It May Concern") is the theoretical, political manifesto of the Right-Opportunist faculty opposing graduate student demands for representation. Since the meeting was "informal," i.e., not a faculty meeting, no decision-making was "mandated." After interminable discussion (a blow by blow replay of the old SSU debates) Co-Chairman Westley declared that "no decision is made." A straw vote, however, was teken of faculty positions, the voting as follows:

Against the Students, in favor of the Hamilton Statement	Representation for students, with reservations	Representation for students
Westley	Krohn	Wallerstein
Solomon		Ehrensaft
Pinard		Rains
Hamilton (letter)		Dixon
Robinson		
Carroll		
Von Eschen		

DOCUMENT 50

McGILL UNIVERSITY
DEPARTMENT OF SOCIOLOGY

November 20, 1974

TO: Whom It May Concern

FROM: Richard Hamilton

SUBJECT: Governance of the Department

This is an educational institution. Its most important task is the education and training of students. A basic assumption of any such institution is that those charged with offering the education and training have themselves been trained in and become expert in the subject matter of the field. The inverse of this is another basic assumption, namely that the students are not yet trained, they are not yet expert in the subject matter. An institution of this sort is not intended to be a democratic polity with all participants counting as equals. The initial basic assumption is the *inequality* of the current of accomplishment.

Proposals to bring persons who are currently in the process of acquiring that education or training are difficult to reconcile with the "sense" of an educational institution. Being in a position to direct the educational operation assumes a prior knowledge of the education to be directed. If that prior knowledge is not yet there, the contribution to governance is going to be a limited or problematic one.

The quality of decision-making is diluted by such a process and the amount of time spent in departmental governance is increased. That additional time spent in "governance" must be taken from somewhere else. The loss, in most cases, comes from time which would otherwise be spent directly or indirectly in the tasks of education. For both of these reasons I am opposed to the proposed innovation. It is detrimental to the interests of students and faculty and to the interests of the general public who ultimately support the entire enterprise.

For the purpose of the discussion at the special meeting of November 20th, I wish to empower Professor Pinard to represent me in all matters. No decisions, I trust, will be taken at this meeting.

Richard Hamilton

Document #51 (issued in April, 1975) signals the final triumph of the Right-Opportunists and the Von Eschen "desperate need for a methodologist" line that Professor Wallerstein had been fighting since 1972. (Documents #41-43) The debate had continued, taking shape as two opposed positions:

Wallerstein: The very best of the available candidates should be recruited.

Von Eschen-Pinard: Hiring should be determined by "priority", i.e., "need" to develop one of the other speciality which, oddly, enough, always turned out to be quantitative methods.

Professor Wallerstein had opposed the Von Eschen-Pinard "desperate need for a methodologist" not only in the terms spelled out in Document #41, but also by pointing out the obvious: even *if* hiring were limited by the "priority" demand, the priority could hardly be methods, since the Department already had a number of qualified persons (Carroll, Hamilton, Pinard and Von Eschen). Pinard and Von Eschen had been trained at Johns Hopkins by James Coleman when it was a great centre of quantitative methods. (Of course, Professor Wallerstein was too much of a diplomat to point out that he knew very well that the presumably qualified persons were too lazy to offer to teach methods courses.)

Wallerstein's position had been supported by Krohn and Spector, who had pointed out that the department already had quantitative methodologists (but Spector, in his usual honest and direct way, *had* pointed out that the qualified persons were too lazy to teach it). Secondly, all three had further argued that the *one* kind of methodologist the department did *not* have was *historical methods*; if there were going to be priorities, it ought to be where the real need was the greater.[20] But *who*, pray tell, uses historical methods? Wallerstein, Ehrensaft, Dixon and Marxists.

---

20. Professor Wallerstein had given seminars and colloquia on historical methods throughout his residence, i.e., unlike other Sociology faculty, he was competent to teach methods *and* theory to his students.

Von Eschen's memorandum, Document #51, a long, turgid document communiqué makes quite explicit, among other revelations (including his own, Pinard and Hamilton's incompetence to teach quantitative methods — at least according to Von Eschen) that Von Eschen holds to his "desperate need for a methodologist" in order to safe-guard his own politics, which would not be challenged by a politically "safe" technician in quantitative methods. A more pernicious desire of Von Eschen's is also expressed in Document #51 (conforming to his treatment of graduate students in general) that is, a required methods course of the sort outlined would put the political graduate students through the ropes — since such students would be working with variants of Marxist theory and would be employing historical methods in most cases (or would need training in economics). Therefore, to require survey and quantitative methods credits was a way of harassing and discouraging Wallerstein and Ehrensaft's graduate students, or indeed, any politically progressive graduate students.

What the McGill outsider would have great trouble spotting in this effort of Von Eschen's is the disguised attack against Wallerstein coupled with the bizarre listing of the "intellectual" credentials of his friends, Professors Pinard and Hamilton and, of course himself. For example, the following "intellectualese" sounds very profound:

> One of the major works relating social structure to development is Genovese's, referred to above. This work has recently come under heavy attack by Fogel and Engerman in their work, *Time on the Cross,* a work given center-piece reviews in the "New York Review of Books", and the "New York Times Book Review Section", and the like. Fogel and Engerman are econometricians. Without acquaintance with hard methods one can't intelligently read this book. More important, without skills in hard methods, one can't adequately criticize it.

In a review written for the *American Journal of Sociology* of Fogel and Engerman's *Time on the Cross* and Genovese's *Roll, Jordan, Roll,* Wallerstein writes:

> As for the process of evidence and inference, the two books illustrate quite different styles. Fogel and Engerman explicitly present their book as an example of the usefulness of cliometrics, 'a set of tools which are of considerable help in analyzing an important but limited set of problems.' (p. 9) Genovese says, on the other hand that 'the subject of this is the quality of life which largely defies measurement.' The contrast between a "scientistic" and "humanistic" style (which is not at all a distinction, if there be one, between scientific and humane knowledge) is an old one, and despite the brouhaha of the publishers of *Time on the Cross,* no new twists are evident in the work of Fogel and Engerman. I leave quite to the side, furthermore, the criticisms of Fogel and Engerman from other cliometricians who argue that *Time on the Cross* is bad cliometrics, as I do those criticisms of Genovese from other Marxists, that *Roll, Jordan, Roll,* is bad Marxism.
>
> I leave on the side. I do not necessarily agree or disagree. But I do not wish to be diverted from what I think would be the useful things to do: discuss the theoretical adequacy of the interpretations. I do this out of a sense of intellectual priorities at this particular moment in history. I have a feeling that the methodological issues have been for the moment fully explored, at least as far as our governing theoretical frameworks permit . . . In my view, the key intellectual bottleneck at the moment is theoretical. We are facing the need to rethink and restate the conceptual frameworks we have inherited from the nineteenth century in order that we can understand and contribute meaningfully to the long world-

systemic transition to socialism which has begun and in which we are living. Both books illustrate very well the nature of these intellectual difficulties.[21]

Wallerstein then proceeds to do very splendidly what Von Eschen asserts *cannot* be done, that is, to adequately criticize Fogel and Engerman *without* a critique of method. Wallerstein knows very well what Von Eschen refuses to understand: that methods never transcend theory (although they may be determined by theory); a method is no more than a tool to address the central task of theory development, which is why Wallerstein was able to address the theoretical heart of the work of Fogel and Engerman and Genovese alike and in contrast, even though one method is "quantitative" and the other "qualitative". We must conclude, on the basis of Von Eschen's own arguments, that his incompetence in quantitative methods would require that a critique of Fogel and Engerman be done by the future "methods man" for Von Eschen says he is incapable of doing his own critique.

The reader needs also to know a little of the background concerning the "student" referred to in Von Eschen's "manifesto" to the Sociology Department on the Department's incompetence in methods:

> I have a very striking example of this prerequisite. I had one of our brightest and most hard-working students go through a number of these works [attacking "radical", whatever that is supposed to mean, theses on contemporary development]. It turned out that she was unable to really critique them. Yet they are directly relevant to her interests and are attacking her own most deeply held beliefs. Essentially all she could do was reject them on the grounds that they contradicted her beliefs and that, therefore, they must be fundamentally wrong.

In the first case, Von Eschen did not "have" this student — the student in question was doing her thesis with Professor Wallerstein. It would be more accurate to say that she fallen into Von Eschen's clutches. He demanded that she do three times the normal reading for such a course, then rejected the paper she turned in, demanding that she undertake another enormous reading load and re-write the paper, giving a critique of the anti-radical literature. She refused, and he gave her a lower mark. What in fact was going on was a common practice in the Department and a favourite ploy of Von Eschen's: he was attacking Wallerstein through one of his students; by claiming that the student was capable of no more than rejecting anti-Marxist writing "on the grounds that they contradicted her beliefs", he was attacking the training she was receiving from Wallerstein. The whole charade, for which the student was made to pay the price, was an attack on the intellectual and professional work of Professor Wallerstein. Another manifestation of this hostility was found when Von Eschen claimed to "admire" Wallerstein's work on the Capitalist World Economy, but then terms it "economic history" when in fact it is an original and creative extension of classical Marxist theory, as the reviewer in the *New York Review of Books* had recognized. Von Eschen, one must assume from his own testimony, is too theoretically illiterate in Marxism to recognize what Wallerstein's intellectual work is and where its significance lies.

---

21. Immanuel Wallerstein, "American Slavery and the Capitalist World-Economy: A Review Essay," to appear in the *American Journal of Sociology*.

DOCUMENT 51

TO: THE SOCIOLOGY DEPARTMENT

FROM: DONALD VON ESCHEN

RE: PRIORITIES IN HIRING

This is to explain why I think we need a quantitative methodologist. I am doing this in writing because I don't think anyone would have the patience to sit through a verbal presentation this long in a Departmental meeting.

Let me begin by stressing, and I can't emphasize this too much, I am not interested in hiring a quantitative methods person because I think "hard" methods are the only way to truth. I do not. One proof of this is that I have used no hard methods in *any* of the writing that I have done in the last three years. Another is that only a very few of the books that I use in my courses employ quantitative methods. Nor does my taste in general run especially toward quantitative works. Two of my favourite books are Genovese's, *Political Economy of Slavery,* and Barrington Moore's, *Social Origins of Dictatorship and Democracy.* Neither are quantitative. Another is Wallerstein's, *The Modern World System,* and an additional one is Westley's, *Violence and the Police.* The first is historical and the second uses participant observation. I, also, happen very much to like Pinard's, *Rise of a Third Party,* and Hamilton's, *Affluence and the French Worker.* These, of course, both use simple quantitative methods. But I hope this isn't taken to indicate my partiality towards such methods, but rather my eclecticism, my belief that many different methods can lead to high quality work, if wielded by talented individuals. In fact, the essence of my conviction is that many different methods should be pursued in sociology, for each has certain strengths for certain types of problems.

However, I do feel the following very strongly.

1.   Quantitative methods are *one* very important way to truth. Therefore, we should have some full time person in the Department who can effectively teach them in all their complexity.

2.   Command over quantitative methods is essential for participation in intellectual discourse in certain important fields. Some of these are fields we concentrate on at McGill:

a.   *Development.* Let me begin with historical development. One of the major works relating social structure to development is Genovese's, referred to above. This work has recently come under heavy attack by Fogel and Engerman in their work, *Time on the Cross,* a work given center-piece reviews in the "New York Review of Books", the "New York Times Book Review Section", and the like. Fogel and Engerman are econometricians. Without acquaintance with hard methods one can't intelligently read this book. More important, without skill in hard methods, one can't adequately criticize it. Of course, you might say this is an isolated case. But it is not. Much of U.S. economic history is being rewritten, correctly or incorrectly, by econometricians. And now econometricians are beginning to rewrite European economic history. A book has just come out recently on England. Thus, for students to participate intelligently in the discourse in this area, they must be trained in quantitative methods. The same is true for contemporary development. The radical thesis about current development (or more precisely, under-development) has been attacked in a number of major quantitative studies — by Leff, MacBean, Diaz Alejandro, etc. I think each of these studies contains crucial methodological problems. But for a student to see this, he needs to be fairly well trained in quantitative methods. I have a very striking example of this pre-requisite. I had one of our brightest and most hard-working students go through a number of these works. It turned out that she was unable to really critique them. Yet they are directly relevant to her interests and are attacking her own most deeply held beliefs. Essentially all she could do was reject them on the grounds that they contradicted her beliefs and that, therefore, they must be fundamentally wrong. Of course, one could say that only conservatives use quantitative techniques in this field and, because they are obviously biased, quantitative work can thus be ignored. But quantitative work has been used not only to disprove, but also to prove the radical thesis. For instance, one can refer here to the work of Chase-Dunne, which analyses cross-national data through regression analysis. The two radical students here with whom I have talked who have read this work both liked it. But this study, too, contains important methodological problems, and, as far as I can tell, these were not picked up by these students. Finally, turning from empirical studies to theory, one of the major theories underlying the radical thesis about development uses the labor theory of value. I refer here to Arghiri Emmanuel's brilliant work, *Unequal Exchange*. To decide whether or not to adopt Emmanuel's theory in part requires coming to terms with the labor theory of value. And this, in turn, requires the ability to read the literature on the subject. This literature, which is of very high quality, is heavily quantitative and mathematical in character. Could most of our students in development read this literature? I think not . . .

b.   *Economic Sociology.* A number of staff and students in the Department are interested in the functioning of economic institutions in advanced societies. The reason that sociologists are interested in this is because economists have by and large abstracted from these institutions and, thus, ignored crucial variables. Nevertheless, *some* economists do deal with institutions and they have produced a large body of research, much of which is referred to in Scherer's book, *Industrial Market Structure.* Most of this literature uses econometric techniques; that is, it is quantitative. One of our graduate students wrote a field exam in this area. Much of what he wrote was wrong, for he was ignorant of this literature. Furthermore, even if he had been aware of it, it is doubtful if he could have read it, for he was without the quantitative skills to do so. Furthermore, it is not only economists which have used quantitative methods to investigate the functioning of economic institutions. Political scientists and sociologists have also been doing so. See, for instance, the volumes entitled, *Testing Theories of Economic Imperialism,* and *Testing the Theory of the Military Industrial Complex.* These books contain crucial empirical studies. And a substantial proportion of these studies use quantitative methods. Shouldn't our students be able to do such research? And shouldn't they be able to criticize it in depth?

Of course, it may be objected to all this that the literature I have cited is not in sociology but in other areas. I disagree. One of the prime virtues of sociology is that it transcends disciplinary boundaries; that it breaks up the artifical divisions existing in the social sciences, boundaries that in some aspects advance knowledge, but in others inhibit it. Work by sociologists was crucial in transforming what is done in political science. I expect Wallerstein's work in economic history to do the same for that field.

Nevertheless, let's assume for the moment that sociology should stick to its own. Here I point to the character of our own journals. They are full of literature using high powered quantitative methods. Now it is true that most of us don't read the journals. The articles they contain are too diverse (they cover too many fields) and most are dry and uncreative. Nevertheless, we are likely to refer to the journals for evidence for propositions we want to argue for or attack. That is, the quantitative articles — most of which do no more than test hypotheses (which is one of the things that makes them dull) — contain *evidence*. However dull, they are, therefore, nevertheless important. Our students need to be able to read them, and they need to be able to critique them deeply. We need quantitative methods taught by a full time person for that reason alone.

O.K., let's assume that I have convinced you — which of course I probably haven't — that we need to have a full time methods person. Isn't it the case that we already have people who can adequately teach students quantitative methods, or, in a more extreme form, that the Department is being taken over by quantitative methodologists.

Let me take the last argument first. In the Department, there are only 3 persons who use primarily hard data in their writing: Pinard, Hamilton, Carroll. I do not do so now; my interests are historical and theoretical. On the other hand, there are 9 persons who use primarily qualitative data: Solomon, Westley, Wallerstein, Krohn, Robinson, Spector, Rains, Ehrensaft, and I can even include myself. I really don't yet know where to classify Smith and Locher. In any event, it ought to be clear that our Department does not produce primarily quantitative literature. But we can go further than this. Most of the people who do or have produced quantitative work are hardly methodological purists who believe that quantitative work is the only road to truth. Hamilton, for instance generally supplements his quantitative work with a broad knowledge of historical and other qualitative materials, as anyone who has read the extensive footnotes in his books will know. Furthermore, he has often expressed to me his great admiration, for instance, for Whyte's, *Street Corner Society,* a book based exclusively on participant observation. On top of this, he is working on a book on American presidential politics that uses as its main data historical qualitative documents. As for me, I have already stated that I now use non-quantitative methods almost exclusively. Furthermore, until the last few years, I have systematically worked to hire people on the basis of their substantive work, regardless of methods. Generally, I have looked for people with a critical stance. Thus, I supported, for instance, Kay Trimberger, whose work is historical, Barrie Thorne, who used primarily participant observation, and so forth. (Hamilton, too, by the way, supported Thorne.) I only began looking for a quantitative methodologist when I suddenly began to realize that we would not get such a person automatically, and that, furthermore, as we recruited persons — persons that I supported — who did not use quantitative methods, that some of them would be against hiring such a person. I then got panicky and supported a candidate last year that thought sociology was the quantitative study of the relations between indexes rather than people. I regret I did this. It sprang not out of a belief that quantitative methods are the only road to truth, but out of the situation I have described above. That is, out of a realization that we as a Department are becoming dangerously weak in one — not the only — important method, and that some members of the Department were apparently prejudiced against this method. It sprang, in essense, out of my commitment to a range of methods. Pinard, believe it or not, similarly regards a range of methods as legitimate. If this is not visible, it is largely because most of his own work has been quantitative. But it has been quantitative not out of a belief that this is the only way to truth, but because he has a particular talent for survey research. I know from many conversations with him that he appreciates work done with other methods *if* this work is done in a rigorous fashion. This leaves only Carroll. I would have thought that Carroll might be committed to quantitative research as the only real road to truth. But apparently I was wrong. At the last meeting, he hardly showed a compulsion to hire a quantitative methodologist — on the contrary. And even were he a methodological purist, that would make only one person in a department of 15. In short, I reject as nonsense the view that this Department is dominated by quantitative purists.

What about the other objection — that we already have full-time persons here who can adequately teach students quantitative methods? Contrary to Carroll's assertion, neither Pinard, Hamilton, nor I can adequately teach these methods. How can this be, you might ask? We come from two of the most quantitative departments in North America — Columbia and Johns Hopkins University. Let me begin with Hamilton. When he was at Columbia, he ran around with an anti-quantitative crowd. His mentor among the graduate students was Maurice Stein. And he avoided like the plague courses by Lazarsfeld. Essentially, as he will tell you, he never learned to do much more methodologically at Columbia than compute a percentage (which, of course, he already knew). He analyzes survey data (collected by others) using percentages. This is all he does methodologically. His work has the stature it does because of its intellectual — not methodological — content. He is not trained, nor has he acquired the knowledge, to teach hard methods. The same is largely true for Pinard. I was at Hopkins with Pinard. He did not learn a lot of high powered methods there. Many students did, but it was not necessary to get through the program. If one learned survey methods, that was really all the Department required, whatever its external image. Coleman and Stinchcombe — in spite of their own mathematical skills — were much more interested in substance than methods. If you could show that you could do intelligent work using simple methods, as Pinard did by writing a publishable paper (published in the *AJS*) his first year there — that was all that counted. You did not have to become a methodological wizard to get a Hopkins' Ph.D. Thus, Pinard did not learn factor analysis, did not become skilled at regression, etc. Of particular importance, he did not learn statistics. He had the unfortunate experience of being thrown into an advanced statistics course for which he was not prepared (he had never had a beginning statistics course) and which was taught not by the regular professor — who was an excellent teacher but was unfortunately on leave — but by an ex-student who spent almost the whole course on probability theory and hardly got to statistics at all. As with Hamilton, the stature of Pinard's work results not from methodological sophistication, but intellectual content. He, too, is not trained to teach a quantitative methods course. Both Hamilton and Pinard could teach an elementary survey course, and under pressure both probably would agree to do so. However, they cannot fill the need for a full-time person sophisticated in hard methods. As for me, I am somewhat more sophisticated than Pinard or Hamilton — that is, I have had more training. However, for years I have done virtually no quantitative research. I am, as a consequence, hopelessly out of date on recent developments — that is, developments since 1965 (10 years out of date). My future research will not lead me to pick up new techniques. Research, furthermore, is the only way a person picks up such techniques. And, in any event, although I did study quantitative methods, they were hardly my forte or my chief interest. Finally, the only way a student can really learn high powered quantitative techniques is by working with a person that uses them daily in his own research. I say this on the basis of having watched the ways students learn these techniques and fail to learn them. The student I referred to above who couldn't critique the quantitative literature attacking her view had been through Eaton's quantitative methods seminar. Only if there is a full-time person here who constantly uses these methods and inducts students into their use, will these methods be learned. (The proviso, of course, is that the person know how to use his methods to study important problems in an intelligent way. It is for this reason that I regret having supported the candidate last year mentioned above.)

In sum, I think we need a full-time quantitative person, and this should be one of our priorities. The person, of course, should be not only skilled in quantitative methods, but knowledgeable about society and intelligent in their use.

I might conclude this already overly long plea with a statement of why I am so concerned about this. When I entered graduate school many years ago, I was attracted to methods because they seemed to offer a way of rigorously grounding knowledge. At the same time, I was repelled by the conservative, apologetic, non-critical nature of social science. My hope was that in time a new generation of social scientists would create a different kind of social science, one that would combine a critical stance with the rigorous grounding of that stance. That is, I hoped that critical social scientists would arise who also had high methodological skills — both quantitative and qualitative, for, as I have said, I believe that both methods are important for rigorously grounding knowledge. Well, what has social science produced since I left graduate school? It has produced a critical sociology. Thank god for that.* But has it produced a grounded critical sociology? To a slight degree, yes. But much too large a part of critical sociology is assertion rather than research. One of the central tasks lying before social scientists now is to link critical social science with methods. In our Department we already do this in terms of qualitative participant observation. What we need also to do is to do it in terms of quantitative methods.

It would be in error to believe that the procedures and departmental politics of the Sociology and Political Science Departments were atypical of McGill; they are not. They have the merit, however, of being crude, so that departmental procedures and its mentality as well had become transparent to Wallerstein early on in the Dixon case; the same sort of mentality and procedures turned up in the Vaillancourt case; but it was the appeals to the MFU that were to teach Professor Wallerstein that Sociology and Political Science were specific examples of what was generally accepted at McGill. McGill was a branch plant; it was a version of the University College of the Gold Goast. Wallerstein consequently found himself fighting McGill, not only Sociology, Political Science, French and English Departments, not only through MFU, but in the Faculty of Arts as well. It is in Document #44 that the generality of prejudice, arbitrary judgement and political persecution at McGill is revealed. The reader will recall that "incompatibility" was the fundamental ground upon which justification for the attempted dismissals of both Dixon and Vaillancourt actually rested. In Document #44 Wallerstein is seeking to block an attempt to write "incompatibility" as grounds for dismissal into the university regulations:

Grounds for the refusal of tenure may include *inter alia* such factors as serious incompatibility with one's colleagues or with established academic priorities . . .[22]

The Faculty of Arts meeting at which this run-in between Westley, Wallerstein and Hamilton occurred was held on February 19, 1974 (the year that Dixon was due to be reviewed for promotion).

It will surely not be lost upon the reader that the "incompatibility" clause being defended by Westley, echoed by Hamilton, quite literally would make it regulation to dismiss or deny promotion or tenure to any individual who is disliked by any "Renewal, Promotions and Tenure Committee" at McGill. Furthermore, the "academic priorities" criterion makes it possible to fire even charming Marxists. The reader will further note that Professor Wallerstein had been fighting against these "old boy" procedures at McGill since 1971 on behalf of the whole faculty at McGill (cf., The Vaillancourt Precedents). The Sociology Department was convinced, however, that Wallerstein was doing no more than paving the way for Dixon's promotion when he raised objection (Item 606.5). It was clear from Westley and Hamilton that *they were* anticipating what they believed to be a

---

* It would be more appropriate to thank Marlene Dixon, Columbia Graduate Students, David Colfax *et al.* for that; however, since Donald Von Eschen has in practice, opposed critical sociology; certainly has made no contributions to it, invoking supernatural entities is perhaps appropriate to the case.

22. *REPORT OF THE SENATE COMMITTEE ON APPOINTMENTS AND TENURE,* p. 8. The Senate Committee on Tenure was appointed March 1969 to "review the regulations governing the appointment and tenure of teaching staff, and to recommend to Senate revision of these regulations". The Committee submitted a report to Senate at the end of the summer of 1970, which was discussed in a Senate meeting on 25 November 1970. The Faculty of Arts discussion presented here was held in February, 1974.

Dixon promotion/dismissal battle (Items 606.9, 606.12, 606.14, 606.15). It must be granted that Westley-Hamilton were not being selfish in their goal: they were willing to assure the same right to arbitrary dismissal to Political Science (in order to finally rid themselves of Vaillancourt) and indeed, to the whole reactionary old-boy network at McGill.

In Document #44, in Westley and Hamilton's own words, was found proof of the major assertions made in this book:

> Professor Hamilton said that in his view compatibility really was a serious issue and did not present all the difficulties that Professor Wallerstein imputed to it. There were after all people who were seriously incompatible with colleagues and there should be means for removing such persons. (606.9)

> Professor Westley said that the idea of incompatibility perhaps raised ambiguities, but it was nevertheless true that departments were bodies of people who must work together (sic). This being so, there should be room for the expression of serious incompatibility *without placing upon the department concerned the necessity of lying.* Incompatibility was a real phenomenon. (606.12, emphasis added.)

> Professor Westley said that in probationary status, the burden of proof lay on the candidate and that therefore objective proof was not required. *As to the general question of incompatibility, the grounds will be used in any case, whether under other disguises or not.* (606.14, emphasis added.)

DOCUMENT 44

REPORT OF THE COMMITTEE ON APPOINTMENTS AND TENURE (D3-11) A-73-25
DISCUSSION ON TENURE — App. p. 161

606.1 Professor Westley said that the core of the report was a decision that tenure was a desirable thing and that in coming to that conclusion, his committee had rejected arguments that tenure was unnecessary. Earlier arguments for tenure had centred on the protection of members of an academic community from intervention by external and political sources. Now it could be seen to allow members of Faculties to have protection from their colleagues. At the same time, it was certainly possible to use tenure as a crutch — that was to say, as protection in a secure job. The only way to protect tenure was to force Faculty to make a clear and difficult review before tenure were granted. The committee's recommendation of an "up or out" policy had been designed to emphasize this. This was a harder decision than the mere decision to permit tenure, since if a member of Faculty were good enough for tenure, he would under this provision be good enough for promotion. Thus when departments consider this review they will make the review in terms of academic competence, teaching ability and quality of intellectual productivity. The effect of this was not to force the university into a "publish or perish" position, but only to require a hard decision on whether tenure and promotion are proper or improper in particular cases. A second crucial part of the report was the provision of due process for probationary appointments and the underlining of the fact that in probationary appointments the burden of proof lay upon the candidate and not upon the department.

606.2 Professor Malloch said that he considered the most important section of the report to be Section C, the dismissal procedures. So called tenure at McGill was in fact no protection since the Statutes said that the Board of Governors may "remove" for cause. After having considered the well-being of the university the section of the report to which he spoke required arbitration for removal and were Section C of the report to be removed, the report would be much diminished in effect.

606.3 Professor Wallerstein asked what was the Status of the discussion.

606.4 Dean Vogel said that Faculty could move with respect to one part of the report or another for transmission to Senate but that the discussion would also serve to inform the Senators of Faculty's views. Senate would attempt to boil down the report to its basic principles.

606.5 Professor Wallerstein said that he thought it was a fine report and that he agreed the purpose of tenure was not only to protect members of Faculty from public authorities but also from colleagues. He was in general agreement with the report but had two reservations. The first reservation was the phrase in Section B 11 "serious incompatibility with one's colleagues". This phrase opened a Pandora's box, since it was able to cover illegitimate motives for termination. His second objection was an omission, concerning the rights of persons holding a first probationary appointment to have a second one. This he would pursue at a future time.

606.6 Professor Wallerstein *moved* and it was duly seconded "that this Faculty believes from the reasons for denial of tenure ought to be removed the notion of serious incompatibility with one's colleagues". The surrounding text for this section was then read by Dean Vogel from the Senate document D3-63, page R-3.

606.7 Professor Velk said that Faculty ought to go through the document in an orderly way.

Professor Wallerstein said that this was true enough but that in his view the particular thing he had pointed our was most important and ought to be dealt with straightaway.

606.8 Professor Lindeman said that he was in principle in agreement with Professor Wallerstein's motion. It was exactly such a phrase that pointed out that Faculty was engaged in supporting a system of meritocracy and indeed it ought to do so. Nevertheless, the notion of up or out was new and it was very true that this in conjunction with the removal of the requirement for strong compatibility with colleagues would lead to a "publish or perish" situation. It should be pointed out that the incompatibility spoken of was serious and the seriousness of it was after all the point.

606.9 Professor Hamilton said that in his view compatibility really was a serious issue and did not present all the difficulties that Professor Wallerstein imputed to it. There were after all people who were seriously incompatible with colleagues and there should be a means for removing such persons.

606.10 Professor Thompson said that the itemized list of causes were a sufficiency of reasons for any department.

606.11 Professor Malloch said that the report had been drafted in 1970. It was to be hoped that one would be permitted over the years to advance one's own learning. Incompatibility had at one time been part of the CAUT guidelines, but those guidelines had more recently been amended to exclude incompatibility as a cause. He therefore supported Professor Wallerstein's motion.

270

606.12 Professor Westley said that the idea of incompatibility perhaps raised ambiguities, but it was nevertheless true that departments were bodies of people who must work together. This being so, there should be room for the expression of serious incompatibility without placing upon the department concerned the necessity of lying. Incompatibility was a real phenomenon.

606.13 Professor Wallerstein said they had no doubt that this was at the heart of what a lot of people considered tenure. Without the phrase substantive grounds for termination would have to be demonstrated. With the phrase no one would ever win an appeal. There were other grounds and these were grounds which could be evaluated. Scholarship, for example, could be evaluated by the whole academic community and teaching could be evaluated by student reports and evaluations.

606.14 Dean Vogel asked on whom did the burden of proof lie.

Professor Westley said that in probationary status, the burden of proof lay on the candidate and that therefore objective proof was not required. As to the general question of incompatibility, the grounds will be used in any case, whether under other disguises or not.

606.15 Professor Hamilton said that the idea of serious incompatibility was not a triviality.

606.16 Professor Wallerstein said that he had not meant to suggest a shift in the burden of proof, but nevertheless the whole history of professorial protection in North America lay in the overriding of departmental cases by the requirement that grounds be demonstrated.

606.17 Professor Lindeman said that he would vote for Professor Wallerstein's motion, but that nevertheless Faculty should consider seriously the problems of the publish or perish policy which might be implied in the report.

606.18 The question on the motion was put and carried, Faculty then adjourned.

April 8, 1974.

Item 606.6 "Professor Wallerstein *moved* and it was duly seconded 'that this Faculty believes from the reasons for denial of tenure ought to be removed the notion of 'serious incompatibility with one's colleagues'. Professor Wallerstein's motion passed: 50 in favour, 4 against. Two of the nay votes were cast by Professors Westley and Hamilton.

The fact that the Sociology Department was haunted by the fear of a Dixon-Wallerstein-MFU-CAUT style battle for renewal and promotion is signaled not only by the revealing antics in the Senate and Faculty of Arts, but also in an astounding article written by Professor Hamilton laying out the departmental "line" on Dixon *and* on the pernicious consequences of Professor Wallerstein's defense of such "incompetents". Such pre-struggle promotional work was necessitated by the loss of the "compatibility and academic priorities" clause. Of course, *The Montreal Star* had no way of knowing that it was being utilized as part of a propaganda war. The irony of Hamilton's effort was, unknown to the Sociology Department, Professors Dixon, Vaillancourt, Ehrensaft and Wallerstein had *all* decided that they had had enough — more than enough — of Old McGill.

The Dixon Resignation, October, 1974

As a type of social man, the intellectual does not have any one political direction, but the work of any man of knowledge, if he is the genuine article, does have a distinct kind of political relevance: his politics, in the first instance, are the politics of truth, for his job is the maintainance of an adequate definition of reality. In so far as he is politically adroit, the main tenet of his politics is to find out as much of the truth as he can, and to tell it to the right people, at the right time, and in the right way. Or stated negatively: to deny publicly what he knows to be false, whenever it appears in the assertions of no matter whom; and whether it be a direct lie or a lie by omission, whether it be by virtue of official secret or an honest error. The intellectual ought to be the moral conscience of his society, at least with reference to the value of truth, for in the defining instance, that *is* his politics.

C. Wright Mills,
On Knowledge and Power, 1955.

As a type of social woman, the intellectual does not have any one political direction, but the work of any woman of knowledge, if she is the genuine article, does have a distinct kind of political relevance: her politics, in the first instance, are the politics of truth . . .

A sabbatical leave is a truly wonderful opportunity for reflection and study. When I departed McGill, I had opportunity to review what the ravages of fighting on and off for nine years against political repressions and purges in the academy had done to me intellectually, morally and psychologically. The years fighting were in one sense an irreparable loss to me, years stolen from my development and my thought in pursuit of the politics of truth. Reflection led me to an absolute determination that not one more hour should be stolen from me; no power on earth, not promotion, not tenure, not $25,000 a year would have persuaded me to spend one more moment combating the mindless, malevolent stupidity of the McGill Department of Sociology.

I promised that my letter of resignation would be a means to continue the struggle, but this time about *them*: this book is proof of the assertion. The indictment is the resignation itself.

272

DOCUMENT 52

McGILL UNIVERSITY

October 8, 1974

Professor R. Vogel, Dean
Faculty of Arts
McGill University
Montreal, Quebec

Dear Dean Vogel:

This is to inform you that I do not wish to be considered for renewal in the Department of Sociology and wish to resign as of 31st August, 1975. I have come to this decision only very painfully after long consideration. In five years one forms attachments to people and places which are not easily given up. Considerations of justice impel one to demand, or try to demand, a decent hearing on the question of appointment. However, I know that I cannot expect a decent hearing, only a political combat. I would even be willing to engage a political combat if I thought some useful purpose would be served, if some change within the Sociology Department would result from It. However, the last three years have made it plain that no change would result in the presently intolerable conditions. Since I am not the only one who suffers under the repressive conditions that exist, I am taking this opportunity to state openly why I prefer resignation to reappointment.

It was once my belief, which I must now think to have been hopelessly naive, that universities were places in which one furthered intellectual work in a supportive and collegial atmosphere. But what I have experienced at McGill in the Department of Sociology has been an ever increasing atmosphere of repression, vindictiveness and distrust, which leads in turn to such bitterness, anger and disgust that one's whole life becomes corroded by it. For example, consider that the Sociology Department was unable to select a chairman because of the over-riding political considerations and motivations of the entrenched reactionary faculty. To ward off putting the Department into receivership, which ought to have been done, rights to faculty self-government were sacrificed, and explicit recognition was given to the *de facto* dictatorship of the reactionary senior faculty. This decision stripped the minority faculty of any rights or protections within the department.

How does one institute a petty dictatorship? First, one needs the acquiescence of the McGill Administration which has shown itself reluctant to intervene, possibly because the top levels of McGill's administration have no commitment to academic freedom whatsoever, and indeed may well support the suppression of progressive faculty. It was, in fact, only the intervention of CAUT in the Vaillancourt case that stopped a blatant political firing. Or perhaps the administration is unaware of the situation in the Sociology Department? I find that hard to believe. In the first case, the top Administration must be aware that the repressive activities of the reactionaries in the Sociology Department have extended themselves to collateral departments because this was made obvious in the Vaillancourt case. Secondly, the administration must have realized the political motivations which dominated the Sociology Department's inability to select a chairman by normal procedures, since these machinations were made public at the time. One therefore is led to assume that the repression practised in the Sociology Department is given license by the tacit approval of the top University Administration itself.

The faculty reactionaries are always pointing the finger of blame for politicizing the department at progressive faculty. Yet how can that be? The progressive faculty do not form a bloc, nor even represent a single tendency in Sociology. The group of "progressive faculty" exist as such only as a consequence of the polarization created by the systematic persecution of any dissenting faculty of any sociological persuasion by the entrenched senior clique. Furthermore, "dissenting" refers to those faculty with the courage to oppose the oppressive rule of our "benevolent dictators," and not to participation in communist or socialist "plots" to "take over", the department, as was alleged in the fiasco over the non-selection of a chairman. Symbolic interactionists, Marxists, Africanists, and economic sociologists obviously do not form a disciplined organization of political agitators! When socialist plots are not manufactured to disguise the hegemony of the reactionary faculty, then the issue is presented as the "preservation of standards." Yet all that is being preserved are mechanistic, professional "standards" having nothing to do with actual competence or with intellectual excellence. "Standards" serve as a diversion, as a cover for the blatant repression which is required to keep mediocre senior faculty in control of the department. Preservation of "standards" also serves to legitimate the fact that any vigorous intellectual tendency which does not conform to the establishment sociology in vogue ten years ago is slandered as "incompetent" and becomes a non-challenge to the prevailing mediocrity.

The very use of the term professional is important. The "profession" is in fact a hierachical organization in which power in the profession is gained by the same means used in any other bureaucratic organization. Those who control "standards" and "professional criteria" control academic sociology, and the prestige and high salaries and occupational security that goes with professional power. It is thus a situation in which men of a hostile ideology are in a position of defining standards and criteria for those whom they consider to be their enemies! Marxism directly challenges their theoretical hegemony — and their theories themselves. Progressive young faculty demanding restructuring of the university challenge the existing reward system of prestige and salary as well as directly challenging the entrenched power and privilege of senior faculty. That is why academic reform and student participation is opposed, not because of any intrinsic concern for intellectual "standards," which are quite different from professional "standards." Graduate student participation was crushed in the Sociology Department at McGill when their demands extended to participation in faculty hiring, precisely because the power to hire and fire, define "standards," and "judge" the work of junior faculty is the very foundation upon which senior faculty power and privilege has historically rested. What disguises itself as "saving" professional (not again, intellectual) "standards" is in fact a political process by which those entrenched in power stay in power. It is why, for example, the Sociology Department can be so acutely embarrassed when scholars from outside the department and of unquestionable reputation, but *no vested interest,* expose the Department's "judgment" of junior faculty as hopelessly biased. It is why there are two standards of judgment in the Sociology Department, one for the *senior* faculty and those junior faculty who exhibit the proper servility, and another for those junior faculty who do not. It is why standards are applied to junior faculty which the *senior* faculty have not achieved. It is why the Sociology Department at McGill does not conduct evaluations, but vendettas, as several cases at McGill have made clear. In my case, my reputation, controversial as it is, is established, and nothing that the McGill Department says or does accomplishes anything more than strengthening existing opinions. Other junior faculty are not so fortunate.

This reactionary hegemony means that every facet of academic life is in fact politicized. Renewals are based on the individual's alignment or non-alignment with the clique in power. Promotions are given only to those who collaborate with the regime. It means that it is impossible to recruit the most competent candidates for new appointments, as spurious political considerations are always found to block these appointments. It is wonderful to behold how plodding, mediocre candidates somehow excel in "professionalism" and are without "political" taint, that is, so conformist that they seem to present no oppositional danger. Graduate student applications are also scrutinized for possible "political" tendences, and competent graduate students have been refused admission on political grounds alone. Once in graduate school, the students confront politically motivated obstacles to certification. Graduate students have no rights, and are not significantly represented in the governance of the department. The appointment of students to sit on a committee where they have no vote and are never taken seriously is an insult to their intelligence and mine. Having a reactionary without relevant qualifications doublecheck the reading of an exam by progressive faculty, ostensibly to "protect standards", is insufferably oppressive, as are set-up situations where one is expected to "perform" for hostile faculty as a test of "competence," under cover of a seminar.

The real struggle in the Sociology Department is not over "standards" and not occasioned by "socialist plots." It is a struggle for academic freedom. The "dissenting" faculty are those who engage a different sociology and/or have a different conception of graduate education than does the ruling clique. In turn, the ruling clique is not concerned with "standards" and violates academic freedom consistently in order to preserve their power, protect their prestige and mask their mediocrity. *That* is what makes it insufferable. Their right-wing sociology goes hand in hand with their right-wing politics, which makes them attack Marxists with a virulence that is nothing less than persecution. If they singled out only myself, we could certainly classify them as purely motivated by reactionary politics, which would be bad enough. The truth is, they are principally motivated by self-interest *and* reactionary politics. Thus they attack anyone who opposes them in any way and especially those of whom they are "professionally" jealous or who challenges them intellectually from a different tendency within Sociology.

In the Sociology Department it is possible to depict what the triumph of reaction means in terms of daily life. It means, for me, that to accept reappointment in that department would be to continue to try to survive an oppressive, reactionary and vengeful atmosphere. That would be analogous to accepting a prison sentence, to serve time in a prison of the mind and spirit. That is what they have made of "their" department.

However, the McGill Sociology Department raises a much larger issue, the issue of genuine academic freedom. That issue is not confined to McGill, but part and parcel of the general triumph of reaction in North American Universities.

Permit me to recall some of the issues that were important at the time of the last renewal struggle, since those issues are still important. First, there is the politicization of my academic life that began in the 1960's. It was in part the consequence of two sets of events: the regeneration of Marxian sociology out of critical sociology (in which I have been an activist, along with others, to fight for the *right* of a Marxian tradition to co-exist with mainstream sociology) and the struggle for a relevant and responsible university, that grew out of the opposition to the war in Viet Nam that was waged on campuses in the United States. Campaigns in opposition to the war spread to political struggles for a university responsible to the community (which in turn grew out of the civil rights struggle of the Black people); to demands that students had a right to participate in the decisions affecting their lives and their education; and which in turn spread to the struggle for the equality of women. That was how it began.

Against these progressive currents for change, reprisals from those with vested interest in the status quo, the reactionaries, were not long in coming. I was but one of the early activist junior professors purged, and I use the term deliberately and without exaggeration, from American universities. It is now common knowledge how this purge was disguised, hiding behind the assertion that "academic standards" of excellence were being threatened by activists. In my case, the University of Chicago thought it was necessary to fly Edward Shils in from England in order to attack the Doctoral thesis of a junior professor of less than two years standing. I suppose I ought to be flattered. So many others were purged with so much less ceremony.

To those who would quibble that Chicago was not a purge, I answer simply by saving that the faculty where I worked, Human Development, recommended re-appointment for a full three years and never retreated from that position, even when great political pressure was put upon them to do so. The Sociology Department was therefore used as the instrumentality for the purge, a department so previously unconcerned with my academic work that they did not even know I had undertaken a study of Marxian sociology. They did know, however, that I was an organizer of the Sociology Liberation Movement against whom their colleagues in Boston had felt impelled to call the police (under no direct provocation), and they also knew, from a student police informer and a police undercover agent, that the Chicago police department considered my teaching "dangerously persuasive" and myself a subversive. The point is important, since the University knew that the student was an informer as he had undertaken to sue the University. I also knew that the University had consultations with the police. I also know that the student informer was readmitted to the University while I was removed. The case was a classic politically motivated firing, a gross violation of academic freedom. I hope you begin to understand why I use the term *purge*.

The rise of dissent and the slow emergence of Marxism in the 1960's created situations where academic freedom became a central issue. It became the central issue because a real attempt to use academic freedom as something more than empty rhetoric occurred. At that point, internal and external pressures were brought to bear on the universities, calling for the suppression of such "extremists". Universities answered that demand of conducing the purges themselves rather than resolutely defending academic freedom. Universities and related organizations erected structures of procedure behind which to hide their purges, to make it impossible to demand any redress against either direct firings or not very subtle campaigns to hound and persecute people to the point of leaving.

I have included mention of the Chicago affair precisely to underline the point that formalistic, abstract discussions of academic freedom to not touch the roots of the real lack of freedom, the very real oppression and persecution, the injustice, that is common "procedure" in academia today, and that is the common "procedure" in the two universities at which I have spent my academic life: the University of Chicago and McGill University. It is in fact more widespread than these two universities. There has been David Colfax from Washington University, the purge of the Criminology School at the University of California at Berkeley, and a long list of others. All of these cases make it clear that there is seldom genuine redress within the present academic system.

Indeed, it is probable that it is politically impossible to ever have any guarantee of genuine academic freedom. Nonetheless one must raise the issue in hopes that some persons treasure intellectual freedom enough to at least oppose the present condition of unfreedom and repression, to see beyond the strangulating hypocricy of "procedural appeal" in which the accused is assumed guilty and must "prove" innocence, while all means to display that proof are virtually denied. How can one "prove" an institutional process? How does one "prove" the coming and going of police agents? unrecorded phone calls? threats and conspiracies under cover of "confidentiality"? How does one discover perjury without subpoena power and rights to cross-examination? In the Colfax case at Washington University the committee of professors called upon to decide the Colfax case concluded that under the *procedures* for determining *if violations of procedure* constituting violations of academic freedom had occurred, it was impossible for them to find such violations, even though they *knew* there *were* violations, knew that an injustice was being done, were aware that outside political pressure was placed on the university, and knew that Zeitlin and the others were lying. The Committee recommended that procedures be changed. Of course, procedures were not changed.

Herman and Julia Schwendinger have recently completed a book, *The Sociologists of the Chair* (Basic Books, 1974), which represents the most thorough-going treatment of the development of American sociology, and which treats at length the interplay between academic freedom and North American sociology. Their study is pertinent because it reveals such repression is not new, but has characterized the field, determined its theory and development, from the very beginning. It may be said that undue reference should not be made to the United States in regards to a Canadian university. However, since the McGill Department of Sociology is overwhelmingly staffed by American sociologists and is, furthermore, completely oriented to American sociology, it is impossible to speak of academic problems at McGill in isolation from the situation in the United States, reproduced as it is at McGill.

Some of the history of North American departments of sociology as recounted by the Schwendingers is therefore relevant, for the methods of repression have changed very little over time. In 1914 at the annual meeting of the American Sociological Society there was a panel on academic freedom — it could have been transcribed from a panel held today. Consider these statements from the discussants:

As an economist, Nearing (1914: 165-166) pointed out that the issue of academic freedom was not concerned primarily with the protection of the rights of non-conforming faculty, because they were decidedly in the minority. 'The real issue regarding the freedom of teaching,' Nearing insisted, 'lies in an entirely different direction. There are in every college faculty numbers of men who are under the domination of that most rigorous of all taskmasters, the necessity for providing a living for a family. Even when they are willing and anxious to express themselves, they have this necessity constantly confronting them.' (p. 532-533)

In 1914 teachers were usually hired from year to year, with the result that "the extent of occupational insecurity (which) permeated the entire field of higher learning . . (resulted) "in only a minority of institutions in the United States does the question of academic freedom present a significant issue." Things have not changed much. Now a dissenting professor is due after a year and a half to have a "review" to determine if reappointment should be made for a new three year contract. Since a dissenting professor may not safely conclude that he or she will *ever* be promoted, much less given tenure, men and women are broken, purely and simply, by the mechanism of occupational insecurity. It is a singularly brutal method of social control, reprisal and punishment.

E.A. Ross, one of the "founders" of American sociology, commented at the conference that he agreed with Nearing:

He tersely noted that "academic asphyxiation is much more common than is generally realized." He objected to parts of Pritchett's statement . . . which implied that few academics are actually dismissed by universities much less dismissed because of political reasons. Ross commented: "President Pritchett's paper is, I think, far too optimistic. The dismissal of professors by no means gives the clue to the frequency of the gag in academic life." Ross, of course, was not without personal experience in this regard; officially Ross had voluntarily *resigned* from Stanford, although everyone knew that he was, in fact, forced to leave that institution. (p. 533).

The Schwendingers amply document that North American Sociology was ideologically cleansed from its earliest days, which in turn determined its theoretical development culminating in a theoretical sociology which has been incapable of predicting any major contemporary event, and which has been repeatedly exposed over the last ten years to have been a sophisticated exercise in the task of justifying, excusing, rationalizing and promoting the American status quo, and very little else.

It is important that we understand the real nature of the "cleansing process". How is it that a discipline becomes ideologically self-policing in order to avoid the "risk of raising questions of violation of freedom where such questions have no proper place?" In the formative years of American sociology, as Veblen made clear in his analysis, based on the University of Chicago (*The Higher Learning in America: A Memorandum on the Conduct of Universities by Businessmen*), ideological selection and promotion of professors (hand in hand with universal repression of "impossible" socialist or Marxist professors) created an elite within the university agreeable to American capitalism. That elite became intertwined with the administration of the University itself, gaining control over hiring and firing, control of professional journals, promotion and recognition. The results were multiple hegemonic roles in the profession and academy. The findings, as summarized by the Schwendingers:

These repressive relationships, as we have seen, encompass the bureaucratic controls that (as exercised by university administrators and senior academics) have influenced academic working conditions and hiring practices. Furthermore, because of the identification between the academy and social science disciplines, the effects of these controls have been reinforced by the *professional* definitions of the domains of these disciplines and the *professional* criteria for evaluating scholarly competence. In academic life, moreover, both employment practices and professional standards are, to some extent, formulated, *operatively interpreted, and sanctioned by the very same men.* (p. 546 emphasis added)

277

These are the "very same men" whose *professional* power, whose style of "mainstream sociology", rests upon:

> the systematic effects of outright, periodic political repression in this country. Repressive attacks occurred, for example, during and after World War I, toward the end of the Great Depression, prior to and during the McCarthy period, in the later sixties, and at the present time. During these periods, overt repression, added to enduring repressive relationships, have provided multiple guarantees for the long-term domination of liberalism within the academic social sciences. (p. 546-47).

What of the situation today? Has it changed from the early days when socialists and Marxists "ran the everpresent risks of being stigmatized as irrational, incompetent and unprofessional"? The Schwendingers report:

> Flushed with their experience in civil rights and anti-war movements, armed with contempt for liberal platitudes, and equipped with more objective understanding of American society — radical members of the new generation of American sociologists made their first significant critical assault on professional institutions at the 1968 annual conference of the American Sociological Association . . . Many liberal sociologists immediately responded to this assault by deriding the radicals for their "uncouth" manners, their defiant condemnation of the field, and their disrespect for the institutions that academic sociology had served so faithfully. (pp. 564-65).

As one of the organizers of that assault I can testify to the Schwendingers' account. Indeed, we were so "uncouth" that police protection was dramatically, and completely unnecessarily, called in. We also had a slogan, *Knowledge for Whom?*, and we attacked professional complicity in American militarism and the war in Viet Nam. That was the opening battle. In the intervening years the outcome has been the general triumph of reaction by means of systematic repression. How was the reaction manifested?

> By 1971, an unbroken series of articles attacking radical developments in the field began to appear in professional journals such as the *American Journal of Sociology*, the *American Sociological Review*, and the *American Sociologist*. (p. 565).

But was this attack an open intellectual "battle of ideas"? It was not, since prior to the "defense of reason" carried on in the house journals:

> (from 1968 to 1970) in American institutions of higher learning, radical scholars began to experience a wave of political repression. This wave was spearheaded in some instances by institutional trustees. But it was chiefly conducted by academic administrators often operating in collusion with tenured faculty members within social science departments and professional schools, or within academic senates as a whole. (p. 565).

I have made a distinction between *professional* and *intellectual* standards. The professional justifies his judgments on "intellectual" grounds, posing as competent to judge the apparently overwhelming incompetence of radicals and Marxists according to "intellectual merit" and "professional" standards. I submit that they are *not* intellectually competent to judge, even if they were capable of mastering the bias produced by vested interest, which they have proved themselves not to be. Most of them are not competent to judge the work of symbolic interactionists *or* Marxists because they are not trained in these disciplines. Not only are they ignorant of these fields, they are actively hostile to them, and substitute prejudice for judgment. They see these fields as competitive to their own, and often have a vested interest in attempting to discredit the specialties by discrediting the people who practice them. It is but another example of the double standard, one applied to us and quite another to them. It is taken for granted that we must defend the very right for our thought and mode of analysis to *exist* in the face of mindless but well established "professional" prejudice, while the bourgeois ideologists, the "professional" social "scientists" indulge themselves freely in attempting to discredit alternative theoretical systems.

Yet those are the very same men who sit in judgment, hire and fire and renew and "evaluate", the work of Marxists. By what "procedure" is such an absurdly repressive process redressed? Will the requisite number of committees, readings, hearings and appeals educate them? Over-ride their fear and loathing for a theoretical system which has been systematically repressed from the 1880's to the present? and which directly threatens their hegemony, theoretically and professionally? What "academic freedom" is there when considerations of power and prestige are at stake, and when a hostile and self-interested elite *controls* hiring, firing, judgment, determines "standards"? Is, in short, judge, jury and prosecutor.

That such prejudice presented as "standards" is applied in the Sociology Department at McGill became public knowledge with the distribution of the document concerning the Chairmanship. I experienced this prejudice personally in the previous consideration of renewal of contract two years ago. The Sociology Department *habitually* uses "nonprofessional" and certainly "non-intellectual" political considerations in their conduct, hiding behind "confidentiality" to keep people silent who are repelled at what they see and hear, and who quite understandably fear the reprisals and punishments which the senior faculty of the Sociology Department exercise with such readiness. Indeed, there is only one member of the senior faculty who is a genuine intellectual pluralist, and who does have a genuine respect for academic freedom, Professor Wallerstein. However, Professor Wallerstein, whom I did not know prior to his coming to McGill and who agreed to defend my work on his judgment of its merits, thereupon lost all status as an internationally recognized scholar and became no more than a part, as the "secret" document from Sociology testified, of a "radical" conspiracy to "pack" the department, undermine "standards", and generally operate as part of an "international network of socialism" It was not until over fifteen outside scholars, including some who outrank anyone at McGill with the possible exception of Wallerstein, concurred in his evaluation that the august members of the senior faculty lost their nerve in asserting my "incompetence," or "irresponsibility" and my work as "having absolutely no merit". The spite and vengefulness that has persisted over the last three years, the politicization of every facet of departmental life, has been conducted by the right, by the reactionaries, even as they accuse me or Professor Wallerstein of being members of an international socialist plot to subvert professionalism, destroy standards, and seize control of "their" department. I ask the Dean: can you imagine what life in this department must be like for us? Where "it is hard to have one's every utterance examined by hostile eyes, the worst possible interpretation put upon his every act, and harder still to avoid the awkward sentence, the garbled statement, or the misreported utterance that will give... a chance to get rid of him as *incompetent?"* (Schwendinger, p. 537). Where "the students themselves were harmed because freedom of speech and intellectual honesty were greatly undermined in the process." It is an atmosphere in which almost all of one's energy is consumed in purely defensive and generally pointless, skirmishes; where daily life is oppressive, and above all *repressive,* for in such an atmosphere one merely *survives* — one does not grow or develop intellectually except through the most arduous and difficult effort. It is a process designed to break or drive out any dissenters, or even better to significantly cripple their ability to work intellectually as a result of the struggle to survive professionally. It is repression, brutal in its daily manifestation, subtle in its elusiveness. By what "procedure" does one demand relief from this kind of persecution? How can a purely legalistic, and fundamentally hypocritical, form of "academic freedom" protect the objectively powerless from the hostile, powerful men in control by virtue of the structure of academic jobs?

After all this, one might well ask what I do hold academic freedom to be, having spent so many pages trying to show what it is not, and above all, that it is far more than a question of following "correct procedure".

I start with the academic Magna Carta of the University of Wisconsin, inscribed on a tablet on Bascom Hall (1915).

As regents of the university with over a hundred instructors supported by nearly two million people who hold a vast diversity of views regarding the great questions which at present agitate the human mind, we could not for a moment think of recommending the dismissal or even the criticism of a teacher even if some of his opinions should, in some quarters, be regarded as visionary . . . We must, therefore, welcome from our teachers such discussions as shall suggest the means and prepare the way by which knowledge may be extended, present evils removed and others prevented . . . In all lines of academic investigation it is of the utmost importance that the investigator should be absolutely free to follow the indications of truth wherever they may lead. Whatever may be the limitations which trammel inquiry elsewhere we believe the great state University of Wisconsin should ever encourage that continual and fearless sifting and winnowing by which alone the truth can be found.

With this objective in mind, I propose that, to achieve academic freedom:

(1) the spirit of the above "magna carta" of academic freedom be extended to Marxists of *all* persuasions and not only those social "scientists" who fit within the liberal tradition and whose reformism never challenges capitalism, monopoly capitalism, imperialism, and all the consequences of these exploitative, oppressive, alienating and genocidal social systems.

(2) To protect, in reality, the academic freedom of dissenting faculty — indeed of *all* faculty — the link between the profession and employment be abolished, and that employment be regularized in universities as it is in all other unionized bureaucratic institutions, promotion being based upon the principle of seniority in time. Only in this way will the ideological and material tyranny of tenured ranking professors be broken, and the intolerable exercise of the power to withdraw a human being's livelihood be taken out of the hands of the senior professors. Far from the abolition of tenure, I propose its further extension to all.

I am more than aware that to demand the second point may be considered madness or "extremism" by administrators, present tenured faculty, and trustees. I believe, however, that nothing short of the second demand would, in actuality, guarantee academic freedom for dissenting faculty. In the absence of such a system, I am forced to conclude that there is not, nor could there be, academic freedom for real dissenters, given the present organization of the university. It is, furthermore, historically obvious that the only possible source of amelioration or redress of grievances is through the organization of intellectual workers employed on university staff into such a union as to give the dissenting professors the capacity to meet power with power, and so to defend themselves against repression from whatever source.

I will now conclude by stating once again that I resign in order to protest and to bring to the attention of the academic community at McGill University and other interested parties the following intolerable conditions in the Department of Sociology:

(1) The Department is administered in such a fashion as to be intolerably oppressive towards junior faculty and graduate students. That the department is a petty tyranny of senior faculty and has been two years without even the formal pretence of collegial democracy. That its decisions and policies have been based for the last three years on non-academic, politically discriminatory grounds. That individuals have been subjected to treatment that violates academic propriety, in that slander and other blackhanded means have been used against dissenting members of the department.

(2) Much of the source of the oppressive nature of the department results from the intolerance of the reactionary faculty towards, and opposition to, new and progressive, and specifically Marxists, thought. The reactionary faculty have sought only to repress this tendency in the department, to do everything in their considerable power to stop any person of a like persuasion, either as faculty or student, irrespective of intellectual or even "professional" qualifications, to be admitted to the Department. That their unyielding hostility and power tactics have bred such suspicion and resentment, bitterness and hostility among the members of the department that collegial democracy cannot function. That they have created this atmosphere in order to expel dissenting faculty and

students in such a way that they do not "risk raising questions of violation of freedom where such questions have no proper place".

(3)   They have been universally hostile in attitude and punitive in action to any person who has taken a position in favor of the Quebec people and in opposition to the present ruling class in Quebec. Reactionary members of the Sociology Department are so zealous in this aspect of their prejudice that they undertake to attack suspect persons in other departments as well as in their own.

(4)   They have so stripped graduate students of any rights and spread such a general fear of reprisal, based upon actual reprisals which have been taken in the past, that the conduct of graduate education has been seriously affected. Students select faculty and topics of study based upon the political position within the department of the faculty member in question, and in many cases not upon the intellectual considerations. The result has been to create a situation where "the students themselves were harmed because freedom of speech and intellectual honesty were greatly undermined in the process". Students have been admitted on the basis of their apolitical position in the "first place because they were conformists; or faculty members (and students) were indoctrinated under these conditions to the point where they gladly conformed".

(5)   They have presumed to apply to dissenting professors standards which they cannot themselves meet. Thus, they apply inappropriate standards. We have a situation in which assistant professors are sometimes more qualified and have a greater professional standing than full professors. This inequity is maintained in order to shield the mediocrity of the reactionaries and harm or expel younger and more intellectually vigorous junior staff. By so doing, they have substituted professional mechanics for innovating scholarship, Marxist or otherwise, and have actively opposed consideration of genuinely important intellectual questions by junior staff and most particularly by students.

(6)   They have violated the spirit and intent of the norms and values of academic freedom, *even as they would define it.* They have been utterly intolerant of academic freedom in the broader sense discussed in this letter, and their intolerance has been carried to the point where they feel free to act out their personal prejudices through vindictive actions against those less powerful than themselves.

Finally, as the seventh and last point, I wish to resign in order that I cease to lend them my name as an advertisement that the McGill Department of Sociology is a progressive department. I will not any longer have some student come to me, or a professor write to me, saying I have come or I want to come because you are at this department thinking they are going to get something they will not be able to receive, while more than likely receiving much more in the way of punishment and disappointment than they could imagine. Many people assume that the department must be progressive and open because I am here. It is insufferable to permit myself to be used in this way, so that these men may boast of their tolerance while in fact they violate decency, intellectual integrity and academic freedom with such seeming arrogance.

I will not accept employment at any cost, and thus I cannot continue to be a part of what is going on here. Since I have tried, and failed, to change matters, and since I cannot see how the situation can be ameliorated without some form of external intervention, perhaps by the province, I truly believe that the general cause is best served in this way, to expose and bring out into the open what has been hidden behind "confidentiality". Confidentiality is the last resort of academic frauds.

Yours sincerely,

Marlene D. Dixon
Assistant Professor of Sociology

The Vaillancourt Resignation, July, 1975

Surely in the Committee of Enquiry and its decision we see CAUT and the academic community at its best. And yet . . . What is absent? While "due process" in this case, at least, finally produced a just decision, the *cost* of due process, personally and financially, is born by the aggrieved professor. The radical issues, in the sense of *root* issues, *are* circumvented — that is, the issues of the original and fundamental injustices of political, sex and class discrimination that resulted in an unjustifiable refusal to reappoint Professor Pauline Vaillancourt. Indeed, the fight began in October, 1972 only in a technical sense; the fight, in fact, began with the original appointment in 1969 — and yet the resolution was not concluded until September 12, 1973 when the McGill Board of Governors informed Professor Vaillancourt that her contract was to be renewed, on recommendation of the Committee of Enquiry.

A year, at the very least, of Professor Vaillancourt's life was consumed and a not inconsiderable piece of Professor Wallerstein's time was also lost. Literally lost, in the sense that time fighting against an unjust and inappropriate firing cannot be compensated in any terms. Damage is not only done to professional reputations, there is also damage to health, personal relationships and scholarly productivity. When one completes the Ph.D., one has presumably committed one's life to scholarship: to threaten the very basis of an adult's chosen career is to create ferocious stress psychologically and intellectually. Furthermore, Professor Vaillancourt would not return to McGill. If she had returned, she would not have discovered a contrite group of colleagues, but a solid wall of vindictive hatred, so that her life would have been made more intolerable than it had been before, her scholarly work impeded and her human ability to be reasonably happy, safe and guaranteed the minimum tranquility in which to carry out her intellectual work, denied.

Pauline Vaillancourt's professional reputation was vindicated; the accusations against Professor Wallerstein were exposed as malicious and suspect in their motivation; *but at what cost?* And who shall compensate the cost? Not McGill, not CAUT. For beside the personal hardship that these attempted or successful purges imposed, there was the purely intellectual hardship: the energy consumed in defense of the right to exist is energy taken away from scholarly work, from intellectual productivity, from thought and intellectual development. The fact that dissenting faculty may be forced, quite literally, to expend the greater part of their lives fending off repression or finding a means of livelihood is itself a form of political, personal and intellectual repression:

> I myself have not written about the issues posed by the west coast sociology conference primarily because I have been deluged with dissertations, organizational work . . . an unstable job situation, family medical problems, etc. etc. etc. . . . outside of attempts to describe the events surrounding my tenure hearings I have not written anything substantial on any topic of interest to me over the last two years . . .[23]

23. From a friend to the author.

Vindication more often than not does not compensate for the losses:

> Of central importance to the second major finding of the Committee is its criticism of the Department of Sociology to which you refer in the later portion of your statement. The Hearing Committee did indeed judge that conditions in the Department of Sociology had deteriorated to the point that the Committee seriously questioned whether the Department could have made a tenure decision in an acceptable manner. The Committee found that in these circumstances the University's denial of tenure to Professor Colfax created an untenable state of affairs and one requiring relief for Professor Colfax. [24]

The intra-university Committee on Academic Freedom and Tenure's findings were violated in spirit and intent by Washington University (having no Quebec Labour Law or CAUT sponsored Committees of Enquiry) which led, at one point, to a letter from J. David Colfax, stating:

> I am pleased to see that the Administration of Washington University is beginning to recognize its responsibility for the damage done to my career and personal life as a result of the actions of certain tenured members of the Sociology faculty. I am at something of a loss, however, to understand the purpose the offer of one year's salary is intended to serve. It does not begin to redress the grievances I have against the Sociology Department and the Administration which is responsible for the actions of that Department . . . as such it shows little appreciation of the fact that the tenured Sociology faculty, through actions which are now a matter of record . . . have effectively destroyed my professional career, have made it impossible for me to find a teaching position in the United States, interrupted my scholarly work, and severely disrupted my personal life... [25]

Is it any wonder that so many professors decline to stand up for their rights or fail to defend their ideals when the cost is so terrifically high? When procedures (even in the best of circumstances, not true for Professor Colfax, far more true for Professor Vaillancourt) are so constructed as to impose enormous burdens upon those who suffer, and protest, injustice? And when the perpetrators of such violations of the fundamental norms which *ought* to be practiced in the academic community are let off with a tap on the wrist and a short-lived bruise "image-wise"?

The truth is that harassment, isolation and repression are everywhere taking their toll from radical scholars and radical scholarship — which is why more and more critical intellectuals are leaving university life. Most of "the boys" see this trend as a cause for rejoicing, but surely there are other members of the liberal academic community who believe, like the Committee of Enquiry, that:

> A new style of scholarship introduced into a department where a different style has prevailed is very likely to disturb the smooth congeniality of the department. But the claims of congeniality must not be allowed to outweigh the claims of scholarship, and a problem of this kind is an entirely improper reason for nonrewal. [26]

---

24. Professor Edward E. Schwartz, School of Social Work, member of Washington University's Academic Freedom and Tenure Committee in the Case of J. David Colfax, to Dr. William H. Danforth, Chancellor, Washington University, July 10, 1972.

25. J. David Colfax to Mr. Carl A. Dauten, Executive Vice Chancellor, Washington University, December 7, 1972. J. David Colfax is still (1975) black-listed and still unemployed.

26. Report of the Committee of Enquiry, Document #34, Item #34.

The author, who spent four years of her life attempting to secure a right to exist, and to establish the principle of pluralism in her department, asks the liberal members of the academic community: on what real grounds do you challenge us to respect *your* right to teach? Have you defended ours? Have you respected ours? Have you ever been seriously threatened with a purge for what you believe, study, teach? I know and you know that the answer is negative! If the present conditions denying academic freedom to critical social scientists are to be altered, then the academic community itself must engage in collective soul-searching and must find within itself ways to protect and guarantee dissenting thought. For the community is not now adequate to the protection or furthering of the *critical* intellectual enterprise. Failure to engage such a re-examination is itself an accusation: and a confirmation — that liberalism is bankrupt, and the university the most bankrupt liberal institution of them all.

The Committee of Enquiry decision forced McGill to grant, technically, a three-year renewal to Professor Vaillancourt. At the time that the decision was finally made to renew her contract, she was already teaching at the University of Quebec in Montreal. It is probable that McGill never expected that she would return — it is certain that the Political Science Department did everything to discourage her. The Committee of Enquiry decision could not change the basic repressive nature of McGill University, nor grant a true redress of Professor Vaillancourt's grievances — the basic injustice remains untouched. The root of the problem is specified in Professor Vaillancourt's letter of resignation, when she says:

> No legal system to my knowledge allows the same jury, whose verdict is determined unjust by a higher court to continue to sit and judge an individual in all future cases.

The Committee of Enquiry vindicated Professor Vaillancourt's assertion of her competency in her field and her accusations of the unprofessional and unwarranted treatment she received from the McGill Political Science Department. We shall close this section with Pauline Vaillancourt's letter of resignation from McGill University. In the McGill equivalent of the "back room" the boys could now cross off a second name. In June, 1975, Pauline Vaillancourt was elected to the Board of Directors of the Canadian Political Science Association.

DOCUMENT 54

UNIVERSITÉ DU QUÉBEC À MONTRÉAL
DÉPARTEMENT DE SCIENCE POLITIQUE

August 25, 1975

Robert Vogel
Dean of Arts
McGill University
Montreal, Quebec

Dear Dean Vogel:

Thank you for your letter of May 1, 1975. Please accept my resignation effective September 1, 1975. My reasons for resigning are many. I have an offer of a position with tenure at the Université du Québec à Montréal. But this alone is not the decisive factor. The main reason for my resignation is the general intellectual climate of the Political Science Department which results from the political biases, anti-women prejudices, and the overall anti-Quebecois attitudes and informal policies of that department. All of these contribute to create an atmosphere in which academic inquiry and freedom of speech are prohibited. The resultant educational environment is incompatible with learning. The documented effects of these prejudices on my own career are a part of the public record. The second reason for my resignation is that I honestly fear that should I return to McGill, I would continue to be treated in a most inequitable manner. My future would be determined by individuals who are biased against me.

The Political Science Department is anti-Quebecois. While such prejudice is manifested in every dimension of academic life, some concrete examples observed over my four years of participation in departmental affairs illustrate the point. Quebecois graduate students applying to the department must show greater merit than English students to be admitted. Justification for this informal policy, offered in response to my questioning it, was that "Francophones should not take places that rightfully belong to the English. The French should go to their own universities" (Professor Sarf, member of graduate admissions committee). A second form of discrimination was repeatedly drawn to my attention by McGill Quebecois students. They reported that they were afraid to submit written work in French, in spite of Quebec university regulations that authorize it, because certain political science professors give lower grades for work submitted in French.

Next, the Department of Political Science is biased against women. It has continued to administer scholarships designated "men-only" in spite of frequent protests by myself and others. In general the conversation in department meetings is indicative of deeply held convictions that women are inferior. When considering which students should receive even the non-discriminatory fellowships, a typical comment is, "now, for this fellowship, we need a *man* strong in international relations . . ." Higher education is viewed in the old English tradition, as the privileged sanctuary of men. Witness an example of this in a recently published article by one of the most senior and influential members of the Political Science Department. He wrote, "The student whose energy and persistence provide him with a good education . . . is an exceptional *man*" (Professor J.R. Mallory, "Over or Under-Educated", *Bulletin of the Canadian Political Science Association*, vol. 4, #3, Jan. 1975).

It is true that the department has three women professors, but then it is equally true that not one of them has ever effectively raised the women issue. They "count as women" (Professor Waller) but they in no way advance women's interests in the department. They contribute to the department's effort to maintain its "image", but with a minimum of substance.

The Political Science Department is openly anti-Marxist. Student demands that a Marxist be hired to teach the one course occasionally offered by the department on Marxism were met with the response that a Marxist could not objectively teach the topic because "he would be too close to the subject matter" (Professor Nayar). Liberals, however, have been hired to teach courses on liberalism, pro-imperialists to teach courses on the "developing nations". Students graduate and leave McGill knowing little or nothing about Marxism, except what knowledge they have acquired on their own at the risk of being penalized seriously if they use a Marxist approach in their work.

This failure of the Political Science Department to maintain an open, free intellectual environment carries over to the standards applied to politically conservative students and to students with a more progressive ideology. Based on my four years of active service in the Political Science Department (including membership on the PhD and MA examination committees) I am convinced that merit is seldom the exclusive criteria for my McGill colleagues decisions concerning fellowships, teaching assistantships, and PhD and MA exam grades.

If a graduate student who has proven to be "ideologically acceptable" does poorly on an exam for the MA or PhD, the department takes into consideration the fact that he or she was "tense before the exam", that he or she was having "personal problems" and was "not really working up to his or her ability" that day. The individual is given a passing grade or at the very worst obliged to take the exam over. A student whose left-wing opinions are known, seldom benefits from such a generous view.

Students suffer from the departmental atmosphere created by these biases, but the faculty is affected as well. I have been touched personally by these biases. The incompetent, but conservative faculty member is renewed and promoted by the Political Science Department as a matter of routine, even though in some cases the professor may lack a doctorate or a commitment to teaching, and research. Left-oriented professors, of even outstanding merit, find each renewal a hotly contested matter. Needless to say, few are hired and of those who are hired, none ever receives tenure. Their careers are marked by harassment and what they try to accomplish is inevitably stifled.

But it is not just the department's prejudices and biases alone which motivate me to resign. It is the fact that over the years these biases have lead to the creation of an atmosphere which is far from conducive to a high quality academic university life. Characteristic of this is the department's inflexibility with respect to my own now and critical approaches to both teaching and research. The joint CAUT and McGill inquiry committee cited the department's failure to adequately appreciate the innovative character of my work as an important factor contributing to the overall unjust failure of the department to renew my contract. In repeated testimony, members of the Political Science Department complained to the committee that the teacher's role was not to encourage controversy and heated discussion about political issues in political science classroom. The classic characterizations of the university as a place of quest and questioning has ceased to exist. Is it surprising, then, that the reputation of the McGill Political Science Department is at such a low point on campus and in the university community in general?

I made an effort to change the atmosphere of the Political Science Department. But, for example, when I treated all students equally, my political science colleagues condemned me for favoritism towards working-class students, women, Blacks, and French Canadians. My conclusion, after numerous experiences of this nature is that my presence in the department changes little, but serves to legitimize the unjust and unfair procedures and the biased, politically prejudiced decisions it so frequently renders.

I began teaching at McGill in 1969. In the first four years I was a professor at McGill, as you yourself indicated to me and to Professor Wallerstein in conversation, four attempts were made to fire me. The attempts failed each time, but only after the facts of the case became known outside the closed departmental atmosphere. In the most recent attempt, an outside committee of inquiry, of indisputable reputation, judged the department's decision in my case as improper.

You indicated to me in your letters of March 25, 1975 and May 1, 1975 that these same faculty members, who have found it impossible to be objective in making decisions about me in the past, will now be called upon to make judgments concerning my future at McGill (including promotions, committee work, sabbatical leave, and student thesis direction, etc). For example, on the question of a sabbatical leave, according to McGill's policy, two years of service at another university may be counted toward a professor's first sabbatical leave. However, in your letter of March 25, 1975, you informed me that the two years I served the French community by teaching at the Université du Québec à Montréal are not to be so counted. Despite your assurances, it is difficult not to attribute this to the general anti-Quebecois attitudes of McGill.

You confirmed my most pessimistic fears about my future at McGill when you cautioned that even when I am eligible (by your less than generous interpretation of my situation) for a sabbatical, decisions on these questions are at the discretion of the department, its needs, and long range plans. How can anyone seriously expect that the same group of people whose unfavorable judgement concerning me was determined to be unfounded and biased by an impartial body selected by the parties involved, will henceforth judge justly and impartially concerning me. Personally, I have no confidence. Would you?

These are some of the reasons why I have decided to resign, effective September 1, 1975.

Sincerely,

Professor Pauline Vaillancourt

PV/cm

The Wallerstein Resignation, 1975

Immanuel Wallerstein's final communication to the Department announced that he had accepted a post at the State University of New York at Binghamton. The decision to leave, of course, had been made at the time of the Chairmanship struggle in April, 1973. Shortly thereafter, Professor Wallerstein had informed the Department that he was "seriously considering specific offers from three major universities". The final choice for Binghamton was made as a consequence of Wallerstein's convictions:

> The chief danger to academic freedom in the United States today comes not from student disruption but from the self-deceptions of the professoriate itself, because of its reluctance to take moral risks, and the resulting tendencies toward mandarinism, discrimination and collegial pressure . . .

> The chief safeguard of academic freedom would be the transformation of the liberal university into the critical university . . .

McGill's Sociology Department thus lost the best scholar in the history of the Department. Mediocrity and mindless self-interest may perceive the market value of a professional commodity, yet not have the soul to see either the value of the commodity or the resistance of the creative mind to *being* a commodity. Above all, the men of the Sociology Department could not comprehend individuals who are committed to principle, who live by the ideals they propagate. In the end, they won, but won nothing.

The last person remaining in the Sociology Department, Philip Ehrensaft, experienced just such vindictive hostility (being the only remaining target) as he expressed to the author in a letter explaining his resignation.

DOCUMENT 55

Feb. 12, 1976

Dear Marlene,

What you have heard is accurate: I have resigned from McGill and am now teaching at l'Université du Québec à Montréal. As to your questions concerning the reasons why, I can't imagine many details of which you are not already aware. In a nutshell, the Sociology Department's steady attempts at political and intellectual repression on a plethora of matters, major and minor, provoked a constant drain of time and energy. There was no reasonable option but to resign from a department whose behavior contradicts all that university life should be. Having more useful things to do than waste hour after hour battling the endless repressive machinations of what passes for a department of sociology, I have abandonned these charmers to their own devices.

Phil

AFTERWORD: The following document was distributed in July, 1975.

The Annual Report of the Department of Sociology, which follows covers the second year of administration of the Department by a co-chairmanship. This interim arrangement has been very successful in achieving the purposes for which it was devised, and consequently seems likely to continue into the immediate future. Whatever minor disadvantages it may have are greatly outweighed by its advantages, and, on balance, it seems to have greatly improved the conduct of affairs in the Department.

Department of Sociology, McGill University,
Annual Report, 1974-75, David N. Solomon and
William A. Westley, Co-Chairman.

WORLD INEQUALITY

edited by
Immanuel Wallerstein

What has changed with the advent of the modern world since the 16th century is neither the existence of inequalities nor the felt need to justify them ideologically. What has changed is that those who defend the "inevitability" of inequalities argue that eventually, inequality will diminish. This factor is at the base of the debate on "international development."

The current debate however is a variant of the classic debates but a number of new issues have outdated these considerations. The thesis of the contributors to this book is that the modern world comprises more than ever before a single world capitalist economy. It follows from this that nation-states are not societies that have separate, parallel histories, but parts of a whole reflecting that whole. To the extent that stages exist, they exist for the system as whole. To understand the internal class contradictions and political struggles of a particular society, we must first situate it in the world-economy. We can then understand the ways in which various political and cultural thrusts may be efforts to alter or preserve a position within this world system which may be to the advantage or disadvantage of particular groups within a particular society.

Prof. Wallerstein brings together in an impressive international discussion of leading authorities to examine various aspects of development and inequality. These include: Richard D. Wolff, Mohamed Dowidar, Jean Piel, Ervand Abrahamian, Albert-Paul Lentin, Mohamed Harbi, Cary Hector, Bogdan Denitch, Denis Brutus, Jorge Niosi, Mahamed-Salah Sfia and others.

Prof. Immanuel Wallerstein is author of the internationally acclaimed book, *The Modern World-System: Capitalist Agriculture and the Origins of the European World-Economy in the Sixteenth Century.*

225 pages | Hardcover $12.95 | Paperback $3.95
ISBN: 0-919618-66-9/ ISBN: 919618-65-0

Contains: Canadian Shared Cataloguing in Publication Data

BLACK ROSE BOOKS No. E 26

THE QUÉBEC ESTABLISHMENT
The Ruling Class and the State

by Pierre Fournier

This powerful book deals with the questions — who owns Québec and who runs it. It is based on Dr. Fournier's detailed study of economic power and the corporations, the structure of business elites, their ideology and association as well as their relationship to government.

This well-documented study analyzes language and education, social and labour issues, as well as the economic policy of the Québec establishment.

The thesis of the book is based on questionnaires sent to 100 companies in the industrial sector as well as questionnaires sent to business leaders.

300 pages / Hardcover $11.95 / Paperback $4.95
ISBN: 0-919618-28-6 / ISBN: 0-919618-27-8

Date of Publication: Fall 1976

Contains: Canadian Shared Cataloguing in Publication Data

BLACK ROSE BOOKS No. F 30

LET THE NIGGERS BURN!

Racism in Canada
The Sir George Williams Affair and its Caribbean Aftermath

edited by
Dennis Forsythe

From the black point of view, Dennis Forsythe, who teaches sociology at Sir George Williams University has edited a collection of essays by other blacks which include: the problems of the black immigrant, the background to the "Anderson Affair" at Sir George Williams and what happened and the subsequent upheaval in the Caribbean area.

These and other essays in the book contribute to the publication of an important book in the growing literature of social criticism in Canada.

Contributors include: Delisle Worrell, Bertram Boldon, Leroi Butcher, Carl Lumumba, Roosevelt Williams, and Rawle R. Frederick.

200 pages / Hardcover $7.45 / Paperback $2.45
ISBN: 0-919618-16-2 / ISBN: 0-919618-17-0

BLACK ROSE BOOKS No. B 4
Library of Congress Catalog Card Number: 73-76057

QUEBEC LABOUR

*Preface by
Marcel Pépin,
president
of the CNTU*

What is the Confederation of National Trade Unions (CNTU) in Québec? How did it develop from its Catholic origins into a mass militant trade union movement representing 250,000 workers? How does the CNTU differ from the AFL-CIO affiliated Québec Federation of Labour? How did the CNTU move beyond collective bargaining to become a unique trade movement in North America? What is the CNTU's SECOND FRONT and what has been its effect in radicalizing both the organised labour force in Québec and the working population in general?

Why has the CNTU now adopted a uniquely anti-imperialist, socialist, and workers' control policy? What is the relationship of the CNTU to the national liberation movement in Québec? How does the CNTU analyse the 'Quiet Revolution'?

These and other questions are dealt with in this book, the content of which include:

A long historical introduction, the official translation of the document of the SECOND FRONT, and the exclusive official translation of the historic, *"Ne comptons que sur nos propres moyens"*.

2nd Revised Edition
224 pages / Hardcover $10.95 / Paperback $3.95
ISBN: 0-919618-14-6 / ISBN: 0-919618-15-4

Chosen for *Canadian Basic Books*

BLACK ROSE BOOKS No. C 6
Library of Congress Catalog Card Number: 73-76058

THE ANARCHIST COLLECTIVES

Workers' Self-Management in Spain 1936-39

edited by
Sam Dolgoff

"Although there is a vast literature on the Spanish Civil War, this is the first book in English that is devoted to the experiments in workers' self-management, both urban and rural, which constituted one of the most remarkable social revolutions in modern history."
— Prof. Paul Avrich, Princeton University

"The eyewitness reports and commentary presented in this highly important study reveal a very different understanding of the nature of socialism and the means for achieving it."
— Prof. Noam Chomsky, M.I.T. University

194 pages with illustrations / Hardcover $10.95 / Paperback $3.95   ISBN: 0-919618-20-0
ISBN: 0-919618-21-9

BLACK ROSE BOOKS C. 14

The Case for PARTICIPATORY DEMOCRACY

EDITED BY C. GEORGE BENELLO AND DIMITRIOS ROUSSOPOULOS

George Woodcock, Rosabeth Moss Kanter, Murray Bookchin, Christian Bay, Colin Ward, Martin Oppenheimer, Staughton Lynd, William Appelman Williams and others in this symposium have learned from their experience that participatory democracy works. They probe the historical roots of participatory democracy in Western culture, analyze its application to the problems of modern society, and explore the possible forms that it might take on every level of society from the work place to the community to the national level.

"The book is, by all odds, the most encompassing one so far in revealing the practical actual subversions that the New Left wishes to visit upon us."

— Karl Hess, The Washington Post

019 / 386 pages / SBN 670-20595-8
Hardcover $6.75

ESSAYS ON SOCIALIST HUMANISM, in honour of the Centenary of Bertrand Russell

EDITED BY KEN COATES

Contributors include Jean Paul Sartre, Vladimir Dedijer, Noam Chomsky, Lelio Basso, Mihailo Markovic and many others.

"How important... that the publishers should have brought out a volume to honour the Centenary of Bertrand Russell's birth and to explore the relationship between Russell's liberalism, libertarianism and pacifism and recent trends in the socialist movement. Great riches of social and political philosophy are to be found here, and that is not surprising... A very rewarding volume... and a whole range of writers combine a well-knit series of essays."

— Times Literary Supplement

021 / 220 pages / SBN 85124 047x
Hardcover $10.00

Printed by
the workers of
Editions Marquis, Montmagny, Que.
for
Black Rose Books Ltd.